The Morrowind Prophecies

Official Guide to
The Elder Scrolls III: Morrowind™

Bethesda™
SOFTWORKS INC.

ZeniMax™
MEDIA INC.

Published By:
Bethesda Softworks Inc., a ZeniMax Media company

Written By:
Peter Olafson

Dedication:
For Isabel

Acknowledgments:
My heartfelt thanks to the many people at Bethesda Softworks who worked hard to make this book possible—especially to Pete Hines, who allowed me only slightly less latitude in its construction than Morrowind itself, to Todd Howard for putting my name forward and to Vlatko Andonov for agreeing, and to Ken Rolston, Douglas Goodall, and Mark Nelson, who responded to my many small questions about the game's internal workings with speedy, detailed answers, and endless good humor.

Edited By:
Pete Hines

Acknowledgments:
Many thanks to the entire Morrowind team for their tireless effort and extraordinary work, to Peter for his lack of judgment in undertaking this monstrous project, and his patience in getting it finished, to Todd Howard for his guidance and insight, to Todd Vaughn for his levity, to designers Ken Rolston, Douglas Goodall, Mark Nelson, and Brian Chapin for all their help in editing, to Matt Carofano, Brian Chapin, and Ashley Cheng for their assistance in pulling together all the images, to Mike Lipari and Craig Walton for their programming help, to Steve Green, Istvan Pely, and Natalia Smirnova for their help with maps and last minute layouts, and to Shannon and Connor for constant support.

Layout and Design By:
Michael Wagner

ISBN Number: 0-929843-31-2
Printed in the United States of America by Technicolor®.

Table of Contents

⚬ The Morrowind Prophecies ⚬

Introduction

When you arrive on the island of Vvardenfell, your destiny and the fate of Morrowind may seem like rather distant and even confusing matters.

But your small scrapes and discoveries as you find tentative footing in this strange land are played out against a broad tapestry of conflicting internal interests—and the rise of a monstrous outside force.

In an earlier era, Lord Nerevar, the great hero of the Dunmer people (as the Morrowind's native Dark Elves call themselves), defeated the Dwarves and their ally, the Dunmer traitor Dagoth Ur, in a great battle at Red Mountain.

But Dagoth Ur somehow survived, and, dwelling in darkness under the volcano, he lusts for revenge.

Technically, he is imprisoned. The Tribunal Temple (essentially, the church of Morrowind) ringed the volcano's crater with magical wards.

But major bad guys who are merely imprisoned and not utterly destroyed have a way of making a comeback.

And, sure enough, Dagoth Ur is making a comeback.

The Ghostfence has begun to fail. Dagoth Ur's minions roam the ashy wastes around the volcano. Members of a secret cult known as the Sixth House serve as the demon's agents outside the crater, and, operating from hidden bases, turn normal people into babbling assassins.

There is no one to stop them.

Nerevar lost his own life defeating Dagoth Ur. The earthly gods of the Tribunal Temple have retreated from the field, and the Temple suppresses as heresy the hopeful belief in a prophesied resurrection of Nerevar. The Great Houses and the Guilds are busy fighting one another, or simply indifferent to the threat, and Empire's representative on the island typically defers to the Great Houses.

In short, Morrowind lacks a strong center.

This is where you come in. You are the prophesied hero behind whom the land might unite.

But that's a different person than the one you are now. Right now, you're a penniless nobody who just got off the boat, and stand at the beginning of a long and difficult road.

What kind of world does that road cross?

It's a different one than in earlier Elder Scrolls games. Arena and Daggerfall were Imperial in focus and empire-wide in scope.

In Arena, Imperial Battlemage Jagar Tharn imprisoned Emperor Uriel Septim VII in an alternate plane and assumed his identity as the provinces ran riot. A hero reassembled eight scattered pieces of Staff of Chaos, defeated the mage, and returned the emperor to the throne.

1

In Daggerfall, 15 years later, an agent for Septim ran a dangerous gantlet to lay to rest of the ghost of slain Daggerfall King Lysandus and reactivate the Numidium—the great iron golem used by Tiber Septim to forge the Empire.

Here, a decade after the events of Daggerfall, you'll explore just one part of a single troubled Imperial province … and the Empire may seem a ocean away. The aged emperor is more of a facilitator than a player.

You're in the relatively safe western region of Vvardenfell—the area settled by westerners after Morrowind was brought into the Tamrielic Empire by treaty. Ramshackle fishing villages dot the coast. Inland, you'll find large towns with lots of opportunities for work.

To the south, Ebonheart, the Imperial seat in the province, and Vivec, a Tamrielic Venice built in the shape of a cross and entirely over water

In the east, wizard towers erupt like vast weeds in the bosky Grazelands and on islands in Zafirbel Bay.

To the north, a wasteland broken only by shrines to old gods, ancient fortresses, and the rusted towers of the vanished Dwarves.

Between them all is Red Mountain, with Dagoth Ur's citadel at its center. You won't reach it for a long time. You won't be powerful enough, and the means to defeat the demon won't be within your grasp until you are.

Experience it as you wish. There is no wrong or right way to play, and while Morrowind gives you a wink and a nudge at the start, it won't force a particular approach.

You'll find challenges in every corner. You can work for four guilds: Fighters, Mages, Thieves, and shadowy Morag Tong, which handles assassinations. You can become a trooper with the Imperial Legion, a fund-raiser for the Imperial Cult, and a Temple pilgrim.

And darker fates await those who wander in darker places.

Along this hard road, your thoughts may stray more than once back to the Empire. Why has the emperor sent you here? What does Septim know, and how does he know it?

All good questions. But the answers will have to wait for another game. This one is about to begin.

Chapter One: Gameplay

Races

Every race starts with different values for each of the eight attributes. They also differ between sexes. These attributes are further modified by your class' favored attributes and birthsign.

NORD

Attribute	Male	Female
Strength	50	50
Intelligence	30	30
Willpower	40	50
Agility	30	30
Speed	40	40
Endurance	50	40
Personality	30	30
Luck	40	40

REDGUARD

Attribute	Male	Female
Strength	50	40
Intelligence	30	30
Willpower	30	30
Agility	40	40
Speed	40	40
Endurance	50	50
Personality	30	40
Luck	40	40

BRETON

Attribute	Male	Female
Strength	40	30
Intelligence	50	50
Willpower	50	50
Agility	30	30
Speed	30	40
Endurance	30	30
Personality	40	40
Luck	40	40

IMPERIAL

Attribute	Male	Female
Strength	40	40
Intelligence	40	40
Willpower	30	40
Agility	30	30
Speed	40	30
Endurance	40	40
Personality	50	50
Luck	40	40

WOOD ELF

Attribute	Male	Female
Strength	30	30
Intelligence	40	40
Willpower	30	30
Agility	50	50
Speed	50	50
Endurance	30	30
Personality	40	40
Luck	40	40

HIGH ELF

Attribute	Male	Female
Strength	30	30
Intelligence	50	50
Willpower	40	40
Agility	40	40
Speed	30	40
Endurance	40	30
Personality	40	40
Luck	40	40

DARK ELF

Attribute	Male	Female
Strength	40	40
Intelligence	40	40
Willpower	30	30
Agility	40	40
Speed	50	50
Endurance	40	30
Personality	30	40
Luck	40	40

KHAJIIT

Attribute	Male	Female
Strength	40	30
Intelligence	40	40
Willpower	30	30
Agility	50	50
Speed	40	40
Endurance	30	40
Personality	40	40
Luck	40	40

ARGONIAN

Attribute	Male	Female
Strength	40	40
Intelligence	40	50
Willpower	30	40
Agility	50	40
Speed	50	40
Endurance	30	30
Personality	30	30
Luck	40	40

ORC

Attribute	Male	Female
Strength	45	45
Intelligence	30	40
Willpower	50	45
Agility	35	35
Speed	30	30
Endurance	50	50
Personality	30	25
Luck	40	40

SKILL BONUSES

Each race receives bonuses to different skills, based on their inherent abilities and attributes. Knowing these bonuses is helpful when choosing a class, or creating your own custom class.

	Nord	Redguard	Breton	Imperial	Wood Elf	High Elf	Dark Elf	Khajiit	Argonian	Orc
Acrobatics					5			15		
Alchemy			5		5	10			5	
Alteration			5			5				
Armorer										10
Athletics		5					5	5	15	
Axe	10	5								5
Block										10
Blunt Weapon	10	5		5						
Conjuration			10			5				
Destruction						10	10			
Enchant						10				
Hand-to-Hand				5				5		
Heavy Armor	5	5								10
Illusion			5			5			5	
Light Armor				5	10		5	5		
Long Blade	5	15		10			5			
Marksman					15		5			
Medium Armor	10	5							5	10
Mercantile				10						
Mysticism			10				5		5	0
Restoration			10							
Security								5		
Short Blade		5					10	5		
Spear	5								5	
Speechcraft				10						
Sneak					10			5		
Unarmored									5	

CHARACTER GENERATION Q&A

If you decide to answer the series of questions to choose your class, you will be asked 10 questions. Below is a chart showing how you answers help determine your character, and a list of the questions and answers according to stealth, combat, or magic. Each class has numbers in up to three columns, which show the number of answers of that type (e.g., stealth) you need to create that type of character. So if you select four stealth answers and four magic answers, you'll create a Nightblade.

		Stealth Answer	Combat Answer	Magic Answer
Stealth	Thief	7		
	Agent	6	1	3
	Assassin	6	3	1
	Acrobat	6	2	2
	Monk	5	3	2
	Pilgrim	5	2	3
	Bard	3	3	3
Combat	Warrior		7	
	Barbarian	3	6	1
	Crusader	1	6	3
	Knight	2	6	2
	Scout	2	5	3
	Archer	3	5	2
	Rogue	4	4	
Magic	Mage			7
	Sorcerer	2	2	6
	Healer	3	1	6
	Battlemage	1	3	6
	Witchhunter	2	2	5
	Spellsword		4	4
	Nightblade	4		4

Question 1
On a clear day you chance upon a strange animal, its leg trapped in a hunter's clawsnare. Judging from the bleeding, it will not survive long.

Combat: Draw your dagger, mercifully ending its life with a single thrust?

Magic: Use herbs from your pack to put it to sleep?

Stealth: Do not interfere in the natural evolution of events, but rather take the opportunity to learn more about a strange animal that you have never seen before?

Question 2
One summer afternoon your father gives you a choice of chores.

Combat: Work in the forge with him casting iron for a new plow?

Magic: Gather herbs for your mother who is preparing dinner?

Stealth: Go catch fish at the stream using a net and line?

Question 3

Your cousin has given you a very embarrassing nickname and, even worse, likes to call you it in front of your friends. You have asked him to stop, but he finds it very amusing to watch you blush.

Combat: Beat up your cousin, then tell him that if he ever calls you that nickname again, you will bloody him worse than this time.

Magic: Make up a story that makes your nickname a badge of honor instead of something humiliating.

Stealth: Make up an even more embarrassing nickname for him and use it constantly until he learns his lesson.

Question 4

There is a lot of heated discussion at the local tavern over a group of people called 'Telepaths'. They have been hired by certain City-State kings. Rumor has it these Telepaths read a person's mind and tell their lord whether a follower is telling the truth or not.

Combat: This is a terrible practice. A person's thoughts are his own and no one, not even a king, has the right to make such an invasion into another human's mind.

Magic: Loyal followers to the King have nothing to fear from a Telepath. It is important to have a method of finding assassins and spies before it is too late.

Stealth: In these times, it is a necessary evil. Although you do not necessarily like the idea, a Telepath could have certain advantages during a time of war or in finding someone innocent of a crime.

Question 5

Your mother sends you to the market with a list of goods to buy. After you finish you find that by mistake a shop-keeper has given you too much money back in exchange for one of the items.

Combat: Return to the store and give the shopkeeper his hard-earned money, explaining to him the mistake?

Magic: Decide to put the extra money to good use and purchase items that would help your family?

Stealth: Pocket the extra money, knowing that shopkeepers in general tend to overcharge customers anyway?

Question 6

While in a market place you witness a thief cut a purse from a noble. Even as he does so, the noble notices and calls for the city guards. In his haste to get away, the thief drops the purse near you. Surprisingly, no one seems to notice the bag of coins at your feet.

Combat: Pick up the bag and signal to the guard, knowing that the only honorable thing to do is return the money to its rightful owner?

Magic: Leave the bag there, knowing that it is better not to get involved?

Stealth: Pick up the bag and pocket it, knowing that the extra windfall will help your family in times of trouble?

Question 7

Your father sends you on a task which you loathe, cleaning the stables. On the way there, pitchfork in hand, you run into your friend from the homestead near your own. He offers to do it for you, in return for a future favor of his choosing.

Combat: Decline his offer, knowing that your father expects you to do the work, and it is better not to be in debt?

Magic: Ask him to help you, knowing that two people can do the job faster than one, and agree to help him with one task of his choosing in the future?

Stealth: Accept his offer, reasoning that as long as the stables are cleaned, it matters not who does the cleaning?

Question 8

Your mother asks you to help fix the stove. While you are working, a very hot pipe slips its moorings and falls towards her.

Combat: Position yourself between the pipe and your mother?

Magic: Grab the hot pipe and try to push it away?

Stealth: Push your mother out of the way?

Question 9

While in town the baker gives you a sweetroll. Delighted, you take it into an alley to enjoy, only to be intercepted by a gang of three other kids your age. The leader demands the sweetroll, or else he and his friends will beat you and take it.

Combat: Drop the sweetroll and step on it, then get ready for the fight?

Magic: Give him the sweetroll now without argument, knowing that later this afternoon you will have all your friends with you and can come and take whatever he owes you?

Stealth: Act like you're going to give him the sweetroll, but at the last minute throw it in the air, hoping that they'll pay attention to it long enough for you to get a shot in on the leader?

Question 10

Entering town you find that you are witness to a very well-dressed man running from a crowd. He screams to you for help. The crowd behind him seems very angry.

Combat: Rush to the town's aid immediately, despite your lack of knowledge of the circumstances?

Magic: Stand aside and allow the man and mob to pass, realizing that it is probably best not to get involved?

Stealth: Rush to the man's aid immediately, despite your lack of knowledge of the circumstances?

WEAPONS

There are a wide variety of weapons to use in Morrowind. Below is a basic list of non-magical weapons, organized by weapon Skill. If you use a shield, you should note the number of Hands the weapon uses. Value is the base value of the item. Enchant represents how much enchantment you can put into the weapon. Health is how much damage the weapon can take. Speed is a factor in how quickly you can repeatedly attack with the weapon. Chop, Slash, and Thrust show the min/max damage ranges for each type of attack.

AXE Type	Skill	Hands	Weight	Value	Enchant	Health	Speed	Chop	Slash	Thrust
Daedric Battle Axe	Axe	Two	90	50000	16	4800	1	1-80	1-60	1-8
Dwarven Battle Axe	Axe	Two	30	750	5	3000	1	1-35	1-33	1-15
Iron Battle Axe	Axe	Two	30	50	5	1200	1	1-32	1-24	1-3
Steel Battle Axe	Axe	Two	30	100	5	1800	1	1-36	1-27	1-4
Chitin War Axe	Axe	One	12	19	2	640	1.25	1-11	1-6	1-2
Daedric War Axe	Axe	One	72	30000	15	3200	1.25	1-44	1-24	1-6
Dwarven War Axe	Axe	One	24	450	5	2000	1.25	1-24	1-13	13
Ebony War Axe	Axe	One	48	15000	10	2400	1.25	1-37	1-20	1-5
Glass War Axe	Axe	One	14.4	12000	3	640	1.25	1-33	1-18	1-5
Iron War Axe	Axe	One	24	30	5	800	1.25	1-18	1-10	1-2
Silver War Axe	Axe	One	19.2	120	4	720	1.25	1-20	1-11	1-3
Steel War Axe	Axe	One	24	60	5	1200	1.25	1-20	1-11	1-3
Steel Axe	Axe	One	24	60	4	1200	1	1-18	1-10	1-2

BLUNT Type	Skill	Hands	Weight	Value	Enchant	Health	Speed	Chop	Slash	Thrust
Chitin Club	Blunt	One	6	6	2	320	1.5	3-3	2-2	1-2
Daedric Club	Blunt	One	36	10000	12	1600	1.5	10-12	4-8	4-8
Iron Club	Blunt	One	12	10	4	400	1.5	4-5	3-3	1-3
Steel Club	Blunt	One	12	20	4	600	1.5	4-5	3-4	3-4
Daedric Mace	Blunt	One	45	24000	15	4800	1.3	3-30	3-30	2-4
Dwarven Mace	Blunt	One	15	360	5	3000	1.5	5-17	5-17	1-2
Ebony Mace	Blunt	One	30	12000	10	3600	1.5	7-26	7-26	1-3
Iron Mace	Blunt	One	15	24	5	1200	1.3	1-12	1-12	1-2
Steel Mace	Blunt	One	15	48	5	1800	1.3	3-14	3-14	1-2
Daedric Staff	Blunt	Two	24	14000	21	1200	1.75	2-16	3-16	1-12
Ebony Staff	Blunt	Two	16	7000	90	900	1.75	2-16	3-16	1-10
Glass Staff	Blunt	Two	4.8	5600	4	240	1.75	2-12	3-12	1-9
Silver Staff	Blunt	Two	6.4	56	5	270	1.75	2-7	3-7	1-5
Steel Staff	Blunt	Two	8	28	7	300	1.75	2-7	3-7	1-5
Daedric Warhammer	Blunt	Two	96	30000	16	8000	1	1-70	1-60	1-4
Dwarven Warhammer	Blunt	Two	32	600	5	5000	1	1-39	1-33	1-2
Iron Warhammer	Blunt	Two	32	40	5	2000	1	1-28	1-24	1-2
Steel Warhammer	Blunt	Two	32	80	5	3000	1	1-32	1-27	1-2

LONGBLADE Type	Skill	Hands	Weight	Value	Enchant	Health	Speed	Chop	Slash	Thrust
Ebony Broadsword	Long Blade	One	24	15000	10	1800	1.25	4-26	2-26	2-26
Iron Broadsword	Long Blade	One	12	30	5	600	1.25	4-12	2-12	2-12
Steel Broadsword	Long Blade	One	12	60	5	900	1.25	4-14	4-14	2-14
Daedric Claymore	Long Blade	Two	81	80000	21	5600	1.25	1-60	1-52	1-36
Dwarven Claymore	Long Blade	Two	27	1200	7	3500	1.25	1-33	1-29	1-20
Glass Claymore	Long Blade	Two	16.2	32000	4	840	1.25	1-45	1-39	1-27
Iron Claymore	Long Blade	Two	27	80	7	1400	1.25	1-24	1-21	1-14
Silver Claymore	Long Blade	Two	21.6	320	5	1260	1.25	1-27	1-23	1-16
Steel Claymore	Long Blade	Two	27	160	7	2100	1.25	1-27	1-23	1-16
Daedric Dai-katana	Long Blade	Two	60	120000	21	7200	1.35	1-60	1-52	1-30
Steel Dai-katana	Long Blade	Two	20	240	7	2700	1.35	1-27	1-23	1-14
Daedric Katana	Long Blade	One	54	50000	18	4800	1.5	3-44	1-40	1-14
Steel Katana	Long Blade	One	18	100	6	1800	1.5	3-20	1-18	1-6
Daedric Longsword	Long Blade	One	60	40000	18	3200	1.35	2-32	1-44	4-40
Ebony Longsword	Long Blade	One	40	20000	12	1600	1.35	2-27	1-37	4-34
Glass Longsword	Long Blade	One	12	16000	3	480	1.35	2-24	1-33	4-30
Iron Longsword	Long Blade	One	20	40	6	800	1.35	2-13	1-18	4-16
Silver Longsword	Long Blade	One	16	160	4	640	1.35	2-14	1-20	4-18
Steel Longsword	Long Blade	One	20	80	6	900	1.35	2-14	1-20	4-18
Iron Saber	Long Blade	One	15	24	5	700	1.4	5-18	4-16	1-4
Steel Saber	Long Blade	One	15	48	5	1050	1.4	5-20	4-18	1-5

MARKSMAN Type	Skill	Hands	Weight	Value	Enchant	Health	Speed	Chop	Slash	Thrust
Dwarven Crossbow	Marksman	Two	10	1200	50	750	1	30-30	0-0	0-0
Steel Crossbow	Marksman	Two	10	160	50	550	1	20-20	0-1	0-1
Daedric Long Bow	Marksman	Two	24	50000	105	1000	1	2-50	0-0	0-0
Steel Longbow	Marksman	Two	8	100	35	600	1	1-25	0-1	0-1
Chitin Short Bow	Marksman	Two	2	20	10	500	1	1-10	0-0	0-0
Daedric Dart	Marksman	Thrown	0.4	4000	45	90	1	2-12	0-1	0-1
Ebony Dart	Marksman	Thrown	0.4	2000	30	60	1	2-10	0-1	0-1
Silver Dart	Marksman	Thrown	0.2	6	12	24	1	2-5	0-1	0-1
Steel Dart	Marksman	Thrown	0.2	6	15	150	1	2-5	0-1	0-1
Glass Throwing Knife	Marksman	Thrown	0.2	25	9	80	1	1-6	0-1	0-1
Iron Throwing Knife	Marksman	Thrown	0.3	3	15	100	1	1-3	0-1	0-1
Steel Throwing Knife	Marksman	Thrown	0.3	4	15	150	1	1-4	0-1	0-1
Chitin Throwing Star	Marksman	Thrown	0.1	3	7	40	1	2-3	0-1	0-1
Ebony Throwing Star	Marksman	Thrown	0.2	2000	30	900	1	2-10	0-1	0-1
Glass Throwing Star	Marksman	Thrown	0.1	20	9	40	1	2-9	0-1	0-1
Silver Throwing Star	Marksman	Thrown	0.2	16	12	45	1	2-5	0-1	0-1
Steel Throwing Star	Marksman	Thrown	0.1	3	15	75	1	2-5	0-1	0-1

SHORTBLADE Type	Skill	Hands	Weight	Value	Enchant	Health	Speed	Chop	Slash	Thrust
Chitin Dagger	Short Blade	One	1.5	6	10	380	2	3-3	3-3	4-4
Daedric Dagger	Short Blade	One	9	10000	60	700	2.5	8-12	8-12	8-12
Glass Dagger	Short Blade	One	1.8	4000	12	300	2.5	6-15	6-15	6-12
Glass Netch Dagger	Short Blade	One	1.8	4900	12	400	2.5	7-9	7-9	6-9
Iron Dagger	Short Blade	One	3	10	20	400	2.5	4-5	4-5	5-5
Silver Dagger	Short Blade	One	2.4	40	16	400	2.5	4-5	4-5	5-5
Steel Dagger	Short Blade	One	3	20	20	450	2.5	4-5	4-5	5-5
Chitin Shortsword	Short Blade	One	4	13	20	540	2	3-7	3-7	4-9
Daedric Shortsword	Short Blade	One	24	20000	120	1500	2	10-26	10-26	12-24
Dwarven Shortsword	Short Blade	One	8	300	40	1050	2	7-14	7-14	8-15
Ebony Shortsword	Short Blade	One	16	10000	80	1200	2	10-20	10-22	15-25
Iron Shortsword	Short Blade	One	8	20	40	600	2	4-9	4-9	7-11
Silver Shortsword	Short Blade	One	6	80	36	570	2	5-10	5-10	7-10
Steel Shortsword	Short Blade	One	8	40	40	750	2	5-12	5-12	7-12
Daedric Tanto	Short Blade	One	12	14000	66	1100	2.25	9-20	9-20	9-20
Iron Tanto	Short Blade	One	4	14	22	500	2.25	5-6	5-6	6-6
Steel Tanto	Short Blade	One	4	28	22	600	2.25	5-11	5-11	6-11
Daedric Wakizashi	Short Blade	One	30	48000	135	1100	2.25	10-30	10-25	7-11
Iron Wakizashi	Short Blade	One	10	24	45	500	2.25	7-12	5-10	1-5
Steel Wakizashi	Short Blade	One	10	48	45	600	2.25	8-11	7-12	2-7

SPEAR Type	Skill	Hands	Weight	Value	Enchant	Health	Speed	Chop	Slash	Thrust
Dwarven Halberd	Spear	Two	24	600	70	1000	1	3-17	1-13	5-28
Glass Halberd	Spear	Two	8.4	16000	30	600	1	1-6	1-6	5-38
Iron Halberd	Spear	Two	14	40	50	700	1	1-3	1-3	5-20
Steel Halberd	Spear	Two	14	80	50	1000	1	1-4	1-4	5-23
Chitin Spear	Spear	Two	7	13	25	500	1	1-2	1-2	5-13
Daedric Spear	Spear	Two	42	20000	150	1000	1	2-9	2-9	6-40
Dwarven Spear	Spear	Two	14	300	50	1400	1	2-5	2-5	5-21
Ebony Spear	Spear	Two	28	10000	100	1200	1	2-8	2-8	5-32
Iron Spear	Spear	Two	14	20	50	600	1	2-4	2-4	6-15
Silver Spear	Spear	Two	11.2	80	40	500	1	1-4	1-4	5-23
Steel Spear	Spear	Two	14	40	50	1000	1	2-5	2-5	6-17

ARROW Type	Skill	Hands	Weight	Value	Enchant	Health	Speed	Chop	Slash	Thrust
Chitin Arrow	Arrow		0.1	1	8	1	1	1-2		
Daedric Arrow	Arrow		0.3	20	45	1	1	10-15		
Ebony Arrow	Arrow		0.2	10	30	10	1	5-10		
Glass Arrow	Arrow		0.15	8	9	10	1	1-6		
Iron Arrow	Arrow		0.1	1	0	10	1	1-3		
Silver Arrow	Arrow		0.1	3	12	10	1	1-3		
Steel Arrow	Arrow		0.1	2	15	10	1	1-4		
Iron Bolt	Bolt		0.1	1	20	10	1	2-3	0-1	0-1
Silver Bolt	Bolt		0.1	8	16	10	1	3-3	0-1	0-1
Steel Bolt	Bolt		0.1	2	20	10	1	2-4	0-1	0-1

ARMOR

Armor can be divided into the three Skills used to wear armor, and further categorized according to the type of armor. The armor listed here does not include the many kinds of magical and enchanted armor that can be found throughout Morrowind. Value is the base value of the item. Enchant represents how much enchantment you can put into the armor. Health is how much damage the armor can take. Armor Rating is how much protection that piece adds to your total armor rating. Greaves, Bracers, and Gauntlets all have separate pieces for the right and left side.

LIGHT ARMOR TYPE	Weight	Skill	Value	Enchant	Health	Armor Rating
Chitin Boots	6	Light	13	4	100	10
Glass Boots	3	Light	8000	10	500	50
Heavy Leather Boots	8	Light	100	2	500	50
Netch Leather Boots	8	Light	10	2	50	5
Nordic Fur Boots	6	Light	10	2	50	5
Chitin Cuirass	6	Light	45	10	300	10
Glass Cuirass	18	Light	28000	12	1500	50
Imperial Newtscale Cuirass	9	Light	100	10	300	10
Imperial Studded Leather Cuirass	9	Light	65	6	300	10
Netch Leather Cuirass	12	Light	35	6	150	5
Nordic Bearskin Cuirass	9	Light	35	6	150	5
Nordic Fur Cuirass	9	Light	35	6	150	5
Chitin Greaves	5.4	Light	29	1	100	10
Glass Greaves	9	Light	17600	10	500	50
Netch Leather Greaves	7	Light	22	1	50	5
Nordic Fur Greaves	5.4	Light	22	1	50	5
Chitin Helm	1	Light	19	12	100	10
Chitin Mask Helm	1	Light	19	12	100	10
Glass Helm	3	Light	12000	15	500	50
Netch Leather Helm	3	Light	15	7	50	5
Nordic Fur Helm	1.5	Light	15	7	50	5
Redoran Watchman's Helm	1	Light	24	12	110	11
Cloth Bracer	1.5	Light	3	6	20	4
Leather Bracer	1.5	Light	5	6	20	5
Nordic Fur Bracer	1.5	Light	5	6	25	5
Glass Bracer	3	Light	4000	10	400	50
Chitin Gauntlet	1	Light	9	10	50	10
Netch Leather Gauntlet	3	Light	7	6	25	5
Nordic Fur Gauntlet	1.5	Light	7	6	25	5
Chitin Pauldron	2	Light	16	1	100	10
Glass Pauldron	3	Light	9600	1	500	50
Netch Leather Pauldron	4	Light	12	1	50	5
Nordic Fur Pauldron	3	Light	12	1	50	5
Chitin Shield	4	Light	22	25	200	10
Chitin Tower Shield	6	Light	32	37	240	12
Glass Shield	9	Light	13600	30	1000	50
Glass Tower Shield	9	Light	20000	45	1100	55
Netch Leather Shield	6	Light	17	15	100	5
Netch Leather Tower Shield	9	Light	25	22	100	5
Nordic Leather Shield	4.5	Light	25	15	100	5

MEDIUM ARMOR TYPE	Weight	Skill	Value	Enchantment	Health	Armor Rating
Bonemold Boots	16	Medium	100	7	150	15
Orcish Boots	17	Medium	800	10	300	30
Bonemold Cuirass	24	Medium	350	16	480	16
Imperial Chain Cuirass	21	Medium	90	14	300	12
Imperial Dragonscale Cuirass	24	Medium	340	16	600	20
Nordic Ringmail Cuirass	21	Medium	80	14	300	10
Orcish Cuirass	26.5	Medium	2800	24	900	30
Bonemold Greaves	13.4	Medium	220	2	150	15
Imperial Chain Greaves	10	Medium	50	7	200	20
Orcish Greaves	13.45	Medium	1760	3	300	30
Bonemold Helm	4	Medium	150	20	180	18
Imperial Chain Coif	3.5	Medium	35	17	100	10
Imperial Dragonscale Helm	4	Medium	130	20	200	20
Orcish Helm	4.4	Medium	1200	30	300	30
Redoran Founder's Helm	4.4	Medium	150	20	180	18
Bonemold Bracer	4	Medium	50	16	75	15
Orcish Bracer	4.4	Medium	400	24	150	30
Bonemold Pauldron	8	Medium	120	1	150	15
Orcish Pauldron	8	Medium	960	2	300	30
Bonemold Shield	10	Medium	170	40	300	15
Bonemold Tower Shield	13	Medium	250	60	340	17
Orcish Tower Shield	13.4	Medium	2000	90	640	32
Redoran Banner Shield	13	Medium	250	60	340	17
Redoran Guard Shield	13	Medium	250	60	340	17

HEAVY ARMOR TYPE	Weight	Skill	Value	Enchantment	Health	Armor Rating
Daedric Boots	60	Heavy	20000	26	800	80
Dwemer Boots	20	Heavy	300	8	200	20
Ebony Boots	40	Heavy	10000	17	600	60
Imperial Steel Boots	19	Heavy	50	8	170	16
Imperial Templar Boots	20	Heavy	50	8	180	18
Indoril Boots	18	Heavy	2000	2	450	45
Iron Boots	19	Heavy	20	2	450	10
Steel Boots	20	Heavy	40	8	150	15
Daedric Cuirass	90	Heavy	70000	60	2400	80
Daedric Cuirass	90	Heavy	70000	60	2400	80
Dwemer Cuirass	30	Heavy	1050	20	600	20
Ebony Cuirass	60	Heavy	35000	40	1800	60
Imperial Silver Cuirass	30	Heavy	280	16	540	18
Imperial Steel Cuirass	29	Heavy	150	20	460	16
Imperial Templar Knight Cuirass	30	Heavy	175	20	540	18
Indoril Cuirass	27	Heavy	7000	18	1350	45
Iron Cuirass	30	Heavy	70	20	2000	10
Nordic Iron Cuirass	35	Heavy	130	20	480	16
Nordic Trollbone Cuirass	32	Heavy	165	16	540	18
Steel Cuirass	30	Heavy	150	20	450	15

HEAVY ARMOR TYPE	Weight	Skill	Value	Enchantment	Health	Armor Rating
Daedric Greaves	54	Heavy	44000	7	800	80
Dwemer Greaves	18	Heavy	660	2	200	20
Ebony Greaves	36	Heavy	22000	5	600	60
Imperial Steel Greaves	17	Heavy	98	2	170	16
Imperial Templar Greaves	18	Heavy	110	2	180	18
Iron Greaves	18	Heavy	44	2	100	10
Steel Greaves	18	Heavy	88	2	150	15
Dwemer Helm	5	Heavy	450	25	200	20
Ebony Closed Helm	10	Heavy	15000	50	600	60
Imperial Silver Helm	5	Heavy	120	20	170	17
Imperial Steel Helmet	5	Heavy	70	25	160	16
Imperial Templar Helmet	5	Heavy	75	25	180	18
Indoril Helmet	4.5	Heavy	3000	22	450	45
Iron Helmet	5	Heavy	30	2	100	10
Nordic Iron Helm	8	Heavy	50	25	160	16
Nordic Trollbone Helm	8	Heavy	65	20	180	18
Redoran Master Helm	4.5	Heavy	3000	22	450	45
Steel Helm	5	Heavy	60	25	150	15
Dwemer Bracer	5	Heavy	150	20	100	20
Ebony Bracer	10	Heavy	5000	40	300	60
Imperial Templar Bracer	5	Heavy	25	20	90	18
Iron Bracer	5	Heavy	10	20	50	10
Daedric Gauntlet	15	Heavy	14000	60	400	80
Imperial Steel Gauntlet	5	Heavy	33	20	80	16
Indoril Gauntlet	4.5	Heavy	1400	6	225	45
Iron Gauntlet	7	Heavy	14	1	50	10
Steel Gauntlet	5	Heavy	28	20	75	15
Daedric Pauldron	30	Heavy	24000	6	800	80
Dwemer Pauldron	10	Heavy	360	2	200	20
Ebony Pauldron	20	Heavy	12000	4	600	60
Imperial Chain Pauldron	10	Heavy	28	7	200	20
Imperial Steel Pauldron	10	Heavy	53	2	160	16
Imperial Templar Pauldron	10	Heavy	60	2	180	18
Indoril Pauldron	9	Heavy	2400	1	450	45
Iron Pauldron	10	Heavy	24	2	100	10
Steel Pauldron	10	Heavy	48	2	150	15
Daedric Shield	45	Heavy	34000	150	1600	80
Daedric Tower Shield	45	Heavy	50000	225	1600	80
Dwemer Shield	15	Heavy	510	50	400	20
Ebony Shield	30	Heavy	17000	100	1200	60
Ebony Tower Shield	30	Heavy	25000	150	1200	60
Imperial Shield	14	Heavy	78	50	320	16
Indoril Shield	13.5	Heavy	2000	45	900	45
Iron Shield	15	Heavy	34	50	200	10
Iron Tower Shield	18	Heavy	50	75	240	12
Nordic Trollbone Shield	16	Heavy	78	40	360	18
Steel Shield	15	Heavy	68	50	300	15
Steel Tower Shield	20	Heavy	100	75	360	18

ALCHEMY AND INGREDIENTS

Ingredients can have up to four effects. The First effect is the one you will get if you successfully eat the ingredient, which is based on your Alchemy skill. The higher your skill, the better the chance you'll get the effect and the longer it will last. In addition, two or more ingredients can be combined to create potions. If at least two of the ingredients have an effect, then that effect will be included in the potion if it is successfully created (again, based on your Alchemy skill). Use the chart below as a guide when combining ingredients to find common beneficial effects for powerful potions. While your character may not be able to identify certain effects, which will be indicated by a question mark (?), using the chart you should be able to determine the unknown effect.

Ingredient	Effects			
	FIRST	SECOND	THIRD	FOURTH
Alit Hide	Drain Intelligence	Resist Poison	Telekinesis	Detect Animal
Ampoule Pod	Water Walking	Paralyze	Detect Animal	Drain Willpower
Ash Salts	Drain Agility	Resist Magicka	Cure Blight Disease	Resist Magicka
Ash Yam	Fortify Intelligence	Fortify Strength	Resist Common Disease	Detect Key
Bittergreen Petals	Restore Intelligence	Invisibility	Drain Endurance	Drain Magicka
Black Anther	Drain Agility	Resist Fire	Drain Endurance	Light
Black Lichen	Drain Strength	Resist Frost	Drain Speed	Cure Poison
Bloat	Drain Magicka	Fortify Intelligence	Fortify Willpower	Detect Animal
Bonemeal	Restore Agility	Telekinesis	Drain Fatigue	Drain Personality
Bungler's Bane	Drain Speed	Drain Endurance	Dispel	Drain Strength
Chokeweed	Drain Luck	Restore Fatigue	Cure Common Disease	Drain Willpower
Coda Flower	Drain Personality	Levitate	Drain Intelligence	Drain Health
Cornberry	Drain Fatigue	Restore Magicka	Fire Shield	Reflect
Corkbulb Root	Cure Paralyzation	Restore Health	Lightning Shield	Fortify Luck
Corprus Weepings	Drain Fatigue	Fortify Luck	Drain Willpower	Restore Health
Corpusmeat	Drain Fatigue	Drain Health	Drain Magicka	
Crab Meat	Restore Fatigue	Resist Shock	Lightning Shield	Restore Luck
Daedra Skin	Fortify Strength	Cure Common Disease	Paralyze	Swift Swim
Daedra's Heart	Restore Magicka	Fortify Endurance	Drain Agility	Night-Eye
Diamond	Drain Agility	Invisibility	Reflect	Detect Key
Dreugh Wax	Fortify Strength	Restore Strength	Drain Luck	Drain Willpower
Ectoplasm	Fortify Agility	Detect Animal	Drain Strength	Drain Health
Emerald	Fortify Magicka	Restore Health	Drain Agility	Drain Endurance
Fire Petal	Resist Fire	Drain Health	Spell Absorption	Paralyze
Fire Salts	Drain Health	Fortify Agility	Resist Frost	Fire Shield
Frost Salts	Drain Speed	Restore Magicka	Frost Shield	Resist Fire
Ghoul Heart	Paralyze	Cure Poison	Fortify Attack	
Gold Kanet	Drain Health	Burden	Drain Luck	Restore Strength
Gravedust	Drain Intelligence	Cure Common Disease	Drain Magicka	Restore Endurance
Green Lichen	Fortify Personality	Cure Common Disease	Drain Strength	Drain Health
Guar Hide	Drain Fatigue	Fortify Endurance	Restore Personality	Fortify Luck
Hack-lo Leaf	Restore Fatigue	Paralyze	Water Breathing	Restore Luck
Heather	Restore Personality	Feather	Drain Speed	Drain Personality
Hound Meat	Restore Fatigue	Fortify Fatigue	Reflect	Detect Enchantment
Hypha Facia	Drain Luck	Drain Agility	Drain Fatigue	Detect Enchantment
Kagouti Hide	Drain Fatigue	Fortify Speed	Resist Common Disease	Night Eye
Kresh Fiber	Restore Luck	Fortify Personality	Drain Magicka	Drain Speed
Kwama Cuttle	Resist Poison	Drain Fatigue	Water Walking	Water Breathing
Large Kwama Egg	Restore Fatigue	Paralyze	Frost Shield	Fortify Health
Luminous Russula	Water Breathing	Drain Fatigue	Poison	

Ingredient	Effects			
	FIRST	SECOND	THIRD	FOURTH
Marshmerrow	Restore Health	Detect Enchantment	Drain Willpower	Drain Fatigue
Moon Sugar	Fortify Speed	Dispel	Drain Endurance	Drain Luck
Muck	Drain Intelligence	Detect Key	Drain Personality	Cure Common Disease
Netch Leather	Fortify Endurance	Fortify Intelligence	Drain Personality	Cure Paralyzation
Pearl	Drain Agility	Dispel	Water Breathing	Resist Common Disease
Racer Plumes	Drain Willpower	Levitate		
Rat Meat	Drain Magicka	Paralyze	Cure Poison	Resist Poison
Raw Ebony	Drain Agility	Cure Poison	Frost Shield	Restore Speed
Raw Glass	Drain Intelligence	Drain Strength	Drain Speed	Fire Shield
Red Lichen	Drain Speed	Light	Cure Common Disease	Drain Magicka
Resin	Restore Health	Restore Speed	Burden	Resist Common Disease
Roobrush	Drain Willpower	Fortify Agility	Drain Health	Cure Poison
Ruby	Drain Health	Feather	Restore Intelligence	Drain Agility
Saltrice	Restore Fatigue	Fortify Magicka	Drain Strength	Restore Health
Scales	Drain Personality	Water Walking	Restore Endurance	Swift Swim
Scamp Skin	Drain Magicka	Cure Paralyzation	Restore Personality	Restore Strength
Scathecraw	Drain Strength	Cure Poison	Drain Health	Restore Willpower
Scrap Metal	Drain Health	Lightning Shield	Resist Shock	Restore Intelligence
Scrib Jelly	Fortify Willpower	Cure Poison	Cure Blight Disease	Restore Willpower
Scrib Jerky	Restore Fatigue	Fortify Fatigue	Burden	Swift Swim
Scuttle	Restore Fatigue	Fortify Fatigue	Feather	Telekinesis
Shalk Resin	Drain Fatigue	Fortify Health	Drain Personality	Fortify Speed
Sload Soap	Drain Personality	Fortify Agility	Fire Shield	Restore Agility
Spore Pod	Drain Strength	Drain Fatigue	Detect Key	Paralyze
Stoneflower Petals	Restore Strength	Fortify Magicka	Drain Luck	Fortify Personality
Trama Root	Restore Willpower	Levitate	Drain Magicka	Drain Speed
Vampire Dust	Fortify Health	Fortify Strength	Spell Absorption	Vampirism
Violet Corprinus	Water Walking	Drain Fatigue	Poison	
Void Salts	Restore Magicka	Spell Absorption	Paralyze	Drain Endurance
Wickwheat	Restore Health	Fortify Willpower	Paralyze	Damage Intelligence
Willow Anther	Drain Personality	Frost Shield	Cure Common Disease	Cure Paralyzation

Chapter Two: Creatures

Creatures

Throughout the world you will find a wide variety of fauna in every shape and size. Some are nothing more than a mere nuisance or good target practice, while others can (and should) make you very afraid. Creatures can be organized into four different groups: Creature, Humanoid, Undead, and Daedra. These groups can be particularly important in using magic effects, as certain spells effects only work on a specific creature type.

The following pages list, in alphabetical order, the basic creatures you will encounter in the wild. This is only a basic list, and you will see different forms of these creatures (e.g., blighted or diseased) as well. Also, you may find that you can play the game for hours on end without seeing certain types of creatures. There's a very good reason for that.

Throughout the game you will find hand-placed creatures and leveled creatures. A leveled creature will do a quick check of your Level and pull the appropriate creature from its list. So if you're at Level 1, you may get a rat, but if you're at Level 4, you may face a Cliff Racer. Returning to that area later in the game may spawn yet another type of creature.

So if you're yearning to kill something new and interesting, just keep working on your skills and you'll be knee-deep in Hungers before you know it.

Most of the info we provide you is self-explanatory. Here are a few creature attributes that might need clarification.

Magicka: Particularly important for creatures with a high magic skill and lots of magic to use

Soul: If you trap the creature's soul with a soul gem when it dies, this is the amount you'll be able to use towards enchanting.

Combat Skill: This value is used any time the creature attempts to do a combat-based skill action such as attacking or running.

Magic Skill: This value is used any time the creature attempts to do a magic-based skill action such as casting spells.

Best-Attack: The range of damage the creature can do using its best attack.

Willpower: Determines the creatures magic resistance.

Agility: Determines how easy or hard the creature is to hit.

Magic: This isn't just available spells, but also diseases (e.g., Brown Rot), resistances (e.g., Immune to Disease) and abilities (e.g., Paralyze).

Alit

Type: **Creature**	Combat Skill: **30**
Level: **3**	Magic Skill: **80**
Health: **30**	Best Attack
Magicka: **75**	Min/Max: **1-9**
Fatigue: **400**	Willpower: **40**
Soul: **20**	Agility: **50**

Magic: **None**

The alit is a tailless two-legged predator common to the grasslands and ash wastes of Vvardenfell. Built like its larger and more dangerous cousin, the kagouti, the alit has a large head and protruding jaw, and when running on its short, stumpy legs, it looks like a big toothy mouth with feet.

Ancestor Ghost

Type: **Undead**	Combat Skill: **30**
Level: **1**	Magic Skill: **80**
Health: **23**	Best Attack
Magicka: **400**	Min/Max: **1-5**
Fatigue: **400**	Willpower: **30**
Soul: **100**	Agility: **50**

Magic: **Ghost Curse, Immune to Disease, Immune to Frost, Immune to Normal Weapons, Immune to Poison**

Ancestor ghosts commonly defend the tombs of clan and kin, but may also be summoned and controlled by sorcerers. Ancestor ghosts are aggressive but not very dangerous--IF you have an enchanted or silver weapon, or deadly sorcery.

Ascended Sleeper

Type: **Humanoid**	Combat Skill: **80**
Level: **25**	Magic Skill: **80**
Health: **300**	Best Attack
Magicka: **300**	Min/Max: **25-75**
Fatigue: **400**	Willpower: **100**
Soul: **400**	Agility: **100**

Magic: **Ash Woe Blight, Ash-Chancre, Black-Heart Blight, Chantrax Blight, Dagoth's Bosom, Paralysis, Fire Storm, Frost Storm, Shockball**

The ascended sleepers are distorted, half-human, half-beast creatures transformed by a mysterious force into powerful magical beings. Ascended sleepers are highly intelligent, aggressive, and dangerous. Ascended sleepers are associated in some way with the Devil Dagoth Ur.

Ash Ghoul

Type: **Humanoid**	Combat Skill: **70**
Level: **15**	Magic Skill: **90**
Health: **220**	Best Attack
Magicka: **280**	Min/Max: **15-45**
Fatigue: **400**	Willpower: **100**
Soul: **250**	Agility: **100**

Magic: **Ash Woe Blight, Earwig, Reflect, Spark, First Barrier**

The ash ghoul is a distorted, half-human, half-beast creature transformed by a mysterious force into a powerful magical being. Ash ghouls are highly intelligent, aggressive, and dangerous. Ash ghouls are associated in some way with the Devil Dagoth Ur.

Ash Slave

Type: **Humanoid**	Combat Skill: **50**
Level: **5**	Magic Skill: **90**
Health: **60**	Best Attack
Magicka: **100**	Min/Max: **5-15**
Fatigue: **400**	Willpower: **80**
Soul: **100**	Agility: **100**

Magic: **Ash Woe Blight, Earwig, Reflect, Spark, First Barrier**

The ash slave is a Humanoid creature transformed by a mysterious force into a deranged beast. These creatures are aggressive and dangerous. Ash slaves are associated in some way with the Devil Dagoth Ur.

Ash Zombie

Type: **Humanoid**	Combat Skill: **80**
Level: **8**	Magic Skill: **60**
Health: **90**	Best Attack
Magicka: **100**	Min/Max: **1-20**
Fatigue: **400**	Willpower: **60**
Soul: **100**	Agility: **20**

Magic: **None**

The ash zombie is a Humanoid creature transformed by a mysterious force into a deranged beast. Though their skulls are apparently empty, these Creatures are nonetheless intelligent, aggressive, and dangerous. Ash zombies are associated in some way with the Devil Dagoth Ur.

Betty Netch

Type: **Creature**	Combat Skill: **60**
Level: **10**	Magic Skill: **90**
Health: **113**	Best Attack
Magicka: **75**	Min/Max: **10-30**
Fatigue: **500**	Willpower: **30**
Soul: **75**	Agility: **50**

Magic: **None**

The betty netch is a large hovering beast, supported by internal sacks of magical vapors. The betty netch, the female of the species, is smaller than the male bull netch, but fiercely territorial.

Bonelord

Type: **Undead**	Combat Skill: **60**
Level: **8**	Magic Skill: **90**
Health: **90**	Best Attack
Magicka: **400**	Min/Max: **8-24**
Fatigue: **400**	Willpower: **80**
Soul: **100**	Agility: **50**

Magic: **Grave Curse: Endurance, Grave Curse: Speed, Immune to Normal Weapons, Resist Frost, Resist Poison, Resist Shock, Second Barrier**

The Bonelord is a revenant that protects the tombs of clan and kin. Bonemeal, the finely ground powder made from the bones of the skeleton minions, has modest magical properties.

Bonewalker

Type: **Undead**	Combat Skill: **50**
Level: **4**	Magic Skill: **90**
Health: **60**	Best Attack
Magicka: **80**	Min/Max: **4-12**
Fatigue: **400**	Willpower: **50**
Soul: **75**	Agility: **50**

Magic: **Brown Rot, Grave Curse: Strength, Resist Frost, Resist Poison, Resist Shock**
Bonewalkers are among the distinctive ancestral revenants that guard Dunmer burial sites, and which may be summoned as spirit guardians. Among the Undead, they are less worrisome than their more powerful manifestation, the Greater Bonewalker. They are not to be underestimated, as they are capable of stopping the hardiest of adventurers dead in their tracks with their powerful curses.

Greater Bonewalker

Type: **Undead**	Combat Skill: **50**
Level: **7**	Magic Skill: **90**
Health: **100**	Best Attack
Magicka: **75**	Min/Max: **5-15**
Fatigue: **400**	Willpower: **60**
Soul: **75**	Agility: **50**

Magic: **Brown Rot, Dread Curse: Endurance, Grave Curse: Strength, Resist Frost, Resist Poison, Resist Shock**
Greater Bonewalkers defend the tombs of clan and kin. Greater Bonewalkers are aggressive and dangerous. They are best dispatched from a distance, as close combat can often result in the player afflicted by crippling curses.

Lesser Bonewalker

Type: **Undead**	Combat Skill: **40**
Level: **3**	Magic Skill: **80**
Health: **45**	Best Attack
Magicka: **60**	Min/Max: **1-10**
Fatigue: **300**	Willpower: **40**
Soul: **65**	Agility: **40**

Magic: **Brown Rot, Grave Curse: Endurance, Grave Curse: Strength, Resist Frost, Resist Poison, Resist Shock**
Lesser Bonewalkers are the least powerful of the tomb and spirit guardians that protect Dunmer burial sites.

Bull Netch

Type: **Creature**	Combat Skill: **50**
Level: **4**	Magic Skill: **90**
Health: **45**	Best Attack
Magicka: **100**	Min/Max: **4-12**
Fatigue: **400**	Willpower: **50**
Soul: **50**	Agility: **50**

Magic: **Poisonbloom**
The bull netch is a huge beast that hovers in the air, supported by internal sacks of magical vapors. The bull netch is poisonous.

Centurion Sphere

Type: **Creature**	Combat Skill: **50**
Level: **5**	Magic Skill: **90**
Health: **75**	Best Attack
Magicka: **70**	Min/Max: **5-15**
Fatigue: **800**	Willpower: **70**
Soul: **0**	Agility: **75**

Magic: **Shock Shield**
The centurion sphere is an enchanted animated artifact of Dwemer creation. These aggressive and dangerous devices compress into a ball when inactive, and transform into a mobile warrior when aroused.

Centurion Spider

Type: **Creature**	Combat Skill: **30**
Level: **3**	Magic Skill: **90**
Health: **38**	Best Attack
Magicka: **20**	Min/Max: **1-9**
Fatigue: **400**	Willpower: **60**
Soul: **0**	Agility: **75**

Magic: **Poisonbloom, Immune to Poison**
The centurion spider is an enchanted animated artifact of Dwemer creation. Constructed in the form of large metal spiders, they are aggressive and dangerous.

Clannfear

Type: **Daedra**	Combat Skill: **60**
Level: **7**	Magic Skill: **90**
Health: **113**	Best Attack
Magicka: **100**	Min/Max: **6-18**
Fatigue: **500**	Willpower: **70**
Soul: **100**	Agility: **80**

Magic: **None**
The clannfear is a fierce, green, lizardlike, bipedal Daedric summoning. Daedra hearts have modest magical properties, and are prized by alchemists.

Cliff Racer

Type: **Creature**	Combat Skill: **50**
Level: **4**	Magic Skill: **90**
Health: **45**	Best Attack
Magicka: **20**	Min/Max: **3-8**
Fatigue: **400**	Willpower: **30**
Soul: **20**	Agility: **50**

Magic: **None**
The long-tailed cliff racer is an aggressive, dangerous, flying creature with a large vertical sail along its spine.

Corpus Stalker

Type: **Humanoid** Combat Skill: **50**
Level: **5** Magic Skill: **90**
Health: **60** Best Attack
Magicka: **50** Min/Max: **5-15**
Fatigue: **300** Willpower: **60**
Soul: **100** Agility: **50**

Magic: **Regenerate**

Corpus stalkers are the deformed, deranged victims of corpus disease. Aggressive and dangerous, they also carry corpus disease, a deadly disease profoundly affecting a victim's mind and body.

Daedroth

Type: **Daedra** Combat Skill: **70**
Level: **12** Magic Skill: **90**
Health: **180** Best Attack
Magicka: **195** Min/Max: **12-36**
Fatigue: **600** Willpower: **80**
Soul: **195** Agility: **75**

Magic: **Regenerate, Poisonbloom, Shockbloom, Immune to Normal Weapons, Third Barrier**

The Daedroth are the crocodile-headed Daedric minions of the Daedra Lord Molag Bal. Daedra hearts have modest magical properties, and are also available at reasonable prices and with considerably less excitement from alchemists.

Dremora

Type: **Daedra** Combat Skill: **80**
Level: **9** Magic Skill: **90**
Health: **160** Best Attack
Magicka: **100** Min/Max: **9-27**
Fatigue: **400** Willpower: **70**
Soul: **100** Agility: **50**

Magic: **Reflect, Immune to Normal Weapons, Second Barrier**

The Dremora are a class of intelligent, powerful war spirits in the service of the Daedra Lord Mehrunes Dagon. Daedra hearts have modest magical properties, and Dremora often carry powerful weapons to aid them in combat.

Dremora Lord

Type: **Daedra** Combat Skill: **90**
Level: **12** Magic Skill: **80**
Health: **280** Best Attack
Magicka: **200** Min/Max: **12-36**
Fatigue: **500** Willpower: **80**
Soul: **200** Agility: **70**

Magic: **Reflect, Fire Storm, Immune to Normal Weapons, Fourth Barrier**

Stronger, faster, and tougher than typical Dremora, the Dremora Lords are truly foes to be feared. Like their lesser counterparts, they wield powerful weapons that can be an excellent source of income to the very powerful (or the very brave and lucky).

Dreugh

Type: **Creature** Combat Skill: **50**
Level: **5** Magic Skill: **90**
Health: **60** Best Attack
Magicka: **75** Min/Max: **5-15**
Fatigue: **400** Willpower: **70**
Soul: **75** Agility: **50**

Magic: **None**

Dreugh are ancient sea monsters, half-human, half-octopus in appearance. Dreugh are hunted for their hides, which are used for making armor, and dreugh wax, a tough, waxy substance with modest magical properties, scraped from dreugh shells.

Dwarven Spectre

Type: **Undead** Combat Skill: **50**
Level: **5** Magic Skill: **90**
Health: **60** Best Attack
Magicka: **75** Min/Max: **5-15**
Fatigue: **400** Willpower: **50**
Soul: **200** Agility: **50**

Magic: **Grave Curse: Luck, Grave Curse: Willpower, Chameleon, Reflect, Immune to Normal Weapons**

Dwarven Spectres are encountered in the ancient abandoned Dwemer ruins. They are aggressive and dangerous, but ectoplasm, a filmy residue that remains after the revenant spirit of a Dwemer has been banished from the mortal plane, is a rare, valuable substance with modest magical properties. Normal weapons do not harm them; only enchanted or silver weapons or deadly spells affect them.

Flame Atronach

Type: **Daedra** Combat Skill: **60**
Level: **7** Magic Skill: **90**
Health: **75** Best Attack
Magicka: **105** Min/Max: **7-21**
Fatigue: **600** Willpower: **70**
Soul: **105** Agility: **50**

Magic: **Reflect, Firebloom, Immune to Fire, Immune to Normal Weapons, Weakness to Frost**

The flame atronach is a powerful Daedric summoning associated with elemental fire. Crystalline elemental fire compounds called fire salts may be salvaged from the remains of banished fire atronachs.

Frost Atronach

Type: **Daedra** Combat Skill: **60**
Level: **9** Magic Skill: **90**
Health: **105** Best Attack
Magicka: **135** Min/Max: **9-27**
Fatigue: **600** Willpower: **80**
Soul: **138** Agility: **50**

Magic: **Reflect, Frostbloom, Immune to Frost, Immune to Normal Weapons, Weakness to Fire**

The Frost Atronach is a powerful Daedric summoning associated with elemental frost. Crystalline elemental frost compounds called frost salts may be salvaged from the remains of banished frost atronachs.

Golden Saint

Type: **Daedra**	Combat Skill: **80**
Level: **20**	Magic Skill: **90**
Health: **250**	Best Attack
Magicka: **755**	Min/Max: **20-60**
Fatigue: **700**	Willpower: **100**
Soul: **400**	Agility: **50**

Magic: **Dispel, Reflect, Immune to Normal Weapons, Resist Fire, Resist Frost, Resist Shock, Shock Shield**

These magical females are spawn of Sheogorath. Their hearts have modest magical properties.

Guar

Type: **Creature**	Combat Skill: **30**
Level: **3**	Magic Skill: **90**
Health: **38**	Best Attack
Magicka: **5**	Min/Max: **1-9**
Fatigue: **400**	Willpower: **40**
Soul: **20**	Agility: **50**

Magic: **None**

The guar is the dominant domesticated herd animal of Morrowind, useful as a pack animal and for its meat and hides. Some guar, however, remain feral and aggressive.

Hunger

Type: **Daedra**	Combat Skill: **60**
Level: **11**	Magic Skill: **90**
Health: **170**	Best Attack
Magicka: **250**	Min/Max: **11-33**
Fatigue: **400**	Willpower: **80**
Soul: **250**	Agility: **50**

Magic: **Disintegrate Armor, Disintegrate Weapon, Paralysis, Immune to Fire, Immune to Frost, Immune to Normal Weapons, Immune to Poison, Immune to Shock**

The Hunger is one of the many voracious servants of the Daedra Lord Boethiah. Daedra hearts have modest magical properties.

Kagouti

Type: **Creature**	Combat Skill: **50**
Level: **4**	Magic Skill: **90**
Health: **45**	Best Attack
Magicka: **10**	Min/Max: **4-12**
Fatigue: **400**	Willpower: **50**
Soul: **20**	Agility: **75**

Magic: **None**

The kagouti is a large, aggressive, dangerous, short-tailed, bipedal creature with huge tusks.

Kwama Forager

Type: **Creature**	Combat Skill: **30**
Level: **2**	Magic Skill: **90**
Health: **23**	Best Attack
Magicka: **15**	Min/Max: **1-3**
Fatigue: **300**	Willpower: **10**
Soul: **15**	Agility: **20**

Magic: **None**

The kwama forager scouts the surface of the land and natural underground passages, searching for suitable locations for new colonies and hunting for prey. Foragers are aggressive but not very dangerous.

Kwama Queen

Type: **Creature**	Combat Skill: **60**
Level: **6**	Magic Skill: **90**
Health: **68**	Best Attack
Magicka: **30**	Min/Max: **6-18**
Fatigue: **1000**	Willpower: **50**
Soul: **30**	Agility: **50**

Magic: **None**

The kwama queen is the huge, bloated kwama that produces the nest's eggs. They are too large and fat to move, and all their needs are attended by kwama worker.

Kwama Warrior

Type: **Creature**	Combat Skill: **50**
Level: **3**	Magic Skill: **90**
Health: **45**	Best Attack
Magicka: **12**	Min/Max: **3-9**
Fatigue: **400**	Willpower: **50**
Soul: **20**	Agility: **50**

Magic: **Kwama Poison**

The kwama warrior defends the kwama colony's tunnels and chambers. Warriors are aggressive and dangerous.

Kwama Worker

Type: **Creature**	Combat Skill: **30**
Level: **2**	Magic Skill: **90**
Health: **30**	Best Attack
Magicka: **8**	Min/Max: **1-6**
Fatigue: **300**	Willpower: **30**
Soul: **8**	Agility: **50**

Magic: **None**

The kwama worker digs the colony's tunnels and chambers and tends the queen and the eggs. Workers are unaggressive, but not completely helpless.

Lame Corprus

Type: **Humanoid**	Combat Skill: 60
Level: 8	Magic Skill: 90
Health: 90	Best Attack
Magicka: 160	Min/Max: 8-24
Fatigue: 400	Willpower: 70
Soul: 160	Agility: 100

Magic: **Black-Heart Blight, Regenerate**

The lame corprus is a deformed, deranged victim of corprus disease. Aggressive and dangerous, they carry corpus disease, a deadly disease profoundly affecting a victim's mind and body.

Mudcrab

Type: **Creature**	Combat Skill: 30
Level: 1	Magic Skill: 90
Health: 15	Best Attack
Magicka: 5	Min/Max: 1-1
Fatigue: 400	Willpower: 0
Soul: 5	Agility: 15

Magic: **None**

They are small creatures with a hard shell. They live mostly along the coast and they're usually not aggressive...but if they ever get the taste of meat, they become hunters.

Nix-Hound

Type: **Creature**	Combat Skill: 30
Level: 2	Magic Skill: 90
Health: 23	Best Attack
Magicka: 10	Min/Max: 1-6
Fatigue: 400	Willpower: 30
Soul: 10	Agility: 50

Magic: **None**

The nix-hound is a medium-sized, aggressive pack predator.

Ogrim

Type: **Daedra**	Combat Skill: 60
Level: 11	Magic Skill: 90
Health: 170	Best Attack
Magicka: 165	Min/Max: 11-33
Fatigue: 1000	Willpower: 80
Soul: 165	Agility: 50

Magic: **Regenerate, Immune to Normal Weapons**

Ogrim are massive, powerful, dimly intelligent servants of the Daedra Lord Malacath.

Rat

Type: **Creature**	Combat Skill: 30
Level: 2	Magic Skill: 90
Health: 23	Best Attack
Magicka: 10	Min/Max: 1-2
Fatigue: 300	Willpower: 0
Soul: 10	Agility: 20

Magic: **None**

The rat is a hardy, abundant hunter-scavenger, found on the land surface and in natural and excavated underground environments.

Scamp

Type: **Daedra**	Combat Skill: 50
Level: 5	Magic Skill: 90
Health: 45	Best Attack
Magicka: 100	Min/Max: 5-15
Fatigue: 400	Willpower: 70
Soul: 100	Agility: 20

Magic: **Immune to Normal Weapons, Resist Fire, Resist Frost, Resist Poison, Resist Shock**

The scamp is a weak, cowardly servant of Mehrunes Dagon. Scamps may be summoned by conjurers, and their skin is sought by alchemists for its magical properties.

Scrib

Type: **Creature**	Combat Skill: 30
Level: 1	Magic Skill: 80
Health: 8	Best Attack
Magicka: 12	Min/Max: 1-2
Fatigue: 300	Willpower: 0
Soul: 10	Agility: 20

Magic: **Paralysis**

The scrib is a late larval form of the kwama. While typically weak and non-aggressive, their bite has the ability to paralyze attackers, making them dangerous to less experienced adventurers.

Shalk

Type: **Creature**	Combat Skill: 60
Level: 6	Magic Skill: 90
Health: 38	Best Attack
Magicka: 30	Min/Max: 6-18
Fatigue: 400	Willpower: 25
Soul: 30	Agility: 30

Magic: **Firebite, Immune to Fire, Weakness to Frost**

The shalk is a large, moderately aggressive beetle. Shalk resins are used as glues and stiffeners in manufacturing bonemold and chitin armors.

Skeleton

Type: **Undead**	Combat Skill: **40**
Level: **3**	Magic Skill: **90**
Health: **38**	Best Attack
Magicka: **30**	Min/Max: **1-9**
Fatigue: **1000**	Willpower: **50**
Soul: **30**	Agility: **50**

Magic: **Immune to Disease, Immune to Frost, Immune to Poison, Resist Shock**

The skeleton is a revenant that protects the tombs of clan and kin. They are capable of using all manner of melee weapons, and often defend themselves with shields.

Skeleton Champion

Type: **Undead**	Combat Skill: **80**
Level: **10**	Magic Skill: **80**
Health: **150**	Best Attack
Magicka: **30**	Min/Max: **10-30**
Fatigue: **1000**	Willpower: **50**
Soul: **200**	Agility: **50**

Magic: **Immune to Disease, Immune to Frost, Immune to Poison, Resist Shock**

The skeleton champion is the most powerful of the animated skeletons that protect Dunmer ancestral tombs.

Skeleton Warrior

Type: **Undead**	Combat Skill: **70**
Level: **7**	Magic Skill: **80**
Health: **80**	Best Attack
Magicka: **30**	Min/Max: **7-21**
Fatigue: **1000**	Willpower: **40**
Soul: **30**	Agility: **50**

Magic: **Immune to Disease, Immune to Frost, Immune to Poison, Resist Shock**

The skeleton warrior is a powerful animated grave guardian found often in Dunmer ancestral tombs.

Slaughterfish

Type: **Creature**	Combat Skill: **30**
Level: **2**	Magic Skill: **90**
Health: **23**	Best Attack
Magicka: **10**	Min/Max: **1-6**
Fatigue: **400**	Willpower: **30**
Soul: **10**	Agility: **50**

Magic: **None**

The slaughterfish is an aggressive creature found both in open waters and subterranean pools.

Small Slaughterfish

Type: **Creature**	Combat Skill: **40**
Level: **2**	Magic Skill: **80**
Health: **15**	Best Attack
Magicka: **10**	Min/Max: **1-5**
Fatigue: **300**	Willpower: **20**
Soul: **10**	Agility: **50**

Magic: **None**

Smaller variety of the slaughterfish.

Steam Centurion

Type: **Creature**	Combat Skill: **60**
Level: **10**	Magic Skill: **90**
Health: **150**	Best Attack
Magicka: **30**	Min/Max: **10-30**
Fatigue: **1000**	Willpower: **70**
Soul: **0**	Agility: **50**

Magic: **Resist Fire, Resist Frost, Resist Poison, Resist Shock**

The steam centurion is an enchanted animated artifact of Dwemer creation. Constructed in the form of an armored warrior, they are aggressive and dangerous..

Storm Atronach

Type: **Daedra**	Combat Skill: **70**
Level: **15**	Magic Skill: **90**
Health: **200**	Best Attack
Magicka: **195**	Min/Max: **15-45**
Fatigue: **600**	Willpower: **90**
Soul: **150**	Agility: **50**

Magic: **Reflect, Shockbloom, Immune to Normal Weapons, Immune to Shock, Resist Poison, Shock Shield**

The storm atronach is a powerful Daedric summoning associated with elemental lightning.

Winged Twilight

Type: **Daedra**	Combat Skill: **70**
Level: **15**	Magic Skill: **90**
Health: **220**	Best Attack
Magicka: **210**	Min/Max: **15-45**
Fatigue: **800**	Willpower: **100**
Soul: **300**	Agility: **50**

Magic: **Reflect, Resist Fire, Resist Frost, Resist Poison, Resist Shock**

Winged twilights are the female-formed Daedric messengers of the Daedra Lord Azura.

Chapter Two: Creatures

Chapter Three: World

I n the Morrowind world maps, we've sought to show significant locations in the game's external world—from bandit caves to Daedric shrines to Dwarven ruins to egg mines to wizard lairs.

Due to an almost fanatical devotion to the artistic virtue called "suspense," the designers have created the world with a wholesome amount of uncertainty. This ensures that you never really know what you're about to experience. Either a) embrace this approach with open arms and enjoy the moments they provide; or b) cower in fear and huddle in the corner. Either way, the designers have produced the intended effect.

Therefore, the references on these maps are representative and not exhaustive. We've noted sites significant in the Main Quest, places where you can receive and perform Faction and Miscellaneous quests, and the characters who play a role in them. We've located characters who have something unusual to offer the player—whether it is training to especially high levels or transportation to a distant town.

We've even put in places like tree stumps where stuff has been tucked away.

And we've tried to give a sense of what creatures you'll face in the wilderness, and where you'll find them.

Note that this has been simplified somewhat, and that your experience with creatures won't exactly match the map.

For one thing, we haven't shown every single location in which a creature might appear. We didn't want to scare you.

Rather, we've sought to show critter clusters, where you might face more than one—places where, sometimes, you could be in danger.

The key word here is "could." Many of the game's creatures will appear in every game. Many other creatures will appear a certain percentage of the time. So it's conceivable, walking into a stony cul-de-sac, that you might face the two rats mentioned in the key, one rat, or, lucky you, no rats at all. You'll also note that you will face new, and tougher, creatures as you rise in level. Consequently, consider the creature locations and numbers as worst-case scenarios.

Use these maps in conjunction with the in-game map, and directions you receive during quests to help pinpoint the location of hard-to-find shrines, caves, ruins, etc. Or, if you perform a more freeform approach, they can serve has helpful "visitor's guides" when wandering the lands.

	A2	A3	A4	
B1	B2	B3	B4	
	C2	C3	C4	C5
	D2	D3	D4	D5
	E2	E3	E4	

ISLAND OF VVARDENFELL, MORROWIND PROVINCE

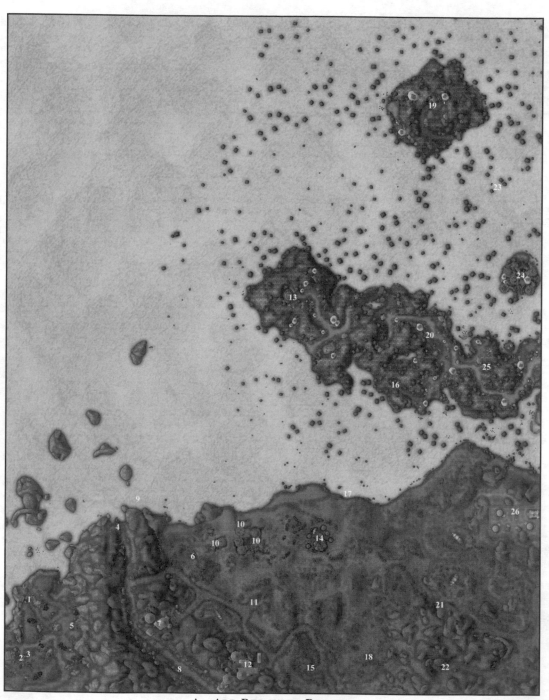

A2: ALD REDAYNIA REGION

A2: ALD REDAYNIA MAP LOCATIONS:

1. **Ashir-Dan:** A smugglers cave-modest in size, but well-stocked.
2. **Panud Egg Mine:** A compact egg mine.
3. A Dreamer.
4. **Derelict Shipwreck:** …with weapon loot below, ingredient loot above, and a grand soul gem in the cabin!
5. A campfire, a bottle of something-or-other, and thou…equals an unprovoked attack by these three renegade Ashlanders.
6. **Ibar-Dad:** Starts out as a regular old cave and turns out to be the hidden Daedric tomb of Mordrin Hannin, with some serious loot-including the artifact Eleidon's Ward.
7. **Druscashti:** Like Galom Daeus, it shows to the world the face of a Dwarven ruin,but this is in fact the headquarters of the Quarra vampire clan.
8. **Sha-Adnius:** A small-ish bandit cave with three bandits, a modest supply of bandit loot…and six Argonian and Khajiit slaves for you to free.
9. Some of the best pearl beds in the game stretch from here to the east.
10. **Assurnabitashpi:** Most Daedric shrines have a single entrance. A few have two. This huge Daedric ruin has three. You'll visit it in a Morag Tong quest to liberate the Ring of Sanguine Silver Wisdom.
11. **Drath Ancestral Tomb:** Small tomb, small risk, small loot.
12. **Bthungthumz:** You'll visit this Dwarven ruin in a House Telvanni quest to retrieve the ring of Dahrk Mezalf.
13. **Ald Redaynia:** And you thought all the renegade wizards who took over the Velothi domes were living. This one is occupied by a Level 20 Skeleton War-Wizard who has the Vampiric Ring artifact.
14. **Urshilaku Camp:** The westernmost of the four permanent Ashlander settlements. You'll spend a good deal of time in and around this camp on the Main Quest and can revisit it in one of the Miscellaneous Quests. You'll find the "index" needed to operate the Propylon Chamber at-the stronghold Valenvaryon on a table in the wise woman's yurt.
15. **Abinabi:** A Sixth House base, deep in the ash desert. Not much loot beyond the great Sixth House Bell Hammer …unless you've suddenly developed a taste for <ulp!> corprusmeat.
16. **Assumanu:** This sorcerers' lair is home to Varona Nelas, from whom you'll attempt to recover an embroidered glove in an Imperial Legion quest.
17. **Madas Grotto:** Obscure, dark, dangerous, and next to empty of loot, Morrowind's grottos are mostly just good for I-found-it bragging rights. Except one. And this isn't that one.
18. **Urshilaku Burial Caverns:** You'll visit this huge mausoleun, consisting of seven linked tombs, on the Main Quest to retrieve the enchanted Bonebiter Bow of Sul-Senipul.
19. **Big Head's Shack:** In fact, this Argonian has a perfectly ordinary-sized head. It's just that what's inside that head has gotten all jumbled up. You'll pay him a visit in one of the Daedric Quests.
20. **Andavel Ancestral Tomb:** A good-sized crypt with so-so loot and Daedric defenders.
21. **Llando Ancestral Tomb:** A small, run-of-the-mill tomb.
22. **Akimaes-Ilanipu Egg Mine:** An egg mine? Out here? Yup. Complete with kwama queen. But watch yourself: The enemies within are blighted.
23. **Obscure Shipwreck:** Some interesting odds 'n' ends at this hard-to-reach site-including some Dwarven loot and amulets useful in a Quarra vampire quest.
24. **Onnissiralis:** A small, deep two-level shrine to Daedric god Sheogorath…with a fair amount of ebony and jewels in the loot.
25. **Sargon:** You'll visit this huge, well-populated and potentially lucrative cave in a Fighters Guild quest.
26. **Valenvaryon:** No, you're not crazy. Valenvaryon is more a stronghold in name than in fact. It doesn't have a proper dungeon-just an assortment of rooftop huts for the stern-looking orcs who live here. One of those buildings is the Propylon Chamber. Here you can teleport you to the strongholds Falasmaryon and Rotheran, if you have the Valenvaryon "index." (It's in the Urshilaku camp.) And Abelle Chriditte is the "secret master" of the Alchemy skill.

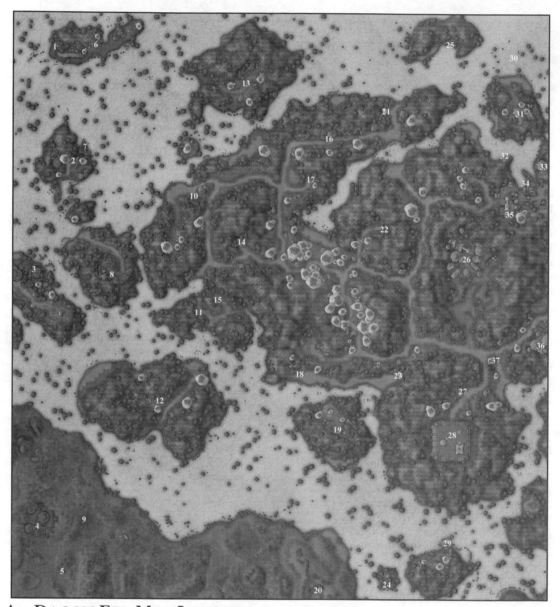

A3: Dagon Fel Map Locations:

1. **Nelas Ancestral Tomb:** A remote crypt with some uncommon loot.
2. **Vas:** You'll escort Buoyant Armiger Ulyne Henim through this Velothi dome in a Fighters Guild quest.
3. **Assurdirapal:** When you activate the statue at this shrine, the Daedric god Malacath will send you on a quest to end the Oreyn family bloodline.
4. **Ebernanit:** This remote shrine is home to Talis Veran, current owner of the Ring of Sanguine Golden Wisdom, which you'll need to obtain in a Morag Tong quest.
5. **Omalen Ancestral Tomb:** A long and well-defended tomb, with a singular letter at its end.

6. A Giant Netch. You'll have to kill it with the Fork of Horripilation in a very strange Daedric quest given you by the god Sheogorath.
7. **Abandoned Shipwreck:** Now and then, you'll stumble onto a quest without anyone actually giving it to you. One such adventure can be uncovered aboard this wreck.
8. **Sanctus Shrine:** In a Tribunal Temple quest, you'll have to travel to this distant island…without uttering a word.
9. Critter alert. Two alits live right around here.
10. **Sud:** A new wizard needs a staff. If you don't have one when it's time for your promotion, your pals in the Mages Guild will suggest, ever so discretely, that you take the staff from Anime, the renegade wizard who lives in this huge lair.
11. **Orethi Ancestral Tomb:** A modest-sized tomb, with commensurate loot and opposition.
12. **Ashmelech:** From the outside, it looks like just another ancestral tomb, but this headquarters of the Aundae clan is effectively a vampire town.
13. **Isle of the Daedra:** The goddess Azura will dispatch you to clear this island of potential distractions in a Daedric quest.
14. **Pudai Egg Mine:** In a Fighters Guild quest, you'll search Pudai for seven fabled Eggs of Gold.
15. **Shara:** The Morag Tong's hit on Telvanni sorcerer Tirer Belvayn will send you to this Velothi dome.
16. **Habinbaes:** A mid-sized bandit cave, with the usual bad guys (plus a pair of nix-hounds) to kill, slaves to liberate, and a good deal of loot to pocket.
17. **Madas-Zebba Egg Mine:** What can we say? Kwama eggs, and lots of them. And a bunch of blighted opponents.
18. **Aharasaplit Camp:** You can visit this renegade Ashlander camp to kill Zallay Subaddamael in a Miscellaneous Quest.
19. **Sendus Sathis:** You'll ferry food to this hermit in a Tribunal Temple quest.
20. **Indaren Ancestral Tomb:** Surprise! You're not alone here. Three smugglers beat you to the punch. And when you're done with them, thar be Daedra!
21. **Sarethi Ancestral Tomb:** An Aundae vampire lair.
22. **Malacath Statue:** You'll deliver an offering of Daedra hearts to the image of this Daedric god in a Tribunal Temple quest.
23. **Dralas Ancestral Tomb:** You'll find two more smugglers in here, and these fellows seem farther along in the process of converting the place to a smugglers' cave. (Crates!) Also, Bonelord!
24. **Ainab:** A Sixth House base, with shrine. Pretty good loot, and lots of baddies.
25. **Malmus Grotto:** How long can you tread water? For a grotto, the loot in the last room isn't too shabby.
26. **Mzuleft:** You'll visit this Orc-infested Dwarven ruin on a Mages Guild quest to get the plans for a Dwemer scarab.
27. **Surirulk:** Bandit cave. Not big enough to get you lost. Well-populated. Good loot.
28. **Rotheran:** Another unconventional stronghold. It's not a dungeon so much as an arena! In an Imperial Cult quest, you're sent there to rescue Adusamsi Assurnarairan and retrieve the Ice Blade of the Monarch.
29. **Ilanipu Grotto:** And a big one, too. Good loot on the two bodies, and potential for more in the plentiful kollop shells.
30. Sunken treasure. There isn't much of it in the game, save in and around full-scale shipwrecks, but here's an exception.
31. **Andre Maul's Tower:** Turning Dwarven towers into living quarters seems to be a trend. Someone should write a Morrowind home-improvement book: "Rusted Gear: Making Yesterday's Dwemer Ruin Tomorrow's Home."
32. **Dagon Fel:** A Nordic village that, like Khuul, is more of a waypoint than a destination. It isn't exceptional in and of itself, but for the easy access it offers to nearby sites
33. **Vacant Tower:** A rather petite Dwemer ruin and home to Khargol gro-Boguk—"secret master"of Unarmored combat.
34. **Haema Farseer:** This gentleman's boat will take you to Khuul, Sadrith Mora, Tel Aruhn, or Tel Mora.
35. **Heifnir: Trader:** The only store in town—and, with End of the World Renter Rooms—the only business, period. Heifnir's got a lot of armor and weaponry on display, but he sells a bit of everything.
36. **Nchardahrk:** A relatively small Dwarven ruin.
37. **Punsabanit:** A large smugglers cave with a ton of loot…and almost as many nix-hounds as smugglers!

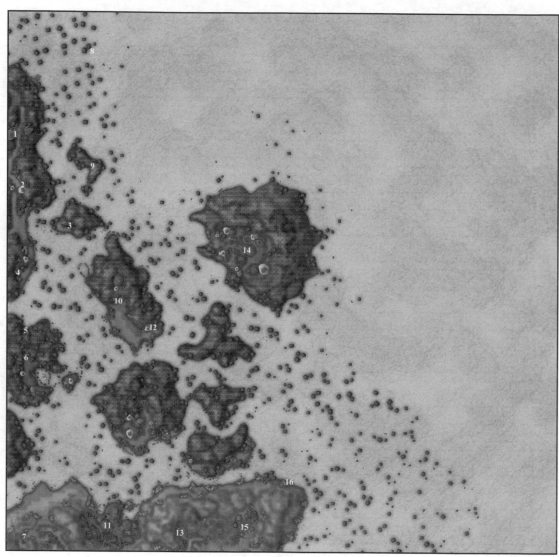

A4: Ald Daedroth Region

A4: ALD DAEDROTH MAP LOCATIONS:

1. **Sorkvild's Tower:** A necromancer lives in this Dwarven ruin just east of Dagon Fel. Your interactions with him are not of the highest quality. You can try to pickpocket him for the Masque of Clavicus Vile from him. And you will be ordered to assassinate him in an Imperial Cult quest.
2. **Senim Ancestral Tomb:** A big tomb with a lot of loot, including a complete set of bonemold armor.
3. **Ancient Shipwreck:** You will find odds 'n' ends of loot aboard this grounded wreck, including an odd little book.
4. **Odirnamat:** Another bandit cave. Like many bandit caves, it's loaded with loot—some quite good and some relatively uncommon.
5. **Shallit:** A bad-guy cave whose link to the vampire lair in Drethan Ancestral Tomb (see item 6) the resident bad guys have exploited. You'll be sent here to kill Rels Tenim in a Fighters Guild quest.
6. **Drethan Ancestral Tomb:** Home to an ancient and powerful vampire named Marara, who has discovered the downside of immortality. You can put her out of her misery in a vampire quest.
7. **Favel Ancestral Tomb:** You'll help Minabibi Assardarainat perform an exorcism in this crypt as part of a Mages Guild quest.
8. **A floating bottle:** Inside, a long note. It may take you a while to realize the writer is no longer of this world.
9. **M'Aiq the Liar:** A fisherman who can't be trusted on any subject. Except two.
10. **Sanni:** Renegades are always in bad moods. That goes for renegade Ashlanders. And it goes for renegade Telvanni sorcerers, which is what you'll encounter in this Velothi dome.
11. **Kushtashpi:** You'll need to do a bit of jumping and running (or know the Levitate spell) to fully explore the underground portion of this Daedric shrine.
12. **Setus Egg Mine:** A rather large, but otherwise undistinguished, egg mine.
13. **Sinamusa Egg Mine:** A relatively compact egg mine. (How much, honestly, can you say about an egg mine?)
14. **Ald Daedroth:** An enormous shrine, where Tribunal Temple Ordinators and Daedra worshippers are having a dust-up. In the Main Quest, you'll add a third party to the equation: the Ahemmusa Ashlanders, who are looking for a safe haven from the Blight (Wrong place to look, folks!) You'll also visit Ald Daedroth on a Morag Tong quest to secure two "Threads of the Webspinner" and a Tribunal Temple quest to recover the "Gambolpuddy." (Don't ask.)
15. **Ahemmusa Camp:** One of two permanent Ashlander settlements in the far north. You'll be a persistent visitor here—on the Main Quest in your campaign to be named Nerevarine and on a range of Faction and Miscellaneous quests.
16. **Eluba-Addon Grotto:** Nobody in here except us pearls.

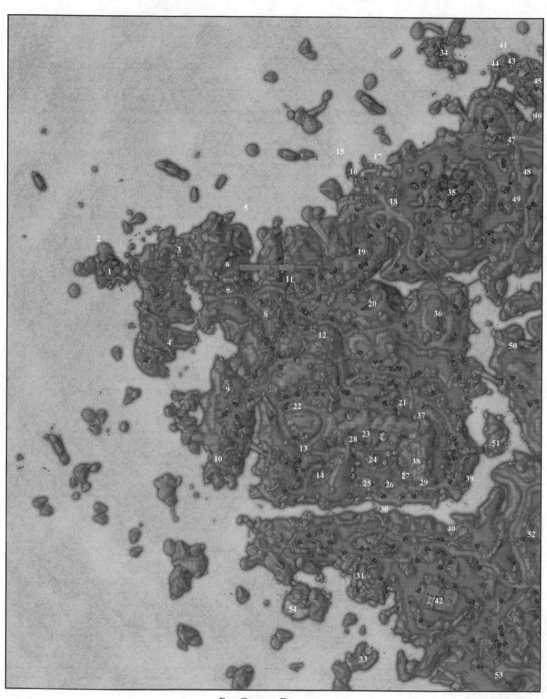

B1: GNISIS REGION

B1: GNISIS MAP LOCATIONS:

1. **Yasammidan:** You'll visit this shrine to Daedric god Mehrunes Dagon in a Morag Tong quest to retrieve the Ring of Sanguine Sublime Wisdom and again in the Daedric Quests to receive a quest from Dagon himself.
2. Unmarked Shipwreck. Until now, that is!
3. Campfire…and a couple of nasties with a chest of gold.
4. **Eluba-Addon Egg Mine:** A small kwama egg mine. Not to be confused with the Eluba-Addon Grotto far to the east.
5. **Forgotten Shipwreck:** Size can be deceptive. This sunken ship is small, but it has a whole lot of loot!
6. **Arkngthunch-Sturdumz:** Edwinna Elbert will ask you to retrieve a Dwemer Tube from this Dwarven ruin in a Mages Guild quest.
7. A lot of loot on a ledge, including a dwarven mace!
8. **Ginith Ancestral Tomb:** The renegade Berne Clan vampire Lord Irarak makes his home here. You'll be asked to kill him in a Quarra vampire quest.
9. Two friendly guys toasting marshmerrow…not!
10. **Ashinabi:** A big (and we mean big) smugglers den, with two sections and, hence, two entrances (east and west).
11. **Synette Jeline and friend:** Help this tender young thing find her lost ring in a Miscellaneous Quest. Do you like surprises?
12. His name is Din. He is ready for the bin. You can escort him to a healer, or you can stick him with a pin. Or cure him yourself, in a Miscellaneous Quest.
13. A Sixth House agent. And this one is talking in his sleep.
14. **The Widow Vabdas' hut:** You'll to be asked to get a deed from this poor lady in an early Imperial Legion quest.
15. **Ald Velothi:** A small and relatively quiet ramshackle fishing village. No fast travel, and not much cooking.
16. **Galyn Arvel:** Abolitionist and leader of the Twin Lamps anti-slavery movement. You'll help her spirit an escaped slave to safety in a House Hlaalu quest, and she can help you by directing marriageable escaped slaves to your stronghold if you're in House Redoran.
17. **Old Blue Fin:** You'll have to kill this slaughterfish in an early House Redoran quest.
18. **Outpost:** The only store in Ald Velothi. Here you can buy a range of items, obtain training and pick up House Redoran faction quests from Theldyn Virith (the village's "sort of" hetman). Oh, and there's the nice view from the tower, too.
19. **Aidanat Camp:** You'll pay these renegade Ashlanders a visit to secure the release of abducted Madura Seran in an Imperial Legion quest.
20. **Llervu Ancestral Tomb:** A small crypt.
21. **Critter alert:** Lots of them roam this wild country, including a hungry alit that's waiting here.
22. Critters here, too. Specifically, a guar.
23. **Gnisis:** It may be a country town, but it's got an Imperial Legion garrison (the source of the most of the quests here), a big old egg mine up on the mountain and a silt strider port.
24. **Gnisis Temple:** The Mask of Vivec is in the basement. You'll make a pilgrimage here in your early quests for the Tribunal Temple.
25. **Gnisis silt strider port:** From here, you can ride Punibi Yahaz's big bug to Ald'ruhn, Khuul or Maar Gan.
26. **Madach Tradehouse:** If you want to join the Legion, you have to go through General Darius. This is where he hangs out.
27. **Gnisis Barracks:** You'll spend some time with the troopers in an Imperial Legion quest to expose a plot against the Emperor.
28. **Arvs-Drelen:** An old Velothi dome that now serves as the residence of rogue Telvanni sorcerer Baladas Demnevanni. You'll become a familiar visitor here. Demnevanni is a Telvanni quest-giver, figures in several quest objectives, and is just a generally knowledgeable fellow. If you don't bore him to tears.
29. **Fort Darius:** The smallest of several Imperial fortifications on Vvardenfell, this is basically just the east gate to Gnisis.
30. **Hentus Yansurnummu:** Someone has stolen his pants. You can get them back for him in a Miscellaneous Quest.
31. **Koal Cave:** You'll escort a pilgrim to a shrine in this seaside cave in a House Redoran quest, twice track down pilgrims who've gotten lost on their way and make a pilgrimage here yourself in one of the early Tribunal Temple quests.
32. **Fedris Tharen:** In fact, here's one of those "lost" pilgrims now, not a stone's throw from the cave door. What an idiot!
33. **Subdun:** One of the bigger bases of the Sixth House cult. If you shut it down, you'll turn off the flow of Dreamers, Sleepers, and nightmares in the Ald Velothi, Gnisis, and Khuul areas.

34. Nothing important. Just a pleasant home away from home for someone in Khuul, no doubt. (Oh, and a locked trunk make it worth your while.)

35. **Ashalmawia:** Three quests will send you to this Daedric shrine—one a Miscellaneous Quest to rescue a woman from cultists, one a House Redoran quest to assassinate the shrine's presiding villain, and one a House Hlaalu quest to rescue an escaped slave.

36. **Palansour:** A smuggler's cave in which you're not the smugglers' biggest problem. You'll learn what we mean in a Miscellaneous Quest. Enter here, or along the river to the northwest.

37. **Mat:** Just your average bad-guy cave.

38. **Gnisis Egg Mine:** Like the Imperial Legion quest that takes you there, this mine has hidden depths-not least of them access to a hidden Dwemer ruin, Bethamez (which you'll visit in a Mages Guild quest)…

39. …and this underwater entrance!

40. **Falas Ancestral Tomb:** Just move along folks. Nothing to see here. Nope. Nothing.

41. **Khuul:** Though rarely itself a destination, this fishing village's tie-ins to Vvardenfell's transportation network means it's often a waypoint on journeys to other destinations.

42. **Berandas:** An ancient Dunmer stronghold. This one's fallen into the hands of Daedra. You'll visit it to recover the Boots of the Apostle in an Imperial Cult quest.

43. **Talmeni Drethan:** This fine fellow will transport you by boat from Khuul to Dagon Fel and Gnaar Mok.

44. A bit of loot someone's squirreled away.

45. **Thongar's Tradehouse:** The only game in town. Thongar sells a wide range of stuff. Ondi will train Imperial Legionnaires. And you'll need to pop in here and nick Shotherra's Amulet of Sanguine Glib Speech in a Morag Tong quest.

46. **Khuul silt strider port:** The estimable Seldus Nerendus will cart your bones (and anyone else's you may be carrying) to Ald'ruhn, Gnisis, and Maar Gan.

47. **Seran Ancestral Tomb:** A small and relatively plain Dunmer crypt.

48. **Asha-Ahhe Egg Mine:** It's an egg mine! It's a witch's lair! It's an egg mine and a witch's lair! The witch is Thelsa Dral, and you'll have to pop her in an Imperial Cult quest.

49. **Shashmanu Camp:** More renegade Ashlanders. As always, they want to have you for dinner.

50. **Rethandus Ancestral Tomb:** A large crypt with a fair amount of loot.

51. **Assarnud:** A big, tough bandit cave.

52. A little kagouti den.

53. **Veloth Ancestral Tomb:** A medium-sized crypt, guarded mostly by Daedra. (When Daedra are in a tomb, should they be called "Deadra"?)

54. A little netch colony.

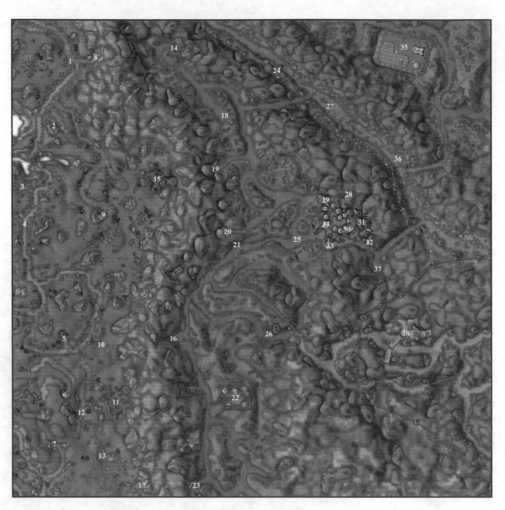

B2: Maar Gan Map Locations:

1. **Sason:** You can get a Miscellaneous Quest from this fellow. His wife has been abducted by cultists and hauled off to the shrine Ashalmawia, near Ald Velothi.
2. A little kagouti lair.
3. Three villains and a bit of loot.
4. Loads of critters east of this road (and some to the west as well).
5. **Salothan Ancestral Tomb:** A small crypt with modest loot.
6. **Mamaea:** In the Main Quest, you'll battle Dagoth Araynys in this huge Sixth House base and claim his Soul Ring. And in a Miscellaneous Quest spin-off from the Main Quest, you'll rescue prisoner Hannat Zainsubani.
7. **Ashimanu Egg Mine:** You'll remove a diseased shalk from this mine in a House Redoran quest.
8. **Alen Ancestral Tomb:** A Quarra vampire lair.
9. **Reloth Ancestral Tomb:** Renegade vampire Merta makes her home here. You'll be asked to kill her in a Berne vampire quest.
10. Future site for the West Gash Petting Zoo. Critter alert!
11. **Dushariran:** A Daedric shrine, it's a long way to the shrine proper, but the loot there makes it worth the trip.

12. **Lucan Ostorius:** He's got a Miscellaneous Quest for you: delivering weapons to Ald'ruhn.

13. A pair of Mabrigash—Ashlander witch women—who behave pretty much like other renegade Ashlanders. (i.e. They attack on sight.)

14. **Yesamsi:** What, did they run out of empty Velothi domes? Two sorcerers are holed up in this cave, along with a good deal of loot and the odd atronach.

15. **Maelkashishi:** You'll visit this shrine on a Tribunal Temple quest to cure an Orc of blight disease, and again to collect the first of the indices needed to operate the Propylon Chambers atop the strongholds. Hope you can Levitate. (The shrine's Forgotten Galleries are immensely high.)

16. **Mila-Nipal:** You'll pop into this renegade Ashlander encampment in a House Redoran quest to free abducted pilgrim Beden Giladren.

17. **Randas Ancestral Tomb:** A mid-sized tomb with decent loot and Daedric defenders.

18. Three Ashlanders stand near a campfire. Two of them are men. One of the men holds a bow. A bottle lies on its side nearby. This can't be good.

19. **Hairat-Vassamsi Egg Mine:** A large egg mine, with blighted enemies, that has already claimed a casualty. (Check out the little shrine back at the Maar Gan Outpost.)

20. **Rothan Ancestral Tomb:** In a House Redoran quest, you'll retrieve lost trader Mathis Dalobar from this crypt, where he's taken refuge from an ash storm, and escort him back to Maar Gan.

21. **Fonus Rathryon:** Also lost is this pilgrim, who was on his way to Koal Cave. You can escort him there in a Miscellaneous Quest.

22. Depends. Seriously. If you haven't built your stronghold, this site will be called Bal Isra, and there won't be anything here. If you have built it, this will be the House Redoran stronghold, Indarys Manor.

23. **Odibaal:** Some hideouts are generic. That is, you're not dealing with bandits, smugglers, or sorcerers—just general-purpose Bad People. This is one of those hideouts. There's a nice, Swiss Family Robinson sort of thing going on in this one.

24. **Shishi:** A Telvanni base-lately crushed by House Redoran. Or maybe not quite so crushed as it appears. You'll explore this Velothi dome for survivors in a House Redoran quest.

25. A Dreamer.

26. Three Mabrigash.

27. **Foyada Bani-Dad:** This lava riverbed is the most direct foot route from Maar Gan to Vvardenfell's north coast and the strongholds in the northern Ashlands.

28. **Maar Gan:** A northwestern complement to Molag Mar, this buttoned-up fortress town lies at the foot of the foyada and so is a natural retreat for a battered adventurer returning from the north.

29. **Andus Tradehouse:** Manse Andus offers bed and barter. Aerin and Bugdurash gra-Gashel offer training. (In fact, Aerin is a "secret master" of Light Armor.) And you'll have to deal with Miles Gloriosus to get a book for a Thieves Guild quest.

30. **Tashpi Ashibael's Hut:** You're sent here in a Mages Guild quest to whack Ms. Ashibael for being a necromancer. (It's a bit more complicated than that, as you'll discover.)

31. **Maar Gan Shrine:** You'll visit the shrine in a Tribunal Temple quest that teaches the value of a good taunt-and again to cop the index for stronghold Falasmaryon's Propylon Chamber. And Salen Ravel has spells, potions, and ingredients for sale.

32. **Hulene's Hut:** There's quite a scene at Hulene's, where an apprentice has summoned a scamp and can't squeeze it back in the bottle. You've got to straighten things out in a Mages Guild quest.

33. **Maar Gan silt strider port:** Daras Aryon will bug you all the way to Ald'ruhn, Gnisis, or Khuul.

34. **Outpost:** A strip mall to serve your hacking 'n' slashing needs. Alds Baro sells and repairs weapons and armor. Saryn Sarothril and Nuleno Tedas offer training. Sedris Omalen sells spells, potions and ingredients.

35. **Falasmaryon:** You'll visit this ancient Dunmer stronghold—now a Sixth House base-to take on Dagoth Tanis in a later House Redoran quest. Missun Akin, in a rooftop hut, is "secret master" of the Marksman skill. With the appropriate index, the Propylon Chamber will zap you to either the stronghold Berandas or Valenvaryon.

36. Two renegade Ashlanders.

37. And two more.

38. **Bthanchend:** A Dwarven ruin. But despite its location inside the Ghostfence, Bthanchend is not an ash vampire citadel.

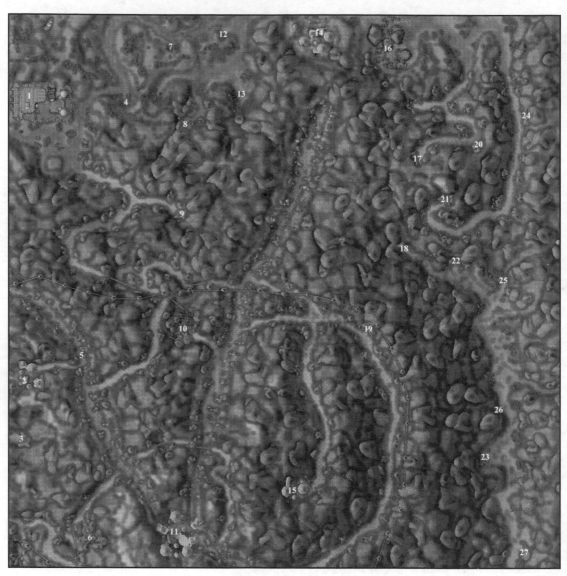

B3: Dagoth Ur Region

B3: Dagoth Ur Map Locations:

1. **Kogoruhn:** It means "unbreakable home," and it may feel unbreakable when you first explore this largest and nastiest of the strongholds-the ancient home of House Dagoth. You'll be sent to Kogoruhn at least twice—once on the Main Quest in order to become a Clanfriend to the Ashlanders and in an advanced Tribunal Temple quest to recover the Hair Shirt of St. Aralor.
2. **Vemynal:** One of five Dagoth citadels in the Red Mountain crater. In the endgame, you'll need to explore it to recover the artifact Sunder and the Amulet of Heartheal.
3. **Mausur Caverns:** A huge abandoned ebony mine. Of course, "abandoned" does not mean "empty"…
4. **Mamshar-Disamus Camp:** More fun with renegade Ashlanders.
5. **Charma's Breath:** The lava tube that links the Red Mountain crater to stronghold Kogoruhn to the north. You'll use it to reach Dagoth Uthol in the endgame.
6. **Ularradallaku:** Life apparently goes on, even deep inside the Ghostfence. This isn't simply a Daedric shrine, but a huge Daedric shrine-with Mehrunes Dagon worshippers and everything! (Even a nasty little trick: The Daedra heart on the altar is cursed. Take it, and a Dremora Lord will appear behind you and attack.)
7. **Drinith Ancestral Tomb:** A big tomb, with Daedric defenders. Big loot, too, but much of it is common.
8. **Kora-Dur:** Molag Bal will send you to this cave to dispatch a lazy follower in one of the Daedric quests.
9. **Ahanibi-Malmus Egg Mine:** A blighted egg mine. This close to Red Mountain, you were expecting they'd be over easy?
10. **Assalkushalit:** A small shrine to Sheogorath.
11. **Dagoth Ur's Citadel:** Your last stop in the Main Quest. In a Tribunal Temple quest, you'll enter the citadel in search of the Crosier of St. Llothi. And in the endgame, you'll come back to kill Dagoth Gilvoth and Dagoth Ur himself. And then run like hell.
12. **Bensamsi:** A big Sixth House base.
13. Two Mabrigash.
14. **Bthuand:** You'll visit this Dwarven ruin to retrieve the enchanted Spellbreaker shield in a vampire quest.
15. **Tureynulal:** Another ash vampire citadel. In a Tribunal Temple quest, you'll enter this stronghold to recover to Cleaver of St. Felms. If you have a "backpath" character and a non-working Wraithguard, you'll also need to get the Planbook from Kagrenac's Library. And in the endgame, you'll return to tangle with Dagoth Tureynul.
16. **Zergonipal:** A small but roomy shrine to the Daedric god Malacath.
17. More fun with renegade Ashlanders. They've got a little loot, too.
18. **Tin-Ahhe:** A small smugglers cave.
19. **Salvel Ancestral Tomb:** Mastrius, imprisoned here, can give you an obscure vampire quest.
20. **Dun-Ahhe:** A sorcerers' hideaway with nice loot.
21. **Cavern of the Incarnate:** In the Main Quest, this is where you'll be acknowledged as the Nerevarine.
22. **Maran-Adon:** A large Sixth House base with good loot.
23. Three rogue Ashlanders.
24. **Dareleth Ancestral Tomb:** A small crypt with OK loot.
25. Three renegade Ashlanders, guarding a bit of loot.
26. **Elith-Pal Mine:** A big ebony mine. The Imperial Guards seem a bit out of place this far east, but they'll make you think twice about stealing this black gold.
27. **Sur Egg Mine:** If it was larger, we could call this the Big Sur Egg Mine. But we won't. Check out the volcanic activity in its depths!

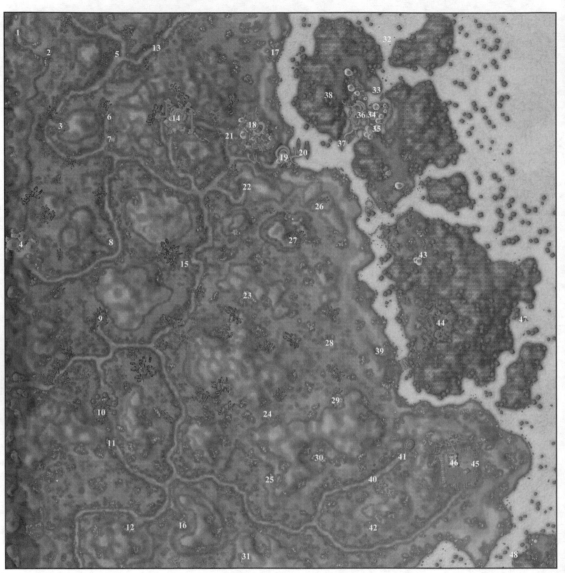

B4: Tel Mora Region

B4: TEL MORA MAP LOCATIONS:

1. **Sanit:** A large Sixth House base.
2. **Ashamanu:** Or, more precisely, the remains of the healer Ashamanu. You'll find her corpse—and amulet—as you follow a white guar in a Miscellaneous Quest.
3. **Nerano Ancestral Tomb:** In the Main Quest, Zainab chief Kaushad will send you here to kill the renegade Berne vampire Calvario.
4. **Nchuleft:** You'll be asked to recover plans from this Dwarven ruin in a Mages Guild quest.
5. The white guar in (2) first appears here.
6. **Mudan-Mul Egg Mine:** A blighted egg mine of modest dimensions.
7. **Tel Vos Dungeon:** This is new construction. As you'll learn from the scattered journal entries of the project foreman, it did not go well.
8. Two renegade Ashlanders.
9. **Venim Ancestral Tomb:** This small tomb contains a potent artifact called the Bow of Shadows and a good deal of other loot. It's guarded by the usual array of tomb critters, and also by necromancer Goris the Maggot King and thief Luven.
10. **Zainab Camp:** You'll visit this permanent Ashlander settlement several times in the Main Quest to complete tasks for its chief. You'll be back for House Hlaalu and Miscellaneous quests. And, at some point along the way, you'll want to train with Ababael Timsar-Dadisun, the "secret master" of the Mercantile skill.
11. **Sethan Ancestral Tomb:** A mid-sized tomb with decent loot.
12. **Aralen Ancestral Tomb:** An Aundae vampire lair.
13. **Athanden Girith:** This merchant has been robbed by a pair of rogue Ashlanders. You can recover his guar hides in a Miscellaneous Quest. See (17) and (34).
14. **Tel Vos:** A tangle of stone fortress and organic wizard's tower, this hilltop stronghold is the base for Telvanni councilor Aryon. If you're Telvanni, he'll be your patron, and this will eventually become a home way from home. You'll need Aryon's support for Telvanni Hortator in the Main Quest, but you can also perform Telvanni quests for him (initially via his "mouth" in Sadrith Mora). In addition, you can pick up a Miscellaneous Quest from Turedus Talanian and perform an assassination in a vampire quest. Finally, the Services Tower offers many of the amenities you'd expect in a town.
15. **Yakaridan Camp:** A renegade Ashlander camp.
16. **Pulk:** A relatively small bandit cave, with the usual huge haul of mundane bandit loot. An exception: the contents of a chest in a deep pool far into the cave.
17. The two Ashlanders who robbed Athanden Girith (13).
18. **Vos Chapel:** Yakin Bael is the "secret master" of Restoration. And Eldrilu Dalen sells spells, potions and ingredients.
19. **Varo Tradehouse:** Burcanius Varo can provide a bed and sells booze and food. Ferise Varo sells spells. Hairan Mannanalit offers training. And you can clear up a little rat problem in the storage room in a freeform quest.
20. Sedyni Veran's boat can take you to Sadrith Mora, Tel Aruhn or Tel Mora.
21. **Vos:** A quiet farm village, with basic services.
22. **Sinarralit Egg Mine:** A good-sized egg mine.
23. **Dubdilla:** It's relatively easy to become a vampire. It is far less easy to return to normal life. To cure your vampirism, you'll have to perform a quest for Daedra god Molag Bal deep within this huge three-level dungeon. Kill his daughter and her atronach consort. Make sure to read the notes of sorcerer Cumanya on the top level before you descend into the Uncharted Caverns.
24. Iveri Llothri is the witch who made off with the barbarian Botrir's axe. (See 40.).
25. Three Mabrigash.
26. Two renegade Ashlanders.
27. A little alit den.
28. **Salit Camp:** The largest of the renegade Ashlander camps.
29. A kagouti lair.
30. **Andalor Ancestral Tomb:** A tiny crypt, with good loot for the little effort required.
31. A small nix-hound den.

32. **Lonesome Shipwreck:** One of a few submerged wrecks, this one has lots of weapons on its lower level. Beware of the dreugh lurking just to the northwest.

33. **Lette:** You'll cure this Redguard of swamp fever in a Tribunal Temple quest.

34. **Berwen: Trader:** You'll remove a corprus stalker from the premises in a Fighters Guild quest, steal a Grandmaster's Retort in a Thieves Guild quest, and pick up a reward for helping Athanden Girith in a Miscellaneous Quest.

35. **Elegnan: Clothier:** A likely Main Quest stopover. Elegnan has the fine outfit needed for the slave you procure as wife for the Zainab Ashlander chief.

36. **Upper Tower:** You'll need Councilor Dratha's support in your Main Quest campaign to be named Telvanni Hortator, and she can give you a single House Telvanni quest as well.

37. Tonas Telvani's boat will carry you to Dagon Fel, Sadrith Mora, Tel Aruhn and ferry you across the channel to Vos.

38. **Tel Mora:** Unlike Vos to the west, which has preserved its own identity in the shadow of Tel Vos, Tel Mora's tied into Telvanni Councilor Dratha's great tower. In addition to quest-related businesses, you'll find an apothecary (Jolda), a smith (Radras), and an inn (The Covenant).

39. **Pinsun:** Lots of loots in this smugglers cave. One other thing: lots of smugglers!

40. **Botrir:** In a Miscellaneous Quest, you can help this barbarian recover his enchanted axe from the witch that stole it. See (24).

41. **Hanud:** Below, a pretty intense undead dungeon. Above, three rogue Telvanni spellcasters, the nastiest being sorcerer Treras Dres in the dome itself.

42. **Massahanud Camp:** Renegade Ashlanders eager to share their special brand of hospitality.

43. And two more of 'em.

44. **Esutanamus:** A small shrine to Daedric god Molag Bal. The ruby on the altar is cursed. The other stuff is all good.

45. **Indoranyon:** Meaning "Blessed greenland," for the Grazelands in which it is sited. But the ancient Dunmer stronghold could be called "Indoor Canyon" just as easily. (As per the note on the door, when you enter, you are transported to someplace very un-stronghold like.) It's used in one of the Morag Tong "Threads of the Webspinner" quests. And Qorwynn, whom you'll find on the way out, is "secret master" of the Enchant skill.

46. **Propylon Chamber:** "Zapping unwary travelers to Falensarano and Rotheran since Vivec-knows-when." If you've got the right index, that is. (It's in Tel Fyr.)

47. **Lost Shipwreck:** little loot in this wreck.

48. **Yassamsi Grotto:** For a grotto, the booty here isn't bad. You can pick up a good chunk of Imperial armor.

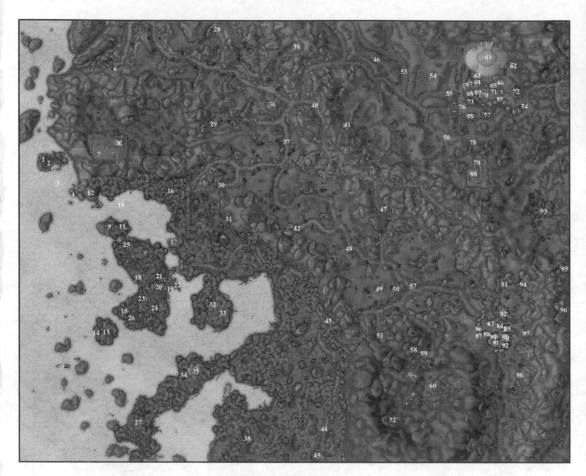

C2: Ald'ruhn Map Locations:

1. Someone's tucked away 125 gold pieces in a tree stump.
2. A chest containing a melee weapon tuned to the player's current level. You'll find more loot in barrels in the water nearby.
3. A capsized longboat conceals more two containers: a small chest with a bit of gold, and a barrel full of shoes.
4. **Neglected Shipwreck:** On the upper level, you'll find a chest full of soul gems.
5. **Shunned Shipwreck:** The cliff racer guarding this wreck must account for the "Shunned" part. The booty's pretty good!
6. **Sariminsun-Assa Egg Mine:** A petite egg mine.
7. **Andasreth:** A large, generic dungeon. You'll have to fight your way into it in a Redoran quest to retrieve the shields of four dead troopers.
8. **Propylon Chamber:** Next stop, Berandas or Hlormaren. Indexes, please! (The Andasreth index is currently doing you a fat lot of good in the dome atop Hlormaren.)
9. **Ilunibi:** The likely site of your first major confrontation with the Sixth House cult. You'll face Dagoth Gares in this five-level base, each level with a name nastier than the last—early in the Main Quest.
10. A bit of Orcish armor amid some bones on sea bottom.
11. An invisibility potion and 100 gold are hidden in a tree stump in a muck pool.
12. The future site of the resurrected shrine of Boethiah—if you perform the god's obscure Daedric quest.

13. Another tree stump, with another cache of gold and a Potion of Shadow.

14. An Abandoned Shack. The last occupant must have left in a hurry. A lot of stuff remains here, just slightly hidden.

15. **Shurinbaal:** You're sent to this smugglers cave in a Redoran quest to kill the ringleaders. But come back soon, finish off their colleagues and loot the place at your leisure. While rather small for a bad-guy lair, Shurinbaal contains no fewer than 27 containers of loot.

16. The two mudcrabs that have been making off with Drulene Falen's guar. You'll have to kill them to finish a Redoran quest. See (29).

17. Two breeding netches, which you'll have to kill to complete an Imperial Legion quest.

18. **Gnaar Mok:** A low-key fishing village…with a slight criminal undercurrent.

19. **Caryarel's Shack:** You'll have to break into this shack in an Imperial Cult quest to steal back a stolen limeware bowl.

20. **Nadene Rotheran's Shack:** In a Romance Quest, you'll kill Camonna Tong thug Daren Adryn in this dwelling.

21. **Dreugh-jigger's Rest:** Himald sells odd 'n' ends and Balan can train you in Athletics, Long Blade and Medium Armor. But the real reason to drop in here is to train with Wardakhu-the "secret master" in the Sneak skill.

22. Vaveli Areklas' boat goes to Hla Oad and Khuul.

23. An invisibility potion, hidden in a tree stump in a muck pool.

24. Same deal, only here it's a glass dagger…and a skull!

25. A Dreamer.

26. **Farvyn Oreyn:** You'll have to whack this rather contemptible "hero" (the two retainers with him are optional) in a quest for Daedric god Malacath.

27. **Addadshashanammu:** A Sheogorath shrine as roomy as its name is long, with a lot of loot. Picking up the pearl on the altar has nasty consequences.

28. Salothran Ancestral Tomb: Tons of loot. You'll probably have a deal with a couple of nix-hounds before you can enter.

29. **Drulene Falen's guar ranch:** You'll help her out by killing a couple of predatory mudcrabs in an early House Redoran quest. See (16).

30. **Telvayn Ancestral Tomb:** A pair of bandits named of Glaum and Gaban-law firm or comedy team?—have taken up residence here. Consequently, loot is better than usual and the tomb-baddie population smaller than usual. (Apart from the bandits, you won't face anything worse than a blighted rat. And the two guar feeding outside the tomb door are benign.)

31. **Mallapi:** Exploring this good-sized sorcerers cave to find the remains of Ruran Stoine is an option in a Fighters Guild quest.

32. **Abernanit:** You're sent into this smugglers cave on an Imperial Legion quest to rescue an abductee named Dandsa.

33. A Fortify Personality potion, hidden in a tree stump.

34. A nice little cache stuffed into a log: 50 gold and a journeyman lockpick and probe. (What, there wasn't a stump handy?)

35. **Aleft:** A Dwarven ruin, with pretty fair loot.

36. A nix-hound lair.

37. **Rasha:** This Argonian will give you a Miscellaneous Quest: Deliver five shirts to Bivale Teneran: Clothier in Ald'ruhn.

38. **Sennananit:** A mid-sized Sixth House base, with respectable loot.

39. **Milk:** This cave is occupied by a Redoran nobleman who lost his mind at the same time he lost his daughter, and has taken to demanding tribute from travelers. You'll try to put things right in a Redoran quest.

40. **Hisin Deep-Raed:** You can cure this barbarian's paralysis with a potion or spell in a Miscellaneous Quest.

41. **Hleran Ancestral Tomb:** A Quarra vampire lair.

42. **Sjorvar Horse-Mouth's guar ranch:** A Blade. Like the six other Blades in the field, he'll allow you to rest at his place and train you. And, if you haven't hit Level 5, he'll urge you to get an enchanted weapon and suggest Galbedir at the Balmora Mages Guild as a source.

43. **Band Egg Mine:** A fairly large mine, with more loot (weapons) than usual. (Egg mines are usually relatively loot-free.)

44. A little cluster of guar.

45. **Norvayn Ancestral Tomb:** A large tomb rich in booty and in enemies.

46. **Drerel Indaren:** Indaren and his wife, Falanu, were separated in a nix-hound attack. You can reunite them in a Miscellaneous Quest. See (53) and (54).

47. **Sosia Caristiana:** She says she's a healer who dealt judiciously with the unwanted advances of the barbarian escorting her. Hlomar Wine-Sot says something else. You will have a chance to reconcile their stories in a Miscellaneous Quest (which comes from Hlomar). See (57).

48. **Pemenie:** She'll start out just seeming flaky. She wants an escort to Gnaar Mok, but instantly seems to have second thoughts about the offered reward. But once you talk to other people about her, after completing this Miscellaneous Quest, you'll realize she was just really shrewd. (And when you try out the reward, you'll feel really stupid!)

49. A rat's nest.

50. **Bugrol gro-Bagul:** An Orc who is hiding out because of…well, something he claims he didn't do. You can serve as messenger between him and his co-conspirator in a Miscellaneous Quest. (See (84), (86), and (89).)

51. **Kudanat:** A big bandit cave, with loot for pocketing (though not so much as you might think), slaves for freeing …and one unusual feature.

52. **Uveran Ancestral Tomb:** A big crypt with good loot, and not all that well-defended.

53. Two nix-hounds.

54. **Falanu Indaren:** Husband and wife have been separated by a nix-hound attack while traveling. See (53) for the husband. This here's the wife. In a Miscellaneous Quest, you can bring them back together. See (46).

55. **Ald'ruhn silt strider port:** You can catch Navam Veran's bug and ride it out to Balmora, Gnisis, Khuul, and Maar Gan.

56. **Viatrix Petilia:** Possibly the most annoying quest-giver in the game. If you take on this Miscellaneous Quest, you will have to escort this rich, scornful pilgrim all the way a Red Mountain shrine. Are the nix-hounds that were bugging the Indarens still around? Yes? Hmmm!

57. **Hlomar Wine-Sot:** This barbarian claims he was seduced by a witch, then paralyzed and left in his undies beside the road. The witch says something else. You can try to figure out who's full of scrib jelly in a Miscellaneous Quest. See (47).

58. **Ashanammu:** In a Fighters Guild quest. you'll be sent to kill four Telvanni agents (who are also Thieves Guild members) holed up in and around this bandit cave. Alveleg (59), just outside the cave, is one of them.

59. **Alveleg:** One of the four Telvanni agents from (58). The other three are in the cave.

60. **Caldera Mine:** This large newly-chartered ebony mine is a source of much bad feeling between Houses Hlaalu (which got the charter) and Redoran (which wanted it). In a pair of Redoran quests, you'll visit the mine to obtain evidence of corruption and then to shut down operations.

61. **Ald'ruhn's Manor District** is "under-skar"-that is, contained within the shell of a prehistoric Emperor Crab. Within, you'll find (alphabetically): Arobar Manor; Bivale Teneran: Clothier; Cienne Sintieve: Alchemist; Llether Vari: Enchanter; Llethri Manor; the Morag Tong Guildhall; Ramoran Manor; the Redoran Council, Sarethi Manor; and Venim Manor.

62. **Morvayn Manor:** Redoran Councilor Brara Morvayn's home has been overrun by Corprus stalkers. In a Redoran quest, you'll be asked to remove the ash statue which drew them there.

63. **Daynes Redothril: Pawnbroker:** One of five local merchants owed money by Ienas Sarandas. You get to be their collections agency in a Miscellaneous Quest.

64. **Codus Callonus: Bookseller:** In the Main Quest, you can find a book of poems here for Hassour Zainsubani. In an Imperial Legion quest, you're called to represent the troopers in a contest of wit and poetry. If your character isn't the brightest lantern in Morrowind, you may need to first visit this shop for a copy of the Red Book of Riddles.

65. **Tiras Sadus: General Merchandise:** Another of Ienas Sarandas' creditors. See (63).

66. **Bevene Releth: Clothier:** And another. See (63) and (65). (The remaining creditors are Llether Vari: Enchanter and Bivale Teneran: Clothier in the Manor District.)

67. **Ald Skar Inn:** Lots of meeting and greeting goes on here. Early in the Main Quest, you'll hook up with Hassour Zainsubani for info on Ashlanders and the Nerevarine cult (and return to him when you've extracted his son, Hannat, from the clutches of Mamaea in a Miscellaneous Quest). And if building a Redoran stronghold, and in need of unmarried females, you can persuade bachelorette #1, Fathusa Girethi, to resettle to Indarys Manor.

68. **Drinar Varyon's House:** A well-known smuggler. You can nail him for ebony smuggling by going undercover in a Hlaalu quest and for Dwemer artifact smuggling by searching his house in an Imperial Legion quest.

69. **Ienas Sarandas' House:** The deadbeat himself. See (63), (65), and (66).

70. **Aryni Orethi's House:** Another potential lady settler for a Redoran stronghold. See (67). (The lady herself is actually outside, and over by the stairs to the north.)

71. **Hanarai Assutlanipal's House:** In a Redoran quest, you'll find she has a Sixth House shrine in her cellar.

72. **Ald'ruhn Temple:** Lloros Sarano will give you Redoran quests, and Tuls Valen will give you Tribunal Temple quests. Methal Seran is "secret master" of the Conjuration skill. And if you've handled the deadbeat Sarandas with kid gloves, he'll turn up here as well.

73. **Ald'ruhn Mages Guild:** Edwinna Elbert offers quests. You can supply books to the guild school in Hlaalu and Thieves Guild quests, and rob the guild blind-which is also a Thieves Guild quest. (Hey, they're thieves. No one ever called them the Consistency Guild!) For a fee, Erranil can teleport you to Mages Guilds in Balmora, Caldera, Sadrith Mora, and Vivec.

74. **Braynas Hlervu's House:** You'll return a locket to Hlervu in a "Bal Molagmer" quest for the Thieves Guild.

75. **Ald'ruhn Fighters Guild:** Percius Mercius is a Fighters Guild quest-giver and general Good Sort of Fellow who will even offer sensible advice on other Guild quest-givers' increasingly agenda-driven assignments. He'll also figures in the Redoran Stronghold quest and a series of critical Thieves Guild quests.

76. **Ano Vando:** You make this vampire hunter dead in a vampire quest.

77. **The Rat in the Pot:** Cornerclub and de facto Ald'ruhn Thieves Guild headquarters. Aengoth the Jeweler is the Thieves quest-giver here, and lots of other tenants figure in Redoran, Fighters Guild, and Miscellaneous quests.

78. **A Dreamer.**

79. **Shardie:** This Imperial trooper is "secret master" of the Block skill.

80. **Buckmoth Legion Fort:** You'll hook up with Buckmoth champion Raesa Pullia here in the Main Quest for your first lead of the Sixth House base at Ilunibi. Imsin the Dreamer offers Imperial Legion quests. Segunivus Mantedius figures in the Hlaalu quest in which you can nail Drinar Varyon for ebony smuggling. (See (68).) Syloria Siruliulus can induct you into the Imperial Cult.

81. **A kagouti den.**

82. **Caldera Governor's Hall:** The place just reeks of corruption. You can get Hlaalu quests here from the corrupt Odral Helvi. (You'll also steal one of his books in a "Bal Molagmer" Thieves Guild quest. See (73).) In an Imperial Cult quest, you'll try to get corrupt Cunius Pelelius to fork over a promised donation.

83. **Surane Leoriane's House:** Another of your buddies from the Blades. Leoriane will give you a place to sleep, train you, and direct you to Llaros Uvayn at the Governor's Hall to learn Detect Enchantment.

84. **Bashuk gra-Bat's House:** You'll ferry notes between gra-Bat and Bugrol gro-Bagul, who's hiding out in the countryside, in a Miscellaneous Quest. (See (50), (86), and (89).)

85. **Elmussa Damori's House:** Damori's a prime suspect in the theft of Caldera mining contracts. You're to track down the perpetrator in a Hlaalu quest.

86. **Valvius Mevureius' House:** If you're curious about what the Orcs gra-Bat and gro-Bagul are up to, check out a note in this house. (See (50), (84), (86), and (89).)

87. **Caldera Mages Guild:** Emelia Duronia can zap you to guilds in Ald'ruhn, Balmora, Sadrith Mora and Vivec using the "guild guide" teleportation service.

88. **Falanaamo: Clothier:** The proprietor will donate a "common shirt" needed in an Imperial Cult quest.

89. **Irgola: Pawnbroker:** Interesting little place. Irgola is the other suspect in the theft of Caldera mining contracts. A note here gives a further hint of the extra-legal activities of Orcs gra-Bat and gro-Bagul. And there's that odd little stone doorstop on the window sill.

90. **Ghorak Manor:** Sculptor Duma gro-Lag will agree to recreate the Shrine of Boethiah in an obscure Daedric quest.

91. **Shenk's Shovel:** Shenk offers the usual room and board, and guests Iratian Albarnian and Ri'Shajirr can train you.

92. **Nedhelas' House:** It's haunted. You've got to roust the ghost in an Imperial Cult quest.

93. **Ramimilk:** Amazing loot in this shrine to Daedric god Molag Bal, including a dwarven mace and ebony wizard's staff. But some of it is cursed (the glass dagger and the emeralds on the altar).

94. **Indalen Ancestral Tomb:** A large, fairly rich tomb with mostly Daedric defenders.

95. **Abaelun Mine:** Morrowind's one and only diamond mine. Small for a mine, but very rich, and guarded by Imperial troopers.

96. **Shushishi:** A hard-to-find bandit cave. You'll explore it in a Miscellaneous Quest to recover family heirlooms for Aeta Wave-Breaker.

97. **Aeta Wave-Breaker:** Speak of the devil. She's been robbed by bandits led by the Khajiit Dro'Zhirr, and…oh, just read (96).

98. **A little alit colony.**

99. **Gildan's House:** Another Blade. Like the other six, he'll put you up for the night, train you, and, if you haven't reached Level 5, offer a suggestion: See Wayn at the Balmora Fighters Guild for jink and spider blades.

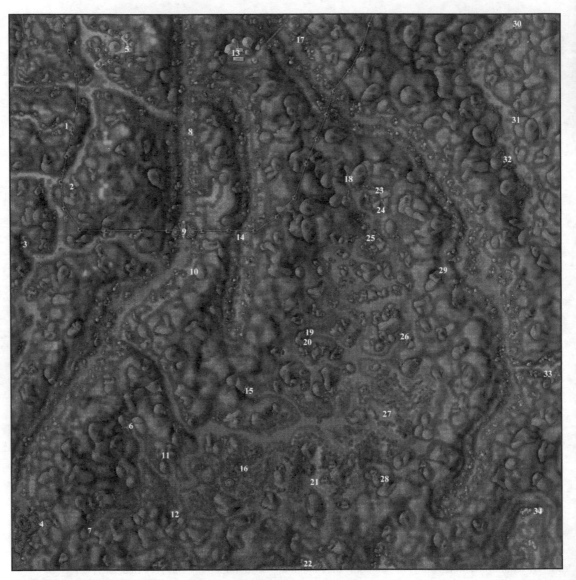

C3: GHOSTGATE MAP LOCATIONS:

1. **Fadathram Ancestral Tomb:** A small tomb with excellent loot.
2. **Panabanit-Nimawia Egg Mine:** An egg mine inside the Ghostfence. Is the sole miner here dead? Yup. Is the adventurer here also dead? Sure. Are the enemies blighted? You betcha.
3. **Sudanit Mine:** A huge Redoran-operated ebony mine. Very rich. And very dark. Shutting it down is an option in Hlaalu quest.
4. **Assarnatamat:** In a Morag Tong quest, you'll visit this small Mehrunes Dagon shrine to recover the Shoes of Sanguine Stalking from Dark Brotherhood agent Thovasi Alen.

5. **Endusal:** A Dagoth citadel. In the endgame, you should kill its resident ash vampire, Dagoth Endus, and take his Amulet of Heartrime. And if you are playing with a "backpath" character (and so can't activate the Wraithguard), you'll need to visit Kagrenac's study to get his journals for Yagrum Bagarn.
6. A rat's nest.
7. **Thalas Ancestral Tomb:** A mid-sized crypt with some interesting bits of loot (like a dreugh shield).
8. **Yassu Mine:** Commerce marches on. Though well inside the Ghostfence, and fairly infested with nix-hounds, this huge Imperial glass mine is still operating.
9. **Ghostgate:** This is Morrowind's Rivendell: the last safe house before you dip into the maelstrom around Red Mountain's crater. In part, it's a barracks for the garrisons of Temple Ordinators and Buoyant Armigers. In part, it's a Redoran hostel for pilgrims. And, in the tower between the two keeps, there's a Temple. You can get Tribunal Temple quests there from Uvoo Llaren. A Telvanni quest takes you into the eastern keep (the Tower of Dawn) in search of an ebony bow that, um, smells faintly of ash yams. (OK, that's it. No more doing anything that involves Therana.) On a Thieves Guild quest, you'll need to sneak a stolen sword into a chest in western keep (the Tower of Dusk). If you're a spearperson, you can train to very high levels with Spear "secret master" Mertis Falandas in the Tower of Dusk. And you'll visit the monastery many times in the endgame to recover from your injuries and load up on supplies. But don't become so inured to the place that you can't see new things within the old. For in the Tower of Dusk, late in the game, you may encounter an old Imperial warrior named Wulf. Speak to him, and accept his gift. He has never been there before, and after you speak with him, he will never be there again.
10. Two angry Ashlanders—so what else is new?—and one who probably would be angry too if he wasn't suffering from a case of the droops. You can cure him in Tribunal Temple quest.
11. **Odaishah:** Two sorcerers and a squad of Daedra in a good-sized cave with good loot.
12. A kagouti lair.
13. **Odrosal:** An ash vampire lair. In the endgame, you'll fight Dagoth Odros here and claim the sword Keening and the Amulet of Heartfire. With the hammer Sunder, Keening is instrumental in destroying the source of Dagoth Ur's power.
14. **Sharapli:** A substantial Sixth House base. And a Daedra seems to have snuck in here as well!
15. **Aryon Ancestral Tomb:** A mid-sized tomb with a fair supply of low-end loot.
16. **Shishara:** Medyn Gilnith, a rogue Telvanni sorcerer and five followers hang their hats here. The loot's mediocre, and most of the books in Gilnith's library are common-save "Nchunak's Fire and Faith."
17. **Yanemus Mine:** A large ebony mine, operated by Ashlanders! (Guess it's more lucrative than harassing passers-by.)
18. **Halit Mine:** A huge Imperial glass mine.
19. **Dunirai Caverns:** You'll run a supply of booze to this large Imperial glass mine in a Fighters Guild quest.
20. A small surprise. The two guys standing next to the campfire here are not Ashlanders. They're High Elves. And maybe it's just the mazte talking, but they're friendly.
21. Two netches
22. Two Ashlanders.
23. **Helas Ancestral Tomb:** A small crypt with OK loot and a mix of standard tomb and Daedric defenders.
24. Two rats.
25. Three Ashlanders
26. Three more Ashlanders.
27. Three Mabrigash. Voted "Most Desolate Spot in Vvardenfell" three years running.
28. **Sanabi:** Now, bandits, we're not trying to tell you your business, but isn't this kind of out in the middle of nowhere for a hideout? Location, location, location. That said, the eight bad guys here don't seem to be hurting for loot, though the cave contains nothing really exceptional.
29. Two more rats.
30. **Sandus Ancestral Tomb:** A large-ish crypt with OK loot.
31. **Maelu Egg Mine:** An ordinary, mid-sized egg mine.
32. A couple of nix-hounds.
33. Two Ashlanders.
34. **Dulo Ancestral Tomb:** An Aundae vampire lair.

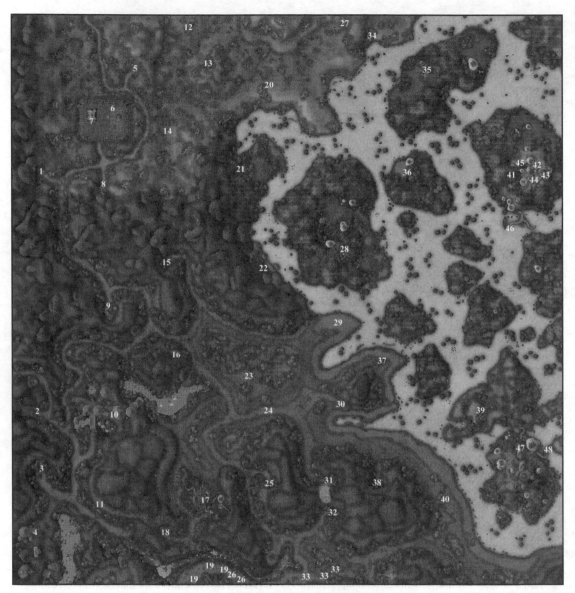

C4: Tel Aruhn Map Locations:

1. **Massama Cave:** A large abandoned glass mine—populated by nothing worse than nix-hounds and rats.
2. **Zalkin-Sul Egg Mine:** A blighted egg mine.
3. **Serano Ancestral Tomb:** A Quarra vampire lair.
4. **Galom Daeus:** This Dwarven ruin and attached observatory serve as the headquarters for the Berne vampire clan. Raxle Berne will give you two Berne-specific quests if you join that clan. You'll also need to get a unique book here to complete the Telvanni stronghold, another for a Mages Guild quest and a third document will be helpful in a vampire quest. In a Tribunal Temple quest, you'll have to kill Berne himself.

5. **Dissapla Mine:** Nix-hounds have gotten into this glass mine, and you'll have to rescue a stranded healer from its depths in a Fighters Guild quest.
6. **Falensarano:** Former Dunmer stronghold. Now big, seemingly empty, dungeon. Not quite. Nasty spellcasters down below. Nice "secret master" Alfhedil Elf-Hewer (Axe skill) up above.
7. **Propylon Chamber:** This chamber will teleport you to strongholds Indoranyon and Telasero. (The index required is in the upper reaches of the shrine Maelkashishi.)
8. Two renegade Ashlanders, who are considerably better equipped than your average renegade Ashlanders!
9. **Gimothran Ancestral Tomb:** The potent Staff of Hasedoki can be found in the possession of Orc sorcerer Koffutto Gilgar at the end of this large and well-defended tomb. (Skeletons!) In a wealth of loot, you'll also find a rare dragonscale helm and another of those adventurer's-last-words scrolls. (For the curious, the companion the writer mentions is in the Baram Ancestral Tomb.)
10. **Mzanchend:** This rather small, but well-defended, Dwarven ruin contains a Dwemer Schematic needed to complete construction of a Telvanni stronghold.
11. Two alits.
12. **Elanius Camp:** A renegade Ashlander settlement.
13. **Ienith Ancestral Tomb:** A large tomb with large loot…and not all that well-defended.
14. Two renegade Ashlanders.
15. **Andules Ancestral Tomb:** A mid-sized tomb, defended by Daedra, and containing a rare mole crab helm. For those times when you want to look like a mole crab.
16. A rat's nest.
17. This will be called Uvirith's Grave if you haven't built a stronghold, and Tel Uvirith if you have. You'll be sent to this Telvanni stronghold in identical Hlaalu and Redoran quests to kill wizard Reynel Uvirith. If this isn't your home park, watch for steam centurions north of the tower.
18. **Shushan:** A good-sized bandit cave with a nice stock of gold and gems.
19. **Fallen pages:** A trail of book pages left by kidnapped hermit Jocien Ancois, whom you'll try to rescue in an Imperial Legion quest. See (26) and (33).
20. Two renegade Ashlanders
21. **Nammu:** In a rather involved Imperial Cult quest, you'll explore this sorcerer's cave to liberate the legendary Ring of the Wind and rescue an apparent prisoner.
22. Two nix-hounds.
23. Rats!
24. **Marsus Tullius:** Two Ashlanders jumped this guy and took his stuff. You've been there, right? But this Miscellaneous Quest has an interesting twist. Look before you leap. See (42).
25. **Zenarbael:** Are they smugglers? Are they bandits? Ah, what's the diff? There are four of them, and they've got a big, interesting cave full of eminently steal-able stuff. An oddity: Zenarbael has a pair of mudcrabs.
26. More fallen pages from Jocien Ancois' book. See (19).
27. **Thiralas Ancestral Tomb:** A tiny tomb without much in it. But it does have some ectoplasm, which is somewhat uncommon.
28. **Yansirramus:** Activate the statue of Molag Bal in this large shrine, and you'll get a quest to kill a lazy Daedroth named Menta Na. (Great loot here—with some killer scrolls at the back.)
29. Two netches.
30. **Ahinipalit:** A big smugglers cave, with lots of loot (27 containers—including two with ash statues) and a glass dagger, a scroll of Invisibility and potion of Shadow lying around loose.
31. **Missir-Dadalit Egg Mine:** A tidy L-shaped egg mine.
32. **Zaintirari:** Sarayn Sadus, the target of a Morag Tong "writ," is hiding out in this all-purpose bad guy cave. Begging to be confused with the Daedric shrine Zaintiraris, which is located south of Molag Mar.
33. Still more pages have fallen from Jocien Ancois' book. See (19) and (26). What's he going to read at the Mabrigash camp? Will he even have time for reading?
34. **Yakin:** You're sent into this large Sixth House base in a Mages Guild quest to capture the soul of an ash ghoul.
35. **Nallit:** An odd trio: a sorcerer, a savant, and a Dremora. Wanna bet the Dremora is the fastidious one?
36. **Ashamanu Camp:** Surprise! Three Mabrigash with a tent…and a man! A dead man. A contradictory dead man at that: a pauper with a unique enchanted weapon called a Banhammer.

37. **Bensiberib Camp**: You'll be ordered to kill Odaishah Yasalmibaal in a Morag Tong "writ" quest.

38. **Andas Ancestral Tomb**: Mid-sized tomb with OK loot—including an uncommon Redoran Watchman's Helm.

39. A netch colony.

40. **Sobitbael Camp**: A renegade Ashlander camp. The tent is "Mal's Yurt." Wait. There's an Ashlander named "Mal"?

41. **Underground**: A north-south tunnel, with a side room that serves as a slave holding area. Check it out. Khajiits and Argonians aren't the only races held in thrall in Morrowind.

42. **Bildren Areleth**: Apothecary: Your best source for the Telvanni bug musk you'll need in the Main Quest to help win the support of the Zainab Ashlander chief. Outside and nearby: Stentus Tullius, father to Marsus. (See (24).) If you complete that get-my-stuff-back quest, Dad will pay you off.

43. **Plot and Plaster**: If you helped Maurrie Aurmine rendezvous with her dashing bandit in a Miscellaneous Quest outside Pelagiad, she'll fix you up with one of her friends. If your character is male, that'll be Emusette Bracques at this bed-and-breakfast. Hubba-hubba.

44. **Tower**: Archmagister Gothren, in the Upper Tower, will give you Telvanni quests, but only through his "mouth" at the Telvanni Council in Sadrith Mora. You don't have to see him in person until you show up to kill him, which you'll have to do sooner or later. In the Living Quarters, you'll have to obtain Senise Thindo's Robe of Drake's Pride in a Telvanni quest. (The Telvanni operate under principles of pure self-interest, and are constantly stealing things from each other.)

45. **Savile Imayn and Falura Llervu**: A slave merchant and a slave, respectively. Both play significant roles in the Main Quest. Imayn sells you Llervu, who you can dress up as a Telvanni lady fit to marry the Zainab Ashlander chief, who will then name you Zainab Nerevarine. Imayn can also (optionally) sell you an egg miner needed for the second phase of the Hlaalu stronghold and marriageable lady settlers needed for the third stage of the Redoran stronghold.

46. Daynas Darys can ship you to Dagon Fel, Tel Mora or Vos.

47. **Tel Fyr**: The home of powerful wizard Divayth Fyr, and a key location in Morrowind. In the Main Quest, you'll visit Tel Fyr and its Corprusarium dungeon to take an experimental cure for your corprus disease. In a Redoran quest, you'll free prisoner Delyna Mandas to restore her father's sanity. (See (39) on Ald'ruhn Map.) In a Telvanni quest, you'll deliver messages between Aryon and Fyr. (The contents are coded, but the context gives them away.) And the tower is also the source of dazzling and barely documented artifacts—one of them at the end of long chain of locked chests.

48. This guy won't ship you anywhere. But Cinia Urtius does happen to be the "secret master" of Medium Armor.

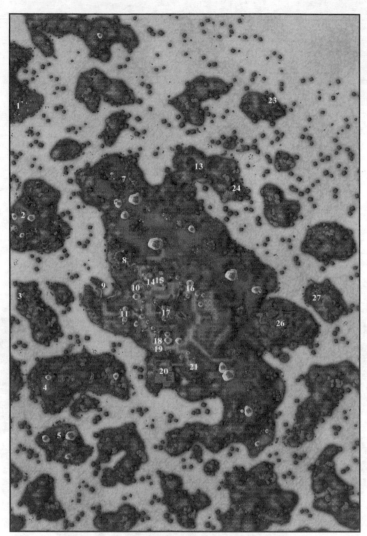

C5: SADRITH MORA MAP LOCATIONS:

1. **Baram Ancestral Tomb:** This large crypt is distinguished only by its size. The "recently slain knight" here is the comrade of the adventurer who left the note in the Gimothran tomb. (See (9) on Tel Aruhn Map.)
2. Two renegade Ashlanders.
3. **Unknown Shipwreck:** You'll find four weapon crates on the lower level.
4. Two kagouti.
5. **Abanabi:** The lair of feared sorceress Draramu Hloran, whom you'll have to dispatch in an Imperial Legion quest to recover a sword of legend.
6. **Dreloth Ancestral Tomb:** A small crypt.
7. **Sadryon Ancestral Tomb:** An only slightly larger crypt.
8. **Telvanni Council House:** The "mouths" in the council room are the source of most Telvanni quests. (One mouth, Raven Omayn, will even give you a vampire quest!) And Llunela Hleran in the Hermitage will be your principal contact on construction of a Telvanni stronghold.

9. **Gals Arethi:** Makes all sorts of trips with his boat—short hops to Tel Mora, medium ones to Dagon Fel and Tel Branora, and long ones all the way to Ebonheart.

10. **Brallion:** You'll need to obtain this well-to-do slave trader's ring in a "Bal Molagmer" quest for the Thieves Guild.

11. **Gateway Inn:** The hotel for outsiders. Technically, non-Telvanni are not supposed to wander or even talk to the locals in Sadrith Mora. But for 25 gold, Angaredhel, the Gateway's greeter, can provide Hospitality Papers that amount to a hall pass. Mostly, you'll stop in here to just put your head down, but occasionally you'll come on business. You'll get the Belt of Sanguine Impaling Thrust—needed in a Morag Tong "Threads of the Webspinner" quest—from Gluronk gra-Shula in north wing's second floor. In a Miscellaneous Quest, you'll have to get rid of the ghost that keeps returning to the South Turret room. An Aundae vampire quest will ultimately lead to Sinyaraman on the inn's second floor. And Ardarume in the west wing is "secret master" of Mysticism.

12. Three renegade Ashlanders.

13. Three netches.

14. **Fara's Hole in the Wall:** A cornerclub. When you need a fancy outfit in the Main Quest, one option is to put the hurt on trader Tolvone Sarendas here and take her duds. In addition, in one Thieves Guild quest, you'll steal a cookbook for Fara from Llethri Manor in Ald'ruhn. And, in another, you can put the squeeze on Fighters Guild steward Hrundi by determining that his lover is Falena Hlaren, who hangs out here.

15. **Anis Seloth:** Alchemist: Your destination in a number of ingredient-related Telvanni quests. In a Thieves Guild quest, you'll need to steal a recipe for a Dispel Magic spell from the shop.

16. **Morag Tong Guildhall:** The headquarters in Vivec may be hidden, but the branch guilds hang out a shingle. You can get "writ" quests (assassinations) here from Dunsalipal Dun-Ahhe. And you'll have to get the ring Black Jinx from Alven Salas in a Telvanni quest.

17. **Tel Naga:** Telvanni Councilor Neloth's tower. You'll need his vote to become Telvanni Hortator in the Main Quest. But mainly you'll come here to wreak various kinds of havoc. In Telvanni quests, you'll procure for Councilor Dratha the Amulet of Flesh Made Whole and dispatch protégé "Fast Eddie" Theman to collect the Ring of Equity. In a Fighters Guild quest, you'll murder a Bosmer mercenary. And you'll need to free hostage Nartise Arobar to secure her father's vote in your campaign to become Redoran Archmagister.

18. **Volmyni Dral's House:** In an Imperial Cult quest, you'll track an embezzling clerk here. (It's his girlfriend's place.)

19. **Pierlette Rostorad: Apothecary:** A reliable source for the Cure Blight scroll needed for the second phase of the Hlaalu stronghold, and for the Cure Blight potion needed in a Telvanni quest to relieve blight problems in Tel Vos.

20. **Wolverine Hall:** An Imperial-style fortress that houses two Sadrith Mora guilds. You can get quests from Hrundi in the Fighters Guild and Skink-in-Tree's-Shade in the Mages Guild. (Skink is also "secret master" of the Speechcraft skill.) At the Mages Guild, Ienith will teleport you to a Mages Guild in Ald'ruhn, Balmora, Caldera or Vivec. The Hall is also a frequent quest destination. On a Telvanni quest, you'll buy the Staff of the Silver Dawn from Arielle Phiencel at the Mages Guild. On Mages Guild quests, you'll drop in here to collect a potion from Skink and try to root out a Telvanni spy. On a Thieves Guild quest, you'll deliver a stolen recipe to Tusamircil at the Mages Guild. And the Miscellaneous Quest to exorcise the Gateway Inn's recurring ghost and an Aundae vampire quest will lead you to that guild as well.

21. **Dirty Muriel's Cornerclub:** The Sadrith Mora Thieves Guild. Big Helende will give you guild quests—in one, you'll escort Tenyeminwe from Dirty Muriel's to the docks—and you'll be ordered to kill that quest-giver in a Fighters Guild quest. And Erer Darothril is "secret master" of the Illusion skill.

22. **Kaushtarari:** Biiig shrine to Daedric god Malacath. If you can just get rid of the two Orcs here, it's all yours. Note that the raw ebony on the altar is cursed.

23. **Hlervi Ancestral Tomb:** A tiny, remote crypt with neat, well-hidden loot. (Check the ledge.)

24. **Strange Shipwreck:** It's only strange this stuff is still here! A useable bedroll and rare book ("The Pig Children") can be found in the cabin. On the upper level, there's a silver claymore on a partially-concealed skeleton. And on the lower, a load of loot, including a chest of soul gems!

25. **Verelnim Ancestral Tomb:** A big crypt, populated by Daedra and blighted rats.

26. **Anudnabia:** A sealed Daedric ruin. You'll search the Forgotten Vaults of Anudnabia for the Skull-Crusher warhammer in an Imperial Cult quest. But you can't enter the ruin at the site itself. You must enter through the…

27. **Omaren Ancestral Tomb:** The tomb part's ordinary. The rest is quite out of the ordinary.

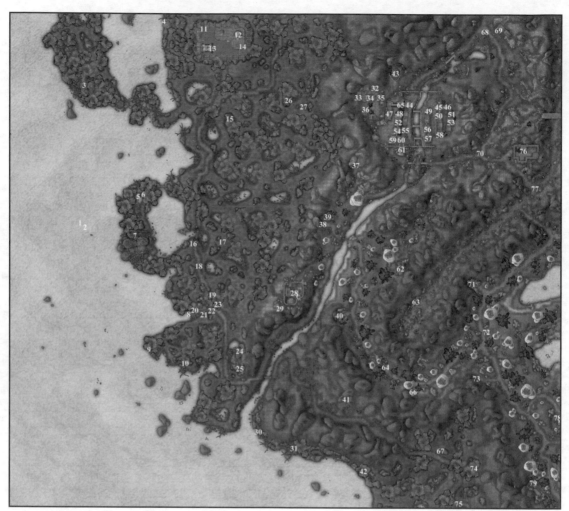

D2: BALMORA MAP LOCATIONS:

1. A dreugh.
2. **The Lost Shrine of Boethiah:** You can sponsor the resurrection of this sunken shrine in a Daedric quest. It will turn up at Khartag Point. See (12) on Ald'ruhn Map (C2).
3. **Ashalmimilkala:** In a Morag Tong quest, you'll deliver an ultimatum to cultist Carecalmo at this huge Mehrunes Dagon shrine. You can return in an Imperial Cult quest to recover the Scroll of Fiercely Roasting.
4. You can get into the extensive sewer for the stronghold Hlormaren via this seaside entrance.
5. A barrel loaded with ingredients-almost invisible inside a tree trunk in a muck pool.
6. **Shal:** On a Mages Guild quest, you'll enter this cave to kill necromancer Telura Ulver. Note the presence of a pet Bonelord.
7. **Ashurnibibi:** You'll rescue knight Joncis Dalomax from this huge shrine to Daedric god Malacath in an Imperial Legion quest.
8. The three floating containers are empty, but a chest full of clothing can be found on the bottom right under Baleni Salavel's boat.

9. **Velfred:** In a Hlaalu quest, you'll be asked to get this outlaw to pay smuggling fees, or kill him.
10. **Heran Ancestral Tomb:** A mid-sized tomb, defended by Daedra, that offers little loot.
11. **Hlormaren:** A big, bad rectangular dungeon. Bigger, in fact, than most of the strongholds, with an underground level that houses slaves and a sewer with its own waterside exit. See (4).
12. **Dome:** The index for the Propylon Chamber at the stronghold Andasreth can be found on a bookshelf in this dome.
13. **Propylon Chamber:** You can teleport from here to strongholds Andasreth and Marandus—with the right index. (The right index is sitting on the windowsill at Irgola: Pawnbroker in Caldera.)
14. **Brilnosu Llarys:** Marked for execution in a Morag Tong "writ" quest.
15. **Zanabi:** Four smugglers are holed up in this large cave with lots of smuggler stuff, a couple of nix-hounds, and a few ash statues.
16. **Fjol:** You can get rid of this outlaw in a Miscellaneous Quest.
17. Three nix-hounds.
18. A Dreamer.
19. **Fatleg's Drop Off:** You'll visit this seedy little whatever-it-is in a Thieves Guild quest to secure some ordered-but-undelivered Dwemer artifacts. In the cellar (a Camonna Tong base), you can pick up a Miscellaneous Quest. Either escort a Khajiit slave to her death in Balmora—or lead her to freedom.
20. Baleni Salavel's boat goes from Hla Oad to Ebonheart, Gnaar Mok, or Vivec's Foreign Quarter.
21. **Murudius Flaeus's House:** Flaeus owes money to a nobleman. You can get it back in a Hlaalu quest. See (22).
22. Fadila Balvel's House: Murudius Flaeus's money is hidden under this house. See (21).
23. **Okur's House:** Okur is being visited by the ghost of a murder victim. In an Imperial Cult quest, you'll try to put the spirit to rest by avenging her death at the hands of smugglers. See (25).
24. A nice cache of loot, including thief tools, weapons, armor, potions, and various odds 'n' ends.
25. **Yasamsi:** The smugglers of (23). And masses of loot.
26. **Andrethi Ancestral Tomb:** A Berne vampire lair.
27. Three kagouti.
28. Odai Plateau, if you haven't yet built a stronghold. Rethan Manor, the Hlaalu stronghold, if you have.
29. In a very few instances, you'll find superb weapons lying undefended in out of the way places. This is one.
30. **Unexplored Shipwreck:** On the lower level, you'll find diamonds, ash statues and ash yams. Debris from the wreck can be found to the southeast-including a chest containing a silver longsword.
31. A tree stump. Inside the stump, a sack. Inside the sack, 100 gold.
32. **Nalcarya of White Haven: Alchemist:** You'll put in here often for ingredients. Occasionally, you'll even pay for them. But not in the Thieves Guild quest in which you're expected to steal a diamond
33. **Morag Tong Guild:** You can get "writ" quests here from Ethasi Rilvayn.
34. **Nerano Manor:** Ondres Nerano has maligned a member of House Redoran. In a Redoran quest, you'll challenge him to a duel.
35. **Hlaalo Manor:** Home of the late Ralen Hlaalo. He's been murdered. In a Hlaalu quest, you must find his killer and settle the score. See (50) and (60).
36. **Hlaalu Council Manor:** You can get Hlaalu quests here from Nileno Dorvayn. Dondos Driler will be your main contact during construction of a Hlaalu stronghold.
37. **Tharys Ancestral Tomb:** A small tomb with OK loot.
38. **Shulk Egg Mine:** You'll kill a pair of kwama egg thieves in this mine in a Fighters Guild quest. You'll be back in an Imperial Cult quest to harvest scrib jelly.
39. No, they're not Ashlanders. What, only Ashlanders can stand around a campfire looking outraged? These two guys are egg miners—and, no, they're not the two who've been stealing the eggs in (38).
40. **Shurdan-Raplay Egg Mine:** You'll have to restore this abandoned (and blighted) mine to productivity to complete the second phase of a Hlaalu stronghold.
41. **Zainsipilu:** Big honking bandit cave with eight baddies to mess up, five slaves to free and 40 containers to paw through. A rare Thief Ring can be found on a rock at cave center.
42. **Samarys Ancestral Tomb:** In an urn marked "Lord Brinne," you'll find a unique artifact called the Mentor's Ring,
43. **Balmora Temple:** Feldrelo Sadri can induct you into the Tribunal Temple.
44. **Fast Eddie's House:** Hey, is this Morrowind or "Happy Days"? If you're Telvanni, "Fast Eddie" Theman (aka Eddie the Rat) will become your protégé, your "mouth" in the Telvanni Council and, finally your quest-doer. Ehhh!

45. **Balyn Omarel's House:** In a Miscellaneous Quest, you'll slip poison into the food of this Morag Tong member, who has been doing freelance executions. (Apparently a no-no.)

46. **Caius Cosades' House:** Your boss in the Blades and your principal Main Quest contact, until he is recalled by the Empire in mid-game.

47. **Dorisa Darvel: Bookseller:** Good bookstore. She has two of the three books Baladas Demnevanni asks you to find in a Telvanni quest, and the "Yellow Book of Riddles," which may prove useful in your Tribunal Temple pilgrimage to Mount Kand.

48. **Balmora Fighters Guild:** It's your first stop on the Main Quest path. Caius Cosades sends you to learn what Hasphat Antabolis knows about the Nerevarine and Sixth House cults. It will become a regular stop if you join the guild; many of the early quests come from Balmora guild steward Eydis Fire-Eye. Even if you don't join, you'll be back to recruit a guard (via Flaenia Amiulusus) if you build a Hlaalu stronghold, and to either bribe Fire-Eye with the Bitter Cup artifact or kill her if you join the Thieves Guild.

49. **Hecerinde's House:** You'll call on this "secret master" of the Security skill in a Thieves Guild quest to beef up defenses at the South Wall Cornerclub.

50. **Nine-Toes' House:** Mr. Toes is the initial suspect in the murder of Ralen Hlaalo. (See (35) and (60).) He's also a Blade. He'll extend to usual professional courtesies, but also gives you, uh, drugs (moon sugar) and proposes that you sell them to Ajira at the Balmora Mages Guild or trader Ra'Virr to raise money for future training.

51. **Vorar Helas' House:** Did you take the Miscellaneous Quest to deliver a slave from Hla Oad to Balmora? (See (19).) If so, this is your destination.

52. **Balmora Mages Guild:** Ajira and Ranis Athrys will offer you quests. Early in the Main Quest, Caius Cosades will send you to Sharn gra-Muzgob for information on the Nerevarine cult. (Naturally, she sends you on an errand on her own.) And Masalinie Merian can teleport you to Mages Guilds in Ald'ruhn, Caldera, Sadrith Mora, and Vivec.

53. **Rithleen's House (upstairs) and Tyemaillin's House (downstairs):** Two more Blades. You guys should start a union. Again, they extend the usual Blade-to-Blade courtesies, and offer useful items. The warrior Rithleen gives you a steel cuirass and helm, and the healer Tyemaillin a Journeyman's Alembic.

54. **Ra'Virr: Trader:** Nine-Toes points you to this trader as a likely buyer for your moon sugar. (Keep track of who buys illegal stuff and who doesn't; some valuable stuff is illegal.) On the legit side, you'll buy a bowl from him in a Mages Guild quest.

55. **Tsiya's House:** You can return belongings found on Ernil Omoran body's (see (69)) to Tsiya in a Miscellaneous Quest.

56. **Drarayne Thelas' House:** Thelas will reward you (albeit rather uselessly) in a super-obscure Miscellaneous Quest if you return the invoice for her pillows from the Abandoned Shipwreck.

57. **Dura gra-Bol's House:** You'll whack this Orc outlaw in a Fighters Guild quest.

58. **South Wall Cornerclub:** If you follow the directions you receive when you are released in Seyda Neen, this will probably your first stop in Balmora. Owner Bacola Closcius will direct you to Caius Cosades. Later on, he'll contribute a bottle of Cyrodilic brandy to a brandy-gathering Tribunal Temple quest. In Fighters Guild quests, you'll be sent here to recover a codebook and kill Sugar Lips Habasi. In a Mages Guild quest, you'll be asked to get Only-He-Stands-There to stop giving unauthorized training in Restoration at the club. In a Miscellaneous Quest, this is where you'll get candidates for the list of the Bad People you're to do in. And, if you join the Thieves Guild, Habasi can give you his own quests. This is the Balmora Thieves Guild, after all.

59. **The Lucky Lockup:** Meril Hlaano has been dissing House Redoran at this cornerclub. In a Redoran quest, you'll try to persuade him to be cool. Benunius Agrudilius will contribute a bottle of Cyrodilic brandy to your Tribunal Temple Quest for Brandy. And, finally, Todwendy is the "secret master" in the Short Blade skill.

60. **Balmora Council Club:** The local Camonna Tong base. You may kill a bunch of people in here before you're through. In a Miscellaneous Quest to rid Balmora of Bad People, you'll murder five of them. See (58) and (76). Thanelen Velas is the most likely suspect in the murder of Ralen Hlaalo. (See (35) and (50).) You'll probably want to kill him, too. And a few folks you'll just engage in pleasant conversation. For example, in a Thieves Guild quest, you can get the key to the top floor of Nerano Manor from Nerano servant Sovor Trandel. (In addition, you can steal from the club's backroom all five bottles of Cyrodilic brandy needed for that brandy quest for the Tribunal Temple.)

61. **Balmora silt strider port:** Selvil Sareloth drives the bug to Ald'ruhn, Seyda Neen, Suran, and Vivec.

62. **Vassir-Didanat Cave:** You can re-discover this lost ebony mine, and turn your knowledge into profit, in a Miscellaneous Quest.

63. **Hassour:** You're sent to shut down this nasty Sixth House base on a Tribunal Temple quest. (In so doing, you'll shut down the flow of Sleepers and Dreamers in the Balmora and Pelagiad area.)
64. **Eight Plates:** In a Tribunal Temple quest, Dulnea Ralaal will donate a bottle of Cyrodilic brandy. You'll also pop in here in a Redoran quest to recover a stolen Founder's Helm from Alvis Teri. And, in a Mages Guild quest, you'll be asked to escort Itermerel from the Eight Plates to the Halfway Inn in Pelagiad.
65. **Nevrasa Dralor:** This pilgrim has lost her way on a trip to the Fields of Kummu. In a Miscellaneous Quest, you can escort her there. (See (14) on the Bal Ur Map.)
66. **Lleran Ancestral Tomb:** A nondescript tomb, but for one ultra-rare item found on a corner of a prayer stool.
67. **Tarhiel:** Did you see him fall? He's been experimenting with a new spell called "Icarian Flight." Also known as "Instant Death."
68. Two alits.
69. The body of Ernil Omoran. You can return the skooma pipe and note to Tsiya in Balmora in a Miscellaneous Quest.
70. A Dreamer.
71. **Adanumuran:** Another of those general-purpose-bad-guy caves-most notable for its nix-hounds and for a chest of books.
72. **Maurrie Aumine: This** young lady is smitten with bandit Nelos Onmar, who just robbed her. Girls do like bad boys, don't they? You can find him, and get the two together, in a Miscellaneous Quest. (See (6) on the Bal Ur Map (D3).)
73. **Ulummusa:** This tiny smugglers cave contains an engraved silver bowl, which you can return to its rightful owner in a Miscellaneous Quest.
74. A firebite dagger and 50 gold, hidden in a tree stump in a muck pool.
75. A Dreamer.
76. **Moonmoth Legion Fort:** Radd Hard-Heart is an Imperial Legion quest-giver, and Legion champion Larrius Varo will give you a pair of Miscellaneous Quests. (You can also try to kill him (fat chance!) in one of the Morag Tong's grandmaster-level "writ" quests.) Somutis Vunnis can sign you up for the Imperial Cult. And Peragon will sell both flowers for one of the Romance quests.
77. **Foyada Mamaea:** A highway to hell. This dry lava river leads southwest to the Sixth House base Hassour and northeast to Ghostgate and the Red Mountain crater.
78. **Junal-Lei's House:** This cute little house isn't important. It signals only that you've reached the west edge of Pelagiad.
79. A guar.

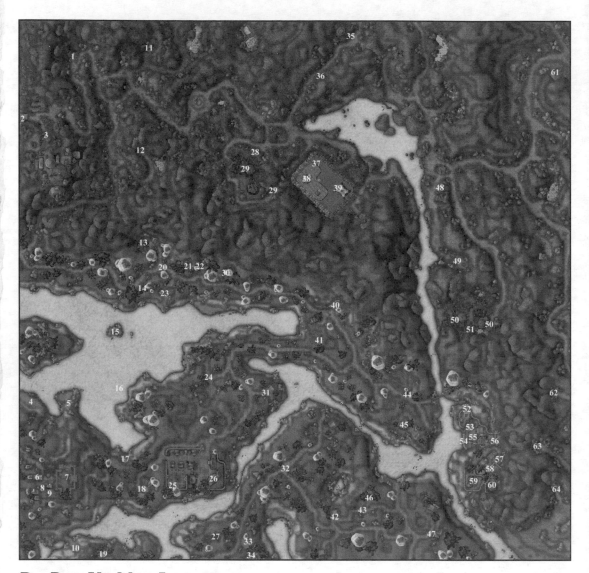

D3: BAL UR MAP LOCATIONS:

1. **Missamsi:** Vast Sixth House base with the usual gang of nasties, but little loot beyond the obligatory Sixth House Bell Hammer.
2. **Snowy Granius:** Just because there's snow on the roof doesn't mean this battlemage doesn't still have a fire in his belly. If you took the silt strider from Sedya Neen, and have been behaving yourself, this could be your first real fight. Nearby: Three crates containing gold and a barrel of Dwarven ingredients.
3. **Arkngthand:** Baby's first Dwemer ruin. This is the ultimate destination on your first Main Quest outing, and the closest source of scrap metal for an Imperial Cult quest out of Moonmoth Fort. It's huge, with six sections, and you won't be able to explore it all until you get the key from Hasphat Antabolis. See (48).
4. A mudcrab colony.

5. **Panat:** Good-sized bandit cave with four baddies, three slaves and one great piece of loot: the Dwarven Halberd in the first room.
6. **Halfway Tavern:** It's the Love Shack! Here you'll find Nelos Onmar, the bandit who stole Maurrie Aumine's heart. (See (72) on the Balmora Map.) If you pay him off (male characters) or kiss him (female characters with bad taste in men), bandit Nels Llendo will turn up here and offer training. (See (2) on Vivec Map.) If your character if male and alive, you can even find love yourself here—her name's Ahnassi—and start up the Romance Quests. The first involves getting the enchanted Belt of Sanguine Fleetness from Hrordis, a guest at the tavern. (This is also a Morag Tong "Threads of the Webspinner" quest.)
7. **Fort Pelagiad:** In a Thieves Guild quest, you can blackmail Shadbak gra-Burbug to force the release of New-Shoes Bragor. And you can join the Imperial Cult by talking to Ygfa.
8. **Mebestien Ence: Trader:** In a Thieves Guild quest, you'll steal a Dwemer Coherer from Ence's private quarters and use it to blackmail Shadbak gra-Burbug at Fort Pelagiad. See (7).
9. **Ahnassi's House:** Your girlfriend's place. If you play your cards right in the Romance Quest, Ahnassi will eventually invite you to stay here with her.
10. **Mannammu:** In a Fighters Guild quest, you'll be asked to kill Dovres Verethi, the leader of a band of smugglers that operates out of this large watery cave. Good loot…and a dreugh.
11. **Saren Ancestral Tomb:** Large crypt with decent loot and Daedra defenders.
12. **Nissintu:** Mid-sized smuggling bandits cave with heroic loot in the depths of its innermost room.
13. **Sarano Ancestral Tomb:** In a Fighters Guild quest, you'll have to kill the Hunger that's gotten into this large crypt and recover the ebony helm it has stolen.
14. **Fields of Kummu Shrine:** You'll make a pilgrimage to this pastoral shrine in your first Tribunal Temple quest. Hence, you'll be well equipped to escort pilgrim Nevrasa Dralor there in a Miscellaneous Quest. Or vice-versa.
15. You'll need a portion of muck in inventory to activate the nearby Fields of Kummu shrine. And look what's here: a cluster of muck-producing muckspunge plants! And a little family of mudcrab custodians!
16. **Desolate Shipwreck:** On the upper level, you'll find a crate of ebony.
17. **Punammu:** You'll find diamonds in this huge bandit cave.
18. **Llovyn Andus and Corky the Guar:** In a Hlaalu quest (from that slimy Odral Helvi), you'll be asked to collect 50 gold for rent and taxes from two farmers. Andus is one. He can't pay and offers the guar, Corky, in lieu of the money. (See (31).) Lloyn's farm's also a good spot to pick up any corkbulb that you can't find in (24).
19. **Balur's Farmhouse:** You'll collect marshmerrow at this farm in an Imperial Cult quest.
20. **Thoronor:** His friend wandered off to investigate an odd animal sound, and hasn't returned. You can find him in a Miscellaneous Quest. See (21), (22), and (30).
21. Two mating kagouti. "Odd animal sound" issue of (20) resolved.
22. Notes on kagouti mating habits, made by Thoronor's pal.
23. **Alof's Farmhouse:** In a Fighters Guild quest, you'll look into a report of Orc meeting at a Daedric ruin near this farm. See (29).
24. **Arvel Plantation:** The suggested site for collecting corkbulb in an Imperial Cult quest.
25. **Hides-His-Foot:** You'll free this slave and escort him to safety in a Hlaalu quest. See (41).
26. **Dren's Villa:** In an advanced Hlaalu quest, you'll have to get Camonna Tong boss Orvas Dren out of the way through assassination, persuasion, or blackmail. In a Thieves Guild quest and a Morag Tong "writ" quest, you'll be ordered to kill Camonna Tong enforcers Navil and Ranes Ienith.
27. Three netches.
28. Two scamps.
29. **Ashunartes:** This small shrine to Daedric god Malacath is the source of Orcs in (23). (Orcs love Malacath.)
30. **Edras Oril:** Thoronor's pal. See (20), (21), and (22).
31. **Manat Varnan-Adda:** The other farmer targeted by Odral Helvi in (18).
32. **Teris Raledran and Rollie the Guar:** In a Miscellaneous Quest, you'll have to find a place for Rollie to wait and then escort Raledran to Vivec's Foreign Quarter.
33. Two more netches.
34. **Gro-Bagrat Plantation:** You can collect willow anther here in an Imperial Cult quest.
35. **Sulipund:** You'll visit this Velothi dome to persuade Llarar Bereloth to join the Mages Guild in a (duh) Mages Guild quest.
36. **Punabi:** And you'll drop in here to persuade Manwe to pay her overdue Mages Guild dues.

37. **Marandus:** A big, brawny dungeon, though on the small side for a stronghold, with lots of folks to kill and stuff to take.
38. You can focus on the stuff-taking by moving directly to the enemy-free zone of this rooftop dome.
39. **Propylon Chamber:** You can teleport from this chamber to the strongholds Hlormaren and Telasero, provided you have retrieved the necessary index from St. Olms Temple in Vivec.
40. **Sandas Ancestral Tomb:** Mid-sized crypt containing the usual undead monsters keyed to the player's current level…and two skeleton champions. Yikes.
41. **Sterdecan:** You'll escort escaped slave Hides-His-Foot (see (25)) and fake escaped slave Tul (see (44)) to this abolitionist's farm in Hlaalu and Miscellaneous quests, respectively.
42. **Piernette's Farmhouse:** You can return the engraved silver bowl found in Ulumussa (see (73) on the Balmora Map) to Piernette Beluelle in a Miscellaneous Quest.
43. Leles Birian is the "secret master" of the Destruction skill.
44. **Tul:** A Camonna Tong assassin who pretends to be an escaped slave so you'll leave him to the abolitionist Sterdecan. You can do so (and then, we hope, kill him quickly) in a Miscellaneous Quest.
45. **Ules Manor:** In the Main Quest, you'll need to win Nevena Ules' support (via Orvas Dren) to be selected as Hlaalu Hortator.
46. Rats!
47. **Paur Maston:** In a Miscellaneous Quest, you can escort him to Molag Mar.
48. **Vandus Ancestral Tomb:** A large, lanky tomb, with ordinary contents.
49. Two alits.
50. **Bal Ur:** You'll visit this big Molag Bal shrine in "The Pilgrimages of the Four Corners" quests for the Tribunal Temple and in the final vampire quest.
51. Two alits. Others roam to the north and east.
52. You can ride Folsi Thendas' silt strider to Balmora, Molag Mar, Seyda Neen, and Vivec.
53. **Desele's House of Earthly Delights:** You can recruit retiring exotic dancers from this cornerclub to settle at your Redoran stronghold. In a Fighters Guild quest, you'll collect a debt from club owner Helviane Desele. And in a Miscellaneous Quest (received from drunken bounty hunter Daric Bielle), you can try to track down escaped slave Haj-Ei.
54. A Dreamer.
55. **Elvil Vidron:** Vidron says he's the Nerevarine. Huh! You can show him the error of his ways—or introduce him to the sharp end of your sword—in a Tribunal Temple quest.
56. **Suran Slave Market:** Dranas Sarthram provides a key piece of info in your search for escaped slave Haj-Ei. See (53).
57. **Suran Tradehouse:** You'll find Haj-Ei here.
58. **Ibarnadad Assirnarari: Apothecary:** If you don't like swimming, you can just buy a portion of muck here for your Tribunal Temple pilgrimage to the Fields of Kummu. See (14).
59. **Oran Manor:** In a Fighters Guild quest, you have to kill the leader of a gang of bandits plaguing the village. Suran Serjo Avon Oran tells you where they're coming from. See (62). You can also extort 1,000 gold from Oran in a Hlaalu quest. See (64).
60. Suran Temple.
61. **Aran Ancestral Tomb:** Lots of equipment in this tomb-including a Dragonscale Tower Shield.
62. **Saturan:** You'll have to kill Daldur Sarys, the leader of the bandits in this cave, in a Fighters Guild quest. See (59).
63. **Umbra:** A world-weary Orc warrior looking for death. You can grant his wish—and inherit an incredible sword—in a Miscellaneous Quest.
64. **Inanius Egg Mine:** You have to sabotage this mine by killing its kwama queen in a Hlaalu quest. You can also extort gold from its owner, Avon Oran. See (59).

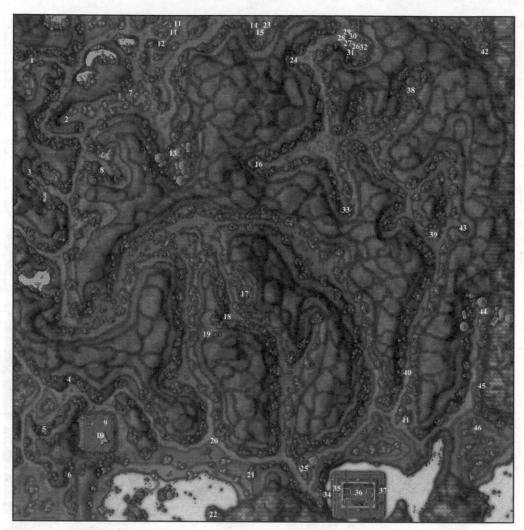

D4: MOLAG MAR MAP LOCATIONS:

1. Two nix-hounds.
2. Two rats.
3. **Piran:** Another huge Sixth House base, with just a smattering of loot.
4. **Kunirai:** Sizeable general-purpose-bad-guy cave. Some bandit loot, some smugglers loot, and some that isn't either, but most of the best stuff is lying around loose.
5. **Vansunalit Egg Mine:** A lot of egg mines share their names, or parts of their names, with grottos. But few of them look like grottos. This one does.
6. **Velas Ancestral Tomb:** Nice loot in this small-ish tomb.
7. More rats!
8. **Mababi:** Four rogue Telvannis have set themselves up in this Velothi dome. Check out the extensive library, which contains the rare volumes "The Pig Children" and "Nchunak's Fire and Faith."

9. **Telasero:** You're supposed to escort scholar Sondaale of Shimmerene into this Dunmer stronghold in a Fighters Guild quest. You'll arrive to discover she's descended without you into what turns out to be a large Sixth House base, and you have to bring her out safely.

10. **Propylon Chamber:** You'll need the index from Telasero's lower level to zap to strongholds Marandus and Falensarano.

11. Still more literary breadcrumbs from kidnapped hermit Jocien Ancois' book. See (19), (26), and (33) on the Tel Aruhn Map.

12. **Shashurari Camp:** And here, finally, is the camp where Ancois is being held by Mabrigash. You can rescue him in an Imperial Legion quest.

13. **Nchuleftingth:** You'll explore this large Dwarven ruin to find a lost guide, and an important book-in a Mages Guild quest.

14. One more page from Jocien Ancois' book.

15. **Reeh-Jah:** An escaped slave. In a Miscellaneous Quest, you can escort him to the Argonian Mission in Ebonheart …or the Slave Market in Tel Aruhn.

16. **Arethan Ancestral Tomb:** What is this thing Hungers have with ancestral tombs? There's one in this crypt as well.

17. **Assu:** In a Mages Guild quest, you can recover the Staff of Magnus from this large sorcerers cave on Mount Kand.

18. **Mount Kand Cavern:** In a Tribunal Temple quest, you'll have to correctly answer riddles from three atronachs in these deep, dark caves.

19. **Linus Iulus:** You must recover the Silver Staff of Shaming from the body of this long-lost acolyte in an Imperial Cult quest.

20. Two nix-hounds.

21. **Raviro Ancestral Tomb:** A Berne vampire lair.

22. Two cliff racers. (A rarity; these creatures typically work solo.)

23. You asked for it, you begged for it, so here it is: one more page from Mabrigash abductee Jocien Ancois' copy of "A REALLY Brief History of the Empire"!

24. **Maren Ancestral Tomb:** You can liberate a great artifact called the Bloodworm Helm from a Nord named Crazy Batou.

25. Dilami Androm will drive you from Molag Mar to Suran or Vivec in his silt strider.

26. **Wise Woman's Yurt:** In the Main Quest, Manirai (your one semi-friendly contact here) will give you the lay of the land at the Erabenimsun Ashlander camp. To wit: To be named Nerevarine, you'll have to kill the current chief and his henchmen.

27. **Ranabi's Yurt:** Take on this guy first.

28. **Ashu-Ahhe's Yurt:** This guy comes second.

29. **Ashkhan's Yurt:** Then beat up on Ulath-Pal and his bodyguard, Ahaz.

30. **Han-Ammu's Yurt:** Now you've just got to persuade this guy to take on the chief's job.

31. **Asaba-Bentus:** The studly young warrior whom you'll trade to the Mabrigash for abducted hermit Jocien Ancois. See (12).

32. **Tinti and Hairan:** The two Erabenimsun warriors who robbed Marsus Tullius of his guar hides. (See (24) on the Tel Aruhn Map.)

33. **Alas Ancestral Tomb:** In a Daedric Quest, you'll be sent to retrieve Mehrunes Dagon's Razor from this crypt.

34. **Vanjirra:** Paur Maston's business partner. She'll reward you once you escort him to Molag Mar. See (47) on the Bal Ur Map.

35. **Waistworks entrances:** Shops and services on Molag Mar's enclosed Waistworks level include a Buoyant Armiger's stronghold where you'll find Giras Indiram. In a Redoran quest, you'll need to coax him into paying an overdue bill.

36. **Molag Mar Temple:** Tharer Rotheloth will give you Tribunal Temple quests. Also here is Ulms Drathan, "secret master" of the Long Blade skill.

37. You might not realize it at first glance, but Molag Mar has boat service. Rindral Dralor can take you to Ebonheart, Tel Branora, and Tel Mora.

38. **Tusenend:** A one-room shrine to Molag Bal, with interesting bits of loot. The ebony on the altar is cursed.

39. **Mount Assarnibibi:** You'll be sent to pray at this shrine in a Tribunal Temple quest.

40. Two cliff racers.

41. **Helan Ancestral Tomb:** Itty-bitty tomb with 100 gold. But the real feature here is the three shrines, which can cure various ailments and temporarily boost certain player stats.

42. **Zebabi:** Big old bandit cave with the usual nice loot—the featured item being a Dwarven battle axe.

43. **Maesa-Shammus Egg Mine:** Blight-schmight. All we know is, there's a dead warrior in here with a Daedric dai-katana and a full suit of Imperial chain armor.

44. **Nchardumz:** Two-level Dwarven ruin, with pretty mundane loot.

45. Two rats.

46. Two alits.

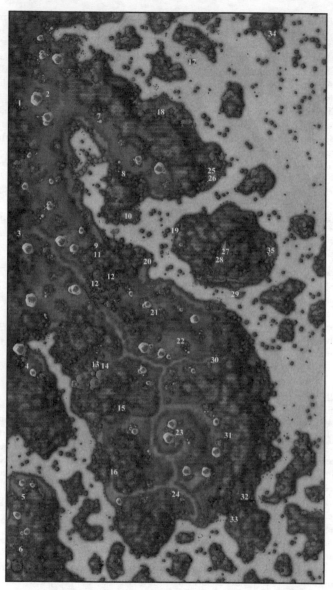

D5: HOLAMAYAN MAP LOCATIONS:

1. **Andalen Ancestral Tomb:** An uncommon Colovian Fur Helm can be found in this crypt.
2. Three renegade Ashlanders, scowling away.
3. **Matus-Akin Egg Mine:** A giant egg mine, with blighted enemies and dead miners.
4. Three Mabrigash.
5. **Savel Ancestral Tomb:** A super-rare Bonemold Founder's Helm can be found in this roomy tomb. (Only three can be found in the game.)

6. **Almurbalarammi:** None of the individual items on this shrine's altar are cursed. But the chest is. Sheogorath's always playing tricks.
7. A rat's nest.
8. An alit lair.
9. A nix-hound den.
10. Two netches.
11. **Ainat:** A sizeable bandit cave, with lots of weapons and armor mixed into the loot.
12. **Shashpilamat:** This ruin has two separate sections, with the Malacath shrine, reached through the western entrance, much larger and immensely rich in gold and precious stones. (But beware of the fiend spear on the altar.)
13. **Nchurdamz:** In an advanced Fighters Guild quest, you'll escort explorer Larienna Macrina through this extremely rich and extremely well-defended Dwarven ruin in search of a Daedroth named Hrelvesuu.
14. **Larienna Macrina:** The lady herself. She's a Level 19 Crusader, decked out in Imperial armor and wielding a steel flamesword. Maybe she should escort you!
15. A cliffracer nest.
16. **Odiniran:** You can play out this scenario from both sides in separate Great House quests. As a Hlaalu, you'll try to rescue the sister of the expedition's leader from the home of necromancer Milyn Faram. As a Telvanni, you'll go in to lift the siege and kill that leader.
17. **Lonely Shipwreck:** Potions on the upper level, food and drugs on the lower.
18. **Arenim Ancestral Tomb:** You'll actually find a Miscellaneous Quest in this tomb. Help Satyana find her father's amulet and she'll help you loot the tomb—the fact that it is her family's vault notwithstanding.
19. **Zalkin Grotto:** Nothing in this dark, "F"-shaped swimming pool save pearls and critters. Depending on your level, they'll range from small slaughterfish up to dreugh.
20. A critter lair. Again what you find here depends on your level. If you're just starting out (and if you are, what are you doing all the way out here?), you could find nix-hounds, alits, or rats. If you're at Level 3, you could find diseased kagouti, rats or alits. Up to a maximum nastiness of blighted alits, kagoutis, or shalks at Level 8.
21. **Ravel Ancestral Tomb:** The loot's excellent throughout this large, Daedra-defended tomb, and one item here is unique: the ashes of "G. Lyngas." It's one of just three instances of named ashes in the game. In each case, they keep company with potent items. Here, it's four of the game's 16 glass throwing stars.
22. A rat's nest.
23. Another level-dependent critter lair. Low end: rats, kwama foragers, and scribs. High end: "Betty" netches.
24. A kagouti lair.
25. **Salmantu:** No loot at all in this comparatively small Sixth House base.
26. A netch colony.
27. **Holamayan:** You'll visit this monastery in middle of the Main Quest to get the lost prophecies. You may be back on a Telvanni quest to collect three books for Baladas Demnevanni. (All are in the monastery's expansive library.) And Taren Omothan is "secret master" of the Hand-to-Hand skill.
28. Another rat's nest.
29. Vevrana Aryon's boat only goes from Holamayan to Ebonheart. (Not that we would even suggest burglarizing the monastery boat, but did you check out the contents of the rusted chest?)
30. **Hlervu Ancestral Tomb:** You'll find a glass dagger in this crypt, but the most distinctive thing about the Hlervu tomb is actually a scroll: the last words of Malaki the Lightfooted.
31. **Ahallaraddon Egg Mine:** For an egg mine, this feels a lot like a grotto.
32. **Shrine of Azura:** If you activate the statue in the shrine, the goddess will give you a Daedric quest: Clear a remote northern island of Daedra.
33. **Aharnabi:** You'll visit this cave on an Imperial Legion quest to kill Honthjolf, a former legionnaire who quit to work for sorceress Llarusea Andrethi.
34. A cliff racer nest.
35. Another level-dependent critter lair.

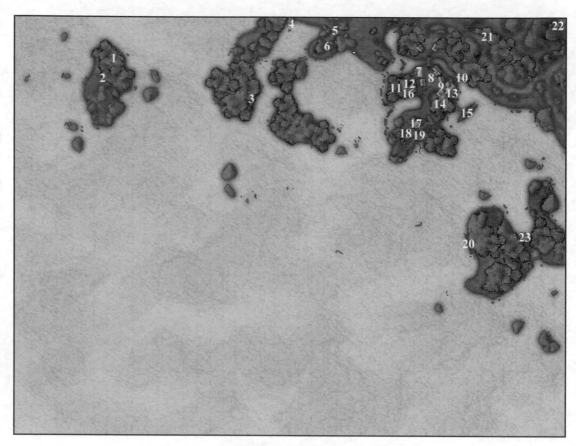

E2: SEYDA NEEN REGION

E2: SEYDA NEEN MAP LOCATIONS:

1. **Aharunartus:** This bandit cave is one of two starter dungeons.
2. **Sarys Ancestral Tomb:** Among the usual tomb creatures, you'll find a bonewalker in this crypt (and more potent variants at higher player levels).
3. **Thelas Ancestral Tomb:** A starter tomb, with a St. Veloth shrine.
4. **Nimawia Grotto:** Just one drowned body in here, but with enough loot on it to make it a worthwhile swim for a starting player.
5. A critter lair, with the type or types of critters depending on the player's level.
6. **Processus Vitellius:** The remains of Seyda Neen's mostly unlamented tax collector. You can track down his killer in a Miscellaneous Quest. See (11), (14), and (17).
7. **Arrille's Tradehouse:** In a Miscellaneous Quest, you can cook up a scheme with Hrisskar Flat-Foot to discover where Fargoth (9) keeps his valuables and then steal them-including his ring (14) if you've already returned it. You'll also find Elone the Scout. Once you're a Blade, she'll offer to train you and give you a copy of "Guide to Vvardenfell."
8. **Vodunius Nuccius:** This fine fellow will refer you to the silt strider port outside town (10) and offer a cursed ring (not Fargoth's) for sale in a very minor Miscellaneous Quest.
9. **Fargoth:** In one Miscellaneous Quest, you can return to Fargoth the enchanted ring you'll find shortly after you create your character-only to steal it back in another Miscellaneous Quest. See (7), (14) and (16).
10. You can ride Darvame Hleran's silt strider to Balmora, Gnisis, Suran, and Vivec. Hleran also tells you that Vodunius Nuccius (8) is unhappy on Vvardenfell.
11. **Foryn Gilnith's Shack:** Gilnith killed tax collector Processus Vitellius. See (6), (14) and (17).
12. **Indrele Rathryon's Shack:** You can return an illicit land deed to Rathryon (the property's rightful owner) in a "Bal Molagmer" Thieves Guild quest.
13. **Census and Excise Warehouse:** You'll be asked to kill Adraria Vandacia in a Fighters Guild quest.
14. **Census and Excise Office:** Here, you'll create your character and pick up whatever loose items you can lay your hands on-including Fargoth's ring, which is in a barrel in the courtyard. (See (7), (9), and (16).) Socucius Ergalla will dispatch you to look into the death of tax collector Processus Vitellius. See (6), (11), and (16).
15. **Imperial Prison Ship:** It brought you to Vvardenfell. And once you enter the Customs and Excise Office, it's gone from the game.
16. **A tree stump:** Fargoth's stuff is hidden here. (This is a frequent practice in this part of Vvardenfell. Always check such places for hidden caches.)
17. **Lighthouse:** It plays a role in your scheme to steal Fargoth's stuff. (See (7), (9), (14), and (16).) Lighthouse keeper Thavere Vedrano was tax collector Processus Vitellius' girlfriend, and can give you a lead on his killer. See (11).
18. An Iron Shardaxe, hidden in a tree stump
19. A silverware cup and 25 gold in a tree stump. Is all this more of Fargoth's stuff? Or someone else's? Either way, it's your stuff now.
20. **Remote Shipwreck:** In one of the crates on the upper level, you'll find a worn Imperial key. It opens the secret door in the shrine below the Imperial Commission in Castle Ebonheart.
21. **Addamasartus:** The other starter dungeon. This large smugglers cave contains another of the game's few Thief Rings.
22. **Andrano Ancestral Tomb:** In the Main Quest, you'll recover the skull of Llevule Andrano from this large and dangerous crypt.
23. **Akimaes Grotto:** Just pearls. So tell us again: Why are we exploring grottos?

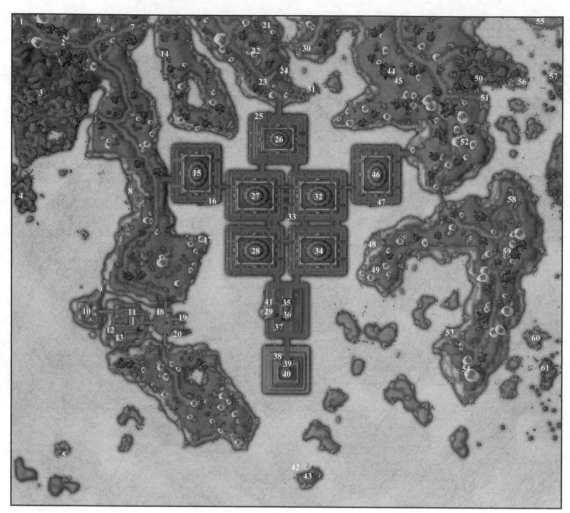

E3: Vivec Map Locations:

1. A Dreamer.
2. **Nels Llendo:** To male characters, he'll appear as a bandit. To females, as a rogue with puckered lips. Either way, satisfying Llendo is a Miscellaneous Quest. See (6) on the Bal Ur Map.
3. **Abaesen-Pulu Egg Mine:** Most of the creatures in this mine are blighted.
4. **Assemanu:** You'll search this giant Sixth House base for the lost Robe of St. Roris in an advanced Hlaalu quest.
5. **Mudan Grotto:** In the final entry on the Seyda Neen Map, we asked why we're exploring grottos. This grotto is the reason you're exploring grottos.
6. **Balur Salvu:** You'll gather marshmerrow in this farmer's fields for an Imperial Cult quest.
7. A pair of bull netches. In an Imperial Cult quest, you'll be assigned to kill a netch for its leather hide, and the one of these two will be the most convenient target.
8. Three mudcrabs.
9. A secret underwater entrance to the caves below Castle Ebonheart. You may discover it in the course of an advanced Imperial legion quest to recover the stolen Lord's Mail.

10. **Castle Ebonheart:** You'll be wearing a groove in the carpets here. You'll visit Duke Vedam Dren, the Imperial representative on Vvardenfell, for a construction contract for your stronghold, and also for advanced Hlaalu quests. Varus Vantinius will offer advanced Imperial Legion quests. Ruccia Conician in the Grand Council Chamber and Lalatia Varian in the Imperial Chapels can sign you up for the Imperial Cult. All Cult quests come from quest-givers in the Chapels, and Llaalam Dredil provides info useful in three of them. You can deliver a letter for Dredil, and receive one back in turn, in a Miscellaneous Quest. In addition, a few quests have destinations here. You'll visit the Imperial Commission in a Romance Quest to snatch Elvul's Black Blindfold, in an Imperial Cult quest to find the aforementioned Lord's Mail (which also leads into the Imperial Guard Garrison) and (maybe) in a Camonna Tong-authored Fighters Guild quest to kill Imperial Magistrate Rufinius Alleius.

11. **Hawkmoth Legion Garrison:** Frald the White offers Imperial Legion quests. Sirollus Saccus is "secret master" of the Armorer skill. And High Elves Landorume or Fanildil provide useful info in your Imperial Cult search for a missing bowl.

12. **Skyrim Mission:** You'll visit this consulate in a fund-raising quest for the Imperial Cult.

13. **Argonian Mission:** Same deal here as in (12), but in a different Cult mission and with addition of an optional, more ruthless approach. In a Miscellaneous Quest, you can escort escaped Argonian slave Reeh-Ja to the Mission.

14. **Othrelas Ancestral Tomb:** A Berne vampire lair. This is about as close as vampires ever get to settled areas in Morrowind.

15. **Vivec:** Hlaalu Compound. See internal maps for detail.

16. Aren Maren's gondola goes to Vivec's Arena, Foreign Quarter, and Temple cantons.

17. Two mudcrabs.

18. **East Empire Company Hall:** You may wind up in here quite a bit, too. In a Hlaalu quest, one option involves persuading boss Canctunian Ponius to buy ebony from your House instead of House Redoran. In an Imperial Cult quest, you've got to get Ponius to pony up a pledged gift. In Miscellaneous Quest, you'll deliver a letter to J'Zhirr. After success in that quest and one other, you can get a third quest here from Bolrin: Get Vivec enchanter Audenian Valius' client list. An alternate solution to a Vivec-based Miscellaneous Quest that has you stealing limeware off the boat Chun-Ook at the Ebonheart docks is to bring the booty to Bolrin to point up the holes in security. And another Vivec-based Miscellaneous Quest requires you to steal Dredil's letter to J'Zhirr. Business really is war.

19. In the Main Quest, Blatta Hateria's boat will take you to the Holamayan monastery.

20. Nevosi Hlan's boat goes to Hla Oad, Sadrith Mora, Tel Branora, and Vivec's Foreign Quarter.

21. A critter lair. (Critter types depend on a player's level.)

22. **Hawia Egg Mine:** No surprises in this mid-sized egg mine.

23. **Tarvyn Faren:** In a Hlaalu quest, you'll escort this merchant to Pelagiad.

24. Adondasi Sadavel's silt strider goes to Balmora, Molag Mar, Seyda Neen, and Suran.

25. Devas Irano's will float his boat to the Arena and the Hlaalu and Telvanni compounds.

26. **Vivec: Foreign Quarter:** See Vivec maps for detail.

27. **Vivec: Redoran Compound:** See Vivec maps for detail.

28. **Vivec: St. Delyn Canton:** See Vivec maps for detail.

29. **Ministry of Truth:** In the Main Quest, you'll rescue Mehra Milo from this Tribunal Temple prison.

30. A Dreamer.

31. Ano Andaram sails to Ebonheart, Hla Oad, Molag Mar, and Tel Branora.

32. **Vivec: Arena**: See Vivec maps for detail.

33. Dalse Adren will ferry you to the Foreign Quarter, the Hlaalu and Telvanni Compounds, and the Temple Canton.

34. **Vivec: St. Olms Canton:** See Vivecl maps for detail.

35. **Danso Indules:** In the Main Quest, this fellow sets up your meeting with Archcanon Tholer Saryoni, who, in turn, sets up your meeting with Lord Vivec. See (40).

36. **Vivec: Temple:** See Vivec maps for detail.

37. A shrine to mark the spot where Lord Vivec stopped a rogue moon from falling on the city. You'll have to activate it in the initial series of Tribunal Temple quests.

38. **The Puzzle Canal:** The true entrance to this puzzle room is on Level 3. You'll have to activate two shrines here in the initial series of Tribunal Temple quests.

39. Two shrines dedicated to the memory of those who died in the last wear against Dagoth Ur. You'll activate them in your initial series of Tribunal Temple quests.

40. **The Palace of Vivec:** Your meeting with the earthly god Vivec atop this great pyramid sets up the Main Quest endgame.

41. Talsi Uvayn's gondola stops at the Arena and the Hlaalu and Telvanni Compounds.
42. A chest, partly buried in the sea bottom. Contents: 25 gold.
43. **Uncharted Shipwreck:** A nice varied haul on this ship, including 100 gold in the cabin and a lot of skooma and moon sugar (if dealing in these illegal substances isn't beneath you). Note: For a shipwreck, it's well guarded.
44. A critter den, with the type of critter depending on the player's current level.
45. **Tinos Drothan:** This guy's just wordless with rage. His escorts just ripped him off. You can save his glass in a Miscellaneous Quest. See (52).
46. **Vivec:** Telvanni Compound. See internal maps for detail.
47. Fendryn Drelvi's gondola goes to the Arena, the Foreign Quarter, and the Temple.
48. Two mudcrabs.
49. **Nund:** This smugglers cave is kind of small, but it's just packed with stuff to steal. Potions, in particular.
50. **Ald Sotha:** You'll be a repeat customer at this giant shrine to Daedric god Mehrunes Dagon. In a Tribunal Temple quest, you'll be here for the Shoes of St. Rilms. A "Pilgrimages of the Four Corners" Temple quest just requires you to activate the statue of Dagon. In a Miscellaneous Quest, you'll search the surface ruin for a rare flower by-product called Roland's Tears. And in a Morag Tong quest, you'll visit Ald Sotha to kill the leader of the Dark Brotherhood.
51. Two mudcrabs.
52. **Beshara:** The bums who stole Tinos Drothan's cargo are in this big smugglers cave with eight of their pals. See (45).
53. Two more mudcrabs.
54. **Ansi:** A large smugglers den distinguished most by its circular layout, a crate full of bonemold armor, and a rather disconcerting number of ash statues.
55. Three mudcrabs.
56. And again with the mudcrabs.
57. **Sinsibadon:** Small bandit cave with nothing amazing in the loot, and more slaves than baddies. (Two nix-hounds, too.)
58. A critter den. Again, what you are is what you get.
59. **Omani Manor:** In the Main Quest, you'll need Velanda Omani's support to be selected as Hlaalu Hortator. And in a Miscellaneous Quest, she'll pay 2,000 gold for the location of the lost Vassir-Didanat ebony mine.
60. Three mudcrabs.
61. Wondering what happened to all that neat out-of-the-way loot you found along the Bitter Coast? Well, that's more of a western Vvardenfell thing. A smuggler kind of thing. But here's a crate of moon sugar that fell off a ship. And a barrel of food is floating just to the northwest.

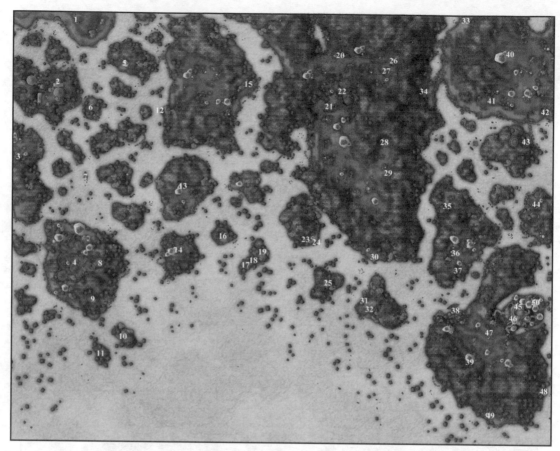

E4: Bal Fell Map Locations:

1. **Minabi:** Big, two-section bandit cave. Lots of beer. And, in the "lair" section, a chest containing 270 gold.
2. **Mzahnch:** Dwarven ruin, also with two sections and a fair number of Dwemer coins. But no beer.
3. **Hinnabi:** Just another bandit cave.
4. **Bal Fell:** Massive Sheogorath temple. Virtually no loot until you reach the inner shrine, and then…
5. **Releth Ancestral Tomb:** Skinny little tomb with unusual loot: a rare Telvanni Dust Adept Helm and a Velothian Shield.
6. The talking mudcrab merchant. (It really does exist.)
7. **Deserted Shipwreck:** Worth the trip. Potions (and tons of 'em) in the cabin, ebony on the upper deck, and a full suit of steel armor plus a steel shield on the lower.
8. Two cliff racers.
9. A netch harem (three bettys and a bull).
10. Two cliff racers.
11. And two more.
12. **Mul Grotto:** Decent loot for a grotto—all of it on or around the corpse in the large southern chamber.
13. **Yakanalit:** 57 containers in this bandit cave. Enough said.
14. **Ashirbadon:** Not many quests way out here in the wild southwest, but here's one. You'll visit this cave on a Mages Guild mission to relieve sorceress Vindamea Drethan of her Warlock Ring.
15. **Masseranit:** Basically, Yakanalit with smugglers. You could spend a day cleaning this place out.

16. **Rissun:** For a Sixth House base, Rissun is small. Great loot in the chest in the final room.
17. Two cliff racers.
18. **The Wreck of the Prelude:** You're sent here to collect a Daedric Wakizashi in a Hlaalu quest. But whatever else you find is yours to keep. If you survive the flanking cliff racers, you will not be disappointed.
19. Two more cliff racers. They must have eaten all the mudcrabs.
20. An alit den.
21. Three clannfear (Ogrim at Level 11).
22. **Zaintiraris:** Great loot behind the altar in this small Sheogorath shrine, but the ebony and candle on the altar itself are cursed.
23. **Marvani Ancestral Tomb:** An obscure Miscellaneous Quest leads you to this remote tomb, where a king's son named Olmgerd was given a Viking burial.
24. A mudcrab and a level-dependent creature (which could be a mudcrab as well).
25. Three cliff racers.
26. **Redas Ancestral Tomb:** In a Redoran quest, you'll try to recover three family treasures from this crypt.
27. **Kaushtababi Camp:** A renegade Ashlander secret master! Adibael Hainnabibi is unequalled in the Athletics skill. And his friends are governed by some passion other than using your head as a soccer ball.
28. A rat's nest.
29. **Eretammus-Sennammu Egg Mine:** Most of the creatures in this good-sized mine are blighted.
30. Two mudcrabs.
31. **Arys Ancestral Tomb:** Do you get the sense someone is using this tomb as a storage compartment? There's a fair amount of gold, and a member of the bonewalker family.
32. Two cliff racers.
33. A critter lair.
34. **Hlaalu Ancestral Tomb:** With the Hlaalu name and all, you might think this would be something special. But apart from one of those Telvanni Mole Crab Helms, it's pretty standard tomb stuff.
35. **Abebaal Egg Mine:** The slaves here have revolted. You'll have to figure out how to handle it in a Telvanni quest.
36. Two nix-hounds.
37. Two cliff racers.
38. Nireli Farys' boat goes to Ebonheart, Molag Mar, Sadrith Mora, and Vivec's Foreign Quarter.
39. Two rats.
40. Two renegade Ashlanders.
41. A rat's nest.
42. **Maba-Ilu:** Lots of scrolls in this sorcerers lair, along with little dashes of ebony, glass, and diamonds in the architecture. Future site of the Maba-Ilu Mine, we suspect.
43. **Mawia:** You'll be sent to this Velothi dome in a Tribunal Temple quest to kill necromancer Delvam Andarys.
44. **Kumarahaz:** Some neat architectural flourishes in this big bandit cave, and a silver claymore in its far reaches.
45. **Tel Branora Upper Tower:** You'll need Telvanni Councilor Therana's support to become Telvanni Hortator in the Main Quest. Of course, killing her is an option, too—as it is with all reluctant-to-commit Telvanni councilors— and you'll also be given also a chance to kill Therana more officially in a grandmaster-level writ quest for the Morag Tong. But you'll be tempted to kill this eccentric wizard long before that—for her response to the clothes you deliver to her in a Telvanni quest and for certain bizarre qualities of the single quest she gives you. (In addition, you can pickpocket her for the key to free the slaves in the Abebaal Egg Mine. If that's too much for you, the key is also in the Lower Tower and in the mine itself. (See (35).) You'll also have to climb the tower in a Thieves Guild quest to get Felen Maryon's enchanted ebony staff. Finally, just outside the door to the Upper Tower is Mollimo of Cloudrest, who gives you a Miscellaneous Quest to deal with Trerayna Dalen and her party. See (47).
46. **Sethan's Tradehouse:** If you completed the Miscellaneous Quest for Maurrie Aumine (see (72) on the Balmora Map), and have a female character, Aumine will try to fix you up with Barnand Erelie at this inn.
47. **Trerayna Dalen:** She's got a bone to pick with Therana. That's not hard to imagine; Therana would be master of the Eccentricity skill, if there were one. You can wipe out Dalen and her party in a Miscellaneous Quest. See (45).
48. **Beran Ancestral Tomb:** A deep and lavishly designed tomb. Fine loot, including a glass poisonsword. At least one atronach is guaranteed to be among the Daedric enemies.
49. **Arano Ancestral Tomb:** An ordinary tomb, defended by Daedra, that's notable most for the number of skulls both inside and outside and an uncommon Nordic Bearskin Cuirass.
50. **Seryne Relas:** A "secret master" of the Alteration skill.

Vivec Maps

ARENA CANALWORKS

EAST SIDE

WEST SIDE

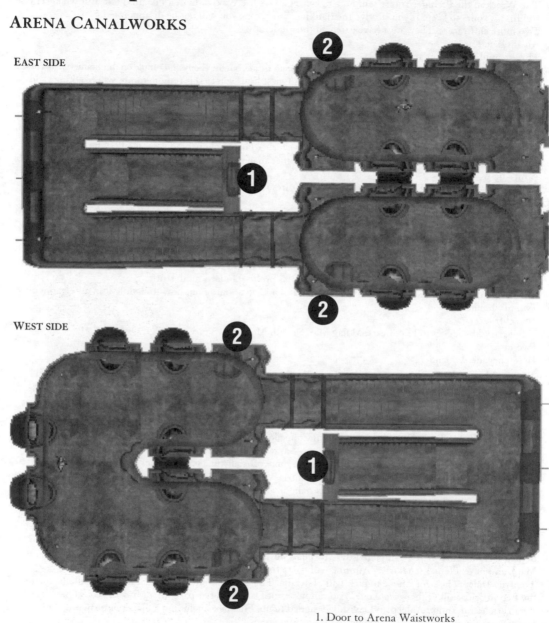

1. Door to Arena Waistworks
2. Trapdoor to Arena Underworks

Chapter Three: World

ARENA PIT

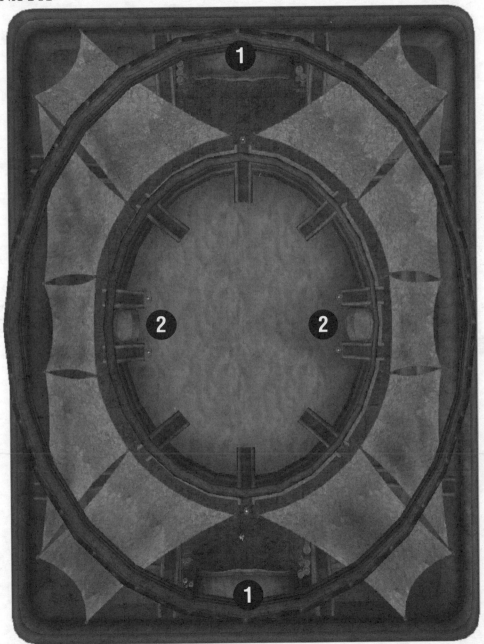

1. Door to Arena Exterior
2. Door to Arena Waistworks

ARENA WAISTWORKS

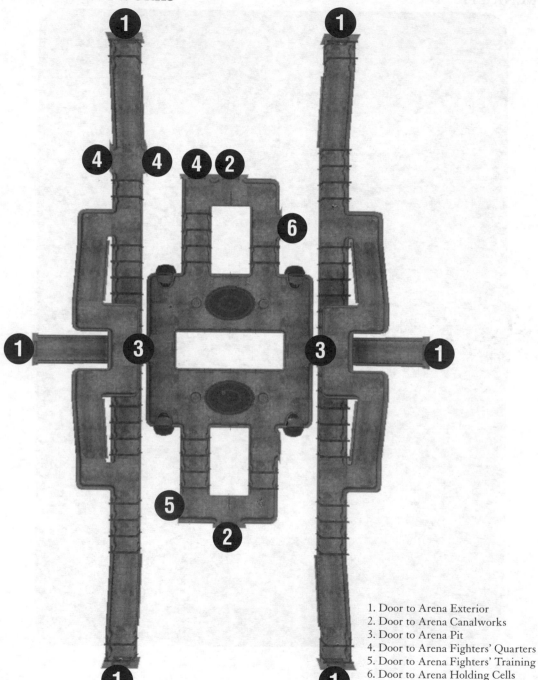

1. Door to Arena Exterior
2. Door to Arena Canalworks
3. Door to Arena Pit
4. Door to Arena Fighters' Quarters
5. Door to Arena Fighters' Training
6. Door to Arena Holding Cells

FOREIGN QUARTER CANALWORKS

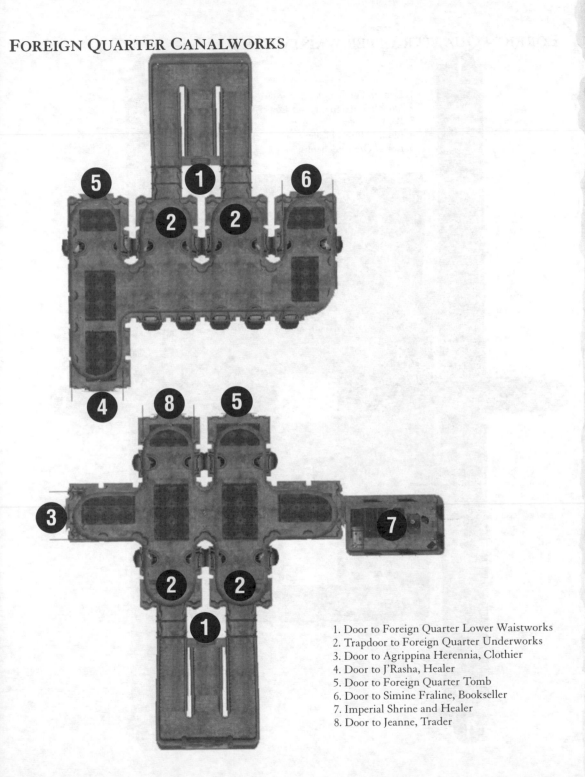

1. Door to Foreign Quarter Lower Waistworks
2. Trapdoor to Foreign Quarter Underworks
3. Door to Agrippina Herennia, Clothier
4. Door to J'Rasha, Healer
5. Door to Foreign Quarter Tomb
6. Door to Simine Fraline, Bookseller
7. Imperial Shrine and Healer
8. Door to Jeanne, Trader

FOREIGN QUARTER UPPER WAISTWORKS

1. Door to Foreign Quarter Exterior
2. Door to Foreign Quarter Lower Waistworks
3. Baissa, Trader
4. Idonea Munia, Healer
5. Rolasa Oren, Alchemist

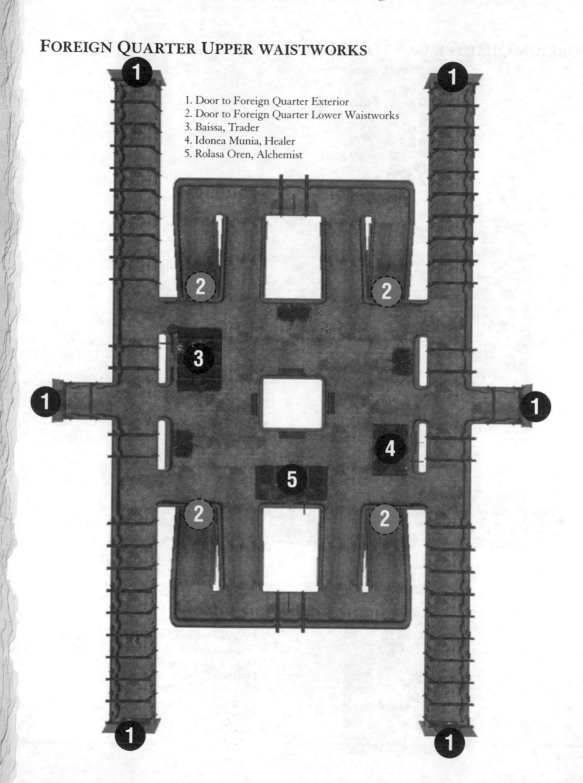

FOREIGN QUARTER LOWER WAISTWORKS

1. Door to Foreign Quarter Exterior
2. Door to Foreign Quarter Canalworks (hidden)
3. Door to Foreign Quarter Upper Waistworks
4. Door to Andilu Drothan, Alchemist
5. Door to Arurane Frernis, Apothecary
6. Door to Black Shalk Cornerclub
7. Door to Miun-Gei, Enchanter
8. Door to Jobasha's Rare Books

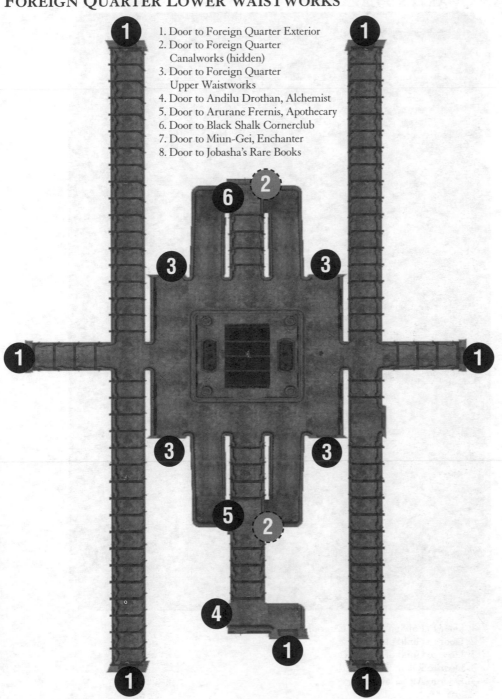

FOREIGN QUARTER PLAZA

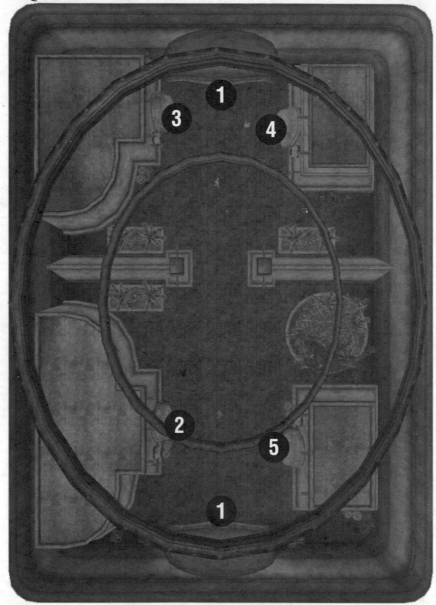

1. Door to Foreign Quarter Exterior
2. Door to Guild of Mages
3. Door to Guild of Fighters
4. Door to Ralen Tivur, Smith
5. Door to Alusaron, Smith

HALL OF WISDOM

1. Door to Vivec Exterior
2. Trapdoor to Hall Underworks
3. Door to Library of Vivec
4. Door to Canon Quarters
5. Door to Canon Offices
6. Door to Milo's Quarters
7. Door to Hall of Justice
8. Door to High Fane (Locked)

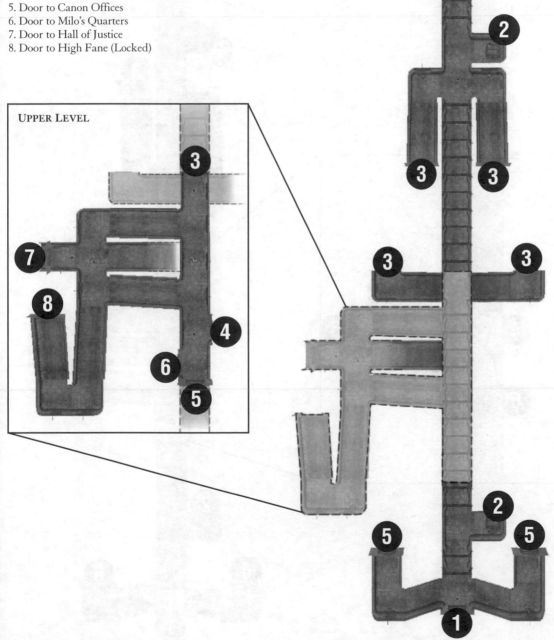

UPPER LEVEL

HALL OF JUSTICE

1. Door to Vivec Exterior
2. Trapdoor to Hall Underworks
3. Door to Justice Offices
4. Door to Office of the Watch
5. Door to Hall of Wisdom
6. Door to Ordinator Barracks

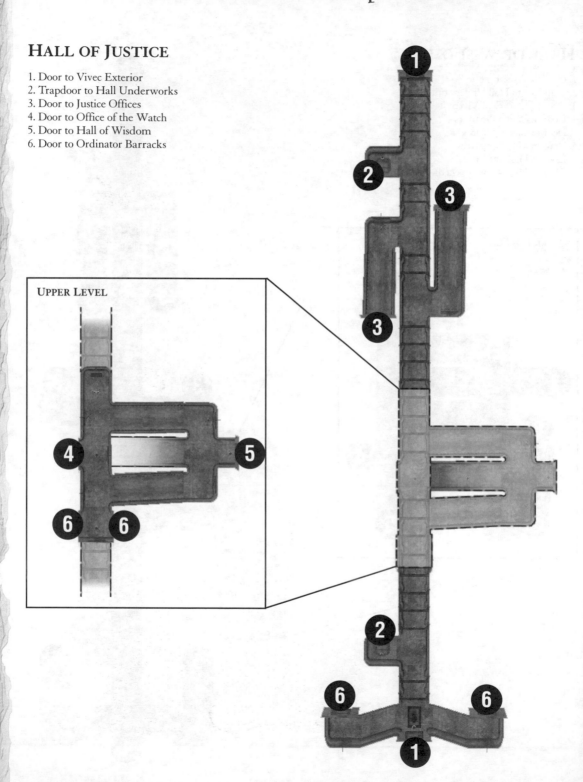

UPPER LEVEL

HIGH FANE

1. Door to Vivec Exterior
2. Door to Hall of Wisdom (Locked)
3. Eris Telas, Apothecary
4. Dileno Lloran, Priest
5. Llandris Thirandus, Enchanter
6. Endryn Llethan, Monk
7. Archcanon Tholer Saryoni

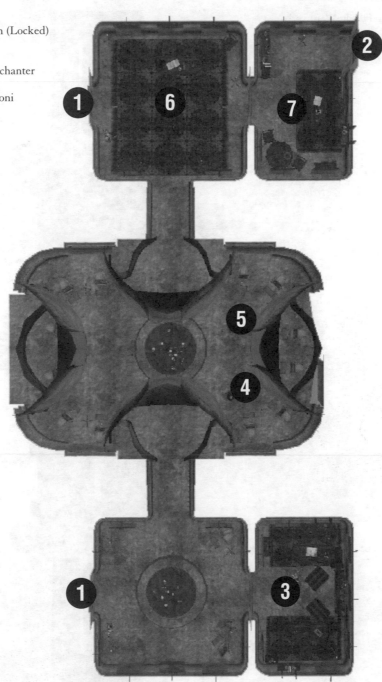

HLAALU CANALWORKS

1. Door to Hlaalu Waistworks
2. Trapdoor to Hlaalu Underworks
3. Door to Hlaalu Ancestral Tomb

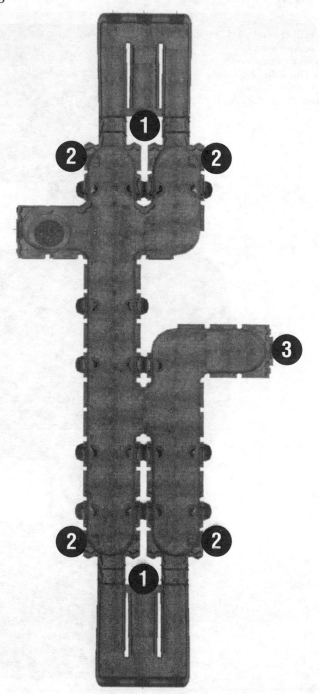

Hlaalu Plaza

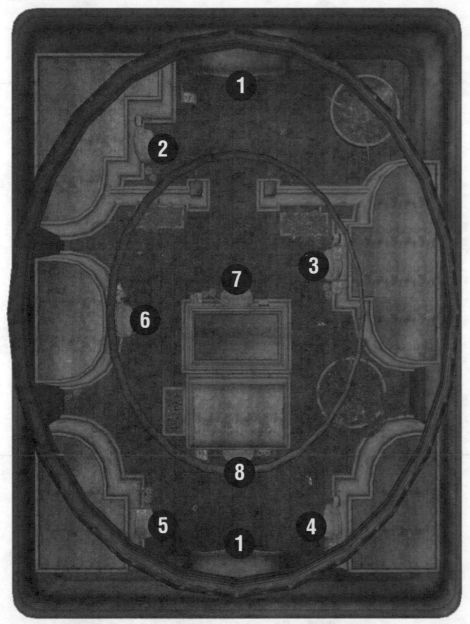

1. Door to Hlaalu Canton Exterior
2. Door to Elven Nations Cornerclub
3. Door to Curio Manor
4. Door to No Name Club
5. Door to Hlaalu Weaponsmith
6. Door to Hlaalu Pawnbroker
7. Door to Hlaalu Alchemist
8. Door to Hlaalu General Goods

HLAALU WAISTWORKS

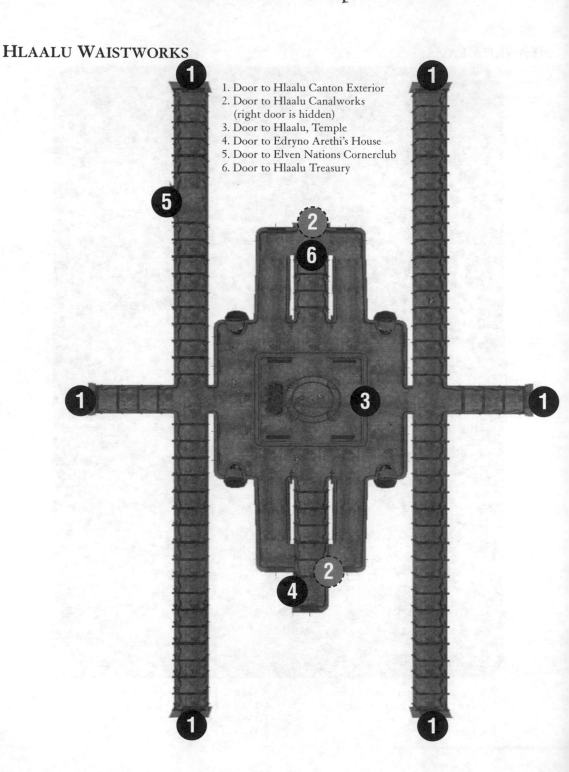

1. Door to Hlaalu Canton Exterior
2. Door to Hlaalu Canalworks
   (right door is hidden)
3. Door to Hlaalu, Temple
4. Door to Edryno Arethi's House
5. Door to Elven Nations Cornerclub
6. Door to Hlaalu Treasury

REDORAN CANALWORKS

1. Door to Redoran Waistworks
2. Trapdoor to Redoran Underworks
3. Door to Redoran Ancestral Tomb

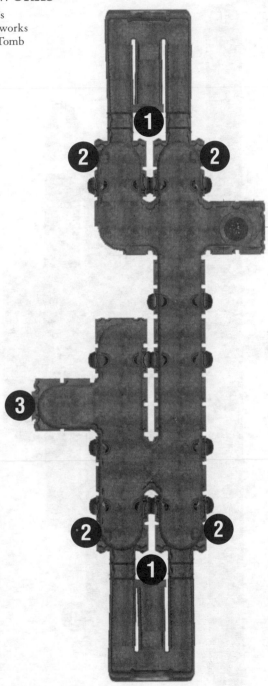

REDORAN WAISTWORKS

1. Door to Redoran
   Canton Exterior
2. Door to Redoran Canalworks
3. Door to Redoran Temple
4. Door to Redoran Records
5. Door to Redoran Scout
   & Drillmaster
6. Door to The Flowers of
   Gold Cornerclub
7. Door to Redoran Prison Cells
8. Door to Redoran Trader
9. Door to Redoran Smith

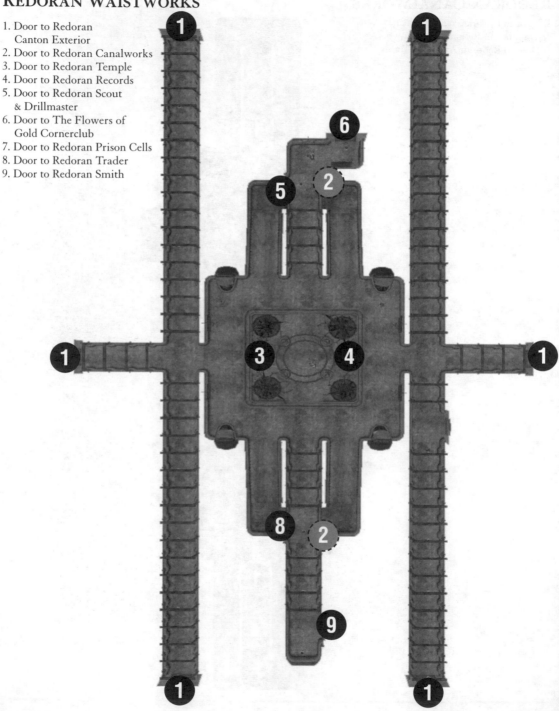

REDORAN PLAZA

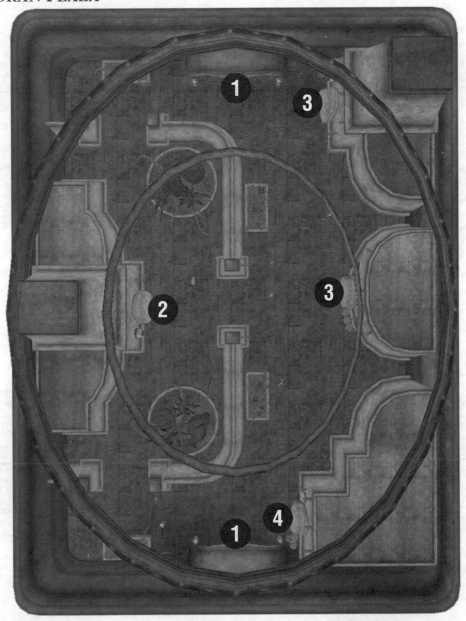

1. Door to Redoran Canton Exterior
2. Door to Dralor Manor
3. Door to Saren Manor
4. Door to Redoran Treasury

St. Delyn Canalworks

WEST SIDE

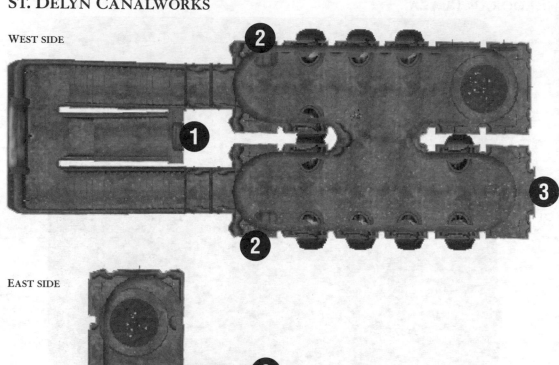

EAST SIDE

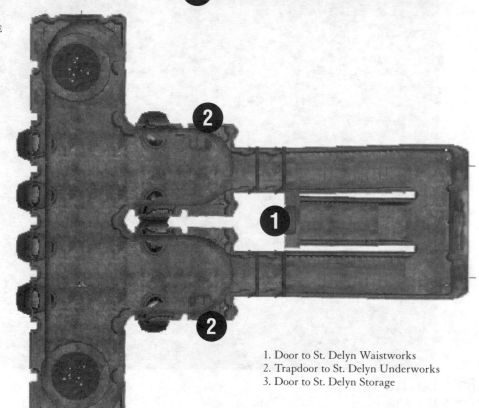

1. Door to St. Delyn Waistworks
2. Trapdoor to St. Delyn Underworks
3. Door to St. Delyn Storage

ST. DELYN PLAZA

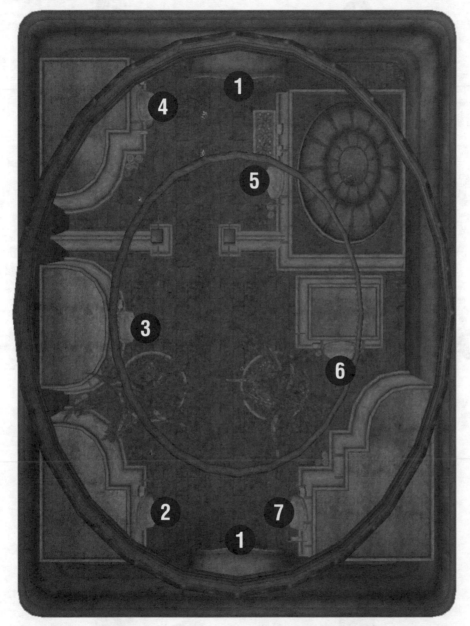

1. Door to St. Delyn Exterior
2. Door to Lucretinaus Olcinius, Trader
3. Door to Mevel Fererus, Trader
4. Door to Glassworkers' Hall

5. Door to The Abbey of St. Delyn the Wise
6. Door to Tervur Braven, Trader
7. Door to Potters' Hall

ST. DELYN WAISTWORKS

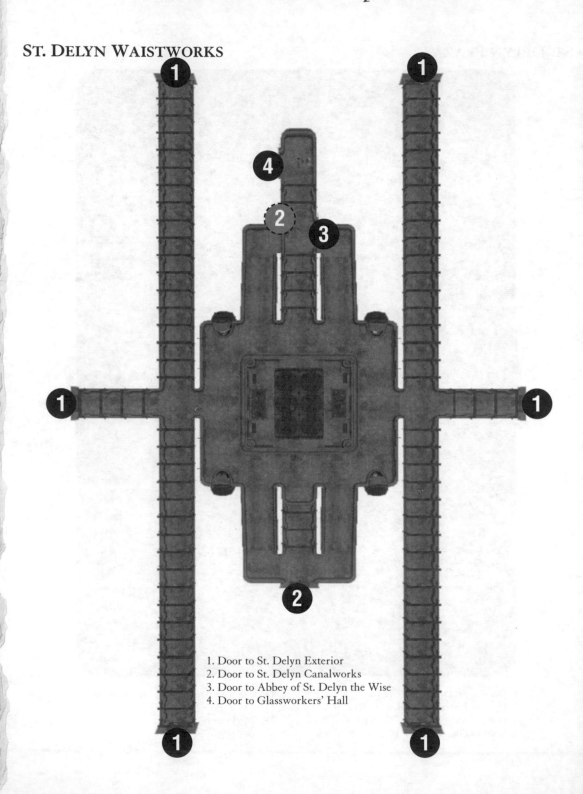

1. Door to St. Delyn Exterior
2. Door to St. Delyn Canalworks
3. Door to Abbey of St. Delyn the Wise
4. Door to Glassworkers' Hall

St. Olms Canalworks

1. Door to St. Olms Waistworks
2. Trapdoor to St. Olms Underworks
3. Door to St. Olms Storage

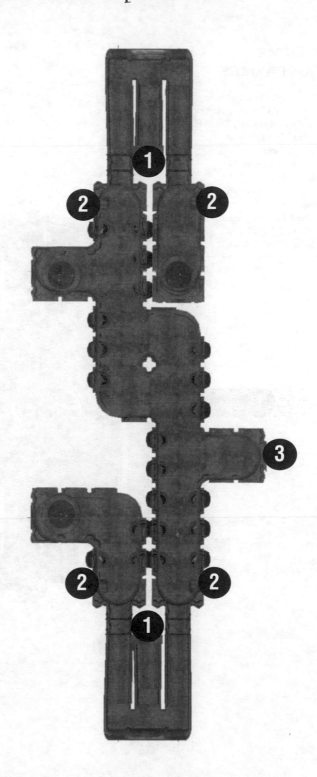

St. Olms Waistworks

1. Door to St. Olms Exterior
2. Door to St. Olms Canalworks
3. Door to Tailors and Dyers Hall
4. Door to Farmers and
   Laborers Hall
5. Door to Tanners and
   Miners Hall
6. Door to Brewers and
   Fishmongers Hall
7. Bervyn Lleryn, Trader
8. Nalis Gals, Trader

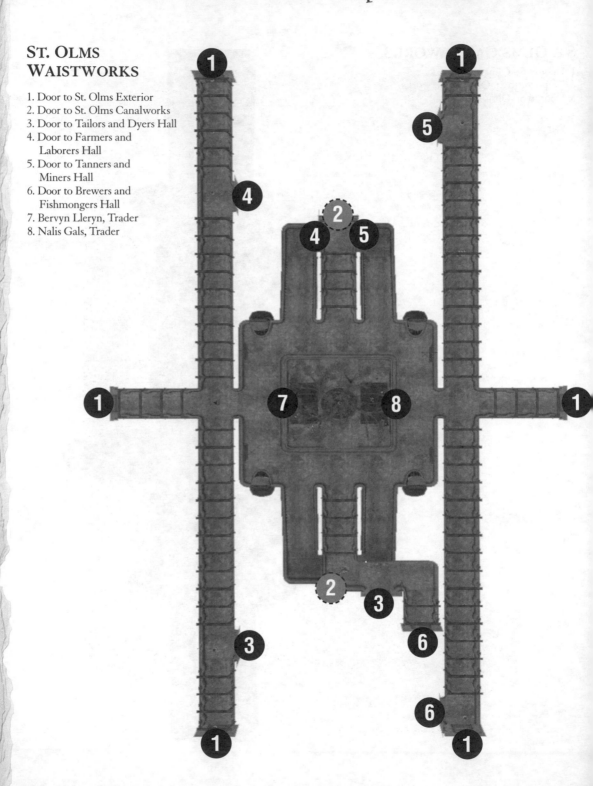

St. Olms Plaza

1. Door to St. Olms Exterior
2. Door to St. Olms Upper-North One
3. Door to St. Olms Temple
4. Door to St. Olms Upper-North Two

5. Door to Haunted Manor
6. Door to St. Olms Upper-South One
7. Door to Yngling Manor

TELVANNI CANALWORKS

1. Door to Telvanni Waistworks
2. Trapdoor to Telvanni Underworks
3. Door to Telvanni Monster Lab
4. Telvanni Slave Quarters

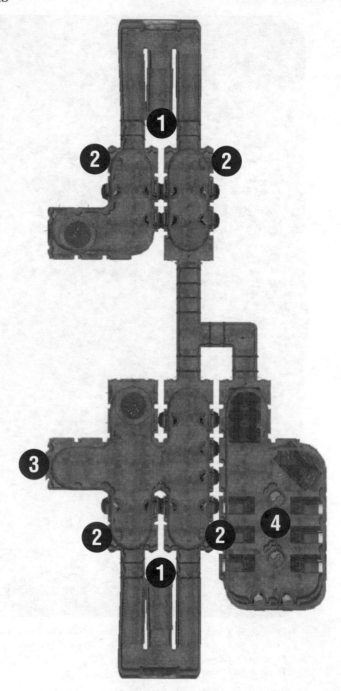

TELVANNI WAISTWORKS

1. Door to Telvanni Canton Exterior
2. Door to Telvanni Canalworks
3. Door to Telvanni Temple
4. Door to The Lizard's
   Head Cornerclub
5. Door to Telvanni Apothecary
6. Door to Telvanni Sorceror
7. Door to Telvanni Mage
8. Door to Telvanni Enchanter
9. Door to Telvanni Alchemist

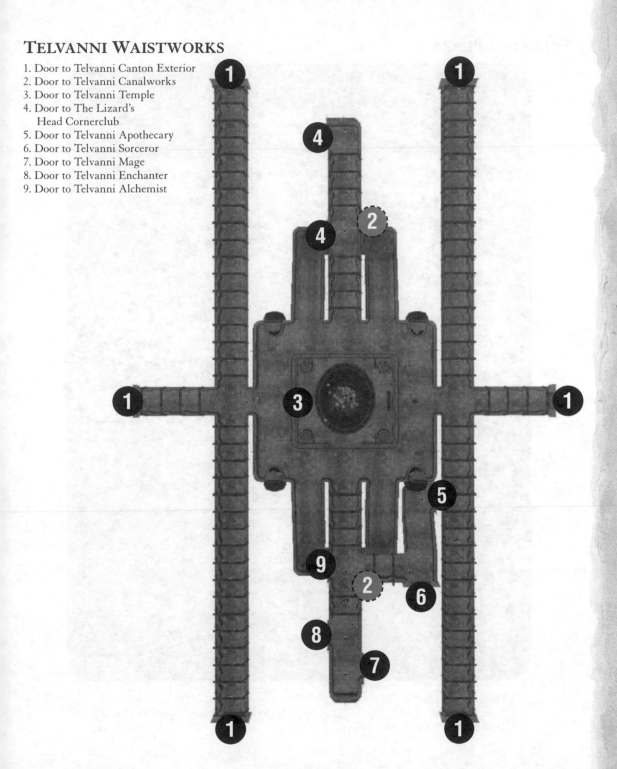

TELVANNI PLAZA

1. Door to Telvanni Canton Exterior
2. Door to Telvanni Tower
3. Door to Hlaren Residence
4. Door to Telvanni Upper Storage
5. Door to Telvanni Temporary Housing

Fast Travel

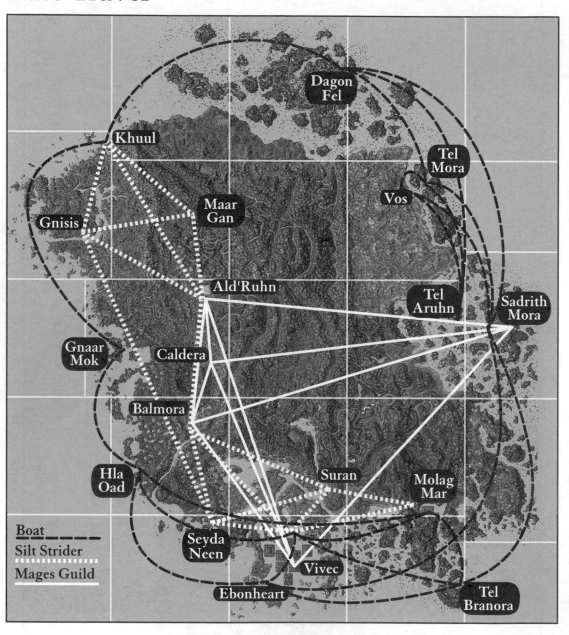

Dagon Fel

Khuul

Tel Mora

Vos

Maar Gan

Gnisis

Ald'Ruhn

Tel Aruhn

Sadrith Mora

Gnaar Mok

Caldera

Balmora

Hla Oad

Suran

Molag Mar

Seyda Neen

Vivec

Ebonheart

Tel Branora

Boat — — —
Silt Strider ·······
Mages Guild ——————

SILT STRIDERS

These giant insect-like creatures roam the ashlands in Vvardenfell. The Dunmer have captured them, lobotomized them, and use them as a means of fast travel among many locations throughout Vvardenfell. Service from each town will visit a handful of locations, so to move across large distances you may need to take several silt striders, or use them in combination with available boat service.

Molag Mar (12,-8) - Dilami Androm
Goes to: Suran (6,-6)
          Vivec (3,-9)

Suran (6,-6) - Folsi Thendas
Goes to: Molag Mar (12,-8)
          Vivec (3,-9)
          Seyda Neen (-2,-9)
          Balmora (-3,-3)

Seyda Neen (-2,-9) - Darvame Hleran
Goes to: Suran (6,-6)
          Vivec (3,-9)
          Balmora (-3,-3)
          Gnisis (-11,10)

Balmora (-3,-3) - Selvil Sareloth
Goes to: Suran (6,-6)
          Vivec (3,-9)
          Seyda Neen (-2,-9)
          Ald'ruhn (-3,6)

Ald'ruhn (-3,6) - Navam Veran
Goes to: Balmora (-3,-3)
          Maar Gan (-3,12)
          Gnisis (-11,10)
          Khuul (-9,16)

Maar Gan (-3,12) - Daras Aryon
Goes to: Ald'ruhn (-3,6)
          Gnisis (-11,10)
          Khuul (-9,16)

Gnisis (-11,10) - Punibi Yahaz
Goes to: Ald'ruhn (-3,6)
          Maar Gan (-3,12)
          Khuul (-9,16)

Khuul (-9,16) - Seldus Nerendus
Goes to: Ald'ruhn (-3,6)
          Maar Gan (-3,12)
          Gnisis (-11,10)

Vivec [3, -9] - Adondasi Sadalvel
Goes to: Seyda Neen (-2,9)
          Suran (-6, -6)
          Molag Mar (12,-8)
          Balmora (-3, -3)

BOATS

Boats provide transport between the coast cities in Vvardenfell and, when used in conjunction with silt striders or Mages Guild teleportation, allow access to and from all major cities and towns.

Khuul (-9,17) - Talmeni Drethan
Goes to: Gnaar Mok (-8,3)
          Dagon Fel (7,22)

Gnaar Mok (-8,3) - Valveli Arelas
Goes to: Khuul (-9,17)
          Hla Oad (-6,-5)

Hla Oad (-6,-5) - Baleni Salavel
Goes to: Gnaar Mok (-8,3)
          Ebonheart (2,-13)
          Vivec, Foreign Quarter (4,-10)

Ebonheart (2,-13) - Nevosi Hlan
Goes to: Hla Oad (-6,-5)
          Vivec, Foreign Quarter (4,-10)
          Sadrith Mora (17,4)
          Tel Branora (14,-13)

Vivec, Foreign Quarter (4,-10) - Ano Andaram
Goes to: Hla Oad (-6,-5)
          Ebonheart (2,-13)
          Molag Mar (13,-8)
          Tel Branora (14,-13)

Molag Mar (13,-8) - Rindral Dralor
Goes to: Hla Oad (-6,-5)
Vivec, Foreign Quarter (4,-10)
Tel Branora (14,-13)

Tel Branora (14,-13) - Nireli Farys
Goes to: Ebonheart (2,-13)
Vivec, Foreign Quarter (4,-10)
Molag Mar (13,-8)
Sadrith Mora (17,4)

Sadrith Mora (17,4) - Gals Arethi
Goes to: Tel Branora (14,-13)
Ebonheart (2,-13)
Tel Mora (13,14)
Dagon Fel (7,22)

Tel Aruhn (15,5) - Daynas Darys
Goes to: Dagon Fel (7,22)
Vos (12,13)
Tel Mora (13,14)

Vos (12,13) - Sedyni Veran
Goes to: Sadrith Mora (17,4)
Tel Aruhn (15,5)
Tel Mora (13,14)

Tel Mora (13,14) - Tonas Telvani
Goes to: Sadrith Mora (17,4)
Tel Aruhn (15,5)
Vos (12,13)
Dagon Fel (7,22)

Dagon Fel (7,22) - Haema Farseer
Goes to: Sadrith Mora (17,4)
Tel Mora (13,14)
Khuul (-9,17)
Tel Aruhn (15,5)

GUILD GUIDES

Teleportation is available between Mage Guilds throughout Morrowind. See the individual listed below for teleportation service in that guild. Service is only available to the other Mages Guilds listed.

Caldera Guild of Mages, Emelia Duronia
Balmora Guild of Mages, Masalinie Merian
Ald'ruhn Guild of Mages, Erranil Ienith

Wolverine Hall: Mage's Guild, Sadrith Mora
Vivec Guild of Mages, Flacassia Fauseius

VIVEC GONDOLAS

Within the vast, ancient city of Vivec, you can use gondolas to as a means of fast travel, when walking gets to be too much. This is a list of available gondoliers and the areas that they serve.

Dalse Adren [arena]
Goes to: Vivec, Temple [3 -13]
Vivec, Telvanni [5, -11]
Vivec, Foreign Quarter [3, -10]
Vivec, Hlaalu [2, -11]

Talsi Uvayn [temple]
Goes to: Vivec, Arena [4 -11]
Vivec, Hlaalu [2, -11]
Vivec, Telvanni [5, -11]

Fendryn Drelvi [Telvanni]
Goes to: Vivec, Arena [4 -11]
Vivec, Foreign Quarter [3, -10]
Vivec, Temple [3 -13]

Devas Irano [foreign Quarter]
Goes to: Vivec, Arena [4 -11]
Vivec, Hlaalu [2, -11]
Vivec, Telvanni [5, -11]

Aren Maren [Hlaalu]
Goes to: Vivec, Arena [4 -11]
Vivec, Foreign Quarter [3, -10]
Vivec, Temple [3 -13]

Chapter Four: Main Quest

Main Quest Walkthrough

The main quest in Morrowind begins innocently enough with a delivery errand. You may not even realize that it has begun.

When it starts, you are basically a nobody—an undistinguished stranger in a strange land. By the time it ends, you will have become more than you can imagine.

CAIUS COSADES

FIND THE SPYMASTER

Your first task is to deliver a package of documents to Caius Cosades in Balmora.

The Census and Excise officer in Seyda Neen will put you on the right track, but he's not Cosades' keeper this week, and you'll need specific directions. (This is often the system you'll use to find your way in Morrowind.) Stop in at the South Wall cornerclub and speak with owner Bacola Closcius about Cosades. He'll direct you to Cosades' home: Out the door, right up the stairs, and left all the way to the end of the street.

Once there, just turn over your parcel and agree to obey Cosades' orders.

Congratulations. You're now a spy. And Cosades is your spymaster.

He inducts you into the Imperial Intelligence Service, known as the Blades. You're just a Novice at the start, naturally, but that will change as you complete quests.

For starters, Cosades advises you to join a guild—depending on your current level, he may steer you to the Fighters and Mages guilds, the Imperial cult, and the Imperial legion, specifically—and to take up the cover of a freelance adventurer. (If you haven't reached Level 4, he'll also turn over 200 drakes in spending money.)

Of course, no one's holding a stopwatch on you, and you don't have to make a beeline north to Balmora. The road holds a few diversions.

For instance, before you leave Seyda Neen, you can run a couple of small errands. Vodunicus Nuccius asks you to mention him to Darvame Hleran, Seyda Neen's silt strider caravaner. Hleran, in turn, mentions that Nuccius isn't happy in Morrowind. And sure, enough, upon your return to Nuccius, he'll offer to sell you a cursed ring for 100 drakes so he can buy passage to somewhere more hospitable. (The ring is a trifle that adds 5 to your Athletics skill, and knocks 10 points off your health, for 60 seconds.)

You can also chat with an elderly High Elf lady, Eldafire, and she'll put you onto a smuggler's cave, Addamasartus, near Seyda Neen strider port—just a small taste of this community's seamy underbelly.

ADDAMASARTUS

(You'll also find Andrano Ancestral Tomb along the road southwest of Pelagiad. But there's little urgency about exploring it, as you will visit it in the course of one of the early main-quest missions.)

When you're ready, and it doesn't have to be right now, just talk to Cosades and select the "orders" topic to get your first quest.

You are on your way, even if you don't know where.

ANTABOLIS INFORMANT

Your first job is right in the neighborhood. Cosades sends you to ask Hasphat Antabolis of the Balmora Fighters Guild about two secret cults: the Nerevarine and the Sixth House.

In Morrowind, as in life, it is rare to get something for nothing. Hasphat requires a favor from you before he'll help. He wants a puzzle box from the Dwemer ruins called Arkngthand, located in the wilderness near Balmora.

To find the ruins, head south out of town, past the silt strider port and cross bridges over the Odai River to the east.

At the signpost, head north toward Pelagiad. On the right, you'll soon see a signpost for Molag Mar. Take this old road up the hill and cross a bridge over Foyada Mamaea. (The bridge is guarded by Snowy Granius—presumably standing watch for the four nasty characters you will find in the ruins. He's a decent opponent in a fight, but you should be able to sneak or race past him.)

Arkngthand is east of the ravine and south of the bridge. A crank on a nearby pipe opens the doors. Inside the Hall of Centrifuge, you find yourself at the top of a high chamber. Work your way down to the floor of the chamber, then look to the west for a second tier above the floor. Climb to the second tier, where you'll find a door to the Cells of Hollow Hand.

You'll find the puzzle box on the back bottom corner of an old three-tier shelf in the Cells of Hollow Hand, in the same room as Boss Crito, an unpleasant and dangerous man. Snatch-grab-and-run, or take Crito down to collect the puzzle box at leisure.

There is a lot more to see here. These cluttered ruins are extensive—both on the surface and underground. You can't explore all of them just yet, and, given the inexperience of your character, you may not want to probe much deeper. But if you do, it's worthwhile. You will find a Dwarven spear, and the odds and ends in the crates can be sold.

Just bring the box back to Hasphat and ask him about the cults. He'll fill you in on the story of the Sixth House—how House Dagoth betrayed the other Houses in the War of the First Council in the First Age and was destroyed for its treachery. He'll also report that Dagoth Ur, the source of the curses that afflict Morrowind, is said to live in the Red Mountain crater.

ARKNGTHAND

This is getting kind of interesting, yes?

Hasphat will also give you notes to deliver to Cosades. Do so, and you're done.

But note that you can come back to Hasphat afterward, ask about the puzzle box and collect a key that opens the lower levels of the ruins. It's not part of the main quest—just a neat extra.

SLEEPERS AWAKE

Not a quest, per se, but an event.

After you start the main quest with the Antabolis Informant mission you just completed, you'll begin to notice strange things happening in Morrowind.

These events, triggered by the broadcasting of Dagoth Ur's dreams through Sixth House bases, consist of player dreams and the appearance of Sleepers, Dreamers, and Ambushers.

The four dream sequences occur only if you sleep in Vivec, Ald'ruhn, or Balmora. Each dream is triggered by the appearance of a specific journal entry in four early missions in the main quest: Antabolis Informant, Addhiranirr Informant, the Mehra Milo segment of Vivec Informants, and Zainsubani Informant.

While the dreams foreshadow the conflict with Dagoth Ur, they won't hurt you. In fact, they don't really affect you at all—except that they become a conversation topic ("disturbing dreams"). You can then relate them to certain characters in the game, who can interpret them for you.

It's just a storytelling device, and having or not having a particular dream has no influence on how the game unfolds.

However, it's a neat thing to experience, and you'll probably want to have all four dreams in order to see Morrowind in all its glory.

But note that there's a certain give and take here. The dreams themselves are harmless, but doing what's required to have them is not. Sleeping in those same three towns opens you up to attacks from Ambushers—Sixth House assassins who assault you from behind as you wake.

Ambushers can be avoided by sleeping in the wilderness or in other towns, but, when encountered, you'll have to kill them.

This is also the only way to deal with Dreamers—people who have been turned into monsters by Dagoth Ur's dream broadcasts.

Dreamers come in two varieties. One type will start talking crazy talk and then attack. You'll find a lot of these folks outdoors. (For instance, one can be found just southwest of Balmora at the crossroads.) The other will attack you on sight. These are also plentiful—especially inside Sixth House bases.

Finally, Sleepers are normal people who suddenly start talking oddly and, later on, may attack you if you provoke them.

Initially, after the Antabolis Informant mission, Sleepers are harmless and just talk wildly—passing on information they've received from Dagoth Ur.

However, once you complete the Sixth House mission, their talk will turn threatening and, as their Disposition drops during dialogue, you may find yourself under attack. After the Corprus Cure mission, their Disposition will drop even more and their inclination to fight increase.

In other words, the earlier you can do something about this, the better.

Be thankful that you can do something about the Sleepers. Don't kill them if you can avoid it. They can be cured if you find the local Sixth House base and kill its priest. Killing Dagoth Hlevul at the Assemanu base (on an island west of Vivec's Hlaalu Compound) will cure Sleepers in Vivec, Suran, and Arano Plantation. Killing Dagoth Fovon at the Hassour Shrine base (at the southwestern end of Foyada Mamaea, south of Balmora) will stop them in Balmora and Pelagiad. And killing Dagoth Draven at the Subdun Shrine (on an island southwest of the Dunmer stronghold Berandas) will shut things down in Gnisis, Ald Velothi, and Khuul.

And what about Ald'ruhn? That's slightly trickier. Visit the basement of Hanarai Assutlanipal to find a Sixth House shrine. Kill her to save the Sleepers here.

But don't think you have to rush out to do all this stuff right now. We mention it here simply so that you understand what's going on behind the scenes. Unless you're quite the freelance adventurer, the task is probably beyond you. Besides, Cosades has another job for you.

Muzgrob Informant

You probably noticed that Hasphat's info covered only the Sixth House. He didn't give you the skinny on the Nerevarine. Cosades sends you off to Sharn gra-Muzgob at the Balmora Guild of Mages to get it.

Ms. Muzgob must have heard from the Fighters Guild about your success collecting the Dwemer puzzle box. She wants a favor as well: the skull of journeyman enchanter Llevule Andrano.

She'll caution you against upsetting the local people. They're not into necromancy, and don't fancy folks poking around in tombs.

What is she up to? If you inquire, she'll deny being a necromancer herself and tell you she can't teach you spells.

Muzgrob

But methinks she doth protest too much. Maybe it wouldn't be a bad idea to poke around a little in Mages Guild before you set out. Sure enough, you'll find her copy of the book "Legions of the Dead" in a chest. Confronted with the evidence, Muzgrob finally allows that she's a necromancer and agrees to teach you to Summon Ancestral Ghost spell if you'll keep a lid on her hobby. (This isn't required to complete the quest, but hey, a free spell is a free spell.)

You'll find the skull in the Andrano Ancestral Tomb—located off the road south of Pelagiad, just before the fork where roads head southwest toward Seyda Neen and southeast to Vivec. Other skulls may be found in the vault as well, but Andrano's is distinguished by its ritual markings.

You're going to see dead people, and you probably need an enchanted blade to deal with them, as ordinary weapons can't touch some of the spirits here. Muzgrob provides an old dagger and some scrolls that should help.

Get the skull, return it to Muzgrob, and ask about Nerevarine and Nerevarine cult. Like Hasphat, she'll give you notes to return to the spymaster.

This'll kick you up the Blades ladder from Novice to Apprentice. Be sure to talk to Caius about the topic "Blades Apprentice" to get a nice little present. If you're Level 3 or higher, your boss already has a new assignment for you.

VIVEC INFORMANTS

You've done everything you can do in the Balmora area for the time being. Now, you're off to Vivec—a substantial city at the southern tip of Morrowind.

ADDHIRANIRR

If you fancy a bit of dungeon-delving along the way, note that the road south passes by the Adanumuran and Ulummusa dungeons.

In Vivec, Cosades has set you three tasks. You'll need to obtain information about the two cults from Addhiranirr, an operative of the Khajiit Thieves Guild; Huleeya, an Argonian in the Morag Tong; and Mehra Milo, a Temple priestess.

It's a bit involved. We'll take it one step at a time.

Your first target is Addhiranirr. She is not easy to find. Three people here know her whereabouts: Sevisa Teran at St. Olms Canalworks, and Adaves Theryn and Aldyne Arenim, both at St. Olms Waistworks. You may have to throw your money or weight around to get them to open up.

It turns out Addhiranirr is hiding in "underworks" (i.e., the sewers) to avoid the taxman—a Census and Excise agent named Duvianus Platorius. You can reach her only by swimming down to the exterior sewer drains and entering the sewers there, or, more easily, by entering through trapdoors found on the floors of St. Olms Canalworks.

Go talk to her. And find out she won't talk to you until Platorius is gone.

In short, it's favor time. Ideally, you'll want to waylay or kill the taxman, who can be found in the St. Olms Waistworks.

If you choose the peaceful route (usually a good idea, if you want to keep up your Reputation), just tell him his quarry has left for the mainland by gondola. He'll tell you he's headed that way himself, and you can go back to Addhiranirr with the good news.

But let's just suppose you're uncomfortable lying to government officials—you'll get over that quickly once you start killing them—or just feeling contrary by the time you run into the taxman.

Well, Platorius doesn't ask for a favor, but you can do him one anyway. Tell him where Addhiranirr is hiding out.

Of course, you'll annoy the hell out of her, and you'll then have to raise her disposition to 70 to get her to talk.

(Before you get too grumpy about the sewers, note that they connect to a particularly unpleasant dungeon. Safety first. Stay out.)

When Addhiranirr does talk, it's interesting stuff. She reports that smugglers are working for the Sixth House. She doesn't know what they are smuggling. However, word is that the cult wants to get rid of the Temple and foreigners and restore things to the way they were before the Empire.

One down, two to go.

Fortunately, your second informant is not in hiding. Huleeya can be found in Black Shalk Cornerclub, located in the Foreign Quarter Waistworks

Unfortunately, his situation here does not permit the free and open exchange of ideas. Three thugs offended by the sight of a free Argonian have surrounded him and are making trouble. You have to shepherd Huleeya to his friend's store, Jobasha's Rare Books on the same Waistworks level, where you'll be able to talk in peace.

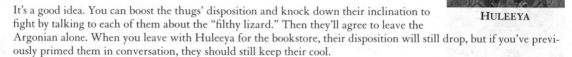

It's a short trip: right out of the door and then straight west, across the atrium.

But that's easier said than done. The thugs are a volatile bunch, and leaving the cornerclub with your contact may ignite combat. Huleeya's no coward, but he doesn't want to fight in his friend's club or besmirch his own honor by killing the thugs.

He suggests you try to talk sense into them.

HULEEYA

It's a good idea. You can boost the thugs' disposition and knock down their inclination to fight by talking to each of them about the "filthy lizard." Then they'll agree to leave the Argonian alone. When you leave with Huleeya for the bookstore, their disposition will still drop, but if you've previously primed them in conversation, they should still keep their cool.

On the other hand, if you leave with your contact without first talking down the bad guys, fighting may break out. If it does, you must protect Huleeya. Kill the thugs if you want to get him out alive.

At the bookstore, just talk to Huleeya and he'll give you notes to carry to the spymaster. He's not up on the Sixth House, but knows something of the Nerevarine. Apparently the Temple's dispute with that cult relates to old grievances between the Ashlanders and the Great Houses.

Two down. Let's go find Mehra Milo.

She's actually the quickest of the informants to open up. Make your way to the Temple District and then find the library in the Hall of Wisdom. Talk to the folks here. They will tell you Milo either is in the library or in her room. Find her. She is being watched, and so won't talk immediately, but if you follow her to the back of the library, she'll tell you about the Nerevarine cult.

In a nutshell, the Temple considers Nerevar a saint, but treats prophecies of his reincarnation as heresy. A group called the Dissident Priests dispute Temple doctrines on these prophecies. An outlawed pamphlet, "Progress of Truth," describes their beliefs. You need to get one for Cosades.

You have two options here. The safe route is just to revisit Jobasha's Rare Books and buy a copy there. The library does have a copy—it's the tall book on a shelf in the southeast corner, opposite a column—but you'll have to deal with the Temple's Ordinator guards and pay a fine if you take it.

Milo also has one other rather alarming bit of info: She says to tell Cosades that she is worried that she is being watched by the Ordinators. If something goes wrong, she will leave a message under the codeword "amaya".

Return to the spymaster for promotion to Journeyman, a reward of 200 drakes...and a little vacation! Cosades needs to peruse all the data you've provided and doesn't have anything for you right away.

Besides, after all that running around in Vivec, you've earned a rest. Allow at least a day to pass, and then return to Cosades for new orders.

MEHRA MILO

ZAINSUBANI INFORMANT

So what do we know so far? A lot, and yet not a lot. We've put together a fair amount of pointed information on the disputes and antipathies that rule this world, but haven't drawn the lines that link those pieces in a bigger picture.

Here, you'll start drawing the connecting lines: Cosades is sending you north to Ald'ruhn to talk to Hassour Zainsubani, an Ashlander who has become a wealthy trader. He is supposed to have information about Ashlanders and the Nerevarine cult.

You must gain his confidence with a gift, and your boss has provided 100 drakes in expense money for this purpose.

A gift is trickier than a favor. It's hard enough to shop for people you actually know. Zainsubani is a stranger. You've got to get to know this stranger a little first.

Happily, you can talk to the man himself. He is staying at the Ald Skar Inn. He'll tell you, rather elaborately, that a gift offered as a courtesy by a stranger should reflect the tastes of the receiver.

For a notion of Zainsubani's tastes, you'll need to talk to the publican—one Boderi Farano, who reports that his guest has a lot of books in his room.

That's a start, but what sorts of books: Romance novels? Science textbooks? Big Little Books?

Well, you're the spy. Go do some spying. Explore Zainsubani's room. This downstairs chamber is unmarked, but it's the only room with books. Among his possessions, you'll find two volumes of poetry: "Words of the Wind," and "The Five Far Stars."

Give Zainsubani a book of poetry. You can find either of the two he already has—and a third, "Ashland Hymns," which he does not have—at Codus Callonus: Bookseller in Ald'ruhn.

Or you can steal one of Zainsubani's own books and return it to him as your gift. Tacky, yes, but Zainsubani won't recognize it as his own, and even if he did, he's the kind of guy who might admire that kind of chutzpah.

(A third option: You don't have to give him a gift at all—just raise his Disposition to 80—and he'll accept your effort in lieu of the actual item.)

In any case, he's now prepared to tell you about Ashlanders and the Nerevarine, and to turn over the notes Cosades requires. Note especially his comments about courtesy and challenges among the Ashlanders and their hatred of foreigners. They will come in handy in the next mission.

And, you know, you can do him a favor after all. Zainsubani mentions that his son, Hannat, means to explore an ancient underground complex at Mamaea, west of Red Mountain. He asks that, should you meet Hannat in the course of your travels, you tell him his father is eager for news of his son.

Red Mountain…now where have we heard that before?

In fact, poor Hannat is stranded in the Mamaea dungeon. This diversion is not required to complete this quest, but Mamaea's not that far away. You can escort Hannat to freedom, and then revisit Hassour with your hand out for a reward.

Well, that was a good day's shopping. Cosades promotes you to Blades Finder and gives you a new assignment—and something to chew on.

MEET SUL-MATUUL

It's here that the story begins to take off. When you return from Ald'ruhn, Cosades reveals your mission—to meet the conditions of the Nerevarine prophecies—and gives you a decoded version of the documents you delivered to him at your first meeting.

You're off to the Urshilaku Camp to speak with chief Sul-Matuul and wise woman Nibani Maesa. Cosades tells you to tell them your story and have them test you against the Nerevarine prophecies.

It's a long haul to the camp—all the way to the north coast of Beden Anmor—and tough to find even with Cosades' directions.

For specifics, talk to a scout in Balmora and another scout in the Maar Gan outpost. (Nuleno Tedas can be found downstairs behind a door.) Follow the Foyada Bani-Dad ravine northwest to the sea. At the shipwreck landmark, swim around the headland to the east. Pass through the ruins of the Daedric shrine Assurnabitashpi, and make your way east to Urshilaku Camp. (Or you could take the safer but longer route, traveling by silt strider to Vivec, then by ship up the west coast to Khuul, then follow the coast east to Urshilaku camp. But then you'll miss all the fun.)

Along the way, you will find loads of potential diversions. The ravine holds not only the usual encounters with monsters but the sorcerer's tower Shishi; the Dwemer site Bthuungthumz; the Sha-Adnius smugglers cave; and the vampire lair Druscashti. (Not to mention the Hairat-Vassamsi Egg Mine near Maar Gan route into the ravine, the Daedric shrine and shipwreck mentioned earlier, and a couple of guys near a campfire!)

That's practically a career, and you haven't even met the Urshilaku yet.

Once you do get to the camp, don't be rash. People live here, and they have customs and traditions. Respect them. Remember what Zainsubani told you and don't enter the ashkhan's tent (called a yurt) without permission. (If you do this by mistake, go have a word with Kurapli the trader.)

Don't kill the Urshilaku, unless you want to make your quest a lot harder.

And follow the pecking order. Start by talking to the garden-variety Urshilaku. Boost their Dispositions to 60 by Persuasion, bribes, gifts (kwama eggs for Tussurradad or trama root for Hainab), and you will be sent to talk to the gulakhan Zabamund. (Trama roots are plentiful in and around Urshilaku camp.) You'll need to persuade Zabamund to allow you to see Ashkhan Sul-Matuul.

NIBANI MAESA

The Ashkhan will send you on an initiation rite—a "harrowing" through the Urshilaku Burial Caverns to retrieve his father's magical Bonebiter Bow. This dungeon can be found south-southeast of the camp, through a north-facing door in a little hill halfway between the camp and the Red Mountain. From the camp, go north to the beach, then east along the coast to a cairn (a group of piled rocks), then straight south down a ravine.

Within the caverns, the spirits of Urshilaku ancestors guard seven burial chambers. You can't talk them out of fighting. But you can evade them or force your way past them with weapons and magic. You'll proceed through Astral Burial and Karma Burial to Laterus Burial. In Laterus Burial, you must make your way to the very highest door in this chamber, leading to Juno Burial, where you'll find the Wraith of Sul-Senipul. Kill the wraith—did you bring your enchanted weapon or spirit-searing magic spells? – and take the bow from his etherial remains.

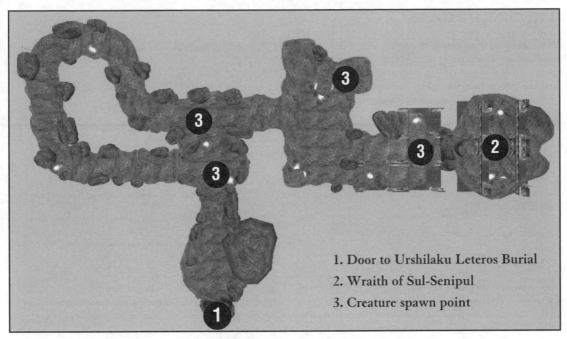

1. Door to Urshilaku Leteros Burial
2. Wraith of Sul-Senipul
3. Creature spawn point

URSHILAKU BURIEL CAVERN

Man, these Ashlanders really put you through the wringer. (You ain't seen nothing yet.)

When you bring Sul-Senipul's bow back to Sul-Matuul, he makes you a Clanfriend (a member of the Ashlander faction) and sends you off to Nibani Maesa, the Urshilaku wise woman, to be tested. (You can't talk to her unless you're a Clanfriend.)

Maesa says you're not the Nerevarine, but could become the Nerevarine. She'll also tell you about the Dissident Priests, the prophecies of the Incarnate, and some Nerevarine prophecies that were hidden, forgotten, and lost by accident or by design.

However, the Dissidents have recorded the Nerevarine prophecies in books. If you choose to be the Nerevarine, Maesa says, bring the lost prophecies they recorded back to her, and she'll serve as your guide.

Basically, she's Yoda, and she just told you that you might be Luke Skywalker.

You may be inclined to start searching for those Dissident Priests right away.

Not just yet. For now, return to Caius Cosades.

THE SIXTH HOUSE

So it's all about you, isn't it? You, you, you. You probably feel like swaggering back into Balmora and asking Cosades for another promotion.

Your boss seems nonplussed by the word that you may be the Nerevarine. And yet he immediately offers what's probably your most dangerous mission yet.

If you haven't reached Level 6, he'll suggest a leave of absence to improve your skills and equipment.

But if you're all pumped up with your new potential-demi-god status, he won't stop you.

Remember the Sixth House smugglers that Addhiranirr told you about back in the Vivec sewers? Well, Buckmoth Fort sent a patrol to Gnaar Mok to hunt them down. It found a Sixth House base and shrine and a half-man priest named Dagoth Gares.

Dagoth Anything is bad news.

You must find the base and kill the priest.

Your first stop should be the fort, which you'll find south of Ald'ruhn's South Gate. Talk to Champion Raesa Pullia for a report on the patrol. It turns out that, fleeing the attacks of cultists and man-beasts, the troopers lost their way in the caves and ran into Dagoth Gares. The priest killed all but one trooper, sparing him so he could bring back ominous messages about a sleeper awakening and the Sixth House rising.

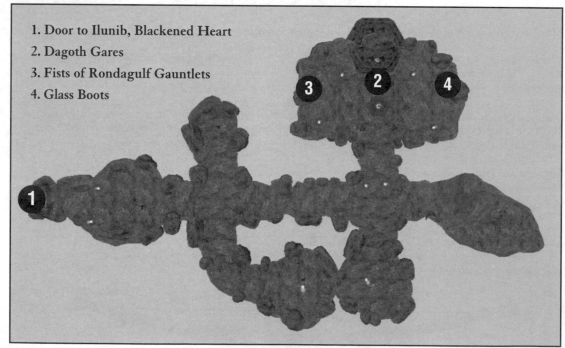

1. Door to Ilunib, Blackened Heart
2. Dagoth Gares
3. Fists of Rondagulf Gauntlets
4. Glass Boots

ILUNIBI CAVERN

DAGOTH GARES

Disfigured with the corprus disease and mad as a March hare, he didn't last long.

Pullia will also try to help you find the cavern. Called "Ilunibi," it's not on the map. She tells you to ask locals in Gnaar Mok to the west. Anybody in Gnaar Mok can tell you that 'Ilunibi' is the name of an old smuggler's cave up on Khartag Point, just north of Gnaar Mok.

From Gnaar Mok, head north for Khartag Point—a little island just north of the village. The cavern opens off the island's north coast. Proceed through Saint's Carcass, Marowak's Spine, and Blackened Heart to Soul's Rattle (the Chamber of Commerce has a charming naming scheme here, eh?), where you'll find Dagoth Gares.

He'll make a little speech. It's one of the privileges of being a "boss" monster. Then you can invoke the privilege of being the player character: Kill him.

But this monstrous priest has the last laugh. As he dies, he curses you with the corprus disease. This just happens to fulfill one of the Nerevarine prophecies.

"Even as my Master wills, you shall come to him, in his flesh, and of his flesh," he says.

Creepy.

There's also opportunity in this mission for some optional side adventures as well—including one involving a missing companion and a mud crab nest.

But you could be forgiven if you're not in the mood. One quest back, you were feeling like king of the hill.

Now, you're just another sick guy with a long walk home.

CORPRUS CURE

On your return to Balmora, you're promoted to Traveler. If that doesn't make you feel better, this may: The spymaster has made inquiries and found a doctor for what ails you.

Regrettably, the wizard Divayth Fyr, who runs a "Corprusarium" for those so afflicted, doesn't make house calls. You'll have to go find him.

We all know how miserable it is to travel when you're sick. At least Cosades helps the process along a bit with a Dwemer artifact (a good gift for always-grumpy wizards), 1,000 drakes for potions and spells, and instructions to ask a scout in Sadrith Mora for directions. He also gives you a couple Levitation potions, because, as he informs you, "Wizards don't use stairs."

Sadrith Mora's a good-sized city halfway up the east coast of Morrowind. The wizard can be found in the tower Tel Fyr—a straight shot southwest of Sadrith Mora, on an island on the southwest edge of Zafirbel Bay. There's no boat, so you'll need to swim, walk on the water or fly.

Once in the tower, talk to the women. Are these Fyr's wives, daughters or just very close female friends? Not important. They will tell you where to find the wizard and how to avoid making him angry.

For starters, do not kill any of the women. (Not that you would, but you know how swords can slip and so on.)

Give Fyr the Dwemer artifact to make him less cranky. It'll kick his Disposition up to around 80 or so. (Alternatively, you can raise it to 70 by other means.) Talk about your disease and brag a little bit about how you may fulfill the Nerevarine prophecies. This seems to confer celebrity status, and Fyr offers you an experimental potion.

He says it might cure you, and it might kill you.

But first you have to go retrieve a pair of enchanted boots from a corprus victim named Yagrum Bagarn down in the Corprusarium—the tower's dungeon. (Yuck. Corprus boots!)

Why do you feel as though you're doing the wizard two favors, and getting half of one back?

Your task here in the Corprusarium is a kind of reverse-dungeoneering. Do not kill any of Fyr's patients, regardless of how monstrous they may look or how bad-tempered they behave. Use stealth and magic to avoid combat, and retreat from any battles you can't avoid.

YAGRUM BAGARN

Better still, find the guarskin drum and give it to Uupse Fyr (standing next to Yagram Bagarn). She will play it, soothe the inmates' savage breasts and so smooth your passage.

Talk to Yagrum Bagarn in the Corprusarium Bowels. Mercifully, he does not want a favor. He'll surrender the boots and tell you about the disappearance of the dwarves. Return the boots to Fyr, and he'll turn over the potion—provided you agree to quaff it right in front of him, so he can observe the effects.

Just do it.

Interesting.

First of all, you're still alive. Second of all, you're not exactly "cured." You still have corprus—but none of its negative symptoms. You're left with the positive symptom: immunity to all disease—another prophesy of the Nerevarine fulfilled.

And, hey, you never actually had to spend most of that 1,000 drakes did you? You're rich, immune, and cured, sort of, and you seem to be fulfilling prophecies at every turn.

Head for Balmora, and strut your stuff.

MILO GONE

Your jubilation is short-lived. Cosades has been recalled to the Imperial City. While you don't know it yet, this is your last mission under his direction.

Before he goes, Cosades promotes you to Operative (which makes you the ranking Blade in the district). He also tells you he thinks you are the real Nerevarine, and instructs you to find the lost prophecies and deliver them to Nibani Maesa—picking up the thread from three missions back.

(Make sure you talk to Caius about 'promoted to Operative,' because that's when the old spymaster gives you some nice things he won't need back in the Imperial City. You get a black shirt with a Fortify Sneak enchantment, black pants with a hefty Chameleon enchantment, and a ring with Fortify Luck and Fortify Security enchantments. These are going to be very helpful in the near future.)

You'll need to visit the Hall of Wisdom and Justice in Vivec. Here, Mehra Milo will tell you how to get the lost prophecies.

But Milo's worst fears from your previous visit have been realized. She has been imprisoned.

Cosades recalled. Milo behind bars. Do you get the idea something's going on?

Word of her confinement doesn't seem to have gotten around. Six people in and around the library will tell you Milo is either in the library or her room across the hall from the Canon Office in the Hall of Wisdom.

Nope and nope. But you want to go to Milo's Quarters in the Hall of Wisdom in any case, as she has left a note to "Amaya" – the codeword for trouble—and two Levitation potions for you on her dresser.

The note is Milo's escape plan. She tells you to bring two Divine Intervention scrolls to the Ministry of Truth—one for each of you—and speak to the entrance guard, Alvela Saram, for admittance. (Don't have any DI scrolls on you? Janand Maulinie at the Mages Guild in Vivec's Foreign Quarter keeps them in stock.)

Fly up to the entrance. Saram gives you the entrance key and instructs you not to kill anyone during the rescue. Apparently sympathy for the captive and the Dissidents exists among the guards, but it will evaporate if someone dies. Instead, use stealth, speechcraft, or limited violence to find the necessary keys and reach Milo's holding cell.

But which way should you choose? Three doors lead into the Ministry. The one next to Saram leads past the Grand Inquisitor's office (good), but also to a locked and guarded door (bad). The door at the other end of the platform is a rear entrance, and the patrols here can be evaded. (The door on the lower platform is also a rear entrance, but it is farther from the door to the Prison Keep, and you'll encounter more guards.)

MINISTRY OF TRUTH

As you enter the rear platform door, be alert. Guards patrol the passage to the left. You want the passage to the right. Follow the passage up and around to a locked door to the Prison Keep. (Watch for a guard, and wait until his patrol carries him away from the door.) Getting through the locked doors should be the least of your problems. The interior locks are all Level 10, and, with any lockpick and the enchanted hand-me-downs Cosades gave you, you should be able to open a Level 10 lock in your sleep.

The Prison Keep is a real problem. When you enter, a team of elite Ordinators stand between you and the cell where Milo is imprisoned. There are three cells, and Milo's cell is the right-hand one. The walkways make it hard to dash past the guards. You want to go around them, not through them. The second Levitation potion Milo gave you will come in handy. Fly over the Ordinators to the right-most cell. You'll take a little punishment as you stand at the door and try to pick the lock. (The key to the cells is in a desk on the walkway; if you're nimble, you might be able to snatch the key as you streak for the cell door.)

Talk to Milo in her cell and give her a Divine Intervention scroll. She'll tell you to go to the East Docks in Ebonheart, find a woman named Blatta Hateria, and tell her that Mehra Milo sent you. Tell Hateria that you want to "go fishing." She'll transport you to the dock at the Holamayan monastery, the refuge of the Dissident priests. Milo, transporting to the Imperial Shrine in Ebonheart, will meet you at Holamayan later.

Upon your arrival, monk Vevrana Aryon will direct you to a stone walkway that leads north to the monastery entrance, which appears only between 6-8 a.m. and 6-8 p.m. (dawn and dusk, foreshadowing a similar event at a key location in the next mission). Inside, you'll be pointed to the library and Master Gilvas Barelo. Ask him about the lost prophecies, and Barelo will give you passages from the Apographa, "The Lost Prophecy" and "The Seven Curses" for Nibani Maesa.

Listen carefully to his analyses of these texts—especially his interpretation of "The Lost Prophecy," which indicates the Nerevarine is an "outlander."

BLATTA HATERIA

Once again, that could be you.

INCARNATE

It may feel strange not to be going back to Cosades' place in Balmora, but events have overtaken your work for the Empire. You're about to assume your real role in this world.

Just don't let it go to your head.

Make for the Urshilaku camp again and speak to Nibani Maesa about the lost prophecies.

She tells you to give her a day to decide what to do. We've already mentioned all the things you can find to do in this area—especially in the Foyada—so go do some of them. When you return, Maesa agrees to be your guide on the path of the Nerevarine.

You must pass the Seven Tests of the Seven Visions. You have already completed two such trials by virtue of your foreign birth and your cured case of corprus. Sul-Matuul, the Urshilaku ashkhan, will send you off on the third.

The first part, the Warrior's Test, takes you to Kogoruhn—the ancient home of House Dagoth and now a Dunmer stronghold—to retrieve three tokens.

To find Kogoruhn, head east along the coast from the Urshilaku camp to a ruined Dunmer stronghold called Valenvaryon. To the southeast, you'll find the ruined Daedric shrine Ebernanit. Kogoruhn lies south of Ebernanit.

The House Dagoth cup can be found on a tabletop in the Dome of Pollock's Eve on the surface. The corprus weepings can be found in the same room, half-hidden under an urn near the dome's supporting column. And the Shadow Shield is at the bottom of this large, tough dungeon.

To reach it, you'll need to pass through the Hall of Phisto and the Hall of Maki, the Nabith Waterway, and Charma's Breath to Bleeding Heart. When you enter Charma's Breath from Nabith Waterway, go right. (Left goes to Bad Places; see below.) The shield can be found on the Tomb of Dagoth Morin in the lava tunnels.

Along the way, you can avoid fighting if you wish. It's not required. (True enough, killing Dagoth Ulen in the Vault of Aerode will give you the key from Hall of Maki to Nabith Waterway, but you can skip that battle and use lockpicks or magic instead.) Combat doesn't even return much loot. You'll actually find more booty on pre-existing corpses and in Bleeding Heart.

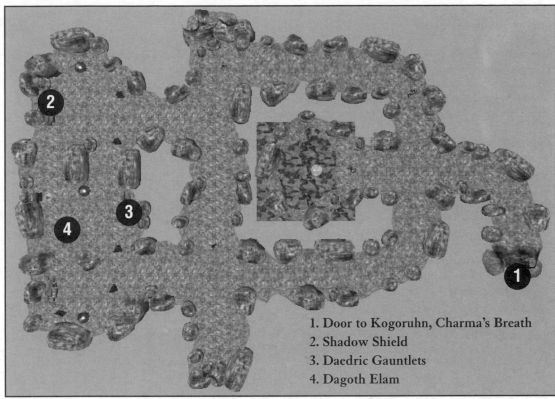

1. Door to Kogoruhn, Charma's Breath
2. Shadow Shield
3. Daedric Gauntlets
4. Dagoth Elam

KOGORUHN

In addition, completists should be aware that it's possible to explore this dungeon a bit too thoroughly and start taking on challenges for which you are not remotely equipped. If you go left to Bad Places instead of right to Bleeding Heart in Charna's Breath, you may get to meet an ash vampire. This is a Bad Thing. And an exit from Charna's Breath leads directly into the Dagoth Ur region, inside the Ghostfence. Where you'll be Very Sad.

With tokens in hand, return to Sul-Matuul, and he'll send you on Wisdom's Test to find the Cavern of the Incarnate. It's different than anything else we've run into so far. He gives you three verses that contain clues to the cavern's location:

> *the eye of the needle lies in the teeth of the wind*
>
> *the mouth of the cave lies in the skin of the pearl*
>
> *the dream is the door and the star is the key*

Nice poem. What does it mean? You must question Ashlander scouts and hunters and Nibani Maesa to find out. (By the way, an Ashlander scout lives in the yurt next to the Ashkhan's yurt in Urshilaku camp.) In so doing, you will learn that the "eye of the needle" is a rock column in the Valley of the Wind on the northeast slopes of Red Mountain. The "skin of the pearl" is a white rock at the top of the Needle. "The star is the key" must refer to Azura's Star, which appears only at dawn (6 a.m. to 8 a.m.) and dusk (6 p.m. to 8 p.m.).

Hence, you can enter the Cavern of the Incarnate when the door at the base of this white-capped rock column is open between those times.

To reach it, travel east along the coast from Urshilaku camp. Pass the Dwemer ruin of Bthuand and the Daedric ruin of Zergonipal, and turn south. Two parallel valleys lead south. The western one, Dry Camp Valley, isn't the one you want (though you will find the Dun-Ahhe dungeon and an outcast camp here). Take the one to the east—the one with the entrance marked by two tall spires called Airan's Teeth. Pass the Dareleth Ancestral Tomb as you follow the valley. Climb to a dead-end, and wait until one of the appointed times to enter.

Inside the cavern, you'll undergo what amounts to a coronation. Approach the statue of Azura to start a cut scene. In this sequence, you receive Nerevar's enchanted ring Moon-and-Star, and learn that you have passed the first three trials, and are, in fact, the Nerevarine.

Congratulations. You've hit a major milestone in the game.

Naturally, you are also set a series of tasks.

You must now go to the councilors of the three Great Houses and ashkhans of the four Ashlander tribes of Vvardenfell and show them your ring. You must persuade each House to acknowledge you as Hortator and each tribe to acknowledge you as the Nerevarine. (These are the titles given to the single war leader behind whom the Houses and tribes, respectively, unite in times of danger.)

However, you'll have to show the danger from Dagoth Ur and the Sixth House to prove such a leader is needed. And you'll have to show that you are that leader—that the Temple has failed the people and is no longer able to contain the threat.

Obtaining the blessing of the Houses and the tribes are the fourth and fifth trials, respectively.

After each is complete, you should return to Maesa for guidance.

What party would be complete without gifts? When the cutscene ends, you can speak with ghosts of failed Incarnates. Each will give you two unique items. Peakstar turns over an embroidered belt and travel-stained pants. (Thanks, Peakstar, but one word: Laundromat. Look into it.) Hort-Ledd: gives you a book (Sithis) and a robe. Erur-Dan offers a spear and cuirass. Idrenie Nerothan provides a Master's Probe and Lockpick, Ane Teria a book (36 Lessons of Vivec, Lesson 12) and a mace, and Conoon Chodala an axe and boots.

Apparently this is a sort of Thrift Shop of the Ages.

This transition is an event in much the same way that starting the main quest was an event. You've suddenly acquired a whole lot of enemies and allies. (You'll discover that your status is posted in cornerclubs and tradehouses.) The Temple becomes your enemy, as does House Redoran (unless you are a member) and the various factions aren't too tickled about it, either.

The world has changed, and there is no going back.

UNIFY URSHILAKU

You don't have to complete these seven quests in any specific order. We've arranged them with the fastest and easiest first.

This one is beyond easy. It's a given that the Urshilaku will give you the nod as Nerevarine. After all, you're family—a Clanfriend—and the tribe's wise woman is your guide on the Nerevarine path.

You have only to return to their camp and talk to Sul-Matuul. He'll explain your new position (and have you recite its requirements so that you're prepared for future encounters), name you War Leader of the Urshilaku and Protector of the People. And he'll give you the Teeth, the tribe's enchanted heirloom and a symbol of its decision.

It could hardly be simpler.

AHEMMUSA SAFE

SINNAMMU MIRPAL

However, don't think for a second that being in good with one Ashlander tribe buys you goodwill with the other three. They're going to make you sing for your supper.

For instance, persuading the Ahemmusa tribe that you're The One requires that you perform an errand with some ingenuity in order to help this troubled people find a new home.

Ashlander scouts and hunters can direct you to their camp. (It's on a point of land at the extreme northeast corner of mainland Vvardenfell.) The chief is wise woman Sinnammu Mirpal, but courtesy dictates that you first speak to three gulakhans—Kausi, Dutadalk, and Yenammu—about Nerevarine before you approach her.

Mirpal is willing to name you Nerevarine, but as always, there is a condition. The Ahemmusa are having trouble with blight creatures and need a safe haven. Your job is to create such a haven at Ald Daedroth, an ancient Daedric site on an island northwest of the camp. Then you'll have to prove to the chief that it's safe by escorting her there to see a great statue.

She does not define "safe." That's up to you.

One obvious way to make Ald Daedroth safe is to make it—ahem—empty. You can simply stomp on everyone you find there who's remotely dangerous

Guess what? They're all sort of dangerous. The site is currently occupied by our old friends, the Ordinators, and a group of Sheogorath Daedra cultists and their priestess. The two sides are not getting along too well, so just do yourself what they're planning to do to each other—wipe 'em all out, hoof it back to the Ashlander camp and take the chief in tow.

It's uncomplicated, it produces loot and, once the slaughter is over, escorting the old lady is a piece of cake.

But this requires a fairly advanced and resilient character and a fair amount of time. And since you'll be killing Ordinators, who are basically good guys temporarily on the wrong side, it doesn't reflect well on your character. (The Nerevarine should be a nice guy, right?)

One alternative is to first wait out the battle between the two sides at the shrine. Don't kill anyone until one side has been wiped out and the other weakened. Then go in and mop up.

But, strictly speaking, you don't have to kill anybody. You can also play this the diplomatic way. You can lie to the Ordinators and tell them you're here to rip off the shrine. Then they'll leave you and the wise woman alone.

The problem is engaging them in conversation to begin with. At this point, the Temple and Nerevarine factions are like diesel fuel and fertilizer—an explosion waiting to happen. However, Calm Humanoid and Charm spells will take the edge off your relationship, and you'll be able to have a chat. There's also an Ordinator standing guard on the island outside the shrine who's willing to talk first and fight later.

On the other hand, negotiating successfully with the Sheogorath cultists means you have to go all the way to the bottom of the shrine, ducking and weaving past hostile cultists, and talk to the cult priestess, Hlireni Indavel, in the Antechamber. If your Speechcraft skill is 50 or greater, you can appeal to the priestess's sense of pity. If it's less than 50, but either your level or reputation is 20 or greater, instead offer to spare her life in exchange for providing a haven for the tribe. Or you can raise her disposition to touch her heart.

In any case, success means the cultists will leave you be.

Then there's the old decoy trick. Attack opponents along your planned escort route and run like hell. Outdoors, lead them into complex terrain that will slow them down and then outdistance them by swimming, flying, or simply moving fast. Indoors, lead them to a distant location and then teleport out.

Finally, the fastest route is to lead Mirpal directly to Ald Daedroth and run interference for the wise woman along the way.

However, there's no practical reason to adopt this approach. Speed isn't relevant. It requires the most flexible tactics. And it's also extremely dangerous—Mirpal being a weak old woman.

In any case, when you're ready, just talk to her and have her accompany you to Ald Daedroth. Lead her to the island and through the Outer Shrine to the Inner Shrine and the statue of a bearded god with a cane and waistcoat. Speak to her again, and she will name you Nerevarine and give you a magic token called the Madstone.

ZAINAB BRIDE

Next is the Zainab tribe. As before, talk to Ashlander hunters and scouts to get directions to the camp. It is located southwest of the village of Vos and southeast from the Cavern of the Incarnate.

This time, you don't have to go through channels. You can go straight to Ashkhan Kaushad.

However, this doesn't mean you have an advantage in these talks. Kaushad is a demanding fellow. For starters, he won't consider your request to be named Nerevarine unless he likes you, and he doesn't like you enough. (Maybe not at all. He uses the words "ignorant outlander.") You need to boost his Disposition to 70.

ASHKHAN KAUSHAD

There's a fast way and a slower way into his affections. See, Kaushad is sort of a hypocrite. The Zainab wise woman, Sonummu Zabamat, will tell you the ashkhan loves exquisite outlander shoes. Bring him a pair to bump up his Disposition by 40 points. (The usual tactics for raising a character's Disposition in smaller increments will also work here.)

OK, now Kaushad likes you, and you can ask him to set you a task to prove your worthiness. He sends you to kill a vampire in the nearby Nerano Ancestral Tomb.

To find the crypt, head west from Zainab camp until you reach the mountains, then turn north. (Keep the mountains on your left for a reference point.). When you pass the ruins of Nchuleft, start watching the east for a tomb entrance flanked by two trees. It's on the western slope of a hill in the center of the Grazelands.

Calvario, a Level 14 vampire, is a difficult but not impossible opponent. And don't forget to pack a few Restore Strength and Restore Endurance potions, just in case you should run into a Greater Bonewalker.

Did you think you were done? I told you Kaushad was demanding. He comes up with one last requirement: a gift. It's not just some trinket, either; Kaushad is asking for a pony among presents. He wants a high-born Telvanni bride.

And she's got to be pretty and plump, with big hips.

It's not going to happen. Speak to the Zainab wise woman, Sonummu Zabamat, and she tells you that a high-born Telvanni lady would not even consider marrying an Ashlander.

However, this wise woman is full of surprises. She sends you to her friend, Savile Imayn, slavemistress of the Festival Slave Market in Tel Aruhn off to the southeast.

Imayn will sell you a pretty Dunmer slave girl, tell you what clothes to buy for her, and then dress her up like a high-born Telvanni lady. You then have simply escort the slave to the Zainab camp and present her to Kaushad.

By George, I think you've got it.

Well, almost.

SONUMMU ZABAMAT   It's a long haul from the Zainab camp to Tel Aruhn. If you learned your lesson from escorting the Ahemmusa wise woman, you'll scout the route before you travel it with a tender young thing in tow. Figure out a path that involves the least possible danger, and kill any wandering enemies (particularly outcast Ashlanders) that might hanker for the Slave Girl Blue Plate Special. (A Heal Companion spell will come in handy, too.)

Sure enough, Imayn says she has just the right slave. She sends you off to Elegnan: Clothier in Tel Mora to buy a fancy shirt, skirt, and shoes.

Return to Imayn with the clothes and she'll dispatch you again in search of Telvanni bug musk. (Yes, it sounds awful, but it's perfume.) You can get this stuff in lots of places, but the closest are Bildren Areleth the Apothecary in Tel Aruhn and Jolda the Apothecary in Tel Mora.

Finally, you have to arrive at a price for the slave. Imayn asks 1,200 drakes, but if you have a Mercantile skill of 40 to 80, you can get away with as little as 600. And if Imayn likes you (Disposition >= 60), she'll settle for 1100 drakes.

Imayn will give you the key to your slave's cage. Give the clothes and bug musk perfume to the young lady (who has the distinctly stripper-like name of Falura Llervu) and she'll follow you all the way to Kaushad's yurt.

As mentioned, it's a haul. Keep an eagle eye on Llervu. She's a good swimmer—and that's a good thing, given all the open water along the way. But she's not exactly a master of self-defense.

Inside the yurt, speak to Llervu and then Kaushad. He's a happy camper (though he manages to work in a complaint about his intended's hips). He names you Nerevarine and gives you the Zainab Thong, an enchanted heirloom of the tribe.

Personally, I don't have much use for a used thong, but it's the symbol of your selection as Nerevarine. (Let's just assume it's a sandal-type thong, OK?) Run to the Erabenimsun camp, before Kaushad assigns you another little task.

WAR LOVERS

The Erabenimsun camp, located to the south in the Great Scathes, is the most remote of the four Ashlander settlements.

This is true both in a physical sense and in a spiritual one.

Located north-northwest of Mount Assarnibibi, and southwest of the Corprusarium, this camp is located far from towns and other convenient reference points. Difficult terrain may make it difficult to find. As usual, your best bet is to ask directions from Ashlander scouts and hunters. These guys know everything.

When you do find the camp, you'll discover the Erabenimsun are remote as well. They don't like outlanders, and they don't like Nerevarines, and you're both. Many of them aren't helpful or pleasant. Some of them will treat you like dirt and threaten you. If you persist in trying to talk to them, some of them will attack you. Fine. Attack them right back. To death. No one will hold it against you.

Those Erabenimsun who talk civilly with you will recommend you see wise woman Manirai. She's the one coopera-tive person here.

Naturally, she has an agenda.

She tells you have no hope of being named Nerevarine by the current Erabenimsun regime. To prevail, you'll have to kill the current Ashkhan, Ulath-Pal, and three of his gulakhans (Ahaz, Ranabi, and Ashu-Ahhe). She offers advice on how to approach each opponent.

You'll fight each battle in a tent, so ranged spells and missile weapons are useless.

Ranabi is the weakest of the gulakhans. Kill him first. He'll summon a skeleton, but you can avoid him by leaving the yurt. When he's toast, get his poisoned dagger.

Fight Ashu-Ahhe next. He's a good challenge, giving and meting out heavy damage, but you shouldn't be at risk in this battle.

On the other hand, you'll have to fight Ahaz and Ulath-Pal together. This is the toughest fight you'll have with the Ashlanders. Take on Ahaz first, and beef up your defense before you start in order to survive the initial two-on-one stage of the battle. Make sure you have a lot of high-level Restore Health supplies ready. If you're a thief or mage, you'll want lots of supplies or magic to keep up your strength.

Once you've completed this dirty work, go have a chat with Manirai's candidate for ashkhan—the gulakhan Han-Ammu, son of the former chief. He's in his gulakyurt.

It turns out he doesn't want the chief's job. (Nor does his tribe want him as chief.) You will have to persuade him.

It's a confidence issue. Manirai has anticipated this. She suggests that if Han-Ammu had tokens recognized as conferring strength, will, and intelligence, he would have the confi-dence to accept the responsibilities of leadership. (Presumably, they'd earn the respect of the tribe as well.)

Now, it just so happens that, in your massacre of the top tier of Erabenimsun government, you now have access to three items that fill the bill. These are the War Axe of Airan-Ammu, Sanit-Kil's Heart of Fire and the Robe of Erur-Dan the Wise.

MANIRAI

Give the items to Han-Ammu to persuade him to become ashkhan. If your Speechcraft skill is 70 or greater, it's enough to simply show them to him and you'll get to keep the cool stuff. If you're not an accomplished talker person, but you've raised Han-Ammu's Disposition to at least 90, he'll allow you to keep the third item you give him. So if you have a favorite, save it for last.

Once Han-Ammu assents, speak to him again and he'll name you Nerevarine. Visit the wise woman one last time to collect the tribe's enchanted token, the Seizing of the Erabenimsun.

That does it for the tribes. By hook or by crook, they have universally acknowledged you as Nerevarine, and you have completed the fifth trial.

The three Great Houses are quite another matter.

REDORAN HORT

You can have two very different experiences with House Redoran.

If you joined this faction before you became Nerevarine-elect back in the Cave of the Incarnate, you're pretty much in like Flynn.

Just pay a visit to Athyn Sarethi at Sarethi Manor in Ald'ruhn and ask to be named Redoran Horator. If you already are a member of his House, Sarethi supports you, and tells you that he can persuade all but one of the other councilors to do the same.

Bolvyn Venim won't toe the party line. With that name, you just knew he wouldn't. Talk to him and you'll learn he won't even consider you for Hortator.

However, if you didn't join House Redoran earlier in the game, you're pretty much a pariah now. Without Sarethi's support, you will have a significant problem talking to Redoran folk without having to beat their heads in. Until then, use bribery and Speechcraft skill to keep things on a civil level.

As you'd expect, Sarethi's support under these adversarial circumstances is not a given. You must rescue his son, Varvur, from Venim's dungeon without killing the councilor and, if possible, without killing his guards. (See " Rescue Sarethi" in the Redoran section for the solution to this challenge. And you'll still need to kill Venim later in a formal duel.)

ATHYN SARETHI

Once this task is complete and Sarethi's support is secured, you'll find dealing with this House much less punishing.

In either case, Sarethi will bring the four other councilors on board, but you'll still need to talk to each of them. And to talk to them, you'll have to find them.

Happily, there's a sort of Redoran councilor directory. You can find their names and residences in the "Red Book of 3E 426." Neminda, at the entrance to the Redoran Council in Ald'ruhn, will give you a copy.

Now you just have to do some running around between the councilors' respective manors and quarters in Ald'ruhn. Miner Arobar, Garisa Llethri, Brara Morvayn and Hlaren Ramoran each will concur and name you Hortator.

Now you must honorably dispatch Bolvyn Venim in a duel. You could just kill Venim outright. But don't. If you do, you'll never win the approval of the other councilors.

To be sure, Venim's a bad guy and he must be killed, but honorably, in a duel. Talk to Venim in his private quarters in Venim Manor (also in Ald'ruhn) and accept his challenge to a duel in the Arena Pit in Vivec.

Expect to spend carefully hoarded potions and scrolls on Bolvyn Venim. Protected by a full suit of ebony armor, and armed with a fearsome Daedric dai-katana, strong and skilled, Bolvyn Venim can kill many characters in a few blows. Only a very powerful, well-armored, well-armed player character can hope to stand toe-to-toe with him in the Arena Pit.

However, mages and rogues with a more flexible sense of honor can perch on the railing above the Arena Pit and drop rocks on him. He has no spells or missile weapons, and is a sitting duck for ranged attacks. Shooting fish in a barrel is a completely respectable way to resolve this affair of honor.

When you have honorably dispatched Bolvyn Venim in the Arena Pit, return to Sarethi to be formally named Redoran Hortator, and to receive the Ring of the Hortator. Sarethi also gives you a sealed package. The note within indicates that, should you succeed in being designated Hortator and Nerevarine, you're invited to a private interview with High Archcanon Saryoni. Hang on to this note; it will be useful later.

Interesting. Suddenly, the Temple wants to talk to you.

HLAALU HORT

You're still a couple of missions from a sit-down with the Archcanon. But, as it happens, you're headed for Vivec anyway.

Bringing House Hlaalu around to the cause is a relatively simple chore, though somewhat expensive.

As in Ald'ruhn, so in Vivec: You'll learn the names and addresses of Hlaalu councilors from a copy of the "Yellow Book of 3E 426." Nileno Dorvayn at the Hlaalu Council Manor in Balmora provides a copy.

If you're a member of the Hlaalu faction, Crassius Curio, found in Curio Manor in Vivec, will take a little sugar or 500 drakes (300 if you bump his Disposition up to 70) to name you Hortator. If you're not a member, buying his good opinion costs 1,000 drakes.

Yngling Half-Troll, at St. Olms Yngling Manor, will take 1,000 drakes if you're Hlaalu and 2,000 if you're not.

But you can save yourself some money by just killing Yngling Half-Troll. Really. Go ahead. No one seems to care. (In fact, two other councilors endorse the idea.) If you taunt him into attacking you, you won't even have to pay the compensation that would be due if you'd murdered him.

Dram Bero at St. Olms Haunted Manor will name you Hortator, but he says that the two remaining councilors are Orvas Dren's creatures. If you are in House Hlaalu, or if she really likes you, Nevana Ules (in Ules Manor across the river from Suran village) will frankly admit she'll do nothing without Orvas Dren's okay; otherwise, she just gives you a cordial run-around. Velanda Omani (in Omani Manor, on Olmas Island east of the Vivec cantons) just acts puzzled. But multiplication tables are a big challenge for Velanda. She does suggest you explain it all to her advisor, Orvas Dren.

To get these last two councilors to name you Hortator, you must kill or blackmail Dren or otherwise force him to step down as head of the Camonna Tong.

YNGLING HALF-TROLL

You can kill Dren (found in the villa on his plantation). But Dren is well-armed and armored, strong and skilled, and supported by two very tough and able bodyguards. Moreover, unlike Bolvyn Venim, Orvas Dren is not easy pickings for ranged attacks, because Dren's Villa is small and cramped.

Characters playing a stealthier game may prefer to take the blackmail route. To do so, you'll need papers hidden behind locked doors in his basement. Dren's bodyguard, Galos Farethi, has the key to the locked doors. Nobel Peace Prize candidates may prefer to raise Dren Disposition to 70 (not easy!), giving the option of saying you want to be Hortator to protect Morrowind from the Empire. Dren will agree to name you Hortator if you select this option.

Speak with Velanda Omani and Nevana Ules again after you've taken care of Orvas Dren. Once everybody's on board, return to Curio to receive the Belt of the Horator. It's probably not the most fulfilling experience—more politics than anything—but it did get the job done.

Now, you just have to deal with the Telvanni.

TELVANNI HORT

ORVAS DREN

A strange quest.

Killing one of the Telvanni councilors is necessary to be named Hortator by this House. But you don't have to stop there. You can kill any of the councilors. You can kill just the ones you can't persuade. Heck, kill them all of them if you want to, and then name yourself Hortator.

Seriously, as long as your rep can stand the pressure, anything goes. This is how the Telvanni settle their differences.

Master Aryon in Tel Vos may have known this going in. He designates you Hortator without conditions. Smart boy. He also advises you that the other councilors, except Archmagister Gothren, can be persuaded to accept you. Of course, Aryon is not exactly Mr. Innocent. Aryon admits Gothren stands in the way of his advancement within the House, and you'd be doing him a favor if you removed this obstacle.

Mistress Dratha, found in the Upper Tower in Tel Mora, also gives you unconditional support—if you're a woman. If you're a guy, you'll have to nudge her Disposition up to 80 and make a little scene. (Mention that Azura is your patron to impress her.) But if you're a guy, and not a member of House Telvanni, then chances are you CAN'T raise her Disposition to 80—with negative modifiers for membership in other factions, she may be very hard to persuade. If that case, it may have to be over her dead body.

The flighty Mistress Therana, found in the Upper Tower in Tel Branora, needs to be in an identically good mood. But she'll also accept you if her Disposition is as low as 30, provided you have a Speechcraft skill of 30 and use it to charm the lady.

Master Neloth, at Tel Naga in Sadrith Mora, is a grumpy guy, but names you Hortator if he has a Disposition of 70.

Master Baladas, at Arvs-Drelen in Gnisis, may become a Telvanni councilor if you're a member of the House. He's easy, requiring only a Disposition of 30 to name you Hortator.

And what to make of Gothren?

When you first visit him in the Upper Tower in Tel Aruhn, he appears persuaded but asks for time to reflect.

But giving him time doesn't help. He's against you, and more time just makes him more specific about why he's against you. He even threatens to kill you if you keep bugging him.

Aryon was telling the truth. Gothren isn't giving you any choice. You will have to kill him. But it won't be easy.

Gothren has a nasty spell that paralyzes you for several rounds while it burns, freezes, poisons, and shocks the meat off you. And while you're paralyzed, his two Dremora bodyguards will pound on you merrily. His quarters offer no room for ranged attacks or maneuver. There is no single elegant and cunning solution to this combat, and no alternative peaceful resolution. One hint may help: remember your Shadow Shield—go invisible to stop combat, then move someplace safe to heal, restore, and plan the next phase of your battle.

When Gothren is dead, and all other councilors have either voted yes, or died, Aryon will give you the Robe of the Hortator.

You're Hortator and Nerevarine both.

Now it's time to go to church.

MEET VIVEC

Back in the days when House councilors were people to be respected, rather than exterminated, you got a note inviting you to arrange an interview with Tholer Saryoni once you became Hortator of the three Great Houses and Nerevarine of the four Ashlander tribes.

That time is now. You're to speak to Danso Indules, the healer of the High Fane of Vivec, to make the arrangements. Indules can be found in Vivec, in the north-south tunnel through the exterior of the High Fane. He tells you to talk to Saryoni in his private quarters. He also tells you to avoid trouble with the Ordinators.

Saryoni's private quarters are inside the High Fane, in the east wing. Problem is, the door is locked, and an Ordinator is standing right there, watching. But there is a back entrance from the Hall of Wisdom. That door is locked, too, but there's no vigilant Ordinator. Whip out your lockpicks or your spell or scroll of Ondusi's Unhinging and pop open the door.

VIVEC

Speak to Saryoni. Basically, he blinks—allowing that the Temple's unenlightened Nerevarine policy may change. Agree to a private meeting with Lord Vivec. The Archcanon gives you two keys, one to his own back door (which allows you to exit through the Hall of Wisdom) and the other to a secret entrance to Vivec's Palace.

Inside the palace, speak to Vivec. Accept the Wraithguard from him and swear to dedicate yourself to the destruction of Dagoth Ur and the preservation of Morrowind. Vivec then teaches you how to use this powerful artifact, offers to answer questions and gives you documents describing Dagoth Ur's plans and his own suggestions for dealing with the enemy.

OOPS

OK, we're all the same page, right?

Right?

Uh-oh.

There are a couple of reasons you might not be on the same page. One of them involves doing some wrong. The other involves doing something that's simply different.

Here, we'll get you sorted out and then move on into the endgame.

You can botch things up in any number of ways in the earlier stages of the game. The possibilities are legion. Somehow, somewhere, you step off the Main Quest trail into the wilderness and never quite find the path again.

Be thankful that the game has a kind of guide rail.

Provided you have become the Nerevarine, have a Reputation of at least 50 and are at least Level 20, you can return to the path of the righteous by talking to Archcanon Tholer Saryoni.

Of course, without help, you might never bump into this guide rail. So signs directing you to it have been spread all around Morrowind. Six familiar characters can steer you to Saryoni: Athyn Sarethi of House Redoran, Hlaalu Councilor Crassius Curio, the wizard Divayth Fyr, Ashlander wise woman Nibani Maesa, Mehra Milo from the Temple library or Master Gilvas Barelo from the Holamayan monastery.

Each asks why you haven't fulfilled the Nerevarine prophecies and points you toward the Archcanon.

Saryoni, in turn, will put you back in the saddle and in touch with Vivec.

But this is not to say you have to play the game as we've outlined. One of Morrowind's special qualities is its openness. As such, you can skip the Main Quest almost entirely, and still finish the game.

Think of it as a vegetarian Thanksgiving: No turkey for me, please, Aunt Juniper, but please pass the yams, the green beans and the cranberry sauce. You can live off the side dishes.

In so doing, it's possible to create a "backpath" character sufficiently powerful to acquire the key to Vivec's Palace and then get hold of Wraithguard and the necessary documents without following the story.

Ah, but there is a hitch. If you take this route and want to use the Wraithguard, you're going to have to wait for dessert a bit longer than if you'd followed the story.

You'll recall an earlier reference to Vivec showing you how to use the Wraithguard? Well, if you kill Vivec, this doesn't happen.

"WHAT? Kill Vivec? You gotta be kidding. He's a god."

Right. He is very, very, very, very hard to kill. Don't even think about it unless you've got a plan that will handle an opponent with thousands of Health, Magicka, and Fatigue points. But he can be killed.

Anyway, like I was saying, if you kill Vivec, you can take Wraithguard from his corpse, but it's an inactive Wraithguard, and you won't know whom to turn to for help turning it on and equipping it. You won't even know if there's anyone who can help.

You won't even know what it is.

At this stage, and under these circumstances, it's simply a unique but useless Dwemer artifact.

Do you think we'd let that happen to you?

Oh, maybe for just a little while, so we can watch you sweat, thrash around, beat up on innocent characters.

OK, that's enough.

In fact, there is one other person in Morrowind who can help you activate and equip Wraithguard.

Remember Yagrum Bagarn from the Corprusarium? You got some enchanted boots from him for Divayth Fyr and chatted a bit about the disappearance of the dwarves? And maybe he did a translation for you? And you maybe you borrowed his book, "Tamrielic Lore," which gives the background for a lot of cool items in the game? (We'll talk about the book in another chapter.)

Bagarn once worked with the great Dwarven inventor Kagrenac. If you take the artifact to Bagarn, he'll identify it as the Wraithguard in dialogue (though it remains "unique Dwemer artifact: in your inventory).

No, it's not that simple.

You'll have to meet one of three conditions just to get the dwarf to agree to help you. You'll need a Reputation of 20 and Bagarn a Disposition of 90, or a Reputation of 30 (with no Disposition requirement), or the documents "Dagoth Ur's Plans" and "The Plan to Defeat Dagoth Ur" in your inventory.

(If you've got the Wraithguard, the plans documents will be a piece of cake. They're on a podium on the south side of Vivec's chamber.)

OK, Bagarn's in.

But while he helped make the Wraithguard, that doesn't make him an expert on its operation. He says he might be able to figure it out with Kagrenac's Planbook and Kagrenac's Journals and suggests that the player search Dwemer ruins for them.

The Planbook is in Kagrenac's Library in Red Mountain citadel Tureynulal. Kagrenac's Journals are in his study in the citadel Endusal.

Bring these books to Bagarn, and the last dwarf will enable the device.

Naturally, there's this one other hitch. You've backed into the ending, and can't expect everything to come off like clockwork. So the first time you use this jury-rigged Wraithguard, it will backfire. Bigtime. When it backfires, it will do between 201 and 225 points of damage to the player. The only way you can guarantee your survival is to have more than 225 hit points and be at full health.

If you have 202 or more hit points, you should save your game someplace safe, and work through the backfires until you survive one. If you have 201 or fewer hit points, you are out of luck, and will need to level up before you can proceed.

But from this point on, the artifact performs exactly like the real Wraithguard.

VIVEC'S PLAN

In the meantime, follow Vivec's plan. It is a blueprint for winning the game. It consists of five broad steps leading up to the climactic battle with Dagoth Ur.

First, you'll need to make probing raids inside the Ghostfence. Your purpose here is to kill off non-respawning monsters and to learn the lay of the land. If you've spent much time inside the Ghostfence, you know it is not an orderly world, and it will take a while to learn how to get around.

You should get some help from folks in Ghostgate. With the end of the Meet Vivec quest, your relationships with the Temple and House Redoran should finally cool down. This means services previously unavailable at Ghostgate should become available. And Buoyant Armigers in Ghostgate are now under orders to provide maps and intelligence on the region within the Ghostfence.

GHOSTGATE

It's nice having friends again, isn't it?

While you're getting all comfy cozy on the enemy's doorstep, it's also not a bad idea to create a local headquarters where you can sleep safely and ferry supplies. Clear out one of the enemy citadels for this purpose. Stock up on all the consumable resources you'll need for a protracted campaign— restore health, fatigue, and magicka potions, repair tools, and in particular, restore attribute potions. Magical attacks of the Sixth House enemies often burn your attributes to nubbins, and you'll need more than nubbins to deal with Dagoth Ur.

Your second step should be to take down the remaining ash vampires, and recover artifacts from their bodies.

Each ash vampire has a special enchanted item that will help you defend yourself in the final battle. The hitch is that getting those artifacts means you're going to have to fight a whole bunch of increasingly nasty bosses pretty much in a row.

ASH VAMPIRES

Tackle Dagoth Uthol first. It's the easiest of the seven ash vampires to kill. Indeed, if you were incredibly thorough in your exploration of the Dunmer stronghold of Kogoruhn, you may have already killed it and recovered its Belt of Heartfire.

If not, Uthol is in Kogoruhn's Charma's Breath section. Even though Kogoruhn is located outside Red Mountain and well north of Ghostfence, this level is reached most easily through Red Mountain.

Next are Dagoth Endus at Endusal and Dagoth Tureynul at Tureynulal. Get their amulets of Heartrime and Heartthrum, respectively.

You'll take on the remaining ash vampires as you close in on Dagoth Ur.

ENDUSAL, KAGRENAC'S STUDY

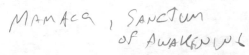

MAMAEA, SANCTUM OF AWAKENING

KEENING

We're close enough to the end to taste it—but not quite ready. You need to recover the artifact blade Keening from citadel Odrosal, located just northeast of Ghostgate.

It's a straightforward mission. To reach the citadel, head north from Ghostgate to the highest point of the terrain, then turn east and peer down into Odrosal.

An interior door leads to the tower. Naturally, it is locked, and, naturally, Dagoth Odros has the key. Kill him and claim his Amulet of Heartfire. In the tower, climb the ladder and retrieve Keening.

Now, be careful. We know you're eager to get on with things,. But don't equip Keening without having Wraithguard equipped first. This super-weapon, and its companion Sunder, can waste anything Morrowind throws at you. But Wraithguard is the buffer that protects you from their awful power.

SUNDER

Retrieval of the hammer Sunder is a bit trickier. Like Keening, it's in a citadel—Vemynal—on Red Mountain inside the Ghostfence, and guarded by Dagoth Vemyn, a high-level Ash Vampire. Kill him to get the real Sunder and the Amulet of Heartheal.

Now that you've got Keening and Sunder, if you have any loose cash, consider a little excursion back to civilization to train with Blunt Weapons and Short Blade if you don't already have those skills at high levels. If these skills are below 20, paying for training is cheap, and tormenting hapless wilderness creatures will quickly raise the skills through practice.

A DETOUR

We've been fighting the ash vampires in order of strength, and it's all been laid out in pretty convenient fashion. Of the seven ash vampires, five are found in Red Mountain citadels and the one in Kogoruhn is reached more easily through the volcano than through the stronghold.

Naturally, one of the strongest is off on his own. It's possible you found Dagoth Araynys if you ventured into Mamaea (located east of the stronghold Berandas) on the Miscellaneous Quest to rescue Hannat Zainsubani.

It's also possible that you got your ass kicked all the way to Gnisis. Araynys is a monstrous opponent—a Level 30 ash vampire with 400 health, 500 spell points, wildly high stats and the ability to do up to 100 points damage with a single blow.

If you've already managed to eliminate him and liberate his Soul Ring, we bow to you. If not, now's the time. We know you have your eyes on the prize. But inconvenient as this detour may be, its impact on your battle with Dagoth Ur will make it worth your while.

DESTROY DAGOTH

Let's take a quick look at what we've achieved.

In Keening and Sunder, you have the two artifacts required destroy Dagoth Ur. And in the Wraithguard, you have the means to use them without killing yourself. And you have beefed up your own defenses substantially by salvaging artifacts from Dagoth Ur's ash vampire brethren..

DAGOTH UR

You're not quite ready for the big bad guy himself, but you're ready to knock on his front door. Enter Dagoth Ur's citadel.

How do you get in? The door appears to be a sphere, but no activation message is displayed upon your approach. It's just like the door to Arkngthand, your first Dwemer ruin outside Balmora. There's a crank on a pipe to the left of the door. Turn the crank, run back before the sphere closes again and enter the citadel.

The last ash vampire is here. Kill Dagoth Gilvoth in the Lower Facility and recover the Blood Ring from his remains.

You're now as well protected as you're going to be. It's time to fight the big bad guy.

Make your way through the citadel to the Facility Cavern. Speak with Dagoth Ur. You'll both have a chance to ask and answer questions. And then, as your journal entry says, the time for words will be past. Dagoth Ur is a well-bred supervillain; he leaves it to you to take the first blow. So take the opportunity to prepare for this climactic battle.

If you have any summon creature scrolls or enchantments, summon them to soak up Dagoth Ur's attacks. Then cast all the enchantments from the ash vampire artifacts, and any other spells or enchantments you have that boost attributes or skills or protect from magic or physical damage. When all your summoned servants and magical enchantments are ready, attack Dagoth Ur, and keep attacking him until he vanishes.

The game isn't over. He's not dead. He can't be killed as long as the Heart of Lorkhan sustains him. But he does leave his very nice enchanted Heart Ring on the floor of the spherical Dwemer door as his disembodied spirit flees to Akulakhan's Chamber.

Enter Akulakhan's Chamber. Within, you will find the towering bulk of Akulakhan, a titanic metal automaton that Dagoth Ur plans to use to conquer the world. The Heart of Lorkhan, which is to serve as the power to animate Akulakhan, hangs inside Akulakhan's torso. You need to get down to heart, strike it once with Sunder, then five times with Keening, in order to destroy the enchantments and sever Dagoth Ur's life line.

When you enter the chamber, you are immediately confronted by a re-embodied Dagoth Ur and Sixth House enemies. It would be smart to avoid them if you can. (Peakstar's gift of Travel-Stained Pants or the Shadow Shield might come in handy here.) A stylish feat of derring-do would be to leap from the upper platform down to the rope bridge to Akulakhan's torso.

DON'T forget to have Wraithguard equipped before you equip Sunder or Keening. Or you will die very fast.

When the enchantments on the Heart are destroyed with Sunder and Keening, Dagoth Ur dies the final death. And so do any ash vampires you haven't already sent to their makers. You've also triggered a catastrophic collapse of Akulakhan, so you might want to get off Akulakhan and back up to the ledge where you can watch the fun from a safe perch. After you've watched Akulakhan collapse, leave the way you came in. (You'll need to find a standard-issue Dwarven crank on a nearby pipe to open the exit doors.)

In the Facility Cavern, you'll meet the spirit of your patron, Azura, and receive her well-deserved praise and a reward (a ring) for destroying Dagoth Ur. Dagoth Ur is gone. The Blight is gone. You have achieved your destiny.

Now what?

That's up to you. The story has ended, but the game isn't over. It's a big world out there, Nerevarine, and it is yours for the taking.

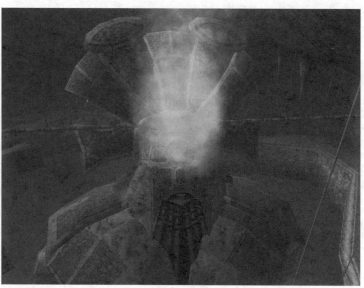

AKULAKHAN

Chapter Five: Faction Quests

So what do you do in Morrowind when you have nothing to do? What happens when Caius Cosades or another of your mentors along the path of Morrowind's Main Quest says you're not quite ready for prime time?

You perform Faction Quests. While the Main Quest is a binder that holds everything together, the Faction Quests give Morrowind its texture. If the Main Quest is the stuff of heroes, the Faction Quests are more the stuff of life.

Vvardenfell has more special interest groups than you can shake a stick at, and, throughout the game, they're all shaking sticks at each other. You'll forge connections with many of these groups—the three Great Houses, the three Guilds, the Tribunal Temple, the Morag Tong assassin's guild, and so forth—and grow in standing, wealth and power by performing their errands and receiving rewards.

They start simple—retrieving an item or escorting a merchant—and move on to major tasks like building a Stronghold, locating impossibly obscure sites, killing off the officers of a rival Guild, and even attempting to solve one of the game's deepest mysteries.

Onward, and downward.

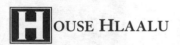OUSE HLAALU

House Hlaalu has always been loyal to the Emperor and the Empire. Hlaalu welcomes Imperial law and the Legions, and freedom of trade and religion. They respect the old Dunmer ways, the ancestors, the Temple, and the noble houses.

Once you've joined House Hlaalu, your initial quests can be obtained by talking to either Nileno Dorvayn or Edryno Arethi. These two series of quests are not inter-dependent, and you can follow them either concurrently or separately.

Favored Skills

Speechcraft	Short Blade
Mercantile	Light Armor
Marksman	Security

Advancement

Rank	Speed	Agility	One Favored Skill at	Two Other Favored Skills at
Hireling	30	30	0	0
Retainer	30	30	10	0
Oathman	30	30	20	0
Lawman	30	30	30	5
Kinsman	30	30	40	10
Hourse Cousin	31	31	50	15
House Brother	32	32	60	20
House Father	33	33	70	25
Councilman	34	34	80	30
Grandmaster	35	35	90	35

Faction Reaction

HATED ENEMY	ENEMY	HOSTILE	FRIENDLY	ALLY	BELOVED ALLY
	Ashlanders Clan Aundae Clan Berne Clan Quarra	House Redoran House Telvanni Thieves Guild	Mages Guild Imperial Cult Temple Camonna Tong Fighters Guild Imperial Legion		

NILENO DORVAYN'S QUESTS

Disguised Armor

NILENO DORVAYN

You'll find Nileno Dorvayn at the Hlaalu Council Manor in Balmora. For your first quest, talk to her, select "business", and then "say that again."

Dorvayn says you sound just like a dead Redoran—Relmerea Saram (if you're a woman) or Felsen Sethandus (if you're a man). She proposes to take advantage of the similarity by sending you to Ald'ruhn in a Redoran helm to take orders from Redoran quest-giver Neminda.

Clever, this Dorvayn.

Neminda can be found at the entrance to the Redoran Council. Make sure you're wearing the helm, then talk to her using the code phrase "Orphan of Arnesia" and collect a parcel. You're supposed to carry it to Maar Gan, but you're Hlaalu so it goes back to Dorvayn in Balmora. Talk to her again on the topic "Orphan of Arnesia" and give her the scroll to complete the quest.

Note that if you're an Argonian or Khajiit, Nileno Dorvayn will not ask you to put on such an unbelievable disguise. Instead, your first quest will be…

Bad Chemistry

This time around, when talking to Dorvayn, select "business" and "alchemical formulas." You'll learn that there's a new alchemist in town and that she's been stealing business from a loyal Hlaalu alchemist. You're to steal one of the newcomer's formulas to help the Hlaalu compete.

Make your way to Aurane Frernis: Apothecary on the west side of Vivec's Foreign Quarter Lower Waistworks and steal a recipe scroll. There's one in plain sight on the table, one in a chest (locked and trapped) at the foot of the bed, and a third on Aurane Frernis herself if you're good at picking pockets. Hoof it back to Balmora, turn any of the recipes over to Dorvayn, and you're done.

Egg Mine

Dorvayn wants you to undermine (so to speak) a rival named Avon Oran. His wealth is based in the Inanius Egg Mine, located across the mountains east of Suran, and Dorvayn wants you to kill the kwama queen there to wreck its operations.

You can also get a little extra cash along the way by using the threat to extort up to 1,000 drakes from Oran—and then kill the queen anyway to get 500 drakes more from Dorvayn. Nice, devious work if you can get it!

An Offer You Can't Refuse

Now you've got to play wiseguy. You're supposed to persuade Rolasa Oren, a vendor in Vivec, Foreign Quarter Upper Waistworks, to buy imported Hlaalu guar hides instead of Redoran ones.

Initially, she won't go for it at all—the imported hides aren't fresh and she's been getting Redoran hides for years—but with either a successful Intimidation or a Disposition of 80 she'll agree. (Killing her will get you through the quest as well, but it's not going to help the Hlaalu guar herders.)

She Spy

On this quest, you're the contact for a House spy named Bivale Teneran—ostensibly an Ald'ruhn clothier—and must deliver her new orders. Teneran's shop is inside the giant crabshell, on the ground level. Just talk to Teneran about "scroll" and turn over her orders. (She'll give you a lavish outfit, to boot.) Get back to Dorvayn to complete the quest.

Retaliation

Your first elaborate quest for the Hlaalu finds you looking into the murder of a nobleman named Ralen Hlaalo. Dorvayn wants you to find the guilty party and kill them.

Start by asking around in Balmora. You'll hear a range of different things—among them that the killer is Nine-Toes the Argonian.

Pay Nine-Toes a little visit at his house in Balmora. He denies committing the murder, and suggests you seek out any remaining servants at Hlaalo Manor.

You'll find Uryne Nirith at the Manor. (Just as a point of interest, you should be able to get this quest from her directly, without going through Dorvayn if you find and examine Ralen Hlaalo's body.)

Uryne Nirith says Hlaalo was murdered by a young Dunmer man with red hair, bonemold armor, and a Dwemer war axe.

Now you have a "murderer's description" you can use in conversation. Ask around some more, and you'll hear that the murderer sounds like Thanelen Velas (of the Camonna Tong), who is at the Balmora Council Club.

Talk to Velas if you want—he's sure it's a coincidence—or simply kill him. If you're not sure Velas is the one, you can kill Nine-Toes instead. And if you can't make up your mind, hey, kill 'em both. It's OK. The rules of evidence don't apply. Just make sure somebody dies. Get back to Dorvayn to finish the quest.

Make Up Your Mine

This time out, you can take the quest in two very different directions. Talk to Dorvayn about "ebony trade" and she'll lay out your options.

You can convince Canctunian Ponius at the East Empire Company in Ebonheart to buy ebony from House Hlaalu instead of House Redoran.

Or you can shut down the Redoran mine in Sudanit.

The first option is shorter if you're skilled in good talking. You'll find Ponius in the Company Hall. Get his Disposition up to 75 and he's in your pocket.

To find the mine, follow the path between Ald'ruhn and the Buckmoth Legion Fort east to the Ghostfence, then bear south until you find the mine. Kill Darns Tedalen to shut down operations, and make your way back to Dorvayn.

If you do both of these—kill Dans Tedalen and convince Ponius—Nileno will give you a suit of Glass Armor.

EDRYNO ARETHI'S QUESTS

Buried Treasure

EDRYNO ARETHI

Edryno Arethi's house is on the south side of the Hlaalu Waistworks. In your first quest for her, you're doing a little "collections" work. Murudius Flaeus of Hla Oad apparently owes Hlaalu nobleman Briras Tyravel a good amount of money. If you collect the loot, you'll keep half.

Meet and greet Flaeus at his home in this seaside community, southwest of Balmora, and talk to him about "debt money."

Initially, he is uncooperative. But with some persuasion—well, actually, a whole lot of persuasion (up to a rolling-on-the-floor-laughing-and-kicking Disposition of 90) or any successful Intimidation—he'll give you a key and confess that a chest is hidden under Fadila's house near the Hla Oad docks. You just have to find it and take the money.

You can skip the persuasion part and just pickpocket the key and find the chest on your own.

In fact, you can skip this deadbeat entirely. Talk to people in town about him, and you'll learn that he often goes swimming near Fadila's house. Follow his example, find the chest on your own, and pick the lock. With money in hand, get back to Arethi to wrap up the quest.

Bank Courier

A simple dispatch job: You're carrying sealed orders to Baren Alen at the Hlaalu Treasury in Vivec. Just talk to Alen when you get there and turn over the orders.

Don't open it. Really. First off, you won't be able to read it—it's in code—and, second, Alen will notice. As a result, you'll sacrifice your reward and compromise your good standing with Arethi. If you're good at Security, you can open some letters like these, and then attempt to reseal them, but if you fail, the seal is broken and Baren Alen will notice.

Escort Merchant

Another fairly simple mission. You're escorting the merchant Tarvyn Faren to the Halfway Tavern in Pelagiad. You'll find him just north of Vivec's North Landing on the road to that town. Talk to him and select "travel together." He'll agree to follow you, and you're off! Go slow, so the trader and his pack guar can follow you. In Pelagiad, Faren will say farewell and you can report back to Arethi for more work.

Odirniran

The Hlaalu are fighting an evil Telvanni sorcerer at Odirniran, located east of Molag Mar. You're to travel there and either help the survivors or take revenge upon the Telvanni.

It's a rather tricky journey, and Arethi suggests you make for Holamayan, which is actually farther away, and then follow the trails southwest.

There are survivors. In fact, the Hlaalu force has done OK for itself, and most of the sorcerer's minions are dead.

However, you'll learn from leader Remasa Othril that the sorcerer himself remains at large and has taken hostage Othril's sister, Vedelea.

Vedelea won't try and follow you until you've killed the wizard. So track down Milyn Faram (he's in the Odirniran Tower section upstairs) and kill him. Get the key from him and go back to Vedelea.

Talk to Vedelea, click on "travel together" and she'll follow you back to Remasa. Head back to Arethi and complete the quest and pick up your reward—500 gold if you simply killed Faram, and another 500 if you saved the girl.

The Exterminator

A weird little mission. A Hlaalu councilor, Yngling Half-Troll, raises game rats to fight in the Arena. A rival has put some diseased rats in with his game rats. You have to kill the diseased rats while sparing the healthy rats.

Find your way to Yngling Manor—it is at the top of St. Olms Canton, near the statue—and make your way to the basement and kill the diseased rats, which are aggressive to you. The healthy game rats will only attack if you attack them first.

You can get away with killing one healthy rat in the process.

You can also visit the Manor proper if you want to talk to Yngling (provided you haven't already whacked him—an option in the Main Quest). Then check in with Arethi to finish the quest.

Ashlander Ebony

If you discuss "ebony trade" with Arethi, you'll learn that the Zainab tribe of Ashlanders has a source of that precious commodity and is selling it to the Empire. House Hlaalu, which had a monopoly on those sales, has had to lower its prices to compete. Your job is to persuade the Zainab to deal only with House Hlaalu.

The real burden here is the long trip. (The Zainab Camp is due southwest of Vos/Tel Mora.) Chat with an Ashlander or two at the camp, and you'll be directed to the yurt of Gulakhan Ashibaal.

Just talk to him. The dialogue will be pretty elaborate, as only dialogue with Ashlanders can be, but in the end you should be able to convince him to trade with the House by choosing the following dialog options: Choice 1: The Zainab are now strong enough to sell ebony. Choice 2: If we both sell ebony the price drops. Then make your way back to Vivec to complete the quest—and snag your share of future profits!

Sunken Treasure

Vvardenfell has a lot of shipwrecks. Arethi has a particular interest in the wreck of the Prelude, east of Bal Fel. An enchanted Daedric Wakizashi can be found on its lower level. Return it to Arethi to complete the quest. Any other loot you recover (and there's a lot!) is yours to keep.

Guard Merchant

Ralen Tilvur's smithy shop in Vivec's Market Canton has been broken into three nights running.

Guess who's been elected to play security guard.

Ralen's shop is the one in the southeast corner of the Foreign Quarter Plaza. Talk to Ralen and the thief, Drarel Andus, will arrive. Once you've dispatched him, get back to Arethi to wrap up the quest and collect your reward.

CRASSIUS CURIO'S QUESTS

I Am Curious, Crassius

If you haven't already figured it out, Hlaalu councilor Crassius Curio likes you.

He really likes you.

But mostly he's subtle about it, expressing his affection in little endearments and overblown rewards.

Well, he's done being subtle.

CRASSIUS CURIO

By now, between Dorvayn's and Arethi's quests, you should have reached at least Rank 3 within House Hlaalu. Once you try to advance farther, people will tell you need a sponsor, and some of them will suggest you talk to Curio.

Curio will sponsor you, all right. He'll sponsor you if you take your clothes off.

Seriously. And that's all of your clothes. No rings. No amulets. (Lucky for you the game doesn't let you take off your underwear.)

While you're in the altogether, talk to Curio again. You've got a patron. Pudding.

When you hit Rank 4, your patron will point you at Odral Helvi.

ODRAL HELVI'S QUESTS

Bank Fraud

More sealed orders. Will you open them this time? And, more to the point, will you give them to the right person?

You'll come back to Curio soon enough. But for the moment, your new quest-giver is Odral Helvi, whom you'll find in the Governor's Hall in Caldera—a rich mining town a short walk north of Balmora.

He's as crooked as the day is long.

For your first quest, he wants you to take the orders, not to Treasury Clerk Baren Alen, as you've done in the past, but to Assistant Clerk Tenisi Lladri in the Hlaalu Vaults (part of the Treasury) in Vivec. You simply have to talk to Lladri, give her the orders and return to Caldera.

Ah, but that's the simple side of things. Helvi seems to hiding something, and you've gotten yourself embroiled in some Hlaalu intrigue.

No fewer than three additional people will accept the orders from you: Alen, Hlaalu nobleman Rovone Arvel at the Arvel Plantation in the Ascadian Isles, and Hlaalu councilor Curio. All of them regard the orders with suspicion.

(Wherever your loyalties lie, it's worth at least experimenting with giving the orders to Curio. He's a scream.)

ODRAL HELVI

However, be advised that while these alternate routes still complete the quest, Helvi won't like it and his Disposition toward you will take a significant drop.

But, as you'll learn from the orders' unintended recipients, he has bigger problems.

Capture Spy

Whatever the tensions in this relationship, your new boss has another job for you. Someone has stolen Caldera mining contracts. You're to recover the documents and kill the thief.

People in town suggest you talk to the two newest people in town: the pawnbroker Irgola and Elmussa Damori.

Irgola flatly denies responsibility. Damori is less convincing. Her denial is defensive. (Not "I didn't do it" but "You have no proof.") She's got lockpicks in her house.

And if you can nudge her Disposition up to 80 (or you belong to the Thieves Guild), she'll admit the theft and surrender the documents.

But she'll plead with you not to tell Helvi.

ELMUSSA DAMORI

You actually have more options than you may have guessed. You can kill Damori as ordered or let her go. You can tell Helvi the truth—at the cost of any standing you may have with the Thieves Guild, which commissioned the theft—or tell him a lie (which he'll swallow if you get his Disposition up to 70).

Once again, it is worthwhile talking to Curio before you complete the quest. He suggests you spare the thief—he wants to talk to her himself—and lie to Helvi about the contracts.

Life as a member of House Hlaalu has suddenly gotten complicated, hasn't it? You can complete the quests in a range of ways. The real question is how you want to play it as a person.

And the irony is that the real spy here is you.

Replace Docs

Talk to Helvi about "erroneous documents" and he will tell you he has found a serious error in the land deeds for the Ascadian Isles. He gives you a new land deed to put in Hlaalu Records in Vivec and asks you to bring him the old one.

You can do as Helvi asks.

Or you can bring Curio in again and give him the fake deed while returning the real one to Helvi. If you don't want to steal from the Treasury and risk being expelled, you can speak with Baren Alen about "erroneous documents" to get a copy of the land deed. This only works after you've given the fake documents to someone. Once again, you can also deliver the documents to Rovone Arvel, but there's no real benefit to going out of your way to do this.

Someone's building a case.

Rent Collector

Now, mysteriously, Helvi wants to collect rent and taxes from Manat Varnan-Adda and Llovyn Andus—two farmers in the Ascadian Isles.

He wants 50 gold from each. And if they won't pay, he wants you to kill them as an example to others.

You can reach Varnan-Adda's farm by heading west out of Suran, crossing the isthmus and then bearing south. Andus' farm is farther west, past the Dren Plantation.

Neither has the money, though Llovyn Andus will offer you his guar, Corky. (If you manage to lead Corky all the way up to Drulene Falen's herd she will pay you 200 drakes for him.)

You can kill the farmers as ordered, but you don't have to. Why do this crooked man's bidding?

Instead, have another chat with Rovone Arvel. He tells you he'll look into the matter himself, and gives you 100 drakes to cover what the farmers owe. Curio's more specific: He thinks Helvi just wants the farmers dead, and suggests you pay the bill yourself.

Any of these solutions is OK. Get back to Helvi and either tell him the farmers are dead (you must have killed them) or pay 100 drakes to complete the quest.

Ebony Delivery

It's ending, finally. You can play it out as a simple errand boy for the bad guy, or as an undercover cop.

Talk to Helvi about a "shipment of ebony," and he'll ask you to take five pieces of raw ebony to Drinar Varyon in Ald'ruhn.

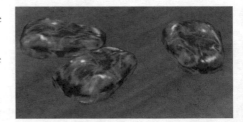

As you may already know, Varyon's a big-time smuggler. Traffic in raw ebony is illegal.

If you're simply an errand boy, just talk to Varyon, give him the ebony and report back to Helvi to complete the quest.

If you're an undercover cop, go see Curio instead. He'll tell you to take the ebony to Segunivus Mantedius at Fort Buckmoth.

Do so, and both Varyon and Helvi will be taken out of circulation.

Now just report back to Curio—your new quest giver—to complete the mission.

Stronghold

By now, Curio may already have mentioned to you something about a stronghold. Once you reach Rank 6 or 7 in your House, councilors and quest-givers will tell you who to contact to build this structure, and where to find them. (However, you don't have to wait to be told, and can start the process on your own any time after Rank 4.)

Stronghold is a sort of maxi-quest, but it isn't simply a quest. It reflects a change in your status within the House and the way you exist in the game world. You're not going to be just a wandering hero any more. You will have a base of operations. (Remember when you finally earned enough money to buy your own house in Daggerfall? It's a little like that. You're getting a place of your own.)

Stronghold construction always has three stages, and it's handled in a similar way from House to House. But the details in each are a little different.

In House Hlaalu, you'll start the first phase by talking about "stronghold" with Dondos Driler at the House's Council Hall in Balmora. Think of him as a general contractor. He will be your principal contact during the construction.

For now, he just needs a construction contract and a land deed.

See Duke Vedam Dren in the Ebonheart's Grand Council Chamber about the contract. He'll ask only for your vow to help his people. Agree, and he'll give you the document. You'll barter for the deed with Baren Alen at the Hlaalu Treasury, in the Hlaalu Waistworks in Vivec.

Take these documents to Driler, and you're on your way.

Now you need to play the waiting game for a bit. Don't sit around and bite your nails. Go knock off a quest. You won't miss anything.

ODAI PLATEAU STRONGHOLD

In a few days, you'll be prompted by a journal entry to talk with Driler about the stronghold. He provides the location (on the Odai Plateau south of Balmora on the northwest bank of the Odai River) and asks that you check in with site foreman Durbul gro-Rush. At the site, you'll learn from that work should be complete within a week.

Report back to Driler. Allow a few more days to pass, and another journal entry will report that Stage 1 of the stronghold is complete.

Start picking out a tile pattern for the kitchen.

On to Phase 2 of Balmora Estates. Check in with Driler again. He says you need to improve business near your stronghold, and suggests you restore productivity the abandoned Shurdan-Raplay eggmine that's located nearby.

Once again, it's a two-step process. The eggmine is abandoned for good reason: The Kwama queen is blighted. You have to cure her and then recruit miners.

Talk to Driler about "Shurdan-Raplay." He'll give you its general location—it's across the Odai from your stronghold—and a couple of sources for Cure Blight scrolls. (Hetman Abelmawia in Gnisis and Pierlette Rostorad in Sadrith Mora both have them in stock.) Descend into the mine's lair—it's different walking through a mine when it's yours, isn't it? – and cure the blighted queen.

Talk to Driler again about "recruit some miners," and he'll mention unemployed ones in Gnisis and Tel Aruhn. Possibilities include Ilasour Tansumiran (who lives on the north side of Gnisis between the Temple and the mines) and Llaals Ores (a former miner, now a slave; Tel Aruhn slave trader Savile Imayn will sell him to you for 200 gold, and with a "good riddance" attached!)

When one miner signs on, go see Driler again to launch the second stage of construction.

Once you reach Rank 7 in the House, and Phase 2 of construction is complete, talk to Driler yet again about "stronghold." He'll tell you that, to encourage people to settle here, you need to get rid of the bandits preying upon commerce in the area. Specifically, you need a guard. He'll point to the Balmora Fighters Guild and the Imperial Legion at nearby Fort Moonmoth as potential sources of recruitment.

This guy knows everything.

The Fort doesn't have anyone to spare, but check with Flaenia Amiulusus at the Guild. She has one candidate named Fjorgeir available for 1,000 gold. Hire him and meet him at your stronghold. Finally, talk to him about "guard against bandits" and he'll tell you where to find them—a small cave called Zainsipilu, across the river and over the hills to the south—and volunteer to fight them with you. (You can also have him patrol the stronghold.)

Head for the cave with your mercenary. Zainsipilu turns out to be pretty good-sized, and fairly thronging in bandits. Wipe 'em out, and go see Driler to begin the third and final phase of construction.

Once the third stage has begun, wait a few days and your journal will be updated that your stronghold is complete. It's moving day…your castle awaits!

ILMENI DREN

ILMENI DREN'S QUESTS

Literacy Campaign

Unlike many of the Hlaalu faction quests, which deal in a currency of corruption and intrigue, the three from Ilmeni Dren (the daughter of Duke Vedam Dren currently slumming in Vivec at St. Delyn Canal South-One) deal in social issues. You can start on these tasks once you reach Rank 4.

Talk to Dren on the topic "people cannot read" to get the first quest. She complains about literacy rates, and reports that teachers in the Mages Guilds often don't have enough books. You're dispatched to find two – "ABCs for Barbarians" and "The Annotated Anuad" – for the school in the Ald'ruhn Mages Guild.

These can be found at better booksellers everywhere. Buy them, deliver them to Vala Catraso at the Ald'ruhn Mages Guild and check back with Dren to complete the quest.

Twin Lamps

Maybe it's because it's an island, but Vvardenfell is not the most enlightened place in the Empire. Slavery still exists here—as does an anti-slavery movement called The Twin Lamps. The abolitionists need your help, and you're off to Ald Velothi to render it.

Seek out and speak with Galyn Arvel by the docks. She reports that a Khajiti slave named J'Saddha was supposed to meet the abolitionists at their boat. (The Lamps often spirit escaped slaves away to the mainland.)

The slave didn't make it. He's hiding in Daedric ruins to the east.

Three slavehunters are prowling the town.

Different approaches should work here. You can kill the slavehunters outright, but this is murder and you may be caught. You can also try to sneak J'Saddha into town.

And, with some diligent speechcraft, you can send the hunters off on wild goose chases. If you can get each slavehunter's Disposition to 60, you can waylay them individually (and only one at a time) by telling one that J'Saddha is in the ruins or has left town. Off that hunter will go. This is best directed against Sadal Doren, as it's comparatively easy to sneak the slave past the other hunters.

Once the way is clear, have J'Saddha travel with you and bring him safely to Galyn Arvel. Then get back to Dren to wrap up this mission and take on another assignment for the Twin Lamps.

Twin Lamps Relit

This time out, you're off to the Dren Plantation to free an Argonian slave named Hides-His-Foot and shepherd him to Sterdecan's Farm.

You'll find him outside. The guards will attack if they see what you're up to, so you may want to consider a two-step process—a preemptive strike to take out the most difficult guards, followed by the actual rescue. Just talk to the slave and have him follow you.

Once you reach Sterdecan's (which isn't that far), the farmer will take over. You just report back to Dren.

This may seem a very minor sort of quest, but it has a very subtle purpose. Hides-His-Foot knows something. Once you deliver him to the farm, ask him about "little secret" and you'll discover he has dirt on his former employer. There's damning evidence in a locked room in Orvas Dren's cellar.

It's also extremely well-guarded dirt—behind heavily-locked and trapped doors and defended by Camonna Tong enforcers. You'll need to visit the villa sooner or later. (If you're in the Thieves Guild or the Morag Tong, you'll have to take the enforcers out in a quest later.)

CRASSIUS CURIO'S QUESTS

Nord Smugglers

If you've reached Rank 4 in the House, and have completed the Odral Helvi missions Bank Fraud and Ebony Delivery, you're ready to work for Curio himself.

Discuss "Velfred the Outlaw" with the colorful Mr. Curio. He asks you to get the outlaw to pay the appropriate smuggling fees to House Hlaalu, or kill him.

And that's about all he says. Curio does not know Velfred's exact whereabouts, but he suggests that you try Hla Oad. Talk to people there about Velfred and his ship, the Grytewake. You'll eventually learn that Velfred's ship is at a secret dock to the southwest.

CRASSIUS CURIO

Now go find Velfred and either wipe the floor with him or get him to listen to reason. Initially, he's unwilling to cut in the Hlaalu—he's already paying off the Empire—but boost his Disposition to 75 and he'll see the light.

Get back to Curio to wrap up the quest and collect a reward of 500 drakes (if you killed Velfred) and 1,000 if you persuaded him.

And get called "dumpling."

Destroy Tel Uvirith

A hit, more or less. Curio sends you off to kill Telvanni sorcerer Reynel Uvirith at the stronghold Tel Uvirith, located in the Ashlands west of Tel Fyr. Note that this quest is virtually identical to the Redoran faction quest Attack Uvirith. When your stronghold goes up, so do unchartered Redoran and Telvanni strongholds. Each Great House has two faction quests in which you launch attacks on its two rivals.

These people never stop fighting.

Bero Support

Curio now tells you that you need the support of another Hlaalu councilor. He puts forward Dram Bero—Bero apparently being the only one hardy (or foolhardy) enough to defy Orvas Dren.

(Orvas Dren, a wealthy man who secretly runs the Camonna Tong syndicate, is the gray eminence behind the Hlaalu Council.)

But Bero is hard to find. Curio suggests you start your search in Vivec.

It's good advice. If you ask around on the streets, you will eventually be directed to the St. Olms Plaza. All the houses up here seem straightforward enough, except for the "Haunted Manor."

Put aside your main question ("So, Mr. Bero, why are you living in a haunted house?") and talk to him about "support on the Council."

As you know by now, no one on Vvardenfell does anything for you without you doing something for them first. Bero wants to see what you're made of by pitting you against his champion, Garding the Bold. He'd prefer you knock him out—a sleep spell will do the trick—so try not to kill him. Garding will also concede if he gets low on health. Once Garding is out cold, talk to Bero again to confirm his support, and then talk to Curio to finish the quest.

Destroy Indarys Manor

Another hit—this one against House Redoran. Curio wants you to put the bag on Lord Banden Indarys at Indarys Manor—along the Ald'ruhn-Maar Gan highway. Get back to Curio when the job is done, and he'll turn over 1,000 gold and promote you to "pudding pie."

DUKE VEDAM DREN'S QUESTS

Win Saryoni

Hlaalu faction quests don't get any more advanced than this. If you've reached Rank 8 in the House, you'll be able to get these last two quests from the Duke in the Grand Council Chamber in Ebonheart.

By now, you have doubtless had painful, first-hand experience with the zealousness of the Ordinators. And apparently you're not the only one. The Temple's security force, under the direction of Berel Sala, has a bad habit of making unfaithful Hlaalu vanish.

DUKE VEDAM

The Duke wants to rein them in. Select "control the Ordinators" in conversation with him, and Dren will ask you to speak with Archcanon Tholer Saryoni on this subject.

Make for the High Fane in Vivec and have a chat with his holiness. In conversation, select "troubling times" and then "Ordinators have failed."

Saryoni, who is a decent fellow, acknowledges the failure and gives you an opportunity to do something the Ordinators couldn't—recover the lost Robe of St. Roris.

It's in a chest at the Assemanu shrine—a lavishly designed cave, with Dagoth Hlevul at its end, on an island in the swamplands on the way to Seyda Neen. Saryoni will give you directions. You will face some tough battles here.

The robe is in a chest on a ledge in the room Dagoth Hlevul is in. The ledge is just above the Sixth House bells, but inaccessible from the ground. You'll need to levitate or use telekinesis to open the chest.

Give Saryoni the Robe and he'll agree to control the Ordinators. Then go see Dren to complete the quest.

Win Camonna

It's all down to one last quest. The Duke tells you that you must win control of the criminal syndicate Camonna Tong from his brother, Orvas Dren, in order to truly assume the role of Hlaalu Grandmaster. You need to do this anyway to get the Hlaalu Council behind you for Hortator.

How to bring it about?

Well, there's killing. But Orvas Dren is exceptionally hard to kill.

There is Persuasion. In dialogue, you can make Dren see that you're a worthy successor. Orvas Dren. A few hints here and there will let you know that Orvas Dren is a nationalist and want to drive the Empire out of Morrowind. If you tell him you want to be Grandmaster in order to do this, he'll agree unless he really dislikes you.

And there's blackmail. Remember what Hides-His-Foot told you. The note from the basement of Dren's villa, implicating him in a conspiracy to kill the Duke, would make him look really bad.

Go have a talk with the druglord to settle accounts. He's upstairs in his villa at Dren Plantation. Once you've succeeded, and Dren has died or stepped down, make your way back to the Duke to be named Hlaalu Grandmaster.

HOUSE REDORAN

House Redoran prizes the virtues of duty, gravity, and piety. Duty is to one's own honor, and to one's family and clan. Gravity is the essential seriousness of life. Life is hard, and events must be judged, endured, and reflected upon with due care and earnestness. Piety is respect for the gods, and the virtues they represent. A light, careless life is not worth living.

Favored Skills

Athletics	Heavy Armor
Spear	Medium Armor
Long Blade	Armorer

Advancement

Rank	Endurance	Strength	One Favored Skill at	Two Other Favored Skills at
Hireling	30	30	0	0
Retainer	30	30	10	0
Oathman	30	30	20	0
Lawman	30	30	30	5
Kinsman	30	30	40	10
House Cousin	31	31	50	15
House Brother	32	32	60	20
House Father	33	33	70	25
Councilman	34	34	80	30
Archmaster	35	35	90	35

Faction Reaction

HATED ENEMY	ENEMY	HOSTILE	FRIENDLY	ALLY	BELOVED ALLY
	Ashlanders	Mages Guild	Fighters Guild	Temple	
	Clan Aundae	House Hlaalu	Imperial Legion		
	Clan Berne	House Telvanni			
	Clan Quarra	Camonna Tong			
		Thieves Guild			

NEMINDA'S QUESTS

Your initial House Redoran quests are offered by Neminda, who can be found at the entrance to Redoran Manor in Ald'ruhn. She is the only one who can recruit you into House Redoran. To join, click on "Join House Redoran" and say you want to join.

Mudcrab Nest

In conversation with Neminda, select "duties" and then "hostile mudcrabs." Neminda will tell you that some mudcrabs have attacked Drulene Falen's guar herd. Follow her directions to the shepherd's hut.

Falen will confirm the attack and report the mudcrabs dragged a guar's body off to the southwest. Follow them. You'll find a dead guar and two mudcrabs nearby. Kill the mudcrabs, return to Falen for a reward of Hackle-lo leaf and then report to Neminda to complete the quest.

Note that while you have to belong to House Redoran, to undertake most of these missions, this quest and the other involving Falen (Guard Guar Herds), don't require House membership.

Courier

Once you've taken care of the mudcrabs, you're good to go for this simple errand. Talking to Neminda, select "duties" and then "cure disease potion." Neminda will ask you to deliver the potion to Theldyn Virith at the Outpost in Ald Velothi. Simply talk to Virith, give him the potion and report back to Neminda.

Now, just suppose for a moment that you're unwell, and need the cure disease potion yourself.

That's OK. Quaff away. You can use any cure disease potion to fulfill the quest. However, no one in Ald Velothi sells potions, so if you drink your cargo, you'll have to find a replacement elsewhere.

Note Virith's remark that he might have duties for you later. He's the source of five relatively mild quests. Once you've finished this one, return to him when you have time or if the core Redoran quests seem a bit too tough.

Find Dalobar

You proved your mettle as an errand boy. Now, how about as an escort? Talk to Neminda about "Mathis Dalobar."

Dalobar is a trader who's gone missing. He passes through Ald'ruhn occasionally, but he's not here now and hasn't turned up in Maar Gan or Gnisis, his likely destinations. Go get him!

Your best bet is to visit those two communities and ask after him. The folks in Gnisis aren't much help; they say only that Dalobar is expected.

But in Maar Gan, you'll get a sense of what might have waylaid the trader: an ash storm. And while discussing that topic, a few villagers mention seeing someone near the Rothan Tomb.

MATHIS DALOBAR

The tomb is on the right side of the road as you head back toward Ald'ruhn. You'll find Dalobar near the entrance. Sure enough, he got stuck in the ash storm and when you click on "travel together," he'll agree to follow you back to Maar Gan. Dalobar should stop following you when you near the temple. If you like, have another chat with him before you say adios, and report back to Neminda in Ald'ruhn.

Founder's Helm

This quest is somewhat more complex. Neminda will tell you that Alvis Teri has stolen a Founder's Helm. The guy's not too subtle about it. He brags about the theft and even wears the helm at the Eight Plates in Balmora.

You've got to get the helm back without murdering Teri, as this would bring dishonor on the House.

Head for the Eight Plates cornerclub and talk to the thief.

He's not just unsubtle. He is rude. You're going to have to use force, subterfuge or persuasion to recover the helm.

There are two ways to go here. You can use persuasion or spells to make Teri like you. If you get his disposition high enough (75 or better), he'll just give you the helm. (But he's still rude.)

Also, you can taunt Teri into attacking you, kill him, and take the helm. This won't be that hard. Teri is predisposed to fight, and he'll want to kick your butt just because you belong to House Redoran.

But whoa there one second. Wouldn't killing him dishonor House Redoran?

No. The prohibition only extends to murder. This may seem like a semantic distinction, but you'll find it useful throughout Morrowind. You can kill Teri and maintain the Redoran honor as long as your victim strikes the first blow—which you, uh, lure him into striking.

Get the helm back to Neminda and we'll explore less morally ambiguous territory.

Guard Guar Herds

Like protecting animals. Nothing morally ambiguous about protecting animals.

If you've killed the mudcrabs and recovered the Founder's Helm, you're eligible for this quest.

Talk to Neminda about "trouble with bandits" to learn that Drulene Falen (from the Mudcrab Nest quest) is having problems again. Bandits have made off with some of her guar. Visit the shepherd's hut and have another chat. She'll tell you that the bandits can be found in a cave to the south.

Go south. You'll come upon two guar. The cave is nearby. Inside, kill the two bandits. You can head straight back to Neminda to complete the quest or drop in on Falen again to collect more of that yummy Hackle-lo leaf.

Note that, as in the Mudcrab Nest quest, you don't have to join House Redoran to perform this mission. You can just go through Falen directly.

Guard Sarethi

In this last quest and the Founder's Helm mission, you've proved yourself as a defender of property. Now, provided you've completed those quests, you'll be asked to defend a person.

Talk to Neminda about "Athyn Sarethi." This will become very familiar name in time.

As you may have already learned, House Redoran has some serious internal problems and Sarethi, an influential Redoran councilor, needs a bodyguard.

Visit Sarethi Manor in Ald'ruhn. You'll find the guards dead.

Uh-oh.

Don't worry; you're not too late. Sarethi still lives. But there has already been one assassination attempt, and Sarethi tells you more may follow.

And how. The moment you stop talking to Sarethi, two assassins appear. They'll attack Sarethi, but he's a hardy soul and likely to survive. Help him as much as you can and, once the assassins are dead, talk to him again.

Sounds like you've got a potential sponsor!

It's probably not the first you've heard about sponsors. Once you reach Rank 3 in House Redoran, Neminda and the other Redoran quest-givers in this section will tell you that you need a sponsor to advance further in House Redoran. They will usually suggest you talk to either Sarethi or a Redoran councilor.

Now you've done that. In the future, you can report directly to Sarethi.

But back to Neminda you go, one last time, to complete the quest.

THELDYN VIRITH'S QUESTS

Old Blue Fin

You can start getting quests from Virith, found at the Outpost in Ald Velothi, as soon as you finish Neminda's Courier quest.

OLD BLUE FIN

We said earlier on that these were mild quests, and they are. In this one, you're going after a fish. It's a slaughterfish called Old Blue Fin, and it's apparently been annoying the dreugh hunters around the Ald Velothi docks something awful. You've just to go whack it. Once it's fish food, report back to Virith.

Ashimanu Mine

You'll need to complete two more of Neminda's quests before Virith offers you another one. Once you've finished Founder's Helm, talk to Virith about the Ashimanu Mine.

Located along the Gnisis-Ald'ruhn trade route, the mine has been invaded by a diseased Shalk. It's been infecting miners and kwama and work has been abandoned. You've got to go in and kill it. No biggie. There's just the one, and it's not quite as tough as other shalk.

Once it's dead, head back to Virith for another job.

Kagouti

Once the Shalk is history, Virith gives you another assignment in that neighborhood—to take out the Kagouti who have been harassing merchants on the same road. However, note that Virith also mentions the Kagouti in his instructions for the Ashimanu Mine quest, so you may have already have taken care of the problem.

Shishi Report

Now, Virith is worried about some soldiers he sent to Shishi—a Velothi tower where the Telvanni have set up a base. He asks you to go see if they're okay and to get a report on the assault.

Again, this is pretty simple. At Shishi, all you have to do is talk to Brerama Selas to get the report and book it back to Virith.

However, you can play this one a bit more elaborately. While you're here, also talk to Temis Romavel to learn that the troops may not have killed all the Telvanni. He keeps hearing sounds from the room below.

But how to get down there? Activating the skull on the table in the room above opens a secret door that's located under the platform near Temis. Kill the Telvanni wizard Faves Andas within and return to Virith for a better reward than you would otherwise have received.

Cult Elimination

Your final assignment from Virith is an assassination, but he'll only give you this quest if you've earned the Rank of House Brother. Talk to him about "Ashalmawia" to learn Virith wants Daedra worshipper Gordol killed for unspecified crimes against the people of Ald Velothi. You'll find the shrine on a high rock just east of that town. Make the hit and report back to Virith.

AHTYN SARETHI

ATHYN SARETHI'S QUESTS

Rescue Sarethi

If you've reached Rank 4 in House Redoran, Athyn Sarethi will send you on this quest to rescue his son, Varvur. He's been accused of murder and is imprisoned in Venim Manor. If you get him back, Sarethi will serve as your sponsor in the House.

However, note that this faction quest is also part of Morrowind's Main Quest. If you've already performed this task in your attempt to be nominated Hortator by House Redoran, you'll skip over this step and move directly to the next quest—Clear Sarethi.

To rescue Varvur, head for Venim Manor in Ald'ruhn. Once inside, make a right and then go through the first door.

Varvur is being held in a room behind a tapestry along the right wall. (If you get confused, a note and a key are on a bench here. The note mentions Varvur's location and the key gets you through the door.) Just look behind the tapestry, open the door, talk to Varvur, and agree to have him follow you. Once you get him back to his Dad, he'll stop following you and you can talk to his father again to complete the quest.

There's one problem en route: the guards in Venim Manor. If they see Varvur, they'll attack.

It's not a big problem. You should be able to run the gantlet of guards and get out of the manor without Varvur taking too much damage. However, if you don't want to feel anything to chance, feel free to kill them or put them to sleep before you attempt the rescue.

Clear Sarethi

Now you just have to clear Varvur's name. It's the most elaborate Redoran quest you've faced to date.

Basically, you're playing detective.

Start by talking to the grateful Athyn Sarethi about "Bralen Carvaren" – the murdered man. He asks you to find out what actually happened.

Varvur says he's innocent—that Bralen was a good friend.

He also mentions he's been having bad dreams.

Talk to Athyn Sarethi again to learn that he thinks his son may have been under a spell. He asks you to search Varvur's room. Do so and collect an ash statue. Keep it in your inventory. Varvur now tells you the dreams began when he got the ash statue, and asks you to take it away.

Question Athyn Sarethi about the statue. He thinks it may have influenced his son, and asks you to take it to Lloros Sarano at the temple.

Go to the Ald'ruhn Temple, talk to Sarano about Carvaren and give him the statue. He will tell you to ask Varvur Sarethi to meet with him. Do so, and then talk to Athyn Sarethi again to receive his thanks.

Note that this story isn't finished. After you've cleared Varvur's name, Sarano will give you the first of four quests: To find out where Varvur got the ash statue. (Sarano's quests are listed separately farther along in this section.) You can jump directly to his Sixth House Base quest now, or save it for later.

Either way, Athyn Sarethi has a new job for you.

Honor Challenge

It's a short step from clearing one member of House Redoran to avenging slander on another. Talk to Sarethi about "slander" and learn that a certain Ondres Nerano has maligned a member of House Redoran. Sarethi wants you to defend the House's honor by challenging Nerano to a duel.

Visit Balmora and ask around town to find Nerano Manor. (You should really know your way around Balmora by this stage of the game, anyway.) Within, talk to Nerano about "slander" and accept his challenge of a duel. You win if Nerano is knocked out, his health drops below 50, or he dies.

Oh, it's OK to kill him—as long as a challenge was issued. (There's that Honor thing again.) Then report back to Sarethi to complete the quest.

Shurinbaal

Another quickie. Sarethi has heard of smugglers operating out of a seaside cave called Shurinbaal, and orders you to shut them down by killing the leaders. It's a small cave, as these things go, and easy to find smugglers Daroder and Enjine. Do the deed and return to Sarethi.

Mad Lord of Milk

Arethan Mandas, a Redoran noble, has gone bonkers. He's holed up in a cave called Milk, and demands tribute from travelers. (Milk money, I suppose.)

This doesn't have to be complicated. You can visit the cave, kill, evade, or sneak past his guards, and then kill Mandras himself.

But there's another way to deal with him. It's a much longer solution, but much more humane, and with a better reward at the end.

When he makes the assignment, Sarethi mentions that you might want to speak with Arethan's father, Llerar, in Ebonheart, Grand Council Chambers.

Llerar Mandas tells you that Arethan went mad after Divayth Fyr kidnapped Arethan's daughter (who is named Delyna), and thinks that his daughter's return might cure Arethan's madness.

ARETHAN MANDAS

So, once again, you're off to the Tower of Tel Fyr on an island in Zafirbel Bay. Make sure you bring a scroll of Open, as otherwise there's a lot of key-finding at the end of this quest.

You've probably already dealt with Fyr on the Main Quest. (He's the demanding and cantankerous wizard who semi-cured your Corprus disease.) And you can deal with him again on the current matter, though it's not required. (Wizards operate on a whole other plane, and he doesn't really care if the girl escapes.)

Delyna can be found behind a locked and trapped door. However, mercifully, Fyr scrimped on the lock and a scroll of open (a la Ondunsi's Unhinging), or picking the lock should open it without any problem.

Delyna will agree to accompany you back to the tower entrance. Once there, talk to her about her father. She will give you an amulet to take back to him with word she is safe.

OK, it's not the girl herself, but it's the next best thing. Go talk to Arethan Mandas and give him the locket. He will pick up some of his scattered marbles and promise to stop demanding tribute. Then return to Sarethi for a respectable reward—not to mention a boost to your reputation within the faction and improvements to the disposition of all Redoran councilors. This will come in handy in the next few quests and in your attempt to be named the Redoran Hortator.

LLOROS SARANO'S QUESTS

GALTIS GUVRON

Sixth House Base

A sequel to the Athyn Sarethi quest Clear Sarethi.

Sarano has an inquiring mind. He wonders where Varvur Sarethi got that ash statue, and asks you to go talk to him again and see what he remembers.

Varvur tells you he got it from Galtis Guvron at The Rat in the Pot Cornerclub in Ald'ruhn. Go talk to Guvron. He will attack you immediately when you bring up the statue.

Well, that isn't good. You didn't get anything out of him, and now he's dead. But you'll find on Guvron's corpse a note on him signed "Hanarai."

Sarano thinks it refers to Hanarai Assutlanipal, who has a house in Ald'ruhn. (You may figure this out yourself if you've explored the town. You don't have to go through Sarano to confirm it.)

Talk to Hanarai about the statue. Ack! She attacks you, too!

Think you're onto something? When she's dead, search her house. Pay special attention to the cellar. Some people have rumpus rooms. Some people have train sets or pool tables.. Hanarai Assutlanipal has a Sixth House shrine. Report back to Sarano.

Find Tharen

Sarano's other three missions involve finding various lost (or dead) people.

The first of these involves a pilgrim named Fedris Tharen. He was supposed to be heading to Koal Cave—a popular destination for pilgrims—but no one has seen him.

The best place to start is the beginning. But in Gnisis, you'll learn only that Tharen has already left for the cave and not returned.

Visit the cave. (It's south of Gnisis' silt strider port.) Tharen should be nearby, next to a tree along a path northeast of the cave entrance. He's sick and can't make it back to Gnisis, and asks that you report his location so he can be cured.

HANARAI ASSUTLANIPAL

However, the best solution is to cure him yourself with a spell or scroll. (In dialogue, Tharen will also accept store-bought cure disease potions—but not home-brewed ones.) You can also report back to Sarano, who says he'll send someone out there to cure Tharen, but you'll get a better reward if you take the DIY approach.

Find Giladren

Pilgrims seem to be disappearing right and left. One named Beden Giladren has vanished on the way to Maar Gan. Lloros wants you to visit that town and see if you can find him.

Folks in Maar Gan will steer you to Tralas Rendas at the shrine. Rendas mentions that Ashlanders recently visited town demanding a ransom for a noble with a similar-sounding name. He tells you how to find them.

Go to the Ashlander camp and talk to leader Manat Shimmabadas. Manat says Giladren is a famous noble and demands 5,000 gold in ransom.

You can simply pay the ransom. (Yeah, right.) You can kill the Ashlanders. Or, once you've gotten Giladren to admit that he's not really a famous noble, you can persuade their leader that Giladren is just a regular guy. (Giladren apparently thought the Ashlanders were going to kill him and made up a story that made him more valuable alive.) Shimmabadas then dramatically revises the ransom downward to…5 drakes.

BEDEN GILADREN

That's almost an insult.

Lost Banner

Finally, Sarano sends you west to discover the fate of four Redoran soldiers who went to the stronghold Andasreth and have not returned. He wants you to rescue them, or, if they are dead, bring back their House Redoran shields.

Regrettably, they are indeed dead. They've been deposited in a locked room on the west side of this enormous fortress' lower level. Find the guards, take their banner shields and deliver them to Sarano to complete the quest. You'll receive a shield of your own for your trouble.

Stronghold

And now, a message from your sponsor: By now, Athyn Sarethi should have told you that you need to get the support of more councilors and build a stronghold.

As in the other Houses, construction has three stages. The first is pretty simple. In House Redoran, you visit Galsa Gindu at her home in Ald'ruhn's Manor District (known as "under Skar"), pay her 5,000 gold to cover labor and materials, and provide her with a construction contract.

The contract will have to come from Duke Vedam Dren in Ebonheart. You'll find him in the Grand Council Chambers. Simply promise to protect Vvardenfell's people, and he'll lay a contract on you. Take the money and contract to Gindu and she'll begin construction.

A few days later, you'll find a new journal entry prompting you to talk with Gindu about the stronghold. She tells you where it is (east of the road between Ald'ruhn and Maar Gan) and asks that you speak with the foreman to make sure work is on schedule. At the site, you'll learn from Bugdul gro-Kharbush that the stronghold should be complete within a week.

Report back to Gindu. After a few days, you should get another journal entry reporting that the first stage of the stronghold is complete.

BAL ISRA STRONGHOLD

How about that? You've got a house.

But it's not exactly a stronghold yet. Gindu won't order further improvements unless the structure is well protected. She asks that you speak with Percsius Mercius at the Fighters Guild and hire some guards.

Mercius will hire some men out to you. But, naturally, he wants a favor first. You must rescue his friend, Frelene Acques, from the prison of the Hlaalu Compound in Vivec.

The prison can be reached through a door off the Hlaalu Treasury. First deal with the guard—who will otherwise attack when you try to release Acques—and have a little chat with the prisoner. She will agree to travel with you out of the area. Once you're clear of the Treasury, Frelene will thank you and tell you she can make her own way back. Or, you can steal the key to her cell—there's one on a desk nearby—and give her the key.

Return to Ald'ruhn and talk with Mercius again. He'll send men to your stronghold. Now you just need to talk to Gindu to get her to start on the second stage of construction. After a few days, a journal entry will tell you that the second stage is complete.

The third stage is somewhat more involved and you won't be able to build Stage 3 until you are a Councilor. This time, Gindu sends you to speak with Hetman Guls from your stronghold's small village. Apparently you need to attract more settlers—specifically marriage-able women settlers.

Just two wives will do, and several different approaches will work.

There are a couple of candidates in Ald'ruhn. Talk to Fathusa Girethi at the Ald Skar Inn. At first, she waffles between uncomprehending and unwilling, but if you can bump her Disposition up to 90, she'll bite.

Same deal with Aryni Orethi, who can be found outside her house in Ald'ruhn.

Alternatively, for 200 gold, you can buy two slaves through slave trader Savile Imayn in Tel Aruhn.

A more ethical route is to deal with abolitionist Galyn Arvel in Ald Velothi. She will agree to send escaped slaves to your stronghold.

Finally, you can visit Helviane Desele at Desele's House of Earthly Delights in Suran. Get her Disposition up to 70 or better, and she'll tell you some of her dancers are ready to retire, and that she'll suggest they retire to your stronghold.

Any one of these will do. Get back to Hetman Guls for his OK and to Gindu to get her to begin work on the last stage of the stronghold. After a few days, a journal entry will tell you that the third stage is complete.

REDORAN COUNCILOR QUESTS

Morvayn Manor

Once the stronghold is built, you need to earn the respect of the other councilors.

While you've been building your home, Mistress Brara Morvayn has lost her home and her husband. Located on the northeast side of Ald'ruhn next to the crabshell, Morvayn Manor has been overrun by Corprus monsters drawn by an ash statue like the one that got Varvur Sarethi into such trouble.

If you've completed the Mad Milk quest and reached Rank 6 within the House, Mistress Morvayn will send you to recover the statue.

The abandoned house is very dark and spooky and those Corprus Stalkers are everywhere. Lucky for you, you don't have to search too hard. It's in an upstairs room in plain sight. Take the statue to our old friend Lloros Sarano at the Ald'ruhn Temple for destruction, then return to Mistress Morvayn for a reward (an amulet).

Tax Collector

Councilor Hlaren Ramoran has the same requirements for this simple quest. You just have to go get the taxes from Hetman Abelmawia in Gnisis, off to the northwest.

Abelmawia can be found in his hut. Talk to him, and he'll give you 60 gold and return to Ramoran.

You can give the councilor the full 60 or just 50. Be honest. It's just 10 stinking gold pieces. Besides, if you short him, Ramoran won't give you his support, or the next quest, and you won't reach the House's highest rank. So there.

Old Flame

But if you're straight with Ramoran, he'll send you on a personal errand. He wants to find what's become of Nalvilie Saren—a girl he loved in his youth.

In the real world, this is usually a mistake. They're not who they were. You're not who you were. But hey, it's none of your business. The guy asked you, so just do it.

Ask around in Ald'ruhn. You'll eventually learn that Saren is in Vivec. In Vivec, you'll further learn that she has a shop in St. Olms Canton or that you can ask her family on top of the Redoran Canton. And, sooner or later, you'll find her store on the south side canal level of the St. Olms Canton.

NALVILIE SAREN

But Saren refuses to speak with Ramoran. Doesn't matter how persuasive you are. Doesn't matter if you don't shoplift while you're in her store. She's absolutely not interested. This is all you need to do. Report back to Ramoran and he's disappointed, but he'll still give you his support.

Maybe there's an alternative. Who knows a councilor better than the councilor's personal guard? Talk to Ramoran's bodyguards. One of them is Nalvyna Sarinith. The name's too similar to the councilor's beloved to be just a coincidence. On top of that, she acts a bit odd when you mention her boss.

Think she might have a thing for him?

Oh yeah. If you take up the topic "Nalvyna Sarinith" with Ramoran, you can convince him to live for today and not for the past. He decides he doesn't want you to find Saren after all, and gives you his support.

Caldera Corrupt

Councilor Garisa Llethri wants to shut down the Caldera Ebony Mines, but risks the House's good name if he tries to do so without evidence. He will send you off to get the goods on House Hlaalu's corrupt operations there.

The mine is southeast of the village of Caldera, which is halfway between Ald'ruhn and Balmora.
The slave Dahleena and Cunius Pelelius will tell you where to look for the evidence—if they like you. (Secunia, who helps run the mines, will need to like you a lot; you'll have to ratchet up his Disposition to a giggling-like-schoolgirl 90 before he'll spill the beans.)

Basically, there are two ledgers. One is a fake for public consumption. The other is hidden (but not that well hidden, it's upstairs in Odral Helvi's chest) and contains the evidence of corruption. Cart the true ledger back to Llethri.

Caldera Disrupt

Llethri sends you straight back to the mines—this time to shut the place down.

Talk to folks in Caldera to get a sense of your options. You can free Dahleena. Without her, the other slaves will not work as hard and may revolt. You can kill her with similar results. (But why kill her?) Or you can kill mine operators Secunia and Stlennius Vibato. This last option gives you a smaller reward. A slave key can be found at the top of the guard tower. Then pop back to Llethri, and finish things up.

Arobar Kidnap

Everybody else gave you a job. Everyone else lined up behind you.

But Redoran Councilor Miner Arobar is uncooperative. He refuses to support you on the council. In fact, he acts rather angry and doesn't talk with you much at all.

What's wrong with this fellow? Go back to Athyn Sarethi for some insight. He thinks House Telvanni is influencing Arobar. He asks you find out how, and to dispel the influence.

Head for the Telvanni town of Sadrith Mora—you can get there most easily by silt strider and boat—and talk to the people on the street. You'll eventually learn that Telvanni councilor Master Neloth is holding Arobar's daughter, Nartise, as a hostage in Tel Naga.

Kidnapping people's kids seems to be a regular way of doing business here. You need to pull off another rescue, and it won't be quite as easy as spiriting Delyna Mandas out of Tel Fyr. She is in the lower levels of Tel Naga on the right side as you enter the main door. Be careful, as she is well-guarded and the guards will attack as you try to escape with her.

Nartise will agree to travel with you to the Telvanni docks, and finds her own way home from there. Go see Sarethi and learn that Miner Arobar is no longer under Telvanni influence. And, if you like, you can revisit Arobar himself to collect to his thanks and a reward.

Archmaster

The only thing standing between you and the post of Archmaster of House Redoran is the objectionable person of councilor Bolvyn Venim.

You could just kill him, but you'd also kill your support from the other councilors, who would see you as a usurper.

However, if Venim were to die in a duel…

Yeah, that's the ticket.

If you've reached Rank 8, built a Stage 2 Stronghold, and earned the support of the other councilors, pay another visit to Athyn Sarethi. He says Venim will fight a duel with you. Go to Venim Manor in Ald'ruhn and issue your challenge. Venim agrees to meet you in the Vivec Arena. Defeat him, and you instantly reach Rank 9. (Note that this duel can also be handled as part of the Main Quest.)

Congratulations, Archmaster!

BOLVYN VENIM

And the Rest

Two other Redoran figures whom you may or may not have met in your travels have quests for you. Neither of them fit directly into your rise up the Redoran ladder—they're not connected to its main story—so we've dealt with them separately here. However, you'll probably want to play some these quests earlier in the Redoran sequence, when the experience they offer will prove more useful.

FARAL RETHERAN'S QUESTS

A short series of quests can be undertaken by talking to Faral Retheran at the Redoran Treasury, Redoran Waistworks in Vivec. The early quests don't have any special requirements beyond completion of their predecessor, but later quests can't be undertaken until you have finish the first phase of stronghold construction.

Hlaano Slanders

MERIL HLAANO

They talk a fair amount of smack in Morrowind, and those that do sometimes get a smack right back for their trouble.

For instance, Retheran has heard that Hlaano noble Meril Hlaano has been slandering House Redoran at the Eight Plates in Balmora. He wants you to convince him to knock it off.

The hardest part is the distance. Shorten it by traveling by silt strider to Balmora. Find the cornerclub, talk to Hlaano and use Persuasion to boost his Disposition to 75, and he'll withdraw his slanders. (Killing him works, too, but obtains no reward aside from the benefit to your reputation.)

Return to Retheran to complete this gig.

Redas Tomb

The last heir of the Redas family has died and, apparently trying to take it with him, has left the family treasures in the tomb. Retheran wants you to go to the Redas Ancestral Tomb south of Molag Mar and recover the Redas Chalice, the Redas War Axe, and the Redas Robe of Deeds.

The robe and chalice are straight ahead from the entrance. The axe is in the last room, and to reach it you'll have to hop in the pool with the slaughterfish and swim there.

You can deliver the items back to Retheran. But, then again, this is precious stuff and you may not want to give it up for a while!

Coward's Disgrace

A junior member of House Redoran, Rothis Nethan, has chickened out of a scheduled duel with Brethas Deras. You're to find Nethan and convince him to be a stand up guy and fight the duel.

Nethan is at the Flowers of Gold cornerclub (how appropriate) in the Redoran compound in Vivec. He pleads that he has no chance against Deras, who is a well-known fighter.

But he's willing to fight if the player brings him 10 standard potions of healing to level the playfield, and you get his disposition to 50.

Jeez, Nethan, how about if you just bring a gun, too?

You should be able to scrape together the potions by visiting a Vivec alchemist or two. As with other quests in Morrowind, homemade potions won't work. Or, at Rothis' suggestion, you can talk to Relms Gilvilo at the Redoran Temple in Vivec. He always has 10. (Has Nethan pulled this stunt before?)

Give the potions to Nethan. He asks you to be his "second" and meet him at the Arena in Vivec. Watch the duel and, at its conclusion, report back to Retheran.

Dagoth Tanis

A Dagoth! They do turn up occasionally outside the Main Quest. Retheran asks you to kill the ascended sleeper Dagoth Tanis, which holds court in a stronghold called Falasmaryon, located close to the Ghostfence to the northeast of Maar Gan. Tanis is in the lower level near the Sixth House altar.

A tough fight.

Attack Uvirith

Once you've established a stronghold, Retheran has another two tasks for you. The first: Go to the stronghold of Reynel Uvirith, a Telvanni wizard in Tel Uvirith, and kill him. This parallels a virtually identical Hlaalu quest, Destroy Uvirith. (Once you build your stronghold, comparable ones appear for the two other Great Houses. In other words, if you were a Telvanni, this would be your stronghold!)

Attack Rethan

The same deal—except this time you're after a Hlaalu lord named Raynasa Rethan who lives on the Odai Plateau southwest of Balmora along the Odai River.

Whatcha trying to do, start a war?

TUVESO BELETH

TUVESO BELETH'S QUESTS

This lady, whom you'll meet at the Redoran Manor in Ald'ruhn, offers two rather personal quests—looking after her son and bill collecting—that require somewhat advanced rank within the House.

Koal Cave

Here Beleth basically hires you as a babysitter. Everyone knows that babysitters have to be responsible, and you won't be sufficiently responsible to perform this quest unless you've reached Rank 3.

Tuveso's son, Deval, wants to make the pilgrimage to the Koal Cave. Beleth doesn't think her son should go alone, and asks you to escort him.

Talk to Deval (he's right next to his Mom) and he'll agree to travel with you to the cave. It's a long trip, but not a dangerous one. When you near the cave, Deval will stop following you, and you can report back to Beleth. (Deval says he will wait for another pilgrim and travel back to Ald'ruhn on his own).

This probably annoys the heck out of his Mom, and perhaps it's not just a coincidence that she doesn't have another quest for you until you hit Rank 5.

Bill Collect

This time out, Beleth wants you to collect debts owed by Giras Indaram for armor repair.

Sounds ordinary enough, right?

Not quite. Indaram is connected. Two of his brothers are among the best of the Buoyant Armigers—the Temple special-forces unit that (among other things) guards the Ghostgate. So you can't just drop by Molag Mar and hand him his head. There could be serious repercussions.

Perhaps Indaram knows this. Because even when you lay it on really thick, he still refuses to pay what he owes.

Ah, but you can find a back door into his wallet. Ask around Molag Mar to learn that Giras' older brothers have to bug him to get him to do anything.

Find and talk to his brother, Tidros. He'll tell you to tell Giras that Tidros said to pay the debt. This time, Giras agrees to pay, but you'll have to prove he owes the money in combat.

Accept the duel. As usual, it ends when Giras is dead, knocked out, or takes a fair amount of damage. Despite his heritage, Giras is something of a wimp, and it shouldn't be hard.

However, do not kill him. His brothers will attack you, and Beleth will not allow you to shovel her driveway.

When you win, talk to Giras and he'll give you the money and you can report back to Beleth.

A safer route for players prone to killing characters they're supposed to just defeat: Ignore all this and just pay the debt yourself. The reward is a poor return for your investment, but you'll avoid doing anything foolish in the heat of the moment.

What's next? Fix the furnace? Clean the gutters?

No. We were just kidding about shoveling her driveway. You're done with Beleth for good.

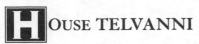

HOUSE TELVANNI

Traditionally isolationist, most House Telvanni wizard-lords pursue wisdom and mastery in solitude. But certain ambitious wizards-lords, their retainers, and clients have entered whole-heartly into the competition to control and exploit Vvardenfell's land and resources, building towers and bases all along the eastern coast. The Telvanni think that wisdom confers power, and power confers right.

Favored Skills

Mysticism	*Alteration*
Conjuration	*Destruction*
Illusion	*Enchant*

Advancement

Rank	Willpower	Intelligence	One Favored Skill at	Two Other Favored Skills at
Hireling	30	30	0	0
Retainer	30	30	10	0
Oathman	30	30	20	0
Lawman	30	30	30	5
Mouth	30	30	40	10
Spellwright	31	31	50	15
Wizard	32	32	60	20
Master	33	33	70	25
Magister	34	34	80	30
Archmagister	35	35	90	35

Faction Reaction

HATED ENEMY	ENEMY	HOSTILE	FRIENDLY	ALLY	BELOVED ALLY
Mages Guild		Imperial Cult Temple House Hlaalu House Redoran Ashlanders Clan Aundae Clan Berne Clan Quarra Imperial Legion			

The Telvanni make getting quests exceptionally easy. Of the six initial quest-givers—those that don't require the player to have first achieved a particular rank in the House—five are in the same room. These quests are all given by "Mouths" – spokespeople for the councilors who actually conduct the day-to-day business of Telvanni government while their patrons dabble in less tangible spheres.

RAVEN OMAYN'S QUESTS

Muck

Raven Omayn is the second from the left of the five "mouths" you see arrayed before you as you enter the Telvanni Council House in Sadrith Mora.

If you've already joined the House, Omayn will start you off with a simple ingredients hunt. She wants five portions of muck to make potions of Cure Disease.

You can buy this slime inexpensively at most alchemist shops—including Anis Seloth's shop in Sadrith Mora—or harvest it from muckspunge pools in the wilderness.

However, you're better off buying it, unless you fancy a really long walk. Even if you don't propose to buy the muck from Seloth, talk to her about it to learn that it grows in the Azura's Coast region to the south and in the West Gash region far to the west.

Deliver the goods to Omayn, and you'll get 100 gold for your trouble, as well as the opportunity to learn the Cure Disease spell.

Black Jinx

Omayn next asks you to obtain a ring called Black Jinx for Telvanni councilor Dratha. It's supposed to be in Sadrith Mora, and that's about all you get out of her.

If you simply ask around enough in town, you'll learn the ring is in the possession of a shadowy league of assassins called the Morag Tong.

There's a Morag Tong Guild in Sadrith Mora. The only person here who's even heard of the ring is Alven Salas, and he's the one who actually has it.

You can't steal the ring. Morrowind characters automatically equip their best items, and you can't steal an equipped item. You'll have to either kill Salas or knock him out. (This carries less of a criminal burden, but it's trickier.)

But there's killing and then there's killing. If you first get Salas' Disposition up to 60, you can challenge him to a duel, and thus avoid becoming a criminal.

ALVEN SALAS

Another interesting wrinkle: If you've been playing as a member of the Morag Tong and have already made Grandmaster, Salas will simply give the ring to you.

Return to Omayn to wrap up the quest. You'll now have a chance to learn the Demoralize spell.

ARARA UVULAS' QUESTS

Sload Soap

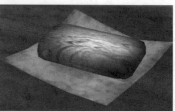

Arara Uvulas is the second Mouth from the right as you enter the Telvanni Council House. Provided you've joined the House, she'll give you the first of two relatively light quests.

It's similar to the errand you may have already received from Raven Omayn. Basically, you're going to the drug store for your Mom. Telvanni councilor Neloth needs five portions of Sload Soap for "research." Uvulas gives you gold and asks you to collect the soap at Anis Seloth's alchemist shop.

Unlike the muck you picked up for Omayn, you can't find Sload in the wild, so just get over to the alchemist's shop and deliver the soap to Uvulas. You'll learn it's a component for an ointment used by the elderly Neloth.

And Mom lets you keep the change.

The Morrowind Prophecies

Silver Dawn

Neloth now wants the Staff of the Silver Dawn. Uvulas understands that someone in the Mages Guild in Sadrith Mora has it, and asks you to get it.

Again, this is a simple retrieval errand. Visit Wolverine Hall and talk to the people in the Mages Guild. They'll direct you to Arielle Phiencel (on your left as you enter the Guild), who confirms she has the staff and is willing to sell. Buy it for 300 gold, return it to Uvulas and receive a Steel Jinkblade dagger.

FELISA ULESSEN'S QUESTS

Therana's Clothes

FELISA ULESSEN

Felisa Ulessen is the Mouth on the far left when you enter the Telvanni Council House. If you've joined the House, she'll start you off with what seems like a standard delivery: She has a new skirt for her patron, Mistress Therana, and asks you to bring it to her in Tel Branora, at the southern tip of the Azura's Coast region.

It's not a standard delivery.

Talk to Ulessen about "new clothes" and learn that Therana can be a difficult mistress. She gives you two scrolls of Almsivi Intervention—just in case.

You need them. An eccentric Level 44 mage is a very dangerous thing. You don't want to wind up as pile of smoking embers, and you'd be wise to plot out an escape route ahead of time.

Head south to Tel Branora. Therana's in her room in the Upper Tower. Make sure you have a Levitate scroll, or you won't be able to reach her. (Learn this spell itself as quickly as you can; it makes visits to these stair-less Telvanni towers much less frustrating.)

Everything should go OK until you talk to Therana about "new clothes." She's concerned that the Khajiit fur skirt you've delivered might be cursed and asks you to wear it.

Do so, and she attacks you.

Don't stick around to see how it ends. Make your escape (you can take the skirt with you) with one of the Almsivi Intervention scrolls (which zap you to the nearest Tribunal Temple) or by other means, such as a Recall spell. (If so, you should set it in motion before you enter the tower.)

Get back to Ulessen for a reward and the Mark and Recall spells.

There's a way around this attack. It's not especially kind, as it makes a victim of an innocent and especially vulnerable party. Near Therana you will see a Khajiit slave named Ra'Zahr. Talk to him about "new clothes" and have him wear the skirt. Therana will attack him instead.

Slave Rebellion

Another quest that tests your moral compass.

The slaves in the Abebaal Egg Mine have revolted. Ulessen asks you put down the rebellion.

You can handle this brutally or humanely. The brutal approach: go to the mine, which is northwest of Tel Branora, and kill the rebel leader, an Argonian named Eleedal-Lei. He's well inside the mine, but Abebaal is very linear in layout, so he's easy to find. If you take this route, you'll have to fight his followers as well.

Then report back to Ulessen and receive rings of Fire Storm and Toxic Cloud.

The humane approach: talk to Eleedal-Lei instead. He seems prepared to die, but offer to free him.

You'll have to find the key to his slave bracers. This key can be found in three places: on Therana's person, on a desk in the Lower Tower in Tel Branora, and in a container in the mine near the Kwama queen.

Once the rebel leader is free, head back to Ulessen to report the slaves missing and learn the Command spell.

BALADAS DEMNEVANNI'S QUESTS

Book Worm

Baladas Demnevanni is a fixture throughout the House Telvanni quests. Though he's the only early quest-giver who doesn't operate out of Sadrith Mora, you're guaranteed to come in contact with him sooner or later.

If you do it sooner, as we propose, it will make dealing with him later that much easier.

You'll find the sorcerer at his spartan home, Arvs-Drelen, on the northwest fringe of Gnisis. The first quest you'll perform for him is actually three separate sub-quests— each with its own impact on your Reputation and the Demnevanni's Disposition. He asks you to find the books "Nchunak's Fire And Faith," "Chronicles of Nchuleft," and "Antecedents of Dwemer Law."

This is easier than it may sound. While some of the books are rare, none of them are unique. And while you can retrieve some books from dangerous places deep under the earth, you don't have to kill yourself to get them.

BALADAS DEMNEVANNI

You don't even have to go that far. All three books can all be found in both the Holamayan monastery (reasonably close to Sadrith Mora as the cliff racer flies) and in the Tribunal Temple's secret library in Vivec. Granted, in each case, you'll pay for the convenience of finding the books together with inconveniences in actually getting them. Holamayan's entrance appears only at dawn and dusk. And stealing from the Temple means running afoul of its Ordinator guards. You can try to divert the guard by picking up something (e.g., a cup) on the other side of the room, paying the fine when he comes to arrest you, and then stealing the book that you want.

If you have the money, the simplest route involves going through two bookstores. You can find "Chronicles" and "Fire" at Dorisa Darvel: Bookseller in Balmora, and "Chronicles" and "Antecedents" at Jobasha's Rare Books in Vivec, Foreign Quarter Lower Waistworks.

Whichever way you go, get the books back to Demnevanni. You'll reap the reward later.

Dahrk Mezalf

The sorcerer never tells you expressly why he wanted the books. But as their delivery is the prerequisite for this next quest, we can only assume that he used them to locate Dahrk Mezalf. You must be Rank 4 (Mouth) or higher to get this quest.

Demnevanni tells you that Mezalf worked as a smith for the great dwarven inventor Kagrenac. He wants one of Mezalf's summoning rings, and believes it can be found in the ruined Dwemer village of Bthungthumz, near the Foyada Bani-Dad (an old lava flow ravine).

From Maar Gan, follow the Foyada north and west. When you see the ruins of Druscashti looming over the eastern edge of the ravine, bear east at your earliest opportunity and follow a trail of vast dead silt striders to the door of Bthungthumz.

It's quite small and you'll have no trouble finding Mezalf, but perhaps a good deal of trouble dispatching his restless spirit. You'll need a good enchanted or silver weapon, or good spells, to deal with the ghost.

Take the ring back to Demnevanni for an extraordinary reward.

Unless you've already killed the creature, he sends his Centurion guard to help you—a retainer who, if well maintained, can fight at your side for the rest the game.

MALLAM RYON'S QUESTS

Spy Baladas

MALLAM RYON

If you've joined House Telvanni, Mallam Ryon, the middle Mouth in the Telvanni Council House, offers you an unusual and somehow very wizardly quest from Archmagister Gothren.

You're to visit Demnevanni again and ask him three questions—about the Disappearance of the Dwarves, Dwemer Artifacts, and the Dwemer Language.

The answers you get depend on how much Demnevanni likes you. If he doesn't, they'll be at best bland and at worst deceptive or snotty.

And that's OK. (And it is strange that it's OK.) You don't have to get answers. You merely have to ask them.

Who can figure the ways of wizards?

Then again, if Demnevanni has a Disposition of 70, he'll tell you something significant on each topic. (If you've already performed the quests he offers, his Disposition should already be high enough that he regards you as a reclaimed son!)

Much of what he says is couched in elaborate language only slightly easier to translate than Dwemer itself. (It's like talking to a scientist who has forgotten he's talking to a non-scientist.) But you'll nevertheless get a general sense of his meaning.

On the Dwarves' Disappearance: they tried to reverse-engineer the laws of nature.

On their artifacts: the Dwarves combined the living and the mechanical in "Animunculi" guardians that sometimes are still active.

On their language: It's unknown. (Actually, you'll find a key to translate Dwemer in a Mages Guild quest.) Here, Demnevanni goes off on a tangent and observes that Dwemer books and other artifacts rarely show signs of age. He suspects the Dwarves created a preservative effect.

When you have asked the questions, report back to Ryon and collect Messenger scrolls as your reward.

Nchuleft Plans

Ryon reports that Gothren has learned the location of the Dwemer ruin Nchuleft. He asks you to recover any plans you can find there, and bring them back to him.

Nchuleft is a small ruin to the west of Vos. (Don't confuse it with Nchuleftingth, which you'll explore in a Mages Guild quest.) The loot is decent and the spider centurions guardians are few, though feisty. The plans (Dwemer Scarab Schematics) are on the bottom shelf of a bookcase in the first room to your left.

If Nchuleft proves too much for you, two other sets of the same plans can be found in the game—at the Dwemer Museum in Tel Vos' Central Tower and in Sorkvild the Raven's Tower in Dagon Fel.

Get the plans back to Ryon, and he'll reward you with an enchanted Cephalopod Helm.

GALOS MATHENDIS' QUESTS

Fyr Message

Galos Mathendis is the Mouth on the far right as you enter the Telvanni Council House. If you've joined the House, he'll first send you to deliver councilor Aryon's coded message to the wizard Divayth Fyr—an important figure in Morrowind who, like Demnevanni, turns up in various connections over the course of the game.

It's not far. Fyr lives in the tower Tel Fyr on an island in Zafirbel Bay. No boat is available, and you'll have to get there under your own steam.

Don't bother trying to read the message; it really is in code. Talk to the wizard, deliver the note, wait for his response (also in code), and bring it back to Mathendis for your reward.

GALOS METHENDIS

Wonder what's going on? All you know is that Fyr said "no."

Cure Blight

Tel Vos is having trouble with blight, and Andil, who runs the apothecary shop there, is running out of Cure Blight potions. Mathendis asks you to deliver three to him.

However, he doesn't give you the potions. You'll have to dig them up yourself.

This isn't hard. You can find two Cure Blight potions without even leaving the Council House. (Look around in the Entry and Chambers areas.) And Pierlette Rostorard: Apothecary in Sadrith Mora sells them, too.

The quickest way to get to Tel Vos is by boat. Simply turn over the potions to Andil and return to Mathendis.

Daedra Skin

Mathendis asks you to get some Daedra skin for Aryon.

You can go hunting for lesser Daedra, such as Scamps, but a lot of the random creatures in this eastern central region are keyed to the player's level and that makes it hard to predict what you'll find. You're best off treating this as another run to the drug store. Anis Seloth in Sadrith Mora has Daedra skin, too.

Once you have the ingredient, take it directly to Aryon in Tel Vos and pick up your reward. (Again, make sure you have a Levitate spell for this purpose.)

Patron

The timing for your visit to Aryon is perfect. By now, you've probably reached Rank 4 (Lawman) in House Telvanni. You will need a patron to advance further, and Aryon is the only councilor who will agree to sponsor you.

This isn't a quest. It's more of a transition. A lot of things will begin happening at this stage of the game.

For starters, Aryon is not just your patron. He is also a client, and from this point on will offer most of the quests that accompany your rise through House Telvanni's upper ranks to Archmagister.

Nor is he alone. Once you hit Rank 4, the other Powers that Be of House Telvanni start taking their former errand boy a bit more seriously and offer you substantial quests—presumably to see what you're made of for the coming vote for Archmagister. We'll deal with those quests and Aryon's quests shortly.

Finally, there's the little matter of your stronghold.

Stronghold

The stronghold is the place you'll hang your wizard's hat in Morrowind—where you're at home when you're at home.

Whichever House you choose, you'll have to build a stronghold, and, in broad strokes, the process is identical from House to House. Once you reach Rank 4, you'll always be nudged toward its construction by your patron and quest-givers as a necessary step to further advancement within your chosen House. You'll always need a contract from the Empire. An Orc will always be foreman on the project, and it will always have three phases.

The differences lie in the details.

Your first stop should be the Hermitage in the Telvanni Council House in Sadrith Mora. You'll want to talk to Llunela Hleran. She tells you need a construction contract from Duke Vedam Dren.

As in the other Houses, the contract is a no-brainer. Just go see the Duke at the Grand Council in Ebonheart. Promise to help his people, and he'll give you a contract. If you relish the role of Telvanni bad boy (or girl), you can slap him around and just take the contract.

Hleran will also give you two Grand Soul Gems for the foundation of your tower, and ask you to fill them with the souls of powerful Daedra. Storm Atronachs are good, but the more potent Winged Twilights and Golden Saints will do as well.

You don't have to go on a Daedra hunt. This is what Summoning spells and scrolls are for. Talk to the Mouths in the Telvanni Council House and they'll suggest you summon Storm Atronachs, cast Soul Trap on them, and kill them.

With the occupied soul gems and contract in your pocket, return to Hleran and she'll order construction of the first phase of your stronghold.

Let the clock run for a while. You'll eventually get a journal entry prompting you to talk to Hleran again. She gives you the stronghold's location—some rather bleak real-estate east of vampire lair Galom Daeus—and tells you to speak with site foreman, Gashnak gra-Mughol. Talk to him and then report back to Hleran.

In a few more days, you should get another journal entry stating that your stronghold is complete. Go check it out. You own a Telvanni tower.

To start the second phase of construction, see Hleran again. She'll ask for 5,000 gold (strongholds not being free) and a Dwemer Schematic from the Dwarven ruin Mzanchend northwest of your stronghold. The Schematic is in its innermost room. Bring Hleran the gold and Schematic and she will order up the next phase of your stronghold.

You may wonder why Hleran needed the Schematic. She was just thinking ahead. For the final stage of construction, Hleran says guards are needed for your stronghold. And to create the guards, she needs a unique book called "The Secrets of Dwemer Animunculi" – found only on a desk in the vampire lair Galom Daeus.

Lucky thing it's right nearby. Unlucky thing that it's a murderously difficult dungeon for anyone save a Berne clan vampire.

Return the book to Hleran, and she'll issue the necessary orders. When the stronghold is complete, go home to check out your new guards. Between the Schematics and "Secrets," Hleran has come up with Dwemer Centurions and Centurion Spheres!

(A side benefit: When you collected the "Secrets" book, you learned the Summon Centurion Sphere spell. It's the only way you can get it.)

THERANA'S QUEST

Auriel's Bow

If Therana was merely eccentric when you met her (in Felisa Ulessen's quest Therana's Clothes), she is now out of her freaking mind.

Once you've reached Rank 4, talk to Therana about "chores," "Auriel's Bow," and "Ash Yams." Therana wants an ebony bow that "smells faintly of Ash Yams." She doesn't explicitly send you anywhere to find it, but she says the smell of Ash Yams is strongest in Ghostgate near the person of Ralyn Othravel.

Humor her and visit Ghostgate.

Well, what do you know? There is a method of sorts to Therana's madness. Ralyn Othravel is in the Tower of Dawn, and he's carrying Auriel's Bow. To complete the quest, you will have to kill him (taunt him into a fight if you don't want to deal with the two Ordinators nearby), and then return the bow to Therana.

Now, we're uncertain of the wisdom of injuring other characters for a madwoman (or giving said madwoman a dangerous ranged weapon, for that matter). After her behavior the last time you brought her something, you could be forgiven for not wanting to deal with Therana at all.

So note that you don't have to perform this quest and that, having obtained the bow, nothing says you have to give it to Therana or even talk to her again. Nothing depends upon it except your reward. It's the only assignment you'll receive from the lady.

But let's just assume you decide to finish the mission. Therana threatens to fly off the handle again. If you refuse to give her the bow, she'll attack you. If you do give it to her, she asks whether you want to be paid.

If you refuse payment, she'll give you 11,111 gold anyway. If you agree to be paid, she'll give you Daedric cuirass and greaves—wonderful enchanted armor that, alas, is unsuitable for most wizards.

Once she receives the bow, Therana keeps it on her person, so, if you change your mind, you'll have to fight her for it…and she fights like a madwoman.

Dratha's Quest

Flesh Amulet

If you've reached Rank 4 in the House, you can get a single quest from councilor Dratha in Tel Mora's Upper Tower. She wants an Amulet of Flesh Made Whole. That it belongs to the captain of councilor Neloth's archers seems not to bother her at all. She sends you to Tel Naga in Sadrith Mora to get it.

The archers' captain isn't mentioned by name—you know only that he's a Bosmer—but this isn't much of an obstacle. Talk to the guards in Tel Naga. If they like you (which requires Dispositions of 60), some will reveal that Berengeval, found in the tower's General Quarters section, has the Amulet.

Find Berengeval, kill him, take the Amulet, and return it to Dratha for a reward—an Amulet of Spell Absorption. (Dratha loathes men and will also give a female character four Summon Golden Saint scrolls—a timely donation if you're still looking for something to plant in the two Grand Soul Gems for your stronghold.)

The implications of this quest are more practical than ethical. For starters, beating up on Berengeval is a crime, even among the ruthless Telvanni, and can get you kicked out of the House. (However, as long as you can pay off the guards, getting booted from House Telvanni is more of an inconvenience than a setback.)

And second, um, that's a really nice Amulet—a unique item and probably better than the reward Dratha offers for it—and you may just want to keep it. (However, if you go this route, don't return to Dratha, as this decision, once declared, takes a chip off her Disposition and adds it to her propensity to fight.)

The situation might be different if you had more quests coming from the councilor, but you don't. The only argument for turning over the Amulet is if you're a male character and you want to be on Dratha's good side (a Disposition of 80) in your Main Quest campaign to be named Telvanni Hortator. (Dratha supports you without conditions if you're female.)

NELOTH'S QUEST

Drake's Pride

Councilor Neloth isn't any better than his colleague. Indeed, he's worse, since his single quest requires you to beat up a servant. A servant, Neloth!

If you've reached Rank 4 in House Telvanni, he'll ask you to get him the Robe of Drake's Pride—currently in the possession of Senise Thindo, who works for Archmagister Gothren.

Simply visit Tel Aruhn (found west-northwest of Sadrith Mora) and talk to people there to be directed to Thindo. She's in the Tower Living Quarters. Kill her, take her robe, and return it to Neloth.

SENISE THINDO

As in Flesh Amulet, you may think twice about whether to turn over the Robe. If you need the resultant bumps up in Reputation and Disposition, fine. But the robe is another unique item, and the reward for liberating it is a pathetic 10 gold.

That is not a typo. Neloth is cheap.

ARYON'S QUESTS

Baladas Ally

Aryon wants an ally on the Telvanni Council. He has in mind Baladas Demnevanni. If you've reached Rank 4 in the House, and have engaged Aryon as your patron, meet with him in his chambers in Tel Vos, and Aryon will send you off to Gnisis to enlist the sorcerer.

Remember what we said about performing Demnevanni's quests sooner rather than later? If you followed that advice, and collected the three books he requested, you've virtually finished this mission. He will join the council "at least for the next century or two."

If not, he'll agree to join provided you get the books for him. See the "Book Worm" quests in Demnevanni's section for details and complete these three assignments. And, either way, once you've secured his agreement, return to Aryon.

Big things happen. You are promoted to Aryon's Mouth—and somehow excused from standing around with the other Mouths in the Telvanni Council House. (Aryon actually goes to the trouble of explaining this dispensation.) You also receive the traditional Silver Staff of Peace.

And the next time you stop in at the Council House, you may notice a subtle change. Former Aryon Mouth Galos Mathendis is gone. And Enar Releth, a new "Mouth" representing Demnevanni, has appeared.

It is a harbinger of bigger things to come.

Mine Cure

But those bigger things are still some ways off.

For now, you have a rather simple task: Cure the blighted kwama queen at the Mudan-Mul Eggmine, located west of your patron's tower.

You'd think you were a novice mage. Aryon practically draws you a diagram for this quest. He offers to teach you the Cure Blight spell. And if you decline, he'll direct you to Hetman Abelmawia in Gnisis for scrolls of Cure Blight.

Whichever approach you take, simply visit the mine, cast the spell to cure the kwama queen and report back to Aryon for a skill book on Alteration.

Wizard Spells

Now your patron wants you to learn some basic incantations: Levitate, Recall and Fire Storm.

You've probably learned some of these already. If so, great. Just talk to Aryon again, and you are done.

If not, the spells can be purchased easily from Feuyn Ralen in Vivec, Telvanni Mage and from Felara Andrethi in Tel Aruhn Living Quarters. Once you've learned them, talk to Aryon again and collect "The Art of War Magic" – a skillbook on the Destruction spell.

Odirniran

Odirniran's the Telvanni side of a House Hlaalu quest of the same name. You're to lift the Hlaalu siege at the home of necromancer Milyn Faram, east of Molag Mar in the Azura's Coast region.

On your way in, kill any Hlaalu you run across. Then go speak to Faram.

The necromancer doesn't seem to take the whole thing that seriously. He's more interested in his work.

But he does ask you to kill Remasa Othril, the leader of the Hlaalu expedition. If you've been thorough and killed her on your way in, he'll thank you. And if you don't kill Othril's sister, Vedelea, who is being held in the "tower" section, Faram will more than just thank you. He will turn over four Summon Daedroth scrolls, and Aryon gives you another skillbook upon your return.

Monopoly

You've scarcely wiped Hlaalu blood from your hands when Aryon sends you into a much more intimidating arena: politics.

The Armistice Treaty allows the Great Houses of Morrowind to offer potions, spells, and magic training only to their members. The Mages Guild has a monopoly on such services to those who aren't House members. (You may have seen in the Mages Guild quests how assiduously it defends its turf.)

Naturally, the mages of House Telvanni want that restriction lifted. There is some support in House Hlaalu for change, but Redoran councilors have resisted.

You're to persuade at least three Redoran councilors to come over to the Telvanni side. That would translate into a majority of the Grand Council, and Duke Dren would change the policy and break the monopoly.

Start with Athyn Sarethi. If you've been following the Main Quest, you know him to be a reasonable man. Even a reasonable man requires some persuasion, however. The Redoran and Telvanni don't get along, and Sarethi initially is cold to the idea.

But if you can get his Disposition up to 50, he'll help you break the monopoly and his support gains you an "appeal to fairness" topic that you can use on other Redoran councilors at a critical moment.

Sarethi also tells you who won't support the change—Archmaster Bolvyn Venim—and he's right. Venim will reject the idea out of hand.

However, Redoran councilors Miner Arobar, Brara Morvayn, Hlaren Ramoran, and Garisa Llethri are all amenable. Get the Dispositions of any two of them up to 40 and then use the "appeal to fairness" topic, and you've got their support. Three's all you need.

It's a good deal of work but you also get a great reward. Return to your patron to collect Aryon's Dominator—a left-handed glove that casts Command Humanoid and Command Creature.

Note that it's also possible to complete the quest, but lose the reward, by fighting instead of talking and exterminating too many Redoran councilors en route.

But even if there aren't enough Redoran councilors left for a quorum, you still get the next quest. And in this one, you're supposed to kill Redorans.

Shishi

Just as Odirniran was the Telvanni side of a Hlaalu quest, so Shishi is the Telvanni side of the Redoran quest Shishi Report.

And, like Odirniran, this is pretty much a commando raid. Redoran forces have attacked a Telvanni base at Shishi, located west-northwest of Holamayan. You're going in to save sorcerer Faves Andas.

Kill the three Redorans warriors on your way in. Brerama Selas, Anise Romoran, and Temis Romavel are all in Shishi's dome. (Note that a number of non-combatants are scattered through the base.)

But where's Andas? You've searched the place from top to bottom. Are you too late?

He's still around, but has taken refuge in a secret room. You just have to find the key.

In his briefing, Aryon said something about moving a skull or bones if you can't find the sorcerer. There's a skull on a table to the right of the door on the dome's upper level. Try to pick it up. You will hear stone grinding on stone. Go downstairs and you'll find a secret door in the floor.

Enter the secret room and talk to Andas, and he'll ask you to kill Redoran leader Selas if you haven't done so. If you have, he'll turn over the skillbooks "The Lunar Lorkhan" (Alteration) and "A Hypothetical Treachery" (Destruction).

Good work. Report back to Aryon, who will bestow on you the Silver Staff of War.

Gee, I hope the Redorans don't use this as an excuse to back out of that Monopoly thing!

Recruit Eddie

If you're going to be a Telvanni councilor, you need a Mouth to speak for you at the Telvanni Council House. Aryon wants you to recruit one.

It's not a matter of who you want as your Mouth—you're not free to pick—but who might agree to serve in the role.

FAVES ANDAS

You find out the same way you find out anything in Morrowind: you ask around. Start with Aryon. You more or less trust Aryon, right? He has heard of a promising candidate in Balmora. However, he doesn't know his name.

Thanks, Aryon. You're a big help.

It turns out, after you've filtered the collective wisdom of the Telvanni, that this candidate is one Edd Theman—aka "Fast Eddie," aka "Eddie the Rat."

"Eddie the Rat"? My protégé is nicknamed "Eddie the Rat"?

If he's still in the game, Caius Cosades, your first mentor on the Main Quest, will provide a succinct rundown on Theman. He's a former Telvanni wizard who has "gone Imperial" and joined the Mages Guild. Cosades says the would-be Mouth is "colorful but unreliable," but a great source of intelligence on doings within House Telvanni.

In other words, you could do better, but you could do worse.

Visit Balmora and drop in on Theman. He'll agree to serve as your Mouth. In return, you have to give him the Silver Staff of Peace you were given by Aryon at Rank 4. If you misplaced it (or <ahem> sold it), you can buy him a new one.

Once the quest is complete, Theman no longer appears at his house in Balmora and instead shows up in the Telvanni Council House. Aryon gives you another neat glove—the right-handed Aryon's helper, which can summon all three atronach Daedra (flame, frost, and storm).

It's going to get even more interesting before it's over.

Attack Rethan

Aryon sends you to kill Raynasa Rethan, master of the new Hlaalu stronghold Rethan Manor along the Odai River outside Balmora. That's it. When it's done, report back to Aryon.

This quest is effectively identical to a Redoran quest of the same name. After the player starts on a stronghold, new strongholds are also built for the two other Great Houses. Each House has two faction quests in which the player is sent to assassinate the masters of its rivals's new strongholds.

Attack Indarys

Ditto—except that this mission is identical to a Hlaalu quest of the same name, and you're after Banden Indarys, master of the new Redoran stronghold Indarys Manor, located east of the road between Ald'ruhn and Maar Gan.

Archmagister

Once you've completed the Kill Indarys quest, Aryon promotes you to Magister—the second highest Telvanni rank and a de facto challenge to current Archmagister Gothren.

To become the new Archmagister, you must secure the support of all the Telvanni councilors—minus any you may have murdered along the way. And if the other councilors won't support you, you can kill them as well.

It's the Telvanni way.

If you have already started your Main Quest campaign to be named Telvanni Hortator, the councilors' numbers may already be reduced. You have to kill Gothren in that campaign. He wouldn't vote for you there, and he won't here.

Indeed, you should refer to the Hortator campaign as the script for your campaign for Archmagister. They're identical. The other councilors will all sign on, though some require a little more work than others. (The bad-tempered Neloth needs a Disposition of 70, and, as mentioned, the man-phobic Dratha a Disposition of 80.)

When you're done, talk to Aryon again, and you're the new Archmagister.

FAST EDDIE'S CHORES

Eddie's Ring

Not "Fast Eddie's Quests?" This is a typo, right?

Nope. Fast Eddie doesn't give quests. He performs them. You've gotten too used to working for someone else.

In these two missions (which you can assign at any point after you complete the Recruit Eddie quest for Aryon), you're the boss.

Sort of. It's different from standard quest-giving in that, rather than you telling Theman what you want, Theman tells you what he can get for you.

Here, he proposes to liberate the Ring of Equity from its hiding place in councilor Neloth's treasury. Just talk to Theman about "chores" and "Ring of Equity" and bring him a Treasury key.

Lots of folks in Tel Naga have the key—including the guards and Neloth himself. Kill one of them (or knock them cold), take the key, deliver it to Theman and wait for a journal entry reporting that he has the ring. Meet him at the Council House and he'll surrender it.

Note his comment about the ring's usefulness in a battle with another wizard; it's designed to help you out in any battles in the quest to become Archmagister.

Eddie's Amulet

The Eddie's Amulet quest is unique in Morrowind. It's the only one not set on Vvardenfell. Theman has to go to the mainland to retrieve this enchanted item.

It's a dangerous quest for Theman—for you, it's just another delivery errand—and he needs five Standard Invisibility potions. You'll be able to obtain these at many alchemist shops, though you may have to go to two or three shops to collect all five. As usual, only store-bought standard potions work.

Once Theman has the potions, he'll vanish for five days. When he's back, you'll get a journal entry. When you talk to him again, you'll get the amulet.

You have become part of the game. You are not just a player. You are a quest-giver.

But does this mean Eddie the Rat could be the Nerevarine?

EDD THEMAN

FIGHTERS GUILD

The Fighters Guild is a professional organization chartered by the Emperor to regulate the hiring and training of mercenaries. Training, goods, and services are cheaper for members, and the Guild Stewards know where to find work. Look for chapters in Balmora, Ald'ruhn, Wolverine Hall in Sadrith Mora, and the Foreign Quarter in Vivec.

Favored Skills

Axe	Heavy Armor
Long Blade	Armorer
Blunt	Block
Weapon	

Advancement

Rank	Strength	Endurance	One Favored Skill at	Two Other Favored Skills at
Associate	30	30	0	0
Apprentice	30	30	10	0
Journeyman	30	30	20	0
Swordsman	30	30	30	5
Protector	30	30	40	10
Defender	31	31	50	15
Warder	32	32	60	20
Guardian	33	33	70	25
Champion	34	34	80	30
Master	35	35	90	35

Faction Reaction

HATED ENEMY	ENEMY	HOSTILE	FRIENDLY	ALLY	BELOVED ALLY
	Ashlanders	Temple	Mages Guild	Imperial Legion	
	Clan Aundae	Camonna Tong	Imperial Cult		
	Clan Berne		House Hlaalu		
	Clan Quarra		House Redoran		

Your tour as a member of Fighters Guild can begin under the tutelage of Eydis Fire-Eye, steward for the Balmora branch, or Lorbumol gro-Aglakh, the steward in Vivec. Both offer a series of low-level quests in which little more than the quest's objective is at stake.

This will gradually change, and you'll begin to see signs of something going on behind the scenes. Watch carefully. By the time you're done with the Fighters Guild, everything will have changed.

EYDIS FIRE-EYE'S QUESTS

Rat Hunt

Nothing like a little rat hunt to help you get comfortable in a new job. Not much chance of getting hurt. Decent pay. Short commute. Low stress.

Except for the rats.

EYDIS FIRE-EYE

At the Guild, talk to Fire-Eye about "cave rat." She'll tell you that Drarayne Thelas has a rodent problem at her home in Balmora.

Thelas' house fronts on the river on the east side of town; it's right at the central bridge.

It's a wonder the rats haven't already been suffocated by all the pillows in here. There's one rat in the bedroom and two more in the storage area upstairs. (Thelas provides a key.) Just kill them, talk to her again to collect your 100 gold and get back to Eydis to wrap things up.

If the rats kill you, well, maybe you should look into a different occupation!

You can do another job for Thelas in the Miscellaneous Quests (see By Region).

Egg Poachers

The rat hunt complete, Fire-Eye has more work for you. This time, talk to her about "egg poachers."

A couple of ex-miners are stealing kwama eggs from the Shulk Egg Mine, located southwest of Balmora near a swinging bridge across the Ouadi Ouadi. The mine's owner, Dram Bero, wants to make an example of them. That means killing them.

However, don't mistakenly kill the two innocent miners standing around a campfire outside the mine. These aren't the guys. Follow the winding path down to the down into the queen's lair, and there you'll find (and kill) Daynila Valas and Sevilo Othan.

Note that Bero has an "egg poachers" topic as well. Use it when you meet him, and you'll get a nice bump in his Disposition.

Telvanni Agents

The meddlesome House Telvanni is behind recent thefts and disappearances at the Caldera mine. Time for payback. Four Telvanni agents are hiding out in and around a cave called Ashanammu in the hills just north of the mine. You're going in to tear them four new ones.

You'll learn from Fire-Eye that the Telvanni agents are members of the Thieves Guild. If you are a member of the Thieves Guild, and you murder a member, you get expelled…but only if the crime is reported. And there are no guards in Ashanammu to report the crime. And YOU'RE not going to say anything, are you?

It's your first taste of the bad blood between the Fighters and the Thieves. It won't be the last.

Three of the agents are in the cave itself—three together, so you'll have to fight them together. The archer outside the entrance seems harmless enough, but he has to die, too. And you'll have to swim with the slaughterfish if you want the contents of the chest at the bottom of a deep watery ravine in the back of the cavern.

You'll come away with some excellent magical weapons—not to mention your gratuity from Fire-Eye.

Sottilde

This starts out sounding like a typical mission. A Guild client wants a code book currently held by Sottilde, who hangs out at the South Wall cornerclub in Balmora. You're to get it back.

But Sottilde won't even admit having it—unless you're a Thieves Guild member. If you are, she'll explain to you what's going on. The code book implicates the criminal syndicate Camonna Tong in the drug trade. When the Thieves break the code, they plan to take the book to the authorities and then assume the drug trade themselves. (Not that they're especially noble or anything; they're a comparatively new power in Vvardenfell, and they're engaged in a turf war with the Tong.)

"The Fighters Guild works for the Camonna Tong since Sjorling Hard-Heart took over," Sottilde tells you. "You have to decide where your loyalties lie."

Do you have any lingering doubts about who that "client" is?

There are a few ways to get the book. You can kill her and take it. You can boost her Disposition to the point where she'll just give it to you. And you can steal it. If you talk with Percius Mercius, another quest giver in the Ald'ruhn Fighters Guild, this will be his suggestion.

PERCIUS MERCIUS

Take the codebook back to Fire-Eye to finish the quest.

A word about Mercius: Now the steward of the Ald'ruhn branch, he used to be Guildmaster, but has been replaced by Sjorling Hard-Heart. He's a good man. Seek his opinion if you're ever of two minds on how to proceed. (And he's not there simply to critique Hard-Heart's decisions; when a quest is legitimate—like the upcoming Orc Bounty—he says so.)

Desele Debt

Helviane Desele, who runs the Desele's House of Earthly Delights cornerclub in Suran, owes money to Manos Othreleth of Dren Plantation. He's hired the Fighters Guild to get it back.

If you talk to Mercius, he'll tell you this may not be a legitimate contract, and you should pay the money yourself. If you're feeling rich after looting the Telvanni, return to Fire-Eye after talking to Mercius and pay the debt. (You'll get half back as your reward.) Otherwise, on to Suran to talk to Desele.

Orc Bounty

An Orc outlaw named Dura gra-Bol, who has a bounty on her head, apparently is living openly in Balmora. The Guild has been asked to "bring her to justice."

Once again, this means killing her. You'll find her upstairs in her home. When it's done, get back to Fire-Eye to complete the assignment and collect your reward.

Alof's Farm

Hey, did someone declare war on the orcs when we weren't looking? You'll need to advance to Protector status in the Guild before you can receive this next quest.

Now Fire-Eye's gotten a contract from Duke Vedam Dren to look into reports of Orcs meeting at a Daedric ruin near Alof the Easterner's farm. You're to meet with the farmer and sort out what needs to be done.

The farm is northeast of Pelagiad and just north of Arvel Plantation. Alof tells you the Orcs are coming from a Daedric shrine known as Ashunartes, and that they would disperse if the leader (Burub gra-Bamog) were out of the picture.

Visit the shrine, kill the leader, and get back to Fire-Eye to claim your reward. There are two entrances to the shrine.

The upper entrance is the one you want in order to take out Burub. However, the lower level does offer some temptation. There are some more orcs down there, and they can be considerably harder to dispatch. One of them, though, is wearing some sweet Orcish armor, so take him out and get that armor for yourself, if you can.

Verethi Gang

This time out, you're trying to put a gang of smugglers out of business. The Verethi Gang works out of a sinewy cave called Mannammu that's found southeast of Pelagiad.

Technically, you only need to kill the gang's leader, Dovres Verethi, but all the other members are between you and him, so you'll probably wind up cleaning a few additional clocks. Then it's back to Fire-Eye to complete the quest and collect your money.

Hunger Loose

The hits just keep coming. A creature known as a Hunger has gotten into the Sarano Ancestral Tomb, located southeast of Moonmoth Fort, and stolen a helm. You must kill it, while dealing with the usual crowd of spellcasting ghosts, return the helm, and report back to Fire-Eye one last time. Keep your eyes open in Sarano tomb. There's a nice dreugh shield hidden behind a rock near where you'll meet the Hunger.

LORBUMOL GRO-AGLAKH'S QUESTS

Debt Orc

Weren't we killing orcs a few missions back? Well, now you're working for one.

Your first mission out of the Vivec Guild finds you trying to recover something called a Juicedaw Feather Ring. Nar gro-Shagramph of Vivec apparently said he'd procure this item for the Guild's client. He hasn't delivered, and Lorbumol sends you to get it.

No sweat. Just bump Shagramph's Disposition up to 60, and he'll turn it over.

But any such Juicedaw ring will do, and if you happen to have picked up another in your travels, you can save yourself the trip.

Tongue-Toad

Hope you brought a toothbrush. You're facing a long trip—a jaunt all the way Ald'ruhn to silence an Argonian named Tongue-Toad. Which you can indeed do.

But when you find him at The Rat in the Pot cornerclub, Tongue-Toad seems genuinely mystified that anyone would want him dead.

This should give you pause. Explore the "kill me" topic for a couple of interesting remarks—one a reference to the Fighters Guild licking the boots of the Camonna Tong, the other a proposal that you allow Tongue-Toad to leave town. (If you consult with Percius Mercius in the Ald'ruhn branch, he'll concur.)

Khajiit Bounty

This quest is much closer to home. You're to kill Dro'Sakhar, a Khajiit outlaw said to be hiding somewhere in St. Olms in Vivec.

Ask around within the canton and you'll learn he lives in St. Olms Canal South-Two—reached through the middle door on the canton's south side.

Just find him, kill him, and get back to Lorbumol to collect the bounty.

Debt Stoine

DRO'SAKHAR

Lirielle Stoine apparently is deep in debt. You're heading to Ald'ruhn's The Rat in the Pot cornerclub to collect.

Again, remember that things sometimes aren't what they seem.

Sure, you could just kill Stoine and report back to Lorbumol to log the quest.

But if you inquire further, either with Stoine herself (provided she likes you enough) or with a good source on all things Ald'ruhn, like Mercius, you'll learn it isn't her debt to begin with. It's her brother's. And Ruran Stoine is already dead.

Mercius suggests you pay the debt yourself.

That's an easy option if you've got the loot. If not, you'll also learn Ruran Stoine died trying to make his fortune in Mallapi, a fairly extensive cave system northeast of Gnaar Mok. You have to wonder how much of his fortune he made before he died. If you explore Mallapi and find him, you'll find it was enough to cover the debt.

Return to Vivec to pay the bill yourself and complete the quest.

It's not quite as clear here as in Telvanni Agents, but this quest is another signal of a brewing war. Note that Lirielle Stoine is with the Thieves and her brother's debt is owed to the Camonna Tong—the Morrowind version of the Mob.

Silence Taxgirl

Another price on another head. Seek out Adraria Vandacia at the Census and Excise Office in Seyda Neen. (You know where this is; it's where you arrived in the game.) The whys and wherefores of this mission aren't spelled out. Someone just wants her dead.

This should make you think twice. Again, go see Percius Mercius at the Ald'ruhn guild. He'll recommend you disobey orders and refuse the contract. In which case, do nothing.

If you're a company man, you can still kill the woman. But watch yourself as you go about it, as there will be guards about.

If you choose to disobey Lorbumol's orders, be warned: He won't give you his Final quest. You'll still be able to get quests from the other questgivers, but you're finished as far as teh orc is concerned. Don't worry, though—you'll be seeing him again later.

Silence Magistrate

The Fighters Guild has become a brutal mistress, and once again, you're off to make a killing.

Apparently no one is safe on Vvardenfell. This time, the victim is a judge.

Something's going on here. Since when did the Guild start acting like criminals? It feels as though someone else is calling the shots.

Again, check with Persius Mercius in Ald'ruhn. And again, his advice is to refuse the contract.

If you're determined to proceed, you'll find Imperial Magistrate Rufinius Alleius at the Grand Council in in Ebonheart. Kill him, again being careful with the guards, and collect your bounty from Lorbumol for the last time.

HRUNDI'S QUESTS

Nchurdamz

Hrundi is the most advanced of the Fighters Guild quest-givers who will offer missions without the player first having reached a particular rank within the Guild. Mercius' former second-in-command, he's based at Wolverine Hall in Sadrith Mora, and the tasks he sets for you are less harsh (though more difficult) than those of his cohorts.

The first of these finds you escorting explorer Larienna Macrina through Nchurdamz, a Dwemer ruin southwest of Holamayan. It's not exactly an easy assignment, and if you haven't reached Level 5, Hrundi will let you know that you might need some more experience first.

But he'll still give you the quest. After all, it's your funeral.

You'll find Macrina just outside the dungeon door. Talk to her and select "explore together," and she'll lay out the story. She's after a Daedric monster called Hrelvesuu. They have fought before, and now the wounded creature has fled to its lair. Macrina basically wants you to watch her back while she goes in to finish it off.

That's actually a useful clue. This isn't some fragile merchant explorer but a resilient explorer—not only a creditable fighter, but healing you on demand—and you'll have to be pretty neglectful to get her killed.

Once Hrelvesuu is dead, get back to Hrundi to finish the quest.

Dissapla Mine

Nix-Hounds have gotten loose in the Dissalpa Mine and are attacking the miners. In this quest (which can be completed without joining the Guild), you'll visit the mine, meet with owner Novor Drethan and do whatever he requests.

The mine is in desolate and empty country northeast of the Dunmer stronghold Falensarano, which is itself west of Tel Aruhn.

When you arrive, hook up with Drethan a short distance inside the mine to learn that one problem has superceded another. The mine's healer, Teres Arothan, went off to look for an apparently lost miner. The lost miner turned up, but now Arothan himself is lost.

Drethan's not looking to have the mine totally cleared out—you just have to rescue the healer—but, naturally, Arothan is lost in the mine's innermost extremity, so you'll probably be fighting a lot.

This can be a rather alarming experience: The insectoid Nix-Hounds are big and scary when they come at you out of the dark. (In the mine's dark depths, use the torches that Drethan provides.)

However, mercifully, with a decent weapon, they're relatively easy to kill.

When you find Arothan, have him travel with you back toward the mine entrance. You can talk to Drethan before you leave, then zap back to Sadrith Mora to get credit for completing the task.

Corprus Stalker

A very traditional, Fighters Guild-type quest (which you should also be able to get without the Guild as middleman). Also, be sure to ask about a second quest before you head out.

A Corprus Stalker is trapped in a shop in Tel Mora. You're supposed to go over an invite it to tea.

Just kidding about the tea. We know it's 3 a.m., wherever you are, and just wanted to make sure you're still paying attention.

Before you leave Hrundi, make sure you also ask him about Rels Tenim. You'll see why in a moment.

The shop with the Corprus critter is Berwen: Trader. The thing is upstairs. It looks like it died two months ago. No way this guy is coming to tea until he takes a shower. Kick his butt. And, if you like, chat with Berwen herself and do a little business on your way out. The shop's open again, and it has some nice magical weaponry.

Now, back to Hrundi to wrap up the…No?

Tenim Bounty

No.

That is, you can return directly to Hrundi, but you don't have to. The Corprus Stalker quest and the Tenim Bounty quest that follows each require only that you've finished Dissapla Mine, and so can be played out as part the same journey—if, as suggested, you had the presence of mind to ask Hrundi about the second quest before you left Sadrith Mora.

Tenim Bounty is even set conveniently on your path back to that town. Rels Tenim is a murderer and Hrundi wants you to track him down.

He was last seen near the town of Vos. Talk to people there. You'll eventually draw a bead on Tenim's general location (a hideout somewhere to the north) and a contact that may be able to stick a pin in your map (the Ahemmusa tribe of the Ashlanders).

Make for the camp, located along the coast northwest of Tel Mora, and talk to the Ashlanders. They'll tell you Tenim is in Shallit.

Now, where in the hell is Shallit?

Good question: It's one of the more remote locations in the game. The hideaway—part waterlogged cavern, part classical ruin—lies beneath a sizeable island southwest of Ald Daedroth. (If you pass a great domed structure on your way from that city, you know you're on the right track; it's the next island to the southwest.)

Be warned: This is not an easy trip. It's probably too far to swim, unless you're really good at it, and flying will require not a few battles with Cliff Racers. By the time you get there, you'll want to kill Tenim just for putting you through this!

Now you can go back to Hrundi.

Dunirai Supply

With these last two quests completed, you're eligible to take on this delivery errand. You may be grateful for its comparative simplicity.

Workers at the Adas Mine are out of sujamma—a popular liquor. The Guild is responsible for supplying Imperial mines on Vvardenfell, and Hrundi has you running a fresh load of booze to Nelacar at the Dunirai Caverns.

Ordinary, right?

What's not so ordinary is the quest's route. If you've been exploring purely by quest, rather than by impulse, you've generally been staying in coastal regions, and it's conceivable this will be your first trip into Vvardenfell's vast, blighted interior. The caverns are southeast of Ghostgate, between the foyadas Esannudan and Ashur-Dan.

Think of it as a preview of what you're up against.

When you've had an eyeful, get back to Hrundi for a small reward to complete the quest.

Telasero

You're playing escort again—this time to a scholar, Sondaale of Shimmerene, who needs to study the stronghold Telasero.

It's located halfway between Suran and Molag Mar. If you haven't visited a stronghold before, it's a fearsome experience—the ashy wind out of the north blowing in your face, the terrain unforgiving, the architecture threatening.

And your client…missing.

She left a note on the door: "Looks safe. Went down to scout it."

For a scholar, she's not too bright. Telasero is a Dreamer motel, to say nothing of other resident creatures keyed to the player's current level.

Beat down the population as thoroughly as you can—Sondaale isn't a Macrina, and will die without your help—and then make a dash for the lower level, where you'll find the scholar <ahem> standing on a table.

Talk to her, select "travel together" and bring her back outside. Then get back to Sadrith Mora and Hrundi.

Note that, if you stumble upon this foolish lady in your travels, you can still get her out of Telasero—lack of Guild membership and technical ineligibility for the quest notwithstanding.

Engaer Bounty

A Guild client has put a price on the head of Engaer—a Bosmer mercenary working for Telvanni councilor Neloth. Proximity and necessity will make this a short mission. Your victim is close by—in Tel Naga, the tower in Sadrith Mora—and he's not alone. Do the deed and get out quickly. Hrundi will reward you well.

Find Pudai

Your final quest for Hrundi involves recovering seven Eggs of Gold that are supposed to be found in the Pudai Egg Mine. If you can return them, the Guild's Telvanni client will pay 10,000 gold.

You will earn it. This quest is difficult. No one knows just where the mine is located. No one. Hrundi says only that it's "on or near" the island of Sheogorad at the northern end of Vvardenfell. That covers a huge swathe of similar territory. In the absence of a recognizable landmark, you could search among these empty beaches, mushroom trees, calm waters, and silent towers of stone for days without finding it.

So here's a landmark: The mine lies west of the great Dwemer ruin at Mzuleft. (If you haven't explored this site, it's south of Dagon Fel.)

It's easiest to fly straight west from Mzuleft's frontdoor. But to reach the mine on foot, head south from Mzuleft and through a gap in the surrounding mountains. You'll find an east-west path. Follow it west to a "T" intersection. Go north. When the path forks northwest and northeast, go northwest. This path will wind west through a grove of those mushroom trees. When it leaves the grove, start looking north. You'll soon see a small door.

This is Pudai. It's a good sized mine. You should be able to find all the Eggs of Gold in the mine proper, but the Queen's Lair is worth checking out as well.

Make your way back to Sadrith Mora to see Hrundi one last time

PERCIUS MERCIUS' QUESTS

Vas

You may already have consulted with Percius Mercius of the Ald'ruhn Fighters Guild on some earlier Guild quests, and in the process may have noted his compassion and thoughtful good sense. He's the soul of the Guild, and if you've reached Rank 3 (Swordsman) in the Guild, you can now work for him directly.

Your first task is to help out a Buoyant Armiger named Ulyne Henim while she goes after a necromancer in Vas on a remote island west of Dagon Fel.

You'll find Henim near the Vas entrance. Talk to her and have her follow you.

She's a reasonably strong fighter, and should be able to account for herself pretty well. But do note Mercius' cautionary description: "young, inexperienced, ambitious, and noble."

There's a small dungeon and tower here The necromancer, Daris Adram, is the tower. Once he's dead, the mission's done and Henim should stop following you. Get back to Mercius to complete the quest.

Beneran Bounty

A straight bounty-hunting job. You're to track down and kill the outlaw Nerer Beneran, a former House Redoran member turned criminal. He's hiding with about a half-dozen other baddies in a fairly large, watery cave called Sargon southwest of Vas. You'll find some of his cohorts in pairs, and he's no slouch either, so be prepared for some fairly protracted fights. (Necromancers like to cavort with Dremora!)

When you've turned the ex-Redoran into an ex-criminal, get back to Ald'ruhn and Mercius to put the quest away.

Suran Bandits

A similar adventure. This time, you're off to the trading village of Suran to talk to the serjo, or mayor, about bandit raids.

DALDUR SARYS

Avon Oran (at Oran Manor) tells you they've been coming from the cavern Saturan, over the mountains to the northeast.

There are a ton of bandits in this large cave. You just to kill the leader, Daldur Sarys. (Apparently the other bandits do not have management aspirations.)

But wouldn't you know? Sarys is at the far end of the cave.

Once you've nailed the bandit, report your success to Oran, and then check in with Mercius for another task.

Elith-Pal Supply

Kind of makes you question your chosen profession when the Fighters Guild keeps making you deliver booze to the mines.

You did it once for Hrundi, and now you're doing it again for Mercius—this time carrying a load of flin to someone named Dangor at the Elith-Pal Mine.

And once again, this quest takes you deep into Vvardenfell's interior. (Elith-Pal is at the base of Red Mountain west of the Zainab Ashlanders' camp. The citizens of Tel Vos can give you directions to the camp.) Drop off the goods, and get back to Mercius to complete the task.

Kill Cronies

You've already gathered that something's been going on behind the scenes between the Fighters and Thieves Guilds.

Now, the curtain rises upon rebellion.

Mercius asks you to kill Vivec guild steward Lorbumol gro-Aglakh. And if you haven't performed the Thieves Guild quest Bitter Bribe, he'll also ask you to kill Balmora steward Eydis Fire-Eye. Both are supporters of Guildmaster Sjoring Hard-Heart.

You may have misgivings about killing characters who've grown familiar. But steel yourself, remember their brutality, and do it. It's better than the alternative. Report back to Mercius when you've finished the job.

Kill Hard-Heart

You've taken out Sjoring Hard-Heart's henchman or henchmen. Now Mercius sends you after the Guildmaster himself.

Talk to him about "Sjoring Hard-Heart" and learn this is the final step in freeing the Guild of corruption—that being the influence of the Camonna Tong.

It won't be easy. Hard-Heart is a powerful character well equipped in conventional weapons. Take Mercius up on the access he grants to his private rooms and take the two suits of armor within.

Then head for the Vivec guild, kill Sjoring, and return to Mercius for promotion to Guildmaster.

That said, you can follow a different, nastier path to the same destination.

SJORING HARD-HEART'S QUESTS

Kill Bosses

SJORING HARD-HEART

If you've hit Rank 7 (Guardian) in the Fighters Guild, and you haven't performed the Thieves Guild quest Kill Hard-Heart or the Fighters Guild quest Kill Hard-Heart, you're ready to take orders from the Guildmaster himself.

After you discover what he's about, you just might change your mind.

Sjoring Hard-Heart can be found in the Guild's Vivec quarters. He is clearly a man with something pressing on his mind.

Talk to him about "Thieves Guild bosses." In essence, he is proposing to commit vendetta against the Thieves Guild. He wants to wipe out its lower-level bosses, and you are his instrument. You are to kill Sugar-Lips Habasi at the South Wall cornerclub in Balmora, Big Helende at Dirty Muriel's in Sadrith Mora, and Aengoth at The Rat in the Pot in Ald'ruhn. He'll even give you gold to pay the inevitable fines.

"You and me are going places," he says.

Ask him about "allies," too. He'll identify them as the Camonna Tong (as you've already been told) and says that, if you can wipe out the Thieves Guild, this Morrowind Mafia will help the Fighters Guild through hard times ahead.

In any event, you can kill the Thieves under-bosses as instructed, and return and talk to Hard-Heart to complete the quest. He'll promote you to Champion, and name you his second in command.

But this course lacks a certain wisdom. If you're in the Thieves Guild, or plan to join, it just doesn't make sense to kill the people who would give you quests. (And if you're already playing as a thief, you know they're decent types who don't send you out to kill folks at every opportunity.)

Look before you leap.

Big Bosses

If you're already committed to this path, there's no reason to hold back the coup de grace: Once you've killed the little Thieves bosses, Hard-Heart sends you after Gentleman Jim Stacey. He tells you kill the Master Thief at Simine Fralinie's bookstore in Vivec.

Do it, and get back to the Fighters Guild and get back to Sjoring.

Somewhere along the way, you might want to steal from Percius Mercius' rooms the armor that he offers you freely in his Kill Hard-Heart quest.

What follows at the Vivec guild may play out in a couple of different ways, depending on how you handle the conversation, but it will end identically. Hard-Heart attacks you. Maybe he's crazy, and maybe he's just evil. Either he sees you as a threat because you're his second in command or because he's just learned you're the new Master Thief.

Once he's dead, you're also Guildmaster.

MAGES GUILD

The Mages Guild is a professional organization chartered by the Emperor to promote study of the arcane arts. Training, goods, and services are cheaper for members, and the Guild Stewards know where to find work. If you're thinking of making wizardry your profession, you should join and work your way up the ranks. Look for guild halls in Balmora, Ald'ruhn, Wolverine Hall in Sadrith Mora, and the Foreign Quarter in Vivec.

Favored Skills

Alchemy	*Alteration*
Mysticism	*Destruction*
Illusion	*Enchant*

Advancement

Rank	Intelligence	Willpower	One Favored Skill at	Two Other Favored Skills at
Associate	30	30	0	0
Apprentice	30	30	10	0
Journeyman	30	30	20	0
Evoker	30	30	30	5
Conjurer	30	30	40	10
Magician	31	31	50	15
Warlock	32	32	60	20
Wizard	33	33	70	25
Master Wizard	34	34	80	30
Arch-Mage	35	35	90	35

Faction Reaction

HATED ENEMY	ENEMY	HOSTILE	FRIENDLY	ALLY	BELOVED ALLY
House Telvanni	Temple	House Redoran	Imperial Cult		
	Ashlanders	House Hlaalu			
	Camonna Tong	Fighters Guild			
	Clan Aundae	Imperial Legion			
	Clan Berne	Thieves Guild			
	Clan Quarra				

EDWINNA ELBERT'S QUESTS

Chronicles of Nchuleft

Once you've joined the Mages Guild, Edwinna Elbert, found at Guild quarters in Ald'ruhn, will shepherd you through many of the early quests. (Ajira, an apprentice at the Balmora chapter, also offers a number of pre-K quests.)

Like most faction quests, Elbert's start simply. In the first, you just have to get her a book for her research.

It's a rare Dwarven tome called "Chronicles of Nchuleft" – a story of the bad blood leading up to the death of Lord Ihlendam.

Elbert doesn't know where to get one, but suggests that you check with booksellers. She will give you 250 gold to cover the purchase. (You can keep the change; that's your reward.)

Ah, but finding it. Booksellers will tell you they don't have a copy. But if you ask around enough, you'll eventually be directed to Jobasha's Rare Books in Vivec, Foreign Quarter Lower Waistworks. He does have a copy. Pick it up and bring it back to give Elbert to complete the quest.

(Note that this isn't the only copy of Chronicles in the game. But Jobasha's is the only place to which you'll be specifically directed.)

Potion

You know what it's like when an item you're expecting doesn't turn up. Well, Elbert's in that predicament now. Skink-in-Tree's-Shade in Sadrith Mora has promised her a Detect Creatures potion, but it's nowhere to be found. You're to talk to Skink and track it down.

You'll find him in Wolverine Hall. The easiest way to get there is through the Mages Guild teleport service. He tells you the potion is ready and turns it over. Just give it to Elbert, and you've wrapped up the quest—and netted a couple of potions to boot. Easy as pie.

Note that, once you've completed this quest, Skink will offer you a number of quests of his own. You'll find them listed farther along in this section.

Steal Book

God save us from mages who want books. Elbert's after another one, and this time she's so desperate that she's willing to have you steal it. (She calls it "borrowing.")

The text, "Chimarvamidium," is part of an "Ancient Tales of the Dwemer" collection, and apparently deals with a golem or centurion of some kind. (Shades of Daggerfall.) Sirilonwe over at the Mages Guild in Vivec seems to have a copy.

SIRILONWE

The book is in a chest in a closet in the Vivec guild. Elbert provides an opening scroll that should help. Just find it, get out of there and give the book to Elbert. If you shut the door again after you enter the closet, you'll almost certainly escape detection.

Along the way, do not speak to the book's rightful owner with "Chimarvamidium" in your inventory. She'll accuse you of stealing it and give you an opportunity to return it. If you don't, prepare to face the consequences. Yelling "Edwinna Elbert made me do it!" is not an option. If you read the book prior to returning it, it will raise your Heavy Armor skill.

The funny part is that the book turns out to be of absolutely no use to Elbert.

Apprentice

A real Sorcerer's Apprentice situation is unfolding at Huleen's Hut southeast of Maar Gan. Huleen's assistant, Listien Bierles, summoned a scamp—essentially, a Daedric imp—to impress his employer and then lost control of it. If he ever had control of it. The Scamp trashed the place and stole the apprentice's clothes and the poor fellow's locked himself in the closet. You can get to Maar Gan via silt strider from Ald'ruhn.

Your job is pretty straight-forward: Kill the scamp and rescue the apprentice from the closet. The door's locked, but there's a key in the scamp and another key on the floor near the door itself. Get back to Elbert to complete the quest and get your reward.

Return Book

That useless book you "borrowed" for Elbert? Sigh. Now she wants to give it back.

Mages really are a pain in the butt.

You have two options here: Put "Chimarvamidium" back in the chest where you found it without getting caught, or forthrightly talk to its rightful owner, Sirilonwe, and just give her the book. Head back to Elbert to finish the quest and pick up a couple of protective amulets as your reward.

Elbert apparently plans to send you into dangerous terrain.

Weird Science

No sooner said than done. If you've reached Rank 4 (Conjurer) in the Guild, Elbert sends you off to the Dwarven ruins at Arkngthunch-Sturdumz in search of an artifact known as a Dwemer Tube. If you aren't yet a Conjurer, you will need to visit another quest giver first. Skink, mentioned earlier in the Potion quest, might be a good choice.
The site is northwest of Gnisis, but it's easier to get there by first heading west from Ald Velothi to the coast. There's not a lot of loot in this modest-sized dungeon, so focus on getting the Tube, getting out, and bringing Elbert her new toy.

Excavation

Now you're off to another ruin—this time to check with Elbert's colleague Senilias Cadiusus to see what's holding up his monthly report on his research at Nchuleftingth.

Elbert will offer two potential routes. You can go around the mountains near Suran and head northeast along the Foyada Nadanat. Or, from Molag Mar, you can head northwest toward Mount Kand, detour north around it, and follow the north side of the Foyada.

You'll find Cadiusus in the upper level of the ruin. Chat with him—first on "excavation report" and then "Anes Vendu."

It turns out that Vendu, the dig's native guide, has disappeared into the ruins lower levels—taking the report with him

Go find him. You'll eventually wind up in a "Test of Pattern" room (mentioned by Cadiusus' daughter, Pania) with three cranks along its left side.

The right-most two cranks are similar. Don't touch them. (They shoot out steam, which injures you.) The one furthest from the entrance is different, and it opens a secret door leading to, alas, the corpse of the unfortunate Vendu. Get the report (which is on Vendu's body) as well as the nearby book, "Hanging Gardens of Wasten Coridale." Check in with Cadiusus and Daughter—Cadiusus is excited about the book—and get back to Elbert.

Elbert also thinks that book you found would be priceless in the right hands. It's written both in Dwemer and Aldmeris and it figures that, if you could find someone who could translate the latter, you could decipher the Dwemer text as well.

The excavation report mentions another Dwemer ruin—foreshadowing your next quest.

Mzuleft

This large and dangerous ruin, south of Dagon Fel, contains blueprints of a Dwemer scarab sought by Elbert. You have to swim in (or fly above) portions of the Sea of Ghosts to get there. A more roundabout way is to buy teleportation in a Mage's Guild to Sadrith Mora, buy passage on a ship to Dagon Fel, which is just north of Mzuleft.

This place is lousy with Orcs! Find the plans—apparently for a large metal insect—and another book called "The Egg of Time." Then get out and reconnect with Elbert.

On your return, she'll mention additional blueprints at another ruin called…

Bethamez

The story goes that the Gnisis eggmine was closed due to the blight, but Elbert has heard rumors that miners broke into the lost Dwemer ruin of Bethamez, and that it contains plans similar to those recovered in Mzuleft.

If you're a Rank 8 Mage, Elbert will dispatch you to retrieve them. The entrance can be found in the lower region of the Gnisis Eggmine. It's not an especially large ruin, as these things go, and its unplundered status means you'll find a number of Dwemer artifacts—including the airship plans Elbert wants.

But this doesn't mean it's not dangerous.

You'll also find another book: "Divine Metaphysics Adapted to the Meanest of Intellects." (Sort of a "Dwemer for Dummies.")

You're done with Elbert—at least for now. But you now have the equipment to perform a key quest for Guildmaster Trebonius Artorius.

AJIRA'S QUESTS

Mushrooms!

The early quests from Ajira, whom you'll meet in the Mages Guild in Balmora, are simple and child-like. The first is the definition of innocence. You're going out into the countryside to pick mushrooms.

Ajira apparently is working on a report on the mushrooms of Vvardenfell's Bitter Coast region and needs samples of four varieties: Luminous Russula, Violet Coprinus, Bungler's Bane, and Hypha Facia. Some will be easier to find than others.

Why do I have the feeling I'm doing my daughter's science project?

The best place to find the mushrooms is the swampy terrain near Balmora. Follow the west bank of the Odai River to the south until you come to a bridge. Then start looking for a path over the hills to the west. It leads straight into the swamps.

Happy pickings. Just watch out for wild critters in the area. With samples in hand, return to Ajira to finish the quest.

Sabotage

One moment, Ajira's doing something sweet and child-like. The next, she's sabotaging another apprentice's project.

Or, rather, she's asking you to sabotage it.

Ajira has made a bet with fellow apprentice Galbedir that she'll make the Journeyman rank before Galbedir does. To guarantee her victory, while Galbedir is away doing research, Ajira has you plant a fake soul gem in Galbedir's desk to make her rival's Journeyman project fail. Her desk can be found on the top floor of Balmora's Guild of Mages.

Simple as that. Report your success, and get the next mission.

Flowers!

Sweet Ajira, evil Ajira, and now sweet Ajira again.

This time she's doing a report on flowers, and sends you off to the shores of Lake Amaya to collect four more ingredients: Gold Kanet, Stoneflower Petals, Willow Anther, and Heather.

The lake is east and south of Balmora. Head south out of town, then east toward the Moonmoth Fort and cross the Foyada Mamaea. Then hook up with the road to Suran, which passes the lake.

When you've got the ingredients, cart them back to Ajira to wrap up the quest…and wait to see whether Jekyll or Hyde turns up next.

Bowl

It's Jekyll. Ajira wants a ceramic bowl from trader Ra'Virr in the working-class section of Balmora. She gives you 10 drakes to buy it. Do so, return, and give it to Ajira. (Note: You may not get this quest if you leave the Mages Guild without talking to Ajira again after completing Flowers.)

Stolen Report

Galbedir, doubtless taking revenge for her spoiled Journeyman project, has stolen Ajira's reports on mushrooms and flowers and hidden them in the Mages Guild. Can't say as I blame her. You just have to find them and return them to Ajira.

They're not that hard to find, and you can search for them on your own. However, if you bump her Disposition up to 70, Galbedir will confess and give you the locations: one under a dresser in the bedrooms and the other among sacks of ingredients. Return the reports to Ajira, and you're good.

Staff of Magnus

After you recover the missing reports, Ajira won't have anything for you for quite a while. But once you've reached the higher ranks of the Guild, return to her for two more quests. (They're actually more in the nature of tips to the location of advanced magic items.)

When you hit Rank 6, go see Ajira for the location of the Staff of Magnus. It's in Assu—a forbidding cave on Mount Kand, which itself lies straight north from Suran.

You'll also find a lot of other loot here—not to mention some tough adversaries. These include the Staff's current owner—a Level 20 Sorceress named Dreveni Hlaren.

Warlock's Ring

Finally, when you hit Rank 8, visit Ajira one last time and she'll put you onto the location of the Warlock's Ring. It's in the possession of sorceress Vindamea Drethan. You'll find her in Ashirbadon, a large and rich dungeon on an island east of the Bal Fell ruins.

SKINK'S QUESTS

Escort Scholar

Once you've completed the Potion quest for Elbert, Skink will offer you assignments as well. You'll find him in Sadrith Mora's Wolverine Hall.

Your first assignment is to accompany a scholar named Tenyeminwe to the ship Elf-Skerring at the Telvanni docks. Evidently, she was involved in some sort of dust-up with a local Telvanni, and now is scared to travel without escort. But Skink's not expecting trouble. She can be found in Dirty Muriel's Cornerclub.

Outside the Hall, talk to the lady about "travel together" and she'll follow you to the docks. Get back to Skink to finish the quest.

SKINK

Vampires of Vvardenfell

As Elbert, so Skink. Mages like books.

Skink is after Volume 2 of "Vampires of Vvardenfell." The Temple has banned it, and it's hard to find.

Skink points you to booksellers and the Temple. Booksellers and Morrowind cognescenti will be more specific and point you to Jobasha's Rare Books or the library in Vivec.

Talk to Jobasha. He does have the book—Jobasha has pretty much everything—but at the steep price of 400 gold.

Another option is to visit the Hall of Justice's secret library in Vivec and steal a copy.

Of course, the guards will pounce on you, so you'd do well to create a diversion first. Steal an insignificant book as far away as possible from the vampires book. Wait for the guards, pay your fine… and then run like crazy, grab the vampires book, and get out before the waylaid guards show up.

Yet another possibility is checking in vampire lairs like Galom Daeus. (Vampires apparently like to read about themselves.)

In any case, once you have the book, turn it over to Skink to wrap up the quest.

Wise Woman

For unstated reasons, your contact wants you to arrange a meeting with an Ashlander wise woman.

But here's the thing: None of the Ashlander wise women want to meet with him. If you like, make the rounds of the Ashlander camps and ask them. They're apparently all washing their hair the rest of their lives.

Skink must be code for "stink." The Ashlanders have no love for foreigners. Skink tells you that your best bet is with the Ahemmusa tribe. They can be found by taking a boat to Tel Vos and heading north along the coast.

To add insult to injury, when you meet with Sinnammu Mirpal, the wise woman for the Ahemmusa tribe, she says she might consider sending her apprentice—and then only to give the girl some useful experience in the errors of foreign ways.

Even the apprentice, Minabibi Assardarainat, isn't immediately available. She is off at the Favel Ancestral Tomb west of the Ahemmusa camp, exorcising a spirit.

Seek out the girl. She says she is too weak to put the ghost of Kanit Ashurnisammis to rest and asks you to do it. Do it. Smack that ghost. Talk to the apprentice again, and then to Mirpal, who agrees to send Assardarainat to the meeting.

The apprentice must be wearing her good sneakers, because she beats you back to the Mages Guild. She'll give you an ancestor's ring for your assistance, and you can check in with Skink to end the quest.

Kill Necromancer

A straight assassination. Skink wants you to kill necromancer Telura Ulver, who lives in Shal.

Shal?

It's a long way from Sadrith Mora, and you'll probably need help to find it.

Find your way to Hla Oad, on the far side of the Vvardenfell. Head north, cross a bridge and follow the coast until you reach a second bridge leading to an island. On the north side of this island, you will find the entrance to Shal in a pool of muck.

TELURA ULVER

When the deed is done, return to Skink.

Soul Gem

If you've reached Rank 7 in the Guild (Wizard), Skink will send you to obtain the soul of an Ash Ghoul.

Any Ash Ghoul will do, but Skink says the closest is in Yakin, an extensive cave system and shrine northwest of Tel Aruhn. He provides two scrolls of soul trap to capture the ghoul (Dagoth Velos), and a soul gem to serve as the vessel. Return the gem to Skink in Sadrith Mora to complete the quest.

Vampire Cure

Skink apparently has been delving into that Vampires of Vvardenfell book you brought him some time ago, and now wants a related manuscript called "Galur Rithari's Papers" – an account of how its author was cured of vampirism.

Check with book vendors and scholarly types for clues. Copies can be found in the Hall of Justice's secret library, Galom Daeus and, if you're especially daring, in Kagrenac's Library in Tureynulal. (Be prepared to make an evening of it; that library holds 70-plus books.)

Return any of these to Skink and receive his amulet.

RANIS ATHRYS' QUESTS

Join Us

When you reach Rank 2 (Journeyman), you'll be eligible to perform this recruitment quest for Ranis Athrys at the Mages Guild in Balmora.

Athrys wants you to persuade Llarar Bereloth, a former Telvanni sorcerer, to join the Mages Guild.

And if he won't join, she wants you to kill him.

Athrys is sort of nasty that way. But you'll find, as you work through her quests, that there are ways around her most brutal solutions, and so there is here.

RANIS ATHRYS

Sulipund's a very nice dome-shaped private house out in the countryside. To reach it, head east from Balmora and pass Fort Moonmoth. Cross a bridge to Molag Amur and continue east to Lake Amaya. (You should see the stronghold Marandus to the south.) Head north up a path between the hills. Before the fork, you'll reach Sulipund.

As usual, it's just a matter of boosting Bereloth's disposition to the necessary level (70, in this case). Bereloth will eventually agree to join the guild the next time he's in Balmora just to get you off his back.

Or if persuasion isn't your strong suit, kill him.

You can return to Athrys at this point to complete the quest. Or, while you're in the neighborhood, you can combine this quest with the next, Pay Dues, and jog west down the road to Punabi.

Pay Dues

In Punabi, you'll find a mage named Manwe who's doing some research. She is behind on her Guild dues. Two thousand gold behind, to be exact.

She doesn't seem to give a hoot, saying she's no longer a member.

Again, making her see the light is just a matter of ratcheting up her Disposition to 60. (This way, you'll get half the take.)

But, as with Bereloth, Athrys has authorized you to <let me guess> kill her if she doesn't pay.

Athrys just doesn't understand the word "no."

You can take pity on her and pay the dues yourself.

In any case, get back to Athrys to wrap up one or both quests.

Stop Competition

Unauthorized magical training makes the Mages Guild go crazy. The current source of its anxiety is an Argonian with the bewildering name of Only-He-Stands-There, who is offering unsanctioned training in Restoration at the South Wall cornerclub in Balmora.

You've got a few options.

Working on his Disposition works. (You'll have to get it up to 60.)

Killing him works. But it would be a shame to kill someone so well-meaning, and who speaks so eloquently to the needs and limited means of his clients.

And then, of course, you could have the Argonian train you in restoration. In return, you'd lie to Athrys that he's agreed to stop. Sounds like a plan!

Just Get His Notes

It's pretty hard to screw up an escort quest when it doesn't matter if your companion survives.

You're asked to accompany Itermerel, a newcomer to Balmora, on his trip from the Eight Plates to the Halfway Inn in Pelagiad.

But Athrys tells you flatly that she doesn't care if he makes it there or not. She just wants his notes.

Resist the temptation to give Athrys an emergency appendectomy. You can kill Itermerel, or allow him to be killed. But if you manage to get him to his destination intact, you'll get the notes as well as a reward.

Deliver the notes to Athrys to complete the quest.

Is She or Isn't She?

There are many things that do not sit well with the Dunmer, and necromancy—raising the dead for fun and profit—is one of them.

Small surprise that, for the second time as a Mages Guild member, you're sent out to whack a necromancer.

This one has the decidedly un-necromantic name of Tashpi Ashibael. She sounds about 13, she probably wears fuzzy pink sweaters, and she lives in a hut in Maar Gan. And, on Athrys' command, you can simply go there and kill her and report back.

That'll work.

TASHPI ASHIBAEL

But, by now, you may have started to question your quest-giver's wisdom and sense of fairness. And you may want to look into this accusation further before you act upon it.

In fact, if you walk around Maar Gan and talk to people, you'll hear that Ashibael is not a necromancer. Nothing like it. She's a healer. The woman herself, astonished, reports that she refused to join the Mages Guild and is surprised that Athrys has carried the grudge so long.

Let Ashibael go into hiding, and tell Athrys you've made the hit.

Spy Catch

Your final quest for Ranis Athrys is a complex and challenging one. You have to root out a Telvanni spy within the Mages Guild.

You're to question Guild members in Balmora, Ald'ruhn, Sadrith Mora, and Vivec. When you find the spy, you're not to take independent action, but report back to Athrys.

Along the way, you'll hear a lot of different things. That there are no spies. That a member of Guild's Ald'ruhn branch belongs to the Dark Brotherhood. (And you're right to be suspicious of Movis Darys, but he's not the one.) That the spy is in Sadrith Mora. And so on.

Your search will eventually take you to Vivec and here you'll begin to hear about a certain Tiram Gadar—an advisor to Arch-Mage Trebonius Artorius who came highly recommended.

It would be great if you could get a look at that recommendation, and you can—either by picking it up near Gadar when you interview him or receiving it directly from Trebonius. You'll find it a transparent forgery. This is your suspect. Tell Athrys, and move on.

But are you sure? Really, really sure? See, there's an alternate approach: You can use this pretext as a way to rid the Guild of this loose cannon of a quest-giver. When you talk to Artorius, report Athrys as the spy. She's out of the loop, and you'll still get credit for the quest. Note that you only get this as an option if you let Itermerel and Tashpi Ashibael live.

TREBONIUS ARTIORIUS' QUESTS

The Disappearance of the Dwarves

TREBONIUS ARTORIUS

Let's face it. Artorius is an idiot. Figuring out how he got to be an Arch-Mage, let alone Guildmaster, could be a quest in itself. He does not have a clue.

In this expansive quest, nor do you. Artorius doesn't tell you squat.

The quest, which he can give you at any time after you join the Guild, involves one of the deepest mysteries of Morrowind: What happened to the Dwarves? Before there was an Empire, they vanished without trace, leaving behind a marvelous technology enshrined in dangerous ruins.

Then again, maybe you already have a clue. What evidence of the Dwarves do you have in your inventory?

If you were thorough in your explorations while on Edwinna Elbert's quests, you should have three Dwarven books: "Hanging Gardens" (from the quest Excavation), "Divine Metaphysics" (from Bethamez) and "The Egg of Time (from Mzuleft).

If not, you need to do some additional dungeon delving.

You should also know from talking to Hasphat Antabolis or Senilias Cadiusus that "Hanging Gardens" is a potential key to the translation of the other two books.

But who can translate Aldmeris? Talk to Elbert, Antabolis, and wizard Divayth Fyr about the books, and you will eventually be pointed to Yagrum Bagarn, a patient in Fyr's Corprusarium, or Telvanni sorcerer Baladas Demnevanni. (Bagarn is a pivotal figure in Morrowind.) Use the topic "Disappearance of the Dwarves," and the books will be translated.

It's frightening stuff. "Divine Metaphysics" explains how to create a god through sorcery. "The Egg of Time" argues that it's not dangerous to interrupt a link to a source of divine power.

Yeah, right. Given how completely the Dwarves vanished—as though some cosmic light switch had been turned off—you may wonder about the value of those conclusions.

Report back to Trebonius. He probably won't understand a word of it, but your reputation within the Mages Guild will go through the roof.

Kill Telvanni

If you've solved Disappearance of the Dwarves, reached Rank 7 within the Guild, and finished the Main Quest, Artorius will give you this rare quest.

He wants you to kill all the Telvanni councilors.

Your initial journal entry on this quest will note: "I'm not sure if he was serious."

Maybe he was and maybe he wasn't. If you question Artorius about "House Telvanni," he'll lay out his wishes in more detail.

But there's a vague dementia lurking around the edges of Artorius' responses.

Then again, a quest is a quest, and this one isn't as hard as it may sound. You've already killed Master Gothren (and conceivably some of his less-agreeable colleagues) as part of the Main Quest, and you don't have to kill the some-times-Telvanni-councilor Baladas Demnevanni (who is useful is his own right). There seems to be no downside, unless you're in House Telvanni and you haven't completed all the quests yet.

Report back to the Arch-Mage and you'll get his staff and the Necromancer's Amulet.

Now you know he's nuts.

Guildmaster

Clearly, the Mages Guild needs a change at the top. That's about to happen.

If you have performed either all of Elbert's quests or all of Skink's, talk to the relevant quest-giver again after you reach Rank 8 to obtain this final mission.

Skink will give you a letter for Artorius. You can read it. It is Artorius' pink slip from the Empire—polite, but unequivocal. Poor fellow. Go talk to him. He'll read the note and name you Arch-Mage. Thus endeth the quest.

The other route is much tougher. If you haven't received Skink's letter, talk to Elbert. She'll tell you to talk to Artorius. Specifically, talk to him about "Arch-Mage," and he will challenge you to a duel to the death in the Vivec Arena. The upside is that you'll get some great equipment off him afterward. The down: He gets to use it against you first.

Advancement Quests

Some promotions within the Guild have special requirements.

When you advance from Rank 3 (Evoker) to 4 (Conjurer), you'll have to pay Guild dues of 200 drakes. Just select "Guild dues," and pay your tab. That's it? That's it—and this one time only. It barely seems like a quest at all.

Moving up to Rank 7 (Wizard) is a more conventional quest. To make this transition, select "Advancement," and learn that you need a Wizard's staff.

You can buy a staff (not cheap at 5,000 gold) and automatically advance. Or you can steal one and then talk to a mage with a rank of 7 or better with the stolen staff in your inventory to get the promotion.

Where to steal one? Well, any staff will do, but the Guild may take some such thefts more in stride than others. Ask about the staff, and you'll learn that the renegade wizard Anime can be found in Sud—a cave on the coast west of Dagon Fell in the far north.

THIEVES GUILD

The Thieves Guild, like any trade guild, is an organization of professionals, except the professionals are thieves and robbers and pickpockets and smugglers and other enterprising operators. They don't have public guild halls, but they do tend to gather at a single location—usually a cornerclub or tradehouse—in larger towns. Look for guild operatives in Balmora, Ald'ruhn, Sadrith Mora, and Vivec.

Favored Skills

Marksman	Acrobatics
Short Blade	Sneak
Light Armor	Security

Advancement

Rank	Agility	Personality	One Favored Skill at	Two Other Favored Skills at
Toad	30	30	0	0
Wet Ear	30	30	10	0
Footpad	30	30	20	0
Blackcap	30	30	30	5
Operative	30	30	40	10
Bandit	31	31	50	15
Captain	32	32	60	20
Ringleader	33	33	70	25
Mastermind	34	34	80	30
Master Thief	35	35	90	35

Faction Reaction

HATED ENEMY	ENEMY	HOSTILE	FRIENDLY	ALLY	BELOVED ALLY
Camonna Tong	Ashlanders	Temple House Hlaalu House Redoran Clan Berne Clan Aundae Clan Quarra Imperial Legion	Mages Guild Imperial Cult		

The Thieves Guild operates in more democratic fashion than other Guilds. You'll be able to obtain quests right away from all four quest-givers—in Balmora, Ald'ruhn, Sadrith Mora, and Vivec. You can perform these in sequence or shuttle back and forth between them as you wish; there are no requirements beyond membership in the Guild and completion of the quest-giver's prior quest.

However, once you hit Rank 2 in the Guild, you can visit Vivec and start on a special, seven-mission sub-quest offered by Master Thief, Gentleman Jim Stacey.

How come all these other folks have Lord of the Rings-type names, and this guy gets one like a riverboat gambler?

One nice bonus to being a Thieves Guild member is the ability to pay off any gold on your head at a discounted rate (50%). In each of the major Thieves Guild locations, you'll find someone who can take care of your bounty problem. They are: Phane Rielle (Balmora), Crazy-Legs Arantamo (Vivec), Rissinia (Sadrith Mora), and Tongue-Toad (Ald'ruhn).

SUGAR-LIPS HABASI

SUGAR-LIPS HABASI'S QUESTS

Diamonds

You'll find Habasi at the South Wall cornerclub in Balmora. As the Khajiit tend to do, she talks about herself in the third-person. Hence, when she tells you "A friend wants a diamond from Habasi," it means she wants you to go get her one.

If you have a diamond in your inventory, great. That'll do fine.

If not, not to worry. You're in the Thieves Guild, remember? Habasi suggests you procure one from Nalcarya of White Haven: Alchemist in the far northwest part of the city.

The Hlaalu guard in the shop proper should serve as fair warning against stealing anything in the shop. And there are a couple of diamonds just sitting on the shelf next to the proprietor, ripe for the picking, if you can get away with it. But Nalcarya's personal quarters upstairs is unguarded. And on the shelf above her bed, in a small chest, you will find three diamonds.

Then again, if you have some misplaced moral compunction against stealing, you can also buy a diamond here, but that gets pricey and…let's face it…if you can't pull this off you've probably joined the wrong guild.

With diamond in hand, return to Habasi at the South Wall to collect a potion and finish the quest.

Manor Key

This time out, Habasi wants the key to the top floor of Nerano Manor in Balmora. (It's just south and around the corner from Nalcarya's.)

Ondres Nerano, who lives there, certainly has a key, but he's not going to just turn it over to you. You'll have to knock him out first or steal it. (Don't kill him. While you'll still complete the quest, it ticks off Habasi and he won't give you a reward.)

A subtler route is to seek out one of Nerano's servants—Sovor Trandel at the Balmora Council Club near the Silt Strider port—and get it from him. (If you have second thoughts, you can turn in the servant and the key to Nerano for a small reward.)

An even more subtle route, for an enterprising thief, is to take the key and clean out Nerano Manor yourself—and then deliver the key to Habasi to complete the quest!

Overdue Payments

Dwemer artifacts. Everyone's fascinated by Dwemer artifacts.

The Thieves Guild is fascinated, too, and has arranged delivery of some of these Dwarven items with Ra'Zhid of Fatleg's Drop Off.

The items haven't turned up. Ra'Zhid asserts that he hasn't received them, but Habasi is hearing a different story from her informants. You're to retrieve the artifacts: a goblet, a bowl, and a Dwemer Tube.

These are all common Dwemer items, and you don't need to turn over the specific ones Ra'Zhid has. However, it's much more fun to show him up as a liar and rob him blind while you're at it. Make your way to Ra'Zhid's shop in

Hla Oad, southwest of Balmora. Talk to him if you want, but it's all different flavors of baloney. The items are in a locked chest behind a couple of barrels that are on your left as you enter the shop. (Note the trapdoor nearby. A quest opportunity can be found in the cellar as well.) Ra'Zhid is pretty likely to notice you stealing his stuff, though, and might decide to fight you. Kill him if you want; he's expendable as far as the quest is concerned.

Get back to Balmora to collect your reward (tools for thieving) and complete the quest.

Vintage Brandy

Ralen Hlaalo is dead. If you're working for House Hlaalu, you may already know this. (As a Hlaalu retainer, you have the opportunity to solve his murder.)

The Thieves Guild sees things a little differently: A dead man with valuable possessions is an opportunity to loot his house. Hlaalo owned some vintage brandy, and Habasi wants it.

Check the bottom floor of Hlaalo's house and you'll find…about a bazillion bottles.

Mercifully, the brandy is easy to pick out; it's in the distinctive bottle on the top shelf.

Bring it back to Habasi for a nice reward. Or drink it, but you won't be able to move to the next quest and you'll receive no reward and no benefits to Reputation or Disposition.

Brother Bragor

The thief New-Shoes Bragor got pinched. He's imprisoned in Fort Pelagiad, and Habasi wants you to get him out.

She has a plan. Shadbak gra-Burbug, who sells weapons and armor at the fort, takes bribes from Pelagiad trader Mebestien Ence, who deals illegally in Dwemer artifacts. You can use this information to blackmail Burburg.

Get the Dwemer Coherer from Ence's shop. (It's in a small chest on a shelf in his private quarters upstairs.)

Now visit the fort and talk to Shadbak. She will agree to let the thief go if you force her admit the bribes, but will attack you if you admit stealing the Coherer. Discretion is the better part of valor and all that.

Stop by the prison to visit New-Shoes, who will give you his new shoes (the reason he got pinched for to begin with, one imagines). And get back to Habasi for another nice payoff.

Balmora Defenses

If you're also working your way through the Fighters Guild quests, you may be aware of the war between the Fighters and the Thieves. Habasi anticipates another attack by the Fighters and Camonna Tong, and thinks the South Wall cornerclub, where the Thieves are based, needs better security.

A master of security lives in Balmora. But who is he? Habasi knows only that he is an Altmer.

This isn't as time-consuming as it may sound. As long as this quest is active, anyone in Balmora (including Habasi) can identify the half-dozen Altmer in town. They are Culumaire at the Lucky Lockup, Estirdalin at the Mages Guild, Imare at the Hlaalu Council Manor, Nalcarya of White Haven (who we've recently ripped off), and Hecerinde and Tyermaillin, who have residences in town.

Now, for fun, you can visit these folks and, in at least some cases, get their takes on the seedy South Wall.

But without knowing it, Habasi has already narrowed the field. Note that most of these folks already have jobs. The two whose jobs aren't listed are your best candidates and one of these—Hecerinde—is our guy. Visit him at his home and talk to him about "South Wall…" He's happy to help. Go see Habasi to wrap things up.

AENGOTH THE JEWELER'S QUESTS

Loot Ald'ruhn Mages Guild

You've picked an auspicious time to visit Ald'ruhn. The mages have split, and a source has told quest-giver Aengoth at The Rat in the Pot that they'll be gone for a while. It's a great time for you to pay them a visit.

The only thing Aegoth wants out of it is a nasty little blade called Anareren's Devil Tanto.

You could be forgiven for harboring a few suspicions. We'll say it again: In Vvardenfell, there are no free rides.

And, sure enough, the Mages Guild is not quite empty. Manis Virmaulese remained behind, and he'll attack you.

AENGOTH THE
JEWELER

Once he's out of the way, steal everything you can lay your hands on. The Devil Tanto you're looking for is downstairs in the room on the right. You'll see a locked chest on the top shelf of a bookcase; that's where you'll find it. Then get back to Aengoth to deliver the tanto and complete the quest.

Master Helm

You're to procure a Redoran Master Helm for a client. Many of the Redoran councilors have these, and Aengoth knows one can be found in Miner Arobar's bedroom.

It's the left-hand bedroom in the private quarters. Note that the Arobars are home at the time, and that a guard occasionally passes through the room, so make sure no one's looking when you snatch the helm off the top of the dresser. Then book, and get back to Aengoth to wrap things up.

Bad Gandosa

For the next quest, your destination is right across the hall.

Arobar's daughter, Gandosa, has a copy of Boethiah's Pillow Book, which has been banned by the Tribunal temple.

"I have to admit I'm a bit curious myself," says Aengoth.

You may be, too. But the book, in a locked chest behind a screen in Gandosa's bedroom, says only, parenthetically, "No words can describe what you see."

We'll leave it at that. Get this scandalous tome back to Aengoth and receive a magic ring and amulet.

Withershins

Aengoth's on a book kick. Now he wants one called "Withershins."

Miles Gloriosus at Maar Gan's Andus Tradehouse has a copy. You'll find it in a locked chest in his room. Of course, he's not going to like you stealing his stuff, but that's sort of your job. Right?

Cart it back to Aengoth for the usual reward. Make sure you give it a read before you hand it over to Aengoth—it also happens to be a Restoration skill book.

Incidentally, "Withershins" is a fairly lengthy (for Morrowind) short story with a "The Twilight Zone" sensibility. Every conversation protagonist Zaki hears is arranged alphabetically.

A game designer's lament?

Ald'ruhn Defenses

A sister quest to Balmora Defenses and Sadrith Mora Defenses, this mission finds you looking for scrap metal so the Guild can build spider centurions—those nasty guardians you've doubtless encountered in Dwemer ruins.

The quest is open in structure. Aengoth doesn't tell you where to get the metal—just that four pieces are needed—and any Dwemer ruin will do. (Two of the closer ruins—Bethamez and Arkngthunch-Sturmdumz—can be found in the Gnisis area.) Or, you can just go buy the metal at Cienne Sintiene's shop. She's right there in Ald'ruhn, under the giant shell.

Bring the metal back to Aengoth. And the next time you're in the cornerclub, keep an eye peeled for some new additions.

Darts of Judgement

Some of Morrowind's faction quests are really just advisories on the location of unique loot. The later quests from Mages Guild apprentice Ajira are two examples. Darts of Judgement is a third.

The Darts, a potent variety of the Daedric dart, are found at Llethri Manor in Ald'ruhn. You've just got to walk over there and grab them off a bed in the guards' quarters. (But let's be clear: You're stealing them. The owner is a Llethri archer named Eindel, and if you ask him about them, he'll tell you it's none of your beeswax.)

Keep them and use them in good health. Or, if you can use the money or you're already burdened with Interesting Stuff, you can sell some or all to the Guild at 500 gold a pop.

BIG HELENDE'S QUESTS

Cookbook Alchemy

The third of the Thieves Guild under-bosses can be found Dirty Muriel's cornerclub in Sadrith Mora. Like her brother thieves, she goes easy on you at the start. Big Helende sends you to the shop of Anis Seloth—the primo alchemist in Sadrith Mora—to find a recipe for a Dispel Magic potion.

The funny thing is, the client turns out to be the Mage Tusamircil. Wouldn't a mage have his own recipe?

Oh, well, yours is not to question why. Yours is simply to poke and prod around the alchemist's shop, without raising the hackles of the guard (as you'll do if you open the locked chest downstairs) until you find the recipe. It's in a crate upstairs in his shop. Careful, though—those guards pack quite a wallop. Deliver the recipe to the mage at Wolverine Hall and then check in with Helende.

Grandmaster Retort

This time around, you're in search of a Grandmaster's Retort.

No, it's not a snappy comeback, but a specialized piece of alchemist's equipment for making potions. You probably found a couple of lower-level versions of the same equipment when you went looking for a five-finger discount at Anis Seloth's shop.

Helende notes that these are not usually for sale, and typically expensive when they are, but that Berwen the Trader in Tel Mora is supposed to have one. Steal that one, or another elsewhere in the game; as is frequently the case, any such item is acceptable. (For instance, there's one in the Services tower in Tel Vos.) Then talk to Helende again, and you're done.

Sadrith Mora Defenses

All the Thieves Guild branches are battening down the hatches for a confrontation with the Camonna Tong and the Fighters Guild. The Balmora branch hired a security expert. The Ald'ruhn branch built spider centurions.

Sadrith Mora being a wizardly world, Helende dispatches you to hire to wizard to protect Dirty Muriel's.

Visit the Mages Guild in Wolverine Hall. The wizards will direct you to Arielle Phiencel. Phiencel, in turn, will direct you to collect four pieces of raw ebony for an experiment.

Like Ald'ruhn Defenses, this quest has no fixed shape. You're free to collect the ebony where you find it—whether in mines like Caldera and Sudanit, or stolen from Anis Seloth's shop (you remember him from the Cookbook quest— that locked chest downstairs has some ebony in it). Once you've found it, talk to Phiencel again, deliver the ebony and she'll send battlemage Natalinus Flavonius to guard the Guild. Check in with Helende to end the quest and collect a Dire Shardbolt ring.

Redoran Cookbook

After that quest, you'd expect the next to be something dark and dangerous—a pre-emptive blow against the Camonna Tong, perhaps.

Not just yet.

It deals with a cooking contest.

Apparently Dinara Othrelas of Ald'ruhn and Fara of Sadrith Mora have an annual cooking competition, and I guess Othrelas has been winning. Fara, who runs Fara's Hole in the Wall, wants a leg up in the next match, and has hired the Guild to swipe the cookbook "Redoran Cooking Secrets" from Llethri Manor, where Othrelas is the cook.

Nice to know the Guild has its priorities straight in these difficult times.

The book is in a locked chest at the foot of Othrelas' bed in Llethri Manor. Othrelas isn't around, so it's simplest to just steal it. If you can't manage the lock's pick setting (50), seek out Othrelas in the Manor entrance and flatter and intimidate her into surrendering the book. You can then take it back either to Fara directly or to Helende to end the quest.

Ebony Staff

Big Helende now sends you to collect an enchanted ebony staff from Felen Maryon, who can be found in his quarters in Therana's Chamber in Tel Branora's Upper Tower.

Don't worry if you don't have the Levitation spell—typically necessary to reach the top section of Telvanni towers. Helende has thought of this and will provide potions that do the trick.

Naturally, Maryon does not simply stand around and watch you steal his staff. He'll fight you over it, and, likely as not, you'll get roughed up by this powerful wizard in the process.

Your best bet is just to take it and run like crazy.

If you give Helende the staff, he'll give you 250 gold and a telekinesis ring (the Ring of Far Reaching).

But if you decide to keep the fruit of your labors, that's OK, too. You'll still get the ring, but not the gold.

GENTLEMAN JIM STACEY'S QUESTS

Stacey offers three different sorts of quests. One consists of standard Thieves Guild jobs. (See Jobs.) These require no special rank within the Guild. Each requires simply that you complete the quest before it.

The second is a series of seven linked missions that comprise in themselves a small campaign. To undertake the Bal Molagmer quests, you must have reached Rank 2 within the Guild.

And when you reach Rank 8, Stacey will give you a final pair of advanced quests that resolve a simmering storyline spread over many Guild missions.

GENTLEMAN JIM STACEY

JOBS

You must have reached the rank of Captain before you can undertake these quests.

Brother Thief

In this quest, which you can get from Stacey, you're searching for a thief named Nads Tharen. He was supposed to deliver an important key to Stacey, but never appeared.

Your first stop should be the Elven Nations cornerclub, where Tharen was a regular. It's located in the Hlaalu Compound—the westernmost of the city's cantons.

You'll find seven people in the tavern. Two of them, proprietor Gadela Andus and Sovali Uvayn, will tell you that Tharen spoke to Arvama Rathri the last time he was there. (More telling is Andus' comment about Rathri if you boost her Disposition to 70.)

Speak to Rathri herself and you'll eventually get a none-too-subtle threat.

You can kill her—persuasion is futile—but it's not necessary, though avenging Tharen does double your reward at quest's end.

Instead, speak to Andus and his patrons about Rathri and you'll learn she lives in St. Delyn Canal South-Two. Visit that address, and you'll find Tharen—dead, but with the key still on him.

Get it back to Stacey, who discloses that it'll help in the Guild's battle with the Camonna Tong. He also suggests you keep an eye on Rathri, as she may be working for that syndicate.

And the key? What about the key?

Not a word.

Enemy Parley

Time to turn things around.

Talk to Stacey about "help us fight." He thinks Percius Mercius, steward of the Ald'ruhn branch of the Fighters Guild, will help the Thieves in their battle with the Camonna Tong.

Mercius was Guildmaster of the Fighters until the Tong got involved, but he's been replaced at the top by Sjoring Hard-Heart.

Nothing like a disgruntled employee to provide good dirt.

Actually, Mercius delivers great dirt. He'll opine that Hard-Heart is too deep in debt to the Tong to back out, and that he's a lost cause. But, with a Disposition of at least 30, he'll suggest that his former second-in-command Hrundi (now Guild steward at Sadrith Mora) can be brought around the Thieves' side. And if you can't, Hrundi apparently has a girlfriend you can squeeze to pressure him.

PERCIUS MERCIUS

Balmora steward Eydis Fire-Eye? Mercius doesn't have specific suggestions, but the thrust of his comments seems to be that she's somehow vulnerable. (Mercius has nothing on Lorbumol gro-Aglakh.)

Return to Stacey with what you've learned to complete the quest.

Bitter Bribe

Stacey has a way to bring Eydis Fire-Eye over to the Thieves' side.

You've learned from Percius Mercius that Fire-Eye worships Clavicus Vile. The Master Thief now asks you to retrieve the Bitter Cup—an artifact sacred to followers of Vile—from the ruins at Ald Reydania.

Could it be any farther away? Ald Reydania is at the western extremity of the northern island of Sheogorad. You'll have to fight your way through various tomb-dwellers before retrieving the Cup, which is located on an altar on the top level.

On your way home to Vivec, talk to Fire-Eye at the Balmora Fighters Guild and give her the Cup. She's all yours. Then talk to Stacey again to complete the quest.

Note that you can follow a different route: You can drink from the cup yourself. This will increase your highest attribute by 20 points and lower your worst by 20—in essence making you more of what you already are.

But it will foul up permanently your attempt to bribe Fire-Eye, as the Cup is a one-use item that then disappears forever.

Hostage

HRUNDI

Now it's Hrundi's turn. Talk to Stacey about "join our cause" and "Hrundi's woman," and then seek out Hrundi at the Fighters Guild in Sadrith Mora.

You can persuade him, and you can blackmail him. Persuasion will take a while, but you'll win his support if you get his Disposition up to 80.

But suppose you only get a "C" in Speechcraft. You'll need to resort to more blatant tactics.

So who's Hrundi's lover? Someone in Sadrith Mora should know. Talk to people, and you'll eventually be pointed to Fara's Hole in the Wall and learn Hrundi goes there to visit Falena Hlaren. (She'll admit it herself if you get her Disposition up to 50.) Bring this fact to Hrundi's attention, and he's also your man. Return to Stacey to wrap things up.

At this point, if you haven't reached Rank 8 (Mastermind) in the Guild, you'll learn from Stacey that you must do so before you can continue.

Check in with Sugar-Lips Habasi, Aengoth the Jeweler, and Big Helende to see if you've overlooked any assignments. And did you perform the Bal Molagmer quests?

THE BAL MOLAGMER QUESTS

In essence, Stacey proposes to resurrect Robin Hood.

Ask him about "Bal Molagmer," and he'll tell you the legend of the "Stone Fire Men" – a group of thieves who stole from oppressors and gave to the oppressed. They disappeared a long time ago, and Stacey feels that, with the bad press thieves have been getting in Morrowind, it's time for them to resurface.

He offers you the chance to play that part.

Next, he offers you a pair of gloves the thieves were said to have worn. When you are prepared to take up this cause, you're to wear the gloves as a symbol, and speak to Stacey again.

Generosity

When you do wear the gloves, he'll ask you, for your first mission, to return the Hlervu Locket to Braynas Hlervu.

Hlervu is a retired egg miner living in Ald'ruhn. He gave up the locket to Redoran Councilor Bolvyn Venim's taxmen, and now it's in Venim Manor. Wearing the gloves, you're to liberate the Locket and bring it back to its owner in the name of <everybody together now> the Bal Molagmer.

Retrieve the locket from a chest in the guard quarters at Venim Manor and return it as planned. Then return to Stacey, and your quest is complete.

If you check in with Hlervu later, you'll learn that Venim's guards came searching for the locket, but that he'd hidden it well and that they left without it. It's too dangerous to keep, and he'll pass it on to his nephew.

Now, we don't know for the life of us why you'd do this. But if you somehow missed the point of the Bal Molagmer story, you can also return the locket to Venim.

However you handle it, it will not go well. In fact, it may go quite badly. Venim will not give you a reward. He may try to kill you. You may have to kill him sooner or later anyway, so the choice is yours. But he is a tough hombre, so later is better than sooner. It's either that, or you'll have to steal the locket a second time.

Yngling

Assuming you pulled off the Generosity mission OK, or, during a temporary blackout, killed the poor old man before you accepted that quest, you're eligible for this one.

Talk to Stacey about "Bal Molagmer" again and then about "corruption." He wants a ledger from Yngling Half-Troll's home—Yngling Manor in the St. Olms section of Vivec—that documents the Hlaalu councilor's corruption. You need simply bring it back to Stacey, and the quest is resolved.

But there are a couple more ways this can play out. Just as you can perversely return the Hlervu locket to Venim, you can perversely offer the stolen ledger to Mr. Half-Troll. No reward is involved and he's mad at you whether you decide to give it to him or not. If you do give it to him, you'll have to steal it back or kill him to finish the quest. If don't, you'll definitely fight.

YNGLING

Finally, you may already have killed Yngling Half-Troll in an entirely different context (your quest to be named Hlaalu Hortator), so this whole thing may just be a relative walk in the park.

Even More Generosity

Bal Molagmer returns. Ask Stacey about that topic again, and then about "forged land deed."

The Hlaalu Council seems to be full of crooks. You've already heard about Yngling Half-Troll's corruption. And now you learn that Councilor Velanda Omani has forged a deed in an effort to take widow Indrele Rathryon's land in Seyda Neen. (Shades of Odral Helvi.)

Unless the Thieves intercede, Omani will bribe her way to success.

The fake deed is in the library in Vivec. (It's lying loose in the middle of the bottom shelf, under a book on the left-most rear bookcase.) Pick it up, take the stilt strider to Seyda Neen, and return the document to Rathryon. (She's near the shacks along the water's edge.) You'll notice that these Bal Molagmer deeds are starting to get a little press with the populace. Nice to get noticed, isn't it?

Now, scoot back down to Vivec and talk to Stacey to wrap things up.

It's also fun to visit Omani with the fake deed in your possession. You can tease her by giving the deed back to her and stealing it back again.

Just watch her squirm.

Enamor

You should be offered this quest an provided you've completed the quest Generosity or if, for some reason, you killed Indrele Rathryon before accepting the quests Generosity or Yngling.

Basically, the Thieves Guild goofed.

Select "Bal Molagmer" and "Enamor" to get the story. One of the Guild members has stolen the sword Enamor from Buoyant Armiger Salyn Sarethi. Turns out the sword was a gift from Lord Vivec himself. Turns out Sarethi's a good guy. Turns out the Guild doesn't want to associated with this sort of thing. (Stacey's seems to be running a sort of politically-correct Thieves Guild.)

Stacey wants you to put the sword back—along with a note of explanation.

Back where? Back in Ghostgate—the fortified monastery that guards the only access through the Ghostfence. It's a long trip north across the Ascadian Isles and the Ashlands. Sarethi's chest is in the lower level of the Tower of Dusk.

Don't forget the note.

Then it's back to Stacey to finish the mission. (Of course, you might want to check around the tower in Ghostgate and practice your thieving skills. Might be a couple valuable things just lying around there....)

You can talk to Sarethi to witness the quest's redeeming impact. But do not kill him. (You know how fights can start by accident.) If you do kill him, Stacey refuses to work with you any more.

Greedy Slaver

It's rare that you perform purely symbolic actions in Morrowind, but this is one of those times.

Talk to Stacey about "Bal Molagmer" and then "Brallion's Ring." He now sends you off to Sadrith Mora to steal a ring from the trader. You're to then deliver it to a Vivec abolitionist named Ilmeni Dren.

BRALLION

If the symbolism is lost on you, Brallion is a wealthy slave trader and Dren an abolitionist. (If you work for House Hlaalu, you can perform quests for her that involve helping escaped slaves.) The transfer of the ring is an emblem of the Bal Molagmer's opposition to slavery.

Brallion can usually be found up a short ramp from an outdoor stall called Dunmer Alchemy. When this quest is active, though, Brallion will be found in Fara's Hole in the Wall, next door. Seems he likes to have a couple belts while there's a quest going on. Ask him about the ring and he'll tell you a terrible, depressing story about how he got it.

You can buy the ring from him for as little as 500 gold if you bump his Disposition up to 60. You can steal it. And you can kill him for it as well, though you won't be able to complete the quest if you do. Logically, that's the sort of thing that would allow the Bal Molagmer to be painted as extremists.

Dren, the daughter of Duke Vedam Drem, can be found in Vivec in St. Delyn Canal South-One. Don't kill her, either, or you'll be unable to complete the next quest. Just give her the ring and hop over to the bookstore to meet with Stacey again.

Plutocrats

This next quest is in the spirit of Ilmeni Dren's Hlaalu quest, Literacy Campaign. (See House Hlaalu Faction quests.) It should be offered to you if you've completed Greedy Slaver or, alternatively, if you killed the trader Brallion but did complete Enamor.

Speak to Stacey yet again about "Bal Molagmer" and then about "history books." He wants you to steal Odral Helvi's copy of "A Brief History of the Empire" from the Governor's Mansion in Caldera and donate it in the Bal Molagmer's name to Vala Catraso at the Ald'ruhn Mages Guild. (You may recall that the Guild runs classes, but doesn't have enough books.)

This four-volume set can be found in a few places in the game—including the library in Vivec and, oddly enough, in the Ald'ruhn Mages Guild itself. While Catraso will accept any of these sets from you, only Helvi's actually completes the quest. Once you've given her the books, she'll mention that she's heard rumors of the return of the Bal Molagmer. She won't believe you're one of them, though, unless you're wearing the gloves. Clothes do make the man. (A side note: Not that you're planning on it, but Catraso's yet another person you shouldn't kill if you want to complete the Bal Molagmer quest.)

Church Police

In this last of the Bal Molagmer quests, Stacey asks you to swipe a large Dwemer goblet from a Temple official and give it to a wandering priest in the name of you-know-who.

To receive the mission, you just have to complete Plutocrats. To get the run-down, select "Bal Molagmer" and "Dwemer goblet."

Again, this quest is largely symbolic, demonstrating to the world that Bal Molagmer is on the side of the angels. The Temple official is security chief Berel Sala. The receiver is Dissident Priest Danso Indules, who wanders about Vivec caring for the sick and is being harassed by Sala's Ordinator guards.

Sound familiar? If you've made good progress in the Main Quest, you know that Indules is the one who made a vital appointment for you with Archcanon Tholer Saryoni, which sets up your meeting with Lord Vivec and the last segment of the story.

The goblet can be found in Sala's office in Justice Offices in Vivec. (It's on the table in front of him.) Indules is in the Temple.

Just don't tell her where you got the goblet, or he won't take it.
Back to Stacey again. You should be ready for the Thieves Guild endgame.

Advanced Quests

Kill Ienith

When you do hit Rank 8 and complete Hostage, you're ready to take the battle to the Camonna Tong. Talk to Stacey about "Ienith."

As in "the Ienith brothers" – the Tong's best enforcers. You're going to take them out. Or at least you're going to give it the old College of Vvardenfell try.

The Ieniths can found in the cellar of Orvas Dren's villa on the Dren Plantation just northeast of Pelagiad. You'll see only Navil. When you attack him, Ranes appears behind you—a la the waking attacks you've doubtless experienced from Sixth House monsters when sleeping in certain towns.

Kill them both, return to Vivec, and talk to Stacey again to complete the quest. They're tough hombres, though, and armed with a couple of nice weapons. You'll enjoy having them when they're dead.

NAVIL IENITH

Kill Hard-Heart

Now you're after the head of the Fighters Guild.

Stacey tells you that all non-violent efforts to come to terms with Sjoring Hard-heart have failed. He seems to take the dispute with the Thieves personally and is plotting an assault on their Guilds.

SJORING HARD-HEART

Kill him, and get back to Stacey.

Your reward is wonderful. Stacey gives you a Skeleton Key. While it has a limited numbers of uses, it will open any door in the game. Save it for those portals and containers that seemed to actively resist your best efforts.

You're not quite done. In conversation, select "duties" again. You have no more duties remaining, but one more reward: Stacey kicks you up to Rank 9.

You are now the Master Thief.

I MPERIAL LEGION

Join up with the Imperial Legion! The Imperial Legion has several fort garrisons here on Vvardenfell. The one near Balmora is Fort Moonmoth, southwest of town. The lower ranks handle law enforcement, escorts, rescues, dangerous predators, diseased and blighted beasts, and so forth. Upper ranks are the Imperial orders of knighthood.

Favored Skills

Athletics   Acrobatics
Spear   Sneak
Long Blade   Security

Advancement

Rank	Endurance	Personality	One Favored Skill at	Two Other Favored Skills at
Recruit	30	30	0	0
Spearman	30	30	10	0
Trooper	30	30	20	0
Agent	30	30	30	5
Champion	30	30	40	10
Knight Errand	31	31	50	15
Knight Bachelor	32	32	60	20
Knight Protector	33	33	70	25
Knight of the Garland	34	34	80	30
Knight of the Imperial Dragon	35	35	90	35

Faction Reaction

HATED ENEMY	ENEMY	HOSTILE	FRIENDLY	ALLY	BELOVED ALLY
	Ashlanders	Temple	Mages Guild	Imperial Cult	
	Camonna Tong	House Telvanni	House Hlaalu	Blades	
	Clan Aundae	Thieves Guild	House Redoran	Fighters Guild	
	Clan Berne	Clan Quarr			

The Imperial Legion is the first faction you will hear about in Morrowind. We can almost guarantee it.

Once you're clear of the Customs and Excise House in Seyda Neen, who's the first person you encounter? OK, there's the handsome face and sparkling repartee of Vodunius Nuccius. But after him? It's the guy with the tight, professional smile and the Imperial purple.

If you ain't misbehaving (i.e., the guard has a Disposition of at least 45), you should be able to talk to any of these guards—the cops for much of western Vvardenfell—about "Imperial Legion" to get a run-down on the Imperial presence on Vvardenfell. The Empire has built Fort Moonmoth at Balmora, Hawkmoth Fort at Ebonheart, Buckmoth Fort at Ald'ruhn, and Fort Darius at Gnisis. (Curiously, they won't mention Fort Pelagiad or Wolverine Hall.)

Note that these bases are entirely on the western side of the island—the area that was settled by the outlanders.

Ask about "join the Imperial Legion" to learn the garrisons are at full strength—except possibly the Deathshead unit near Gnisis. You'll be told to talk to General Darius about that.

JOINING THE LEGION

Signing on with the Legion requires a trip to Gnisis. Far north on the "Smuggler's Coast," it's not exactly on the beaten track. Morrowind won't even send you there as part of the Main Quest (though House Redoran's faction quests will often put you in the Gnisis area).

But be thankful you don't have to walk. The silt striders stop there. It's a quick and inexpensive mode of travel that spares you the indignity of having your inexperienced character dying in the wilderness.

Your natural inclination once there will be to head south toward the distant battlements of Fort Darius. But no need: Darius is at the Madach Tradehouse just east of the silt strider port. The general's office is through the middle door on the bottom floor. He signs you up as a Recruit and gives you an Imperial chain cuirass.

You'll have to wear this armor to talk to him again, so put it on straight away and leave it on for your term in the Legion.

No, we're not telling you to wear crappy armor during a whole bunch of quests. Each time you rise in rank, you'll receive a new piece of standard Legion equipment:

RANK	NAME	ITEMS
1	Spearman	Imperial Steel Shield
2	Trooper	Imperial Steel Cuirass
3	Agent	Imperial Steel Helm & Gauntlets
4	Champion	Imperial Steel Pauldrons & Boots
5	Knight Errant	Templar Cuirass and Greaves
6	Knight Bachelor	Templar Helm & Bracers
7	Knight Protector	Templar Pauldrons & Boots
8	Knight of the Garland	Duke's Guard Silver Cuirass
9	Knight of the Imperial Dragon	Chrysamere and Lord's Mail

In addition, if you ask for orders, Darius will give you your first quest.

(When you become a Knight Protector, you have free access to the "Evidence" chests in the Legion prisons. So if you've had stuff taken from you previously for crimes, feel free to go back and get it. The chests will still be locked, but you can pick them without recourse.)

GENERAL DARIUS' QUESTS

Widow Maker

You may wonder if you've made a mistake. Straight off, Darius asks you to do something repugnant.

Widow Vabdas, who recently lost her husband in the Gnisis Eggmine, holds the deed to land that Darius wants for a new dock. (Between the fort and the nearby barracks, the Empire is already a defining presence in Gnisis.) The general wants the deed, and says he won't take "no" for an answer.

Ask around town about "Widow Vabdas," and you'll learn she lives in a hut west of the village. It's just around the hill.

Ask her about "land deed," and she refuses the surrender it. She'll tell you her husband was murdered by a legionnaire when he went to the closed eggmine east of the village for fresh kwama eggs, and asks you to go the mine and learn the truth.

WIDOW VABDAS

Now, just how bad do you want to be? If the answer is "very," simply kill the widow, take the key you'll find on her body, use it to unlock the chest to the right of the door and take the deed. You can also pick her pocket and simply take the key. Or, if you're already an advanced lockpicker, you can have a go at the chest's Level 40 lock. Then bring the deed back to Darius to wrap up the quest.

Nice. Who're you gonna work for next, the Camonna Tong?

If you don't want to be bad at all, you'll investigate further. Follow the widow's tip and head for the mine itself. It's up on the stony hill east of the village. To get there, you'll need to climb the hill on the north side of town, pass through the tent-like structure and across the bridge.

Talk to the guard, Vatollia Apo, about "egg mine." Since you're in the Legion, he'll just give you the key. You can also get in if you're carrying a miner's pick, or if you can get Apo's Disposition up to 70.

It's a big old mine, and there's a lot going on in here. When you enter the Lower Mine, you'll meet a threatening Orc legionnaire named Lugrub gro-Ogdum who apparently thinks he's your Father and tells you he's going to count to 10.

Don't be intimidated. Walk straight past him and enter the Underground Stream. Here, you'll encounter the ghost of Widow Vabdas' husband. Manoilomat Vabdas reveals how Ogdum killed him on his way out of the mine to hide the fact that the Orc was sleeping on the job when Vabdas entered. As evidence, he directs to you to a broken axe at the bottom of the deep pool behind him, which you should take.

Make your way back down into Gnisis and see Darius again. When he asks for proof of the murder, show him the broken axe. He'll send you to kill Ogdum. Do so and report back to Darius yet again to finish the quest. (It's also OK if you've already killed him.)

LUGRUB GRO-OGDUM

Darius gives you an Imperial broadsword, and his Disposition bump of 20 is twice what it would be if you'd just acted like a stormtrooper with the widow. And this quest alone may be enough to secure your promotion to Rank 1 (Spearman).

In fact, it's even more complex than you may know. If you push deeper into the Underground Stream section of the mine, you'll discover that you can also exit the underground stream into the river! And now, when you talk to Darius about "land deed," it turns out legionaires are now raising money for the widow. You can even make a donation. You've really turned things around.

And did we mention Bethamez? If you've played the Mages Guild quests, you know there's a rumor that the eggmine was closed, not because of the blight, but because miners broke into this lost Dwemer ruin. Like many rumors, it is at least partly true.

Gnisis Blight

In a quest very similar to the Telvanni quest Mine Cure, Darius sends you to play doctor with the Gnisis Eggmine's blighted kwama queen. You need to either cast a Cure Blight spell on the queen yourself or barter for a Cure Blight scroll with village Hetman Abelmawia.

There aren't any surprises or little wrinkles in this one. If you've got the spell, go to the queen in the Lower Eggmine and cast it. If you don't, the Hetman's hut is the northernmost of the three at the west end of the village. Depending on your Mercantile skill, you'll need about 580 gold to buy his Scroll of Daerir's Blessing. (The spell itself can't be purchased at the local Dunmer Temple.)

If you have neither the spell nor the money (which is entirely possible if you've just started), you can go dungeon-delving. Speak to Darius about "little advice" and he'll mention bandit caves to the east. A big, tough one, Assarnud, is located south and east of Gnisis on the island where the river divides.

Once the queen is in the pink, report back to Darius to collect 100 gold. Plus, you can boost the Dispositions of people all over town by talking to them about the eggmine. Yeah, that was me.

Rescue Pilgrim

Word has arrived from Ald Velothi of a kidnapping. Ashlander outcasts are holding hostage a pilgrim named Madura Seran at a camp south of the village. You're to bring her to safety.

MADURA SERAN

Renegade Ashlanders do things like this occasionally. (A similar mission is the Redoran faction quest Find Giladren.) In fact, they're going to do it twice on your watch with the Legion. There's usually a peaceful way around it.

But to negotiate with the Ashlanders, you've got to find them, and "south of the village" may or may not work as directions.

You'll get better ones in Ald Velothi from people with a Disposition of 50 or better. It's a fair jaunt north, and you may encounter distractions en route, but the road is well marked and you'll soon see the Ald Velothi Outpost's tower and the nearby shrine Ashalmawia on the horizon.

Talk to Orero Omothan outside the Outpost about Seran. (Note that you can get this quest from the folks in town without belonging to the Legion.) Omothan says the Ashlanders are on the hill, past a lighted tree. You might well say "which hill?", everything looks like a hill—but if you turn around and look southwest, you'll see a light on the hill to the southwest.

The light will turn out to be a campfire, but it's the right spot. Enter the yurt here and speak to Abassel Asserbassalit. Initially he's adamant about not releasing Seran. But if you can get his Disposition up to 60, he'll let her go for 500 gold.

If you're uncomfortable paying ransom (What sort of message does this send to other rogue Ashlanders?), or just crummy at Persuasion, you can kill the Ashlander, but be advised you'll also need to kill the two Ashlanders outside the yurt.

Once the Ashlanders are assuaged or dead, speak to Seran and have her follow you back to the Outpost. Then make your way back to Gnisis to wrap up the mission, which improves your reputation both in the Legion and Temple.

Rescue Ragash

Darius asks you to find out what's become of a tax collector. Ragash gra-Shuzgub went to visit Baladas Denmnevanni, and hasn't been seen since.

Baladas will prove to be an important part of Morrowind, but, in Gnisis, he's just a weird, reclusive enchanter who took over a Velothi dome on the northwest edge of town. And in the manner of weird recluses everywhere, he has a unique way of dealing with the tax collector: He's thrown her in a cell downstairs.

"I was here before Gnisis, before the Empire of men," he will tell you. "I will be here after Gnisis is gone and after this short-lived Empire has crumbled."

If you're adept at picking tough locks and comfortable with trapped doors, you can get Shuzgub out of Arvs-Drelen without Baladas knowing. Once you've tackled the door, talk to the tax collector, have her follow you out and then lead her toward the Madach Tradehouse.

Another route is to talk to Baladas. (Alone, please. Do not take Shuzgob up to the top level of the dome, as the enchanter will attack her.) If you can get his Disposition up to 60, he'll simply give you the key to Shuzgob's cell.

This is not in itself dangerous, but getting to him may be; Baladas has a Daedroth in his arena and it may seek you out and attack you along the way.

Talos Treason

ARIUS RULICIAN

The Talos Cult isn't itself a problem. The former emperor Tiber Septim is widely worshipped within Tamriel. (In fact, one of Morrowind's own factions is the Imperial Cult.)

But Darius has learned through informants that Talos members within his own Legions' ranks are involved in a plot against the current emperor, Uriel Septim. (Just for background's sake, Septim is now 80 and ill. His manner has never allowed him to ingratiate himself among his people, and now a controversy is brewing back in the Imperial City over who will succeed him.)

The general asks you to investigate this plot.

You won't have to go far. Imperial troopers are all over Gnisis. You can even talk to Nash gro-Khazor, who is in Darius' office. He'll mention that Oritius Maro is a member and suggest you visit the Barracks, where you need to talk to Camp Prefect Optio Bologra.

Bologra is behind the second right-hand door in the Barracks. He's got suspicions of his own. But before you reach him, you'll run into Maro at the base of the first flight of Barracks stairs.

He is pleasant, but uninformative when asked about the Cult. But drive his Disposition up to 70, and he'll ask you if you're interested in joining. When you confirm, he'll give you a key to the Talos shrine, and tells you to speak to Arius Rulician.

(You can also kill him or steal the key, but let's not get ahead of ourselves. So far, all you know is that, yes, Maro is in the Talos Cult. Big deal. That's not a crime.)

Enter the trapdoor in the storage room at the end of the hall and talk to Rulician. He'll tell you to feel free to look around. Take him up on it. Feel very free. Pick the lock on the small chest on the altar and take the note from Maro. It reports rumors that Uriel Septim will visit Vvardenfell and emphasizes the need to strike quickly if opportunity arises.

That's the evidence you need. Taking it is all the provocation Rulician needs to attack you. Kill him. If on the way out of the barracks Maro intercepts you, kill him too. Get back to Darius for an update, and you're done! (If you haven't already killed the plotters, he'll send you off to do so now.)

The Emperor has been saved. But Darius still seems worried—perhaps because of how it reflects on him.

If you ask for orders again, you'll learn that's all he has for you. Your official tour of duty in Gnisis is at an end. Of course, you can stay on and find other things to do—clearing out those bandit caves, searching the wild country to the north for adventure, and plundering the odd ancestral vault. (One along the river surrenders a great enchanted ring.)

But for actual quests, Darius will direct you to the Knight Protectors at the Legion's other forts and, finally, to the Knight of the Imperial Dragon, Varus Vantinius, in Ebonheart.

Vantinius' quests require a Knight Protector, but entry-level quests are available from Imsin the Dreamer at Buckmoth Fort near Ald'ruhn, Radd Hard-Heart at Moonmoth Fort near Balmora, and Frald the White at the Hawkmoth Legion Garrison in Ebonheart.

The most natural choice is Ald'ruhn—a short hop away via silt strider.

IMSIN THE DREAMER'S QUESTS

Smuggler

Buckmoth Fort is south of Ald'ruhn. You'll be grateful just to be inside. This region, just southwest of Red Mountain, is a desert often scoured by a dirty wind. By day, walking can be like swimming against a tide. At night, you may barely be able to see where you're going.

IMSIN

Imsin is on the right side of the fort's central basement room. It's a warm, friendly place; everyone seems to know everyone else. Ask Imsin for orders, and she'll ask you to obtain evidence that Drinar Varyon is smuggling Dwemer artifacts through Ald'ruhn.

You can practically testify to that already. If you've been playing the House Hlaalu faction quests, you already know this fellow is a smuggler. (In the quest Ebony Delivery, you can either participate in an ebony smuggling operation, or go undercover to get Varyon and Odral Helvi on smuggling charges.)

You'll need to get into Varyon's house and look around. Ask around town, and you'll learn that he's in Ald'ruhn studying native pottery (hmmm) and that his house is on the west side of town, across from the Ald Skar Inn.

The door's not locked, and, on top of that, he's home.

Well, this is going to be awkward.

The house is notable to two things: a huge number of redware pots and bowls and three heavily-locked chests.

Don't waste your time fiddling with the chests. While their contents do implicate Varyon in an entirely different type of smuggling (raw ebony), it's too obvious and handling the ebony will start a fight. Killing Varyon will cut in half your Disposition bump from Imsin.

The key is in the pots. It's a sort of "Where's Waldo?" puzzle, only here Waldo is a Dwemer Tube. Look carefully between the pots on the large table where Varyon tends to position himself and you'll find it easily.

Varyon won't react; perhaps he did not notice. That's all good. Hustle the Tube back to Imsin to finish the quest.

Rescue Knight

A knight needs a white knight. Joncis Dalomax, a Knight Errant out of Ebonheart, is being held in the Daedric ruin Ashurninibi, located on island northwest of Hla Oad. You're sent to get him out.

The heaviest burden is just getting there. It's a looong way. Take the silt strider down to Balmora and head southwest to the coast. Hla Oad is a bare wisp of a village halfway between Gnar Mok and Seyda Neen—a seedier version of Khuul. A celebrated outlaw parks his boat here, and the Camonna Tong, the Legion's mortal enemy, has a base under the only store in town.

In short, you'll get no help here.

But you don't need it. You're already close to your target. Make your way north along the swampy coast and you'll soon find Ashurninibi—a fallen-down mass of majestic stone with a hard-to-find door facing west near the ruin's center.

This shrine's totally different from others you've seen. The underground portion of Ashurninibi repeats the devastation of the surface structures, and both paths are broken and often flooded. The path leading directly to the captive is concealed; you'll need Levitate to get in or out.

If you find it, I hope you know how to hold your breath.

Once you've killed the two orcs flanking the statue, Dalomax tells you he can make it out on his own. Get back to the Buckmoth Fort to wrap things up.

A Maiden's Token

If you thought the trip to Ashurninibi was long, wait until you try on Imsin's third and last quest.

A Telvanni outcast is blackmailing a Buoyant Armiger—threatening to expose a love affair using an embroidered glove that was given as a token of affection. Imsin asks you to recover this token "at all costs."

The Telvani, Varona Nelas, is in Assumanu—a cave far to the north in the Sheogorad region.

Take the silt strider to Maar Gan. From there, follow the nearby foyada northwest to the coast, the coast east to the Urshilaku Ashlander camp and, at first opportunity, cross the straits to the north and make your way northwest to Ald Redaynia—the Velothi dome high on a hill at the western end of the island. (You don't need to go inside or even get that close; it's just the nearest convenient reference point.)

Follow the road from Ald Redaynia south. When it reaches a northeast-southwest crossing, head northeast. This path will eventually trail off, but continue around the northern edge of the pool here and it will pick up again farther south. From this point, paths lead east into more open country and south into the hills.

Head south. When the path reaches a dead end, look left, and you'll see a gap between two standing stones. Climb to the top of the low ridge here and follow it a short distance as it winds southeast and then south. It will soon divide into two paths. Take the southerly one. When this ends in a large, puck-shaped boulder, look left and you should see the entrance to Assumanu.

Whew.

This appears to be the home of a little band of rogue sorceresses. If you're heading left at the "T" intersection, you'll go up against Vienne Gilelle and, farther along, Calmaninde.

Heading right, you'll confront a truly formidable opponent: Allimir, Nelas' appointment secretary.

Allimir says you don't have an appointment, and doesn't invite you to make one.

You can kill him, but this will also force you to fight Nelas for the glove.

A better route is to simply push past Allimir or use a Levitate spell to float around him. Then you can talk to Nelas in the next room. Get her Disposition up to 70 with persuasion and bribes and she'll give you the glove.

You can take the glove back to the maiden herself, Ilmeni Dren, in Vivec's St. Delyn Canton. (She's at Canal South-One.)

However, the pay-off you'll get isn't worth the diversion. Dren doesn't give you any good dirt on her affair (and why should she?) or explain why Nelas was blackmailing Dren's lover. Dropping the glove off with Imsin will do.

When you do, the quest is finally done, and so is your Legion work in Ald'ruhn. Silt strider boarding on Ramp One!

RADD HARD-HEART'S QUESTS

Scrap Metal

To find Moonmoth Fort, just bear left out of Balmora's south gate, cross two bridges and keep heading east. It'll appear right in front of you.

Radd Hard-Heart—brother to Fighters Guild guildmaster Sjoring—is also right in front of you when you enter the keep. Ask him for orders, and you'll learn the Legion and the Ordinators are having a contest. The Ordinators are supposed to retrieve the skin of a Corpus beast. The Legion is to recover the remains of a Dwemer centurion.

RADD HARD-HEART

This task has fallen to you.

The only local Dwemer ruin Hard-Heart knows of is Arkngthand to the north. If you've performed the early Main Quest missions for Caius Cosades in Balmora, you already know where that is. If you haven't, there is no time like the present to find it.

Make your way back to the crossroads just west of the fort and follow the sign for Caldera and then the one for Molag Mar. Climb the hill, cross the bridge, and continue up the hill. Welcome to Arkngthand. Open the door by turning the crank on the pipe to the left, and you're in.

You don't even have to kill a centurion. Any Dwemer scrap metal will do. (Not that you'd find a centurion here in any case; but for the handful of wimpy baddies inside, it's safe as the streets of Balmora.)

To find the scrap, descend the three flights of stairs from the southeast corner of the top level. At the bottom, follow the left-hand wall around to the next room, and you'll see two kegs. One should have scrap metal in it. Hustle it back to Hard-Heart, who donates 500 gold to your favorite charity (you) and offers up another assignment.

Rescue the Hermit

Those wacky Ashlanders are at it again. They have kidnapped a hermit, Jocien Ancois, from the Erabinimsun Ashlander camp, where he was educating the tribe in Imperial culture. He's being held at a small camp to the west. As usual, you're going in to ensure his safety and deal with the kidnappers.

There are two ways to find the camps, and two to complete the quest.

It may be shorter trip if you take a ship to Sadrith Mora or Tel Aruhn and then zip down the coast, ducking inland to find the Erabinimsun camp shortly after passing Tel Fyr on your left.

However, this way, you'll probably have to wander around a bit to find one or both camps. (You can find the kidnappers' camp by following a trail of fallen pages from Ancois' books.)

However, if traveling on foot, you can save a step and jump straight to the kidnappers' camp. While this route sends you through a good deal of unforgiving terrain, the path is clear, fairly direct and well marked. Keep following the signs for Mount Assarnibibi. This will eventually bring you to the western edge of a large lava pool. Follow the north edge of the pool, bear straight east and you'll run straight into the kidnappers.

It turns out they are mabrigash, or witch-women, who need a man's "essence" for their magic.

This does not sound like such a bad job.

You can kill all three mabrigash. Or you can talk to Zennammu, their leader, and she'll agree to give up Ancois in exchange for a better man. She even has a better man in mind: a young hunter named Asaba-Bentus from the neighoring camp.

Go enlist him. Assaba-Bentus doesn't bite at first, but he's young and impulsive and, you'll either goad him into accepting by suggesting that he's afraid or by suggesting he can have some fun being a boy toy before he escapes.

Either way, talk to Ancois again after you win his release and he'll find his own way home. Then find your own way home to Moonmoth Fort.

Damsel

You don't get much detail on this one—just that an Imperial citizen named Dandsa has been taken captive by raiders and is being held in a cave called Abernanit southeast of Gnaar Mok. Once again, you're The Rescue Guy.

The fishing village of Gnaar Mok is high up on the Smuggler's Coast. Take the Caldera road north through that town and then follow the signs and make your way west.

The large, swampy island is straight southeast from the village, beyond the Hla Oad boat. The door to Abernanit isn't immediately apparent, but it's in one of those swampy pools. Once past the trapped door within, climb to the second level of this small cave, kill the baddies and have Dandsa follow you outside to safety.

DANDSA

Giant Netch

However, don't run back to Moonmoth Fort just yet. Your next mission is also in Gnaar Mok, and you can tackle it now without first getting it from Hard-Heart.

See those two giant flying jellyfish to the north? They look like baby silt striders, but they are breeding netch. They're dangerous, and they've been getting close to town. Go kill them. You'll get a small bump in Disposition when folks in this otherwise unfriendly village learn you're responsible.

Then it's back to Hard-Heart to get credit where credit is due, and pick up one last quest.

Necromancer

A killing for public-relations purposes.

Necromancy isn't illegal under the Empire, but the Dunmer hate it, and to win their heart and minds, the Legion is going after necromancers. This includes Sorkvild the Raven, who has a tower in Dagon Fel – the northernmost community on Vvardenfell.

Take a ship to Dagon Fel and ask residents about Sorkvild to learn his tower is on the east side of town – he's actually taken over a Dwemer ruin—and that he's unpopular. (You can also get this quest from the locals without first joining the Legion.)

Visit the tower. The folks downstairs are not friendly, and you have to climb through the trap door in the ceiling to meet Sorkvild himself, who will attack you on sight.

Be sure to take his Belt of Nimbleness and Amulet of Mighty Blows. If you talk to the locals on your way back to the ship, they'll express their gratitude. Then check in with Hard-Heart, who will thank you himself and refer you to the Legion's other forts for more work. You've done everything he has to offer.

FRALD THE WHITE'S QUESTS

If you've been following the swath our questing legionnaire has been cutting across western Vvardenfell, you know only one destination remains: Ebonheart.

Built from the same gray stone of the Legion forts, Ebonheart, located just southwest of Vivec, is the seat of Imperial government on Vvardenfell. Most of its offices and services are housed in two forts—Duke Vedam Dren's castle and Hawkmoth Legion Garrison in Hawkmoth Fort. In the second-floor dining room of the latter, you'll find quest-giver Frald the White.

Courtesy

Salyn Sarethi, a Buoyant Armiger (whom you may also meet in a later Thieves Guild quest, Enamor), asserts that the Legion has no courtesy. Frald dispatches you beat the Armiger in a contest of wit and poetry.

Of course, Sarethi is right on the mark about courtesy. Ever talk to a guard? "Move along" is their mantra.

Now, if you're still wondering what courtesy has to do with wit and poetry, go see Sarethi. He is in the lower level of the Tower of Dusk in Ghostgate. (The Legion sure makes you walk a lot.) The Armiger clarifies things for you: He actually said the Legion has no courtesy, wit, poetry, or honor.

Oh.

Ask further about "riddle" and you'll learn about the contest. Sarethi will offer three riddles. Each time, you're to complete them by giving the answer in rhyme.

If your character's intelligence is 50 or better, you won't even break a sweat. It's multiple choice, and for each riddle, the correct answer is the third. Nail all three riddles, and Sarethi relents, allowing that, with wit and poetry, the Legion may have courtesy as well.

If your intelligence is less than 50, Frald will recommend that you first secure a copy of the Red Book of Riddles from the Ald'ruhn bookstore of former Legion champion Codus Callonus. Simply speak to Callonus about the book and he'll give you his copy. Your character may have the intelligence of a slow Nix-Hound, but with the book in inventory, you'll have no trouble with Sarethi's riddles.

Report back to Frald, who gives you a Speechcraft skill book ("2920, Second Seed"). You'll also get nice big bumps in your Faction reputation and Disposition.

SALYN SARETHI

Mind that, if you somehow manage to blow a riddle with or without the book, you'll lose the contest but not the quest, and will still get much more modest Reputation and Disposition bumps for just accepting the challenge. (The only thing you can do wrong here is get ticked off at Sarethi for being a big Buoyant Armiger snob and kill him.)

Traitor Warrior

A "go kill this guy" quest.

Frald sends you after an old colleague in the Order of Ebonheart. Honthjolf quit the Legion and went to work for Llarusea Andrethi at remote Aharnabi, which Frald describes as home to sorcerers and Daedra worshippers.

The Legion's counter-offer: You are so dead.

As in many Legion quests, you'll deal first with simply getting to your destination. Aharnabi is far down on Azura's Coast, and, while a silt strider can take you as far east as Molag Mar, any land route is the hard way.

However, one of the nice things about being quartered in Ebonheart is easy access to ships. Travel to Tel Branora and head northeast up the coast on foot. Look for the giant statue of Azura that marks her shrine. You'll find the entrance to Ahanabi just to the south in a small inlet.

It's a fairly small cave. Frald was right about the enchanters. You'll have to kill one on the way in. Honthjolf is off in the cave's northeast corner. He still has his Imperial armor.

When you've retired him, get down to Tel Branora again and grab a boat back to Ebonheart.

False Ordinator

Another hit, but much closer to home. Suryn Athones, an Ordinator guard in Vivec, has been spreading lies about the Order of Ebonheart. Frald orders you to silence him.

Vivec's close enough that you can walk. In the northwest end of the Hall of Justice, climb the stairs to the Justice Offices, use the door to your left and enter the room on the right at the end of the hall. That's Athones right in front of you. If you ask, he'll continue his slanders. Kill him—this may take a while, as the Ordinators are nothing if not durable—and report back to Frald.

Protect Entius

Saprius Entius, a knight of the Order of Ebonheart, is wanted for murder. Frald doesn't think he can get a fair trial in Vvardenfell and wants to get him in front of an Imperial court on the mainland.

But Entius has gone into hiding in Vivec, and Frald doesn't know where. You have to find him before the Ordinator guards do.

You've got to be squeaky-clean yourself before you can undertake this mission, so before you even accept the quest, turn yourself into the authorities and pay the fines for any outstanding crimes.

SURYN ATHONES

Then start asking after Entius among Vivec's Ordinator guards. This is a huge city; you've got to be able to focus your search on a particular Canton. If you can get a guard's Disposition up to 70, you'll learn he's seen another Imperial legionnaire at the Arena.

Now, where would you hide?

Some place people don't usually go.

An Arena storage area can be found off the Canalworks level. Get down there. Entius is behind the northwest door off the main storage room.

(A side note: This is the only spot in the game where a quest brings you into close proximity to the Morag Tong headquarters. To find it, use the southeast door off the main storage room, and look for a trapdoor in the small chamber beyond.)

Unfortunately, you're only one step ahead of the guards. When you talk to Entius, two Ordinators appear behind you. You'll have to kill them with Entius' help. (And a good thing, too, as they're tough.)

Once they're dead, talk to Entius again. You can have him follow you, but tell him to stay put for now. Happily, the Arena is close to the bridge to the mainland. But you'll want to first scope out a fairly straight escape route that involves crossing paths with the fewest possible guards.

When you've nailed it down, return to Entius, speak to him again and he'll follow you all the way home to Ebonheart. Take him to the Hawkmoth Garrison to finish the quest.

VARUS VANTINIUS' QUESTS

What A Day for a Knight

If you've reached Knight Protector in the Legion, you can go to work for Frald's boss, Varus Vantinius. He's upstairs in the Duke's castle. Use the spiral staircase off the Grand Council Chamber, and you'll suddenly find yourself in very illustrious company.

You may have been to the castle before—either to get a stronghold construction contract or House Hlaalu quests from the Duke, and possibly to perform a questionable assassination for the Fighters Guild.

But if not, finding your way in can be a little tricky. The two forts are connected, and you can get to the castle easily only through Hawkmoth. Climb the stairs outside the door to the Hawkmouth Legion Garrison, and the rest should be simple.

VARUS VANTINIUS

Vantinius tells you that to become a Knight of Garland, you'll have to recover two missing artifacts.

The first is a cuirass called the Lord's Mail, which vanished from the shrine on the lower level of the Imperial Commission. Vantinius will give you a key to the shrine.

Visit the Commission on the ground floor of the castle, and you'll get a definite lead. For starters, Imperial Magistrate Rufinius Alleius suspects the involvement of banished legionaire Furius Acilius, who talked about the armor—and of secret caves under the castle—before he left. He suggests you ask after him at the Imperial Guard Garrison.

A visit to the shrine downstairs answers the question of how the thief got in. There's a secret door in the right wall. Lock Level: 95.

Now, how are you ever going to get past that?

A key would be nice. Check out the Imperial Guard Garrison, which is right next door to the Commission. Descend into the barracks, and talk to the guards to learn Avilius had the southwest room.

A bottle. A cup. Candles. A pillow.

And under the pillow, a key.

The key opens the secret door in the shrine. It leads to a small cave. Turn left at the intersection and you'll find Acilius wearing the armor in question. You can talk to him, but it's going to be a short chat if you discuss the Lords' Mail. Kill him, take the armor, and return it to Vantinius.

Acilius also has a hidden campsite on the ledge above him, which is accessible by levitation. By the way, there's nothing down in the cave beyond what Acilius has on him; the barrel and crate floating in the pool beside him are empty other than a key to the secret door you entered. But check out the pool at the end of the cave's right-hand branch. It leads to an underwater gate, and the gate lets you into the sea. That's how Acilius got in without alerting the guards.

In the second part of the quest, Vantinius sends you after a legendary sword, Chrysamere, which was stolen by another treacherous knight. (Apparently the Legion needs to screen its knights a little better.) Legion spies have learned it is in the possession of sorcereress Draramu Hloran. You're to kill her and recover the blade.

All you know about Draramu is that she lives near Sadrith Mora. Travel there by ship and ask after her. You won't get easy answers.

"I won't speak of her," people will say. "Not out loud."

Even in a town of wizards, people are scared of Draramu Hloran. You'll have the boost the speaker's Disposition to 75 to learn she lives southwest of town in a cave called Abanabi. She's said to have terrifying creatures that guard her lair, and powerful friends.

DRARAMU HLORAN

Even this isn't all that helpful. Zafirbel Bay has a lot of islands and a lot of them are more or less southwest of Sadrith Mora. So we'll need to be really precise. From the front door of Pierlette Rostorard: Apothecary, just north of Wolverine Hall, you'll want to swim and walk (or, ideally, Levitate) in a straight line southwest that will take you over one large island and one small one.

After the small one, you'll see a little beach on your left and a door set in stone. That's the way into Abanabi.

The cave plays with your head a bit. There are two spellcasters in Abanabi. The main tunnel leads to one named Maranique Jolvanne. You should be able to get a word in with her, between killing the creatures she conjures to fight you. She'll say she knows Hloran and identify Chrysamere as a weapon designed to kill spellcasters. But no persuasion or threat will elicit more details.

You'd almost think Hloran had moved on.

She's here. A slightly-concealed side corridor—on the left, before you reach Jolvanne—starts you down toward Hloran's lair. A crooked, narrow stone path, over deep water, leads to the platform where you'll fight her.

And yes, she'll use Chrysamere.

Return the sword to Vantinius for your very own Duke's Guard Armor.

Grandmaster

If you speak to Vantinius again and select "advancement," he'll observe that there can be only one Knight of the Imperial Dragon on Vvardenfell. Select "duel," and he'll tell you he'd rather die than lose his position, and challenge you to a death duel in Vivec's Arena.

Go to Vivec and open one of the two doors to the Arena Pit. If you've already fought all duels to which you've previously committed with other characters, Vantinius should appear.

If you haven't fought all your duels, your opponents will be stacked up waiting for you, like the scene from "Airplane" with the hysterical passenger, and you'll have to complete each of those fights to get to Vantinius. Do so by leaving the Arena Pit after each fight and then returning.

Killing Vantinius can be tough, especially now that he has the armor and weapon you just recovered for him. But once you do, you're head of the Legion. And you get the use the Lord's Mail and the Chrysamere.

IMPERIAL CULT

The missionary arm of the great faiths, the Imperial cult brings divine inspiration and consolation to the Empire's remote provinces. The cults combine the worship of the Nine Divines, the Aedra Akatosh, Dibella, Arkay, Zenithar, Mara, Stendarr, Kynareth, and Julianos, and the Talos cult, veneration of the divine god-hero Tiber Septim, founder and patron of the Empire. Imperial cult priests provide worship and services for all these gods at Imperial shrines in settlements throughout Vvardenfell.

Favored Skills

Speechcraft	*Blunt Weapon*
Unarmored	*Conjuration*
Restoration	*Security*
Mysticism	

Advancement

Rank	Personality	Willpower	One Favored Skill at	Two Other Favored Skills at
Layman	30	30	0	0
Novice	30	30	10	5
Initiate	30	30	20	8
Acolyte	30	30	30	10
Adept	30	30	40	12
Disciple	31	31	50	15
Oracle	32	32	60	18
Invoker	33	33	70	20
Theurgist	34	34	80	25
Primate	35	35	90	25

Faction Reaction

HATED ENEMY	ENEMY	HOSTILE	FRIENDLY	ALLY	BELOVED ALLY
	Ashlanders	Temple	Mages Guild	Imperial Legion	
	Camonna Tong	House Telvanni	House Hlaalu	Blades	
	Clan Aundae	Thieves Guild	House Redoran	Fighters Guild	
	Clan Berne				
	Clan Quarra				

Some factions are fussy about who they take. But it could hardly be easier to join the Imperial Cult.

Don't be put off by the "cult" part. It's just the name for the Imperial religion devoted to worship of Nine "Divines" – including Tiber Septim, who forged the Tamriel empire and served as its first emperor.

To join, you need simply speak to either Ygfa at Fort Pelagiad, Syloria Siruliulus at Buckmoth Legion Fort outside Ald'ruhn, Somutis Vunnis at Moonmoth Legion Fort outside Balmora, or Ruccia Conician or Lalatia Varian at Duke Vedam Dren's castle in Ebonheart. (These last two are in the Grand Council Chambers and Imperial Chapels, respectively.)

You'll make a one-time payment of 50 gold.

And you're in like Flynn.

Advancing is another matter. Like other factions, the Imperial Cult is looking for a particular type of character – in this case, a person who is durable, colorful, and peace-loving without being a weenie—and the more of that sort of character you are, the higher you can rise in its ranks.

When you reach certain ranks and select the "Advancement" topic when in conversation with a quest-giver, you'll receive special magical tokens that, when worn, add five points to certain of your skills.

At Rank 2 (Initiate), you'll receive a Maran Amulet, which adds to your Conjuration, Mysticism, Restoration, and Speechcraft skills. At Rank 3 (Acolyte), you'll get a Stendarran Belt, which supplements your Attack, Blunt Weapons, Enchant, and Unarmored skills. At Rank 5 (Disciple), a Septim Ring adds to your Attack, Blunt Weapons, Speechcraft, and Unarmored skills. And, finally, at Rank 6 (Oracle), you'll get an Akatosh Ring that adds to your Conjuration, Enchant, Mysticism, and Restoration skills.

In some respects, the Imperial Cult's quests operate in a fashion similar to early House Telvanni. The four quest-givers all operate from a single location, and you can start out performing innocent delivery errands. Indeed, two of the Cult quest givers are among the most amiable and flexible in Morrowind. You don't even have to finish their quests. You can turn down or give up on any quest by simply saying so. It's like Quest School, and a great place for a novice Morrowind player to start.

The hitch: If you turn down a quest, the quest-giver will wait a day before giving you another assignment.

SYNNOLIAN TUNIFUS' QUESTS

SYNNOLIAN TUNIFUS

If you liked the early Telvanni quests, when you were looking for spell ingredients, you should look up Tunifus in the lower level of the Imperial Chapels. In his seven "Lay Healer" quests, you are not a killer, a thief, or a spellcaster. You are essentially a guy with a durable pair of shoes and a will to travel.

These missions all require delivery of ingredients. To be sure, Tunifus will offer suggestions on how to acquire the goods, but while these sometimes offer special advantages, they are only suggestions, and you can take or leave them.

Marshmerrow

For your first errand, you're to bring Tufinus five pieces of marshmerrow, an ingredient in Restore Health potions.

He suggests you get them from the fields of Balur Salvu, a Pelagiad-area farmer, and gives you a Fortify Strength potion to give to Salvu as a gift—along with the suggestion that, if you're pleasant, Salvu might be willing to teach you a thing or two.

When you arrive, just speak to Salvu. Your gift is turned over automatically, and the farmer is happy to help—both with the marshmerrow (which can be found in either of his fields) and with an Alchemy skill book. (You'll have to ask him about "do you for" to get this.)

If you like, you can buy the marshmerrow at an alchemist's shop or find it in the wild and keep the Fortify Strength potion for yourself. But then you won't get the benefit of Salvu's teaching.

Return the ingredients to Tunifus for a Restore Health potion, and a mortar and pestle so you can practice making your own potions, and the suggestion that you check your advancement. (You should already qualify for advance to Novice.)

Muck

You've only to speak to Tunifus again to get this two-fer errand.

Ogrul, the chaplain at Fort Darius, has made a deal with Gnisis farmer Abishpulu Shand. You can gather free of charge the five units of muck Tunifus requires from a muckspunge patch near Shand's hut. (Muck is used in potions to cure common disease.) No need to check in with Shand first. (In any case, he's not home.)

And while you're in town, you're also supposed to deliver to the chaplain four Restore Health potions that Tunifus supplies.

It's all pretty straightforward. Take the silt strider to Gnisis from Vivec or Seyda Neen. (Tunifus gives you money to cover this.) The chaplain is in the chapel on the lowest level of the fort. Just talk to him to turn over the potions, and select "return your favor" to get a choice of one of four Restoration spells (strength, willpower, speed, or luck).

The muckspunge patch is between Shand's hut and the Legion Barracks. Note that you can harvest muck only from the larger plants.

Again, if this seems like a long way to go for five units of muck, you can buy or find them instead and keep the potions for yourself.

Return to Tunifus to receive a Cure Common Disease potion, a retort for potion-making, and a collection of 10 alchemical recipes called "The Alchemist's Formulary."

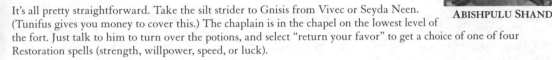

ABISHPULU SHAND

Willow

Now your contact needs Willow Anther for Cure Paralyzation potions. Tunifus confesses that he steals the stuff from flowers around the home of Gurak gro-Bagrat—a skooma smuggler whom he cautions you to avoid.

It's easy to find. Just repeat your trip to Salvu's farm, but this time continue east, across two dock-like bridges, and past any number of wandering netches (which the smuggler raises), and gro-Bagrat's place will soon turn up on the right. You can get the five units of willow anther from the lavender flowers in the box to the right of the front door. Or you can do the buying and finding thing we've already mentioned.

If you are eager to tempt fate, Gro-Bagrat's down in his cellar behind two seriously locked doors—the second one trapped. Let's just say he's not in the mood to talk.

Get the willow anther back to Tunifus for a Cure Paralyzation Potion and his old copy of "The Four Suitors of Benitah," which adds two points to your Restoration skill.

Scrib

You're off to the Shulk Eggmine near Balmora in search of five units of scrib jelly for Cure Poison and Cure Blight potions. Simply kill five scribs, harvest the jelly from their remains and hoof it back to Ebonheart.

As usual, Tunifus can provide detailed directions. Just talk to him and ask after the mine.

You can take the silt strider to Balmora, but it'll take you out of your way at both ends of the journey. And it's safe to walk—provided you don't fall in with bad company. Don't talk to strangers along the way, and just follow the signs north.

South of that large town, you'll find a post with three signs—none of them pointing along an obvious route to the west. Follow this past the Lleran Ancestral Tomb, the pilgrim Nevrasa Dralor, and the Shurdan-Raplay Egg Mine. The path then winds down toward a swinging bridge. In the distance, you should see a campfire. It's right outside the Shulk mine.

The mine's quite large, but relatively safe. Use the Detect Creatures spell Tunifus gives you to avoid any kwama warriors.

Don't worry about the kwama workers; they may look intimidating, but just go methodically about their business. The kwama foragers are numerous and pesky, but easily killed. And the cootie-like scribs themselves are about the least offensive critter in Morrowind; you can kill them almost by looking at them.

However, not every scrib can be harvested for jelly, and you may need to fill out any shortfall in the wilderness or another mine. You can also mooch two units of scrib jelly from one of the miners on break at a fire outside the mine—if he has at least a Disposition of 50. (Avoid the Shurdan-Raplay mine to the east; it is blighted.)

This may be one time you want to buy at least some of the ingredients at an alchemist's shop.

Whichever way you go, you'll get Cure Poison and Cure Blight potions and an alembic when you return to Tunifus.

Corkbulb

Your contact will send you out for five units of corkbulb—a root used in Cure Common Disease and Restore Health potions. Just as the cult has a muck-raking deal in Gnisis, so it has a corkbulb-pulling deal with plantations in the Ascadian Isles region and Tunifus suggests you visit the Arvel Plantation—one of three sited just north of Vivec's Foreign Quarter.

Again, this is simply an extension of an earlier trip. Return to Gurak gro-Bagrat's manor, where you found the willow anther, and this time head north across a strait to Dren Plantation. (If you're scared of the water, Tunifus has taught you a Swimmer's Blessing spell that should ease your passage.) Then continue north, over a rise, to Arvel Manor.

If you can't get all five units of corkbulb here, the Llovyn farm southwest of the Dren Plantation should fill out your supply. And, naturally, any old corkbulb will suffice.

Return to Tunifus for Cure Common Disease and Restore Health potions.

Rat

Tunifus now wants five units of rat meat for Cure Poison potions, and directs you to Vivec's Underworks, or sewers, to find the critters.

Each canton has its own sewer. You can enter them either internally through a trapdoor in the canton's Canalworks level or from the outside using the underwater outflow grates. You should be able to find three or four rats in each.

But just as not every scrib yields jelly, not every rat produces meat and you may have to visit as many as three separate sewers to collect all Tunifus requires.

It's a bit dangerous for an inexperienced character—not so much because of the rats as for what else you may stumble across in the process. The sewers are neither large nor confusing, but they are a place people—sometimes bad people—go to escape. If you're still finding your way in the game, stay focused on the rats and run from anything bigger than a breadbox.

Cart the stuff back to Tunifus for a sample Cure Poison potion. He'll also note that your missions are getting more dangerous and give you a skill book for Unarmored, which boosts that skill by two points.

Netch

Here, you're back in familiar terrain again. To make Cure Paralyzation potions, Tunifus needs the leather hide of a netch—one of those giant flying jellyfish you've spotted previously around Gurak gro-Bagrat's manor.

Pay another visit to Balur Salvu's farm. You should see several netch nearby. All should be close enough to the ground that you can attack them easily, but take Tunifus' tip and look for a bull netch. They are less fierce than the females, but they'll still fight back. You should be able to tackle whatever it dishes out, but if the fight doesn't go your away, feel free to retreat, heal up, and return to the fray.

Gee, hope this wasn't one of gro-Bagrat's netches.

Once the netch is dead, take the leather and return to your contact for an especially nice reward—not only five Magicka Resistance potions, but a Belt of Balyna's Soothing Balm.

And now you've done all the quests Synnolian Tunifus has to offer. That wasn't so hard, was it?

IULUS TRUPTOR'S QUESTS

Well, this is different.

In the seven "Almoner" Quests issued by Iulus Truptor, who shares the downstairs room at the Imperial Chapels with Tunifus, you are a cult fundraiser—collecting gold and the odd item to support the organization's good works.

The quests are of no more than moderate difficulty, but you'll be doing a lot of talking and negotiating and for that you'll need good Personality, Speechcraft, and Mercantile skills.

Skyrim Alms

Your first destination is the mission from the Empire's Skyrim province. It sets the pattern for the early quests in this series. You need to collect 100 gold and return it to Truptor. If you come up with 200, you'll get a bonus. And anything above that is icing and you keep it to cover your "overhead."

The Skyrim and Argonian missions are located close together over in the Hawkmoth part of the fort complex. Don't just blunder in and start asking for moolah. As in most communication in Morrowind, the key is the donor's Disposition. If you ask for "alms for the poor" without using Persuasion or Bribes in preparation, you'll receive a lower donation, and you'll be stuck with it.

However, you should be able to raise the minimum easily. In fact, Mission leader Heidmir will supply it himself at a Disposition of 50 and the full 200 at one of 70. (Everyone else here will give something, and everyone can be nudged to a higher donation with Persuasion or Bribery.)

As a reward, in addition to the usual Faction Reputation and Disposition bumps, you'll get two Fortify Personality potions. At 200 gold, the Faction Reputation and Disposition bumps double in size, and instead of the potions, you'll get the enchanted Shoes of Conviction.

And all you had to do was walk one fort over.

Argonian Alms

At the Argonian Mission, it's pretty much the same story—but at once much simpler and slightly more complicated.

The simpler part: This time, you only have to deal with one person. Everyone else in the embassy defers to Consul Im-Kalaya. With a Disposition of 50, he'll donate 100 gold. At 80, he'll make it 200.

The more complicated part: The 80 Disposition may prove a daunting goal for characters without a high Personality or Speechcraft skill (or deep pockets).

An option for those who find themselves in this position: Explore the embassy. Deep in the bowels of the building, beyond a flooded section of corridor and behind a locked door, you'll find an Argonian slave.

The Argonian mission is spiriting escaped slaves out of Morrowind.

While a noble action, this is also a crime. And while it's pretty contemptible to do so, you can use your new knowledge to blackmail Im-Kalaya by repeatedly mentioning "runaway slave" in conversation to pry the full 200 out of him.

I think I liked collecting spell ingredients better.

With 100 gold, Truptor gives you a pair of Fortify Luck potions. At 200, you'll pick up an enchanted Zenithar Frock.

Buckmoth Alms

Now you're bound for Ald'ruhn to raise money for the "Buckmoth Fund."

It's not exactly hard. But it can take a good long while.

You'll get two kinds of responses to your solicitations.

The Dunmer will say, more or less, drop dead. Don't even bother talking to them.

FORT BUCKMOTH

You'll have better luck with members of other races. Some will give, some won't, and most of those that do will give the minimum donation (10 gold) at a Disposition of 30 and the maximum (20 gold) at 70.

You can put together the 200 from the following eight residents: Aengoth the Jeweller at The Rat in the Pot, Cienne Sintieve at Cienne Sintieve: Alchemist, Codus Colonus at Codus Callonus: Bookseller, Malpenix Blonia at Malpenix Blonia: Trader, Edwinna Elbert at the Mages Guild, and Percius Mercius and Baradras at the Fighters Guild. A number of others will donate smaller amounts.

Turn in your money and Truptor will give a pair of scrolls (Fphyggi's Gem-Feeder and Didala's Knack). If you pull together the full 200, the bonus includes a Mercantile skill book ("The Buying Game").

Shirt

The Harvest's End pageant is coming up, and the cult needs a red shirt and a black vest—a combination known on Vvardenfell as a "common shirt." You're to persuade a clothier to donate the items.

Where to start? Truptor suggests you could find a shop familiar with this Western fashion in Vivec, Balmora, Caldera, or Pelagiad. The closest is Agrippina Herennia on the Canalworks level of Vivec's Foreign Quarter. She doesn't have any, but refers you to High Elf Falanaamo in Caldera.

Use the teleport service at the Mages Guild in Vivec's Foreign Quarter. You'll find Falanaamo: Clothier right next door when you emerge from the Mages Guild in Caldera.

Falanaamo's got the goods…and also the will to be paid for them. You'll need to get his Disposition up to 80 before he'll donate the common shirt. (He'll throw in matching trousers!)

And if you can't manage that, you'll have to steal it —Falanaamo has one with the right colors in a crate upstairs—or even <choke> buy it.

Then again, if you've already blown the whole Persuasion thing, the elf may not even want to sell you the outfit. If so, watch for people on the streets wearing it. It's not a common item, but you'll recognize it when you see it, and you can kill the rightful owner and take it.

We'll just look the other way.

Get the shirt and vest back to Truptor to wrap up the quest and get a Mercantile skill training book as a reward.

Dinner

The cult is holding a high-class fund-raising dinner, and is looking to get the high-class booze for free. You're sent around Balmora taverns and restaurants to round up five bottles of Cyrodilic brandy.

CRATES OF BRANDY

Unfortunately, you can only get donations of three bottles this way. Bacola Closcius at the South Wall cornerclub happily turns over a bottle, and Dulnea Ralaal at the Eight Plates and Benunius Agrudilius at the Lucky Lockup will each give you one, though they need to have their Dispositions stroked first.

Of course, you must buy or find two more.

But hang on: Didn't Closcius say something about the Council Club receiving five bottles of the stuff? You'd never know it: Proprietor Banor Seran either insults you or just kicks you out.

So steal it. It's in a closet in the hall to the right of the bar, and if you close the door before you do the deed, no one will be the wiser.

Bring the brandy back to Truptor for a pair of enchanted gloves—the Right and Left Hands of Zenithar.

Rich

Back to Caldera—this time to persuade Cunius Pelelius, part-owner of the Caldera ebony mine, to follow through on a pledged 500-gold donation to the Imperial cult's Widows and Orphans Fund.

Cunius can be found right inside the door of the Governor's Hall—a large, castle-like structure in the northeast corner of town. Talk to him about the donation, and he'll say he's busy and will discuss it at a later date.

End of story.

Ordinarily, you'd try to bring up Pelelius' Disposition and get him to see the light. But here, Persuasion simply won't work. You'll have to find another way.

Talking to most of the other people in the Governor's Hall isn't productive. But Olumba gro-Boglar in the south upstairs hall is the exception. You can talk to him about Pelelius and learn a rumor that he's solving money troubles by skimming from the mine and by smuggling ebony.

The rumor gains weight when you follow up with slaves in the mine itself—first boosting their Dispositions to 55—and discover Pelelius has been sneaking in at night to steal ebony. Return to the rich man and try on the "donate 500 drakes" topic again and then threaten him with the slaves' account. He'll give you three pieces of raw ebony. Sell it to someone who has a high regard for you—the price depends on their Disposition and your Mercantile skill—and get the 500 gold back to Truptor. In return, he'll give you six scrolls with exotic names.

Admittedly, this is a long road to travel for a mere 500 gold, and none of it is required. If you've done well for yourself, you can simply pay off Truptor from your own resources.

But then you wouldn't get to see that bastard Pelelius squirm.

Ponius

Another deadbeat donor, and another dark tale of corruption in an Imperial enterprise.

In his final quest, Truptor asks you to get Canctunian Ponius of the East Empire Company to pay his pledged gift of 1,000 gold for an Imperial cult mission to the Ashlanders.

Go see Ponius in his office at the rear of the company hall, located near the docks in Ebonheart.

Hey, Ponius, did anyone ever tell you that you look like Napoleon?

CANCTUNIAN PONIUS

The East Empire Company boss is concerned with weightier matters. A seemingly reliable clerk named Mossanon has embezzled 3,000 gold from the company's treasury and vanished. Ponius enlists you to track him down. When you recover the money, he'll make good on the pledge.

You can start tracking right outside Ponius' door. Shazgob gra-Luzgan reports the clerk had been seen coming and going from the teleport service at the Mages Guild in Vivec's Foreign Quarter. And Okan-Shei, in the hall's front room, will give you a sense why he was there: Mossanon has a secret Telvanni girlfriend.

Get over to Vivec and see Flacassia Fauseius at the Mages Guild. Sure, she remembers Mossanon. He went to Sadrith Mora a lot.

And now, so should you.

Did we mention the clerk is a High Elf? Make use of that info. It's going to be important, as it's possible to lose track of Mossanon here by talking to the wrong people. Many people in Sadrith Mora will direct you to a High Elf trader named Sinyaramen at the Gateway Inn. He can't help you, but suggests you talk to Dark Elf females if you're looking for gossip on a Telvanni lady with a High Elf boyfriend.

If you question Dark Elf females in Sadrith Mora about Mossanon, they'll report having seen a High Elf in the company of Volmyni Dral, who lives near Wolverine Hall. They'll even say catty things about her looks.

Go to Dral's House. Look upstairs. (The stairs are on the left; if you can't see them, turn up the Gamma Correction a little.)

Yup, that's Mossanon, all right. Talk to him about "embezzled funds" and he'll admit the deed and say he did it for love.

You have three choices here. You can simply demand the gold. If Mossanon's Disposition is 70 or better and your Speechcraft skill 30 or better, that'll work.

Alternatively, you can promise him secrecy and succeed if his Disposition is 70 or better and your Personality is at least 45 or Reputation at least 10.

Or you can just beat the bejesus out of him and take the money and his enchanted Peacemaker staff.

Now all you have to do is grab a ship home to Ebonheart, return the gold to Ponius, deliver the 1,000-gold pledge to Truptor, and collect the powerful Zenithar Whispers charm amulet.

But how much gold do you return? Ponius doesn't know how much you recovered. You can be honest and give him all of it, like a good would-be Nerevarine. Or you can lie through your teeth, give him just enough to cover his commitment to the Imperial Cult, and keep the rest to cover expenses.

That little twinge is just your conscience.

KAYE'S QUESTS

The "Shrine Sergeant" quests from Kaye, whom you'll find right inside the Imperial Chapels door, are more in line with those you'll perform for other Morrowind factions. Of moderate difficulty, they involve rather more fighting and generally scary situations, and the last, Restless Spirit, pits you against four high-level enemies.

To be sure, as in earlier quests, you don't have to meet any requirements first. But while you can still turn down or back out of quests, there are now repercussions. Kaye gets annoyed at you, and his Disposition drops by 10 points.

Missing Limeware

Seems you just can't leave out the good china when a High Elf is in the house.

KAYE

After treating a High Elf named Caryarel for swamp fever, a rare limeware bowl turned up missing from the Cult's shrine. It's a gift from a benefactor, and its loss would be embarrassing if exposed. You're to track down the thief and retrieve the bowl.

The clues are few. The swamp fever only suggests Caryarel lives along the coast, and Kaye's description of him could fit any number of High Elves. But Kaye also notes that the High Elf community on Vvardenfell is small and tight; one High Elf might know another. He suggests you talk to the High Elves serving in the Hawkmoth Garrison.

While you may have hit a dead-end using a similar approach in the Ponius quest, it works here. At the Garrison, Landorume or Fanildil will point you straight away to the west coast fishing village of Gnaar Mok.

Take a ship there from Ebonheart (Ebonheart to Hla Oad to Gnaar Mok). You'll find Caryarel walking around the village. He allows that he was treated at the chapels, but denies any knowledge of a missing bowl.

His story doesn't have the ring of truth. He's unnecessarily rude, and it's not just the traditional Gnaar Mok rudeness.

He's your guy. But again, as with Pelelius, Persuasion won't make an impression.

Other residents will tell you Caryarel lives in a shack by the docks. It's the last house on the southern side of the docks. Find it, pick the lock, and take the bowl. (It's in a barrel partly hidden by the table.) Return it to Kaye for 200 gold and three Divine Intervention scrolls.

The Haunting

Kaye doesn't have many details—just that a Bosmer named Nedhelas has a ghost in his house in Caldera. A plain old weapon won't touch a ghost, so you'll get 200 gold in front money to buy an enchanted one or some spells.

You may well already have such a weapon. If not, you can pick up one or both in Vivec's Foreign Quarter on your way to the Mages Guild. (Its guild guide teleport service is the fastest way to get to Caldera.) Check out Miun-Gei: Enchanter in the Lower Waistworks.

Once in Caldera, just head south from the Mages Guild and you'll run right into Nedhelas in the street. He thinks the haunt's connected to the cellar—his landlord told him to leave it be—and gives you the key to the trapdoor.

This also opens the front door of the house, located just inside Caldera's south gate. The trapdoor's in the near left corner, and its description should leave you in no doubt of the source of the problem: The house was built atop the Heleran Ancestral Tomb. (One of the designers has apparently has seen "Poltergeist.")

Below is a small crypt-cum-basement, and it's a simple matter to find and beat up the ghost of Galos Heleran. Stop by on your way out to town to tell Nedhelas the good news, and check in with Kaye to get two scrolls of Golnara's Eye-Maze (a Chameleon spell).

Witch

A variation on the ghostbusting of the previous quest, only this time the ghost is a witch named Thelsa Dral and Caldera is the Asha-Ahhe Egg Mine near Khuul.

Again, Kaye doesn't know much—just that Dral is a capable enough spellcaster to summon bonewalkers.

Take ships up the coast from Ebonheart to Khuul, and follow the path south out of town. You'll pass the Panud Egg Mine on your right. When the path splits, go right. You'll eventually come to two intersections set very close to one another. Go straight through the first and turn left at the second, following the signs for Ald Velothi and Gnisis. Over the rise, you'll see the Asha-Ahhe Egg Mine on your right.

Talk to the miners about the mine for a good scare.

But, in fact, Asha-Ahhe is fairly small and linear for an egg mine. Just follow its windings down to the bottom and kill the witch there quickly. Watch out for her Nord barbarian bodyguard, but her Dark Elf healer friend isn't much of a threat. She doesn't offer much in the way of loot (beyond a fancy outfit and an enchanted poison blade). But, back in Ebonheart, Kaye has an enchanted Firestone ring with your name on it.

Silver Staff

The cult's Oracle has had a vision: a Silver Staff of Shaming, lying in a land of burning rock, in the shadow of the Mountain of Fear.

Cult acolyte Linus Iulus vanished with such a staff years earlier. The Mountain of Fear is the old name for Mount Kand. And the shadow (it says here) must mean the staff lies either in the shadow of the rising or setting sun and hence east or west of the mountain.

You're to recover the staff—along with any other of Iulus' personal effects you can lay hand on.

Book passage by ship from Ebonheart to Hla Oad to Molag Mar, and then follow the ashy road north from town. Kaye made the trip sound intimidating. It isn't, really. The road to the mountain is marked and in the one spot where it isn't—branches north and northeast—you just have to remember you're going mountain climbing and follow the uphill path to the north. And if you do get lost, Kaye's provided a Detect Enchantment ring that should lead you by the nose to Iulus' remains.

Near the crest, you'll find a door in the mountainside to your left. Don't enter. You're probably not ready for what's deep under Mount Kand. (Besides, that's a faction quest for a whole different religion.) But use the door as a reference point for your explorations using the ring.

When you locate the unfortunate Mr. Iulus, get his staff, Stendarran Belt and Maran Amulet and make your way down the mountain and back to Ebonheart.

Before you talk to Kaye, look over the booty and figure out what you want to keep. If you have all three items in inventory when you talk to him, you'll turn them all in. In return, Kaye will give you the Silver Staff in addition to a Restoration shirt (which reduces fatigue).

However, Kaye doesn't know what you found, and you can save the Belt, and Amulet for yourself if you dump them before your chat and pick them up again later. If so, you'll just get the shirt. Bear in mind you're going to get your own Belt and Amulet eventually anyway.

Your choice. Greedball.

SMUGGLERS

A Restless Spirit

Okur, an Argonian from Hla Oad, reports that she is being visited by the ghost of a murder victim. The guards apparently can't do anything here (though you were certainly able to act under similar circumstances in the Widow Maker mission for the Imperial Legion) and you're to speak to Okur and see how justice can be served and the spirit allowed to rest.

You'll need to take a ship from Ebonheart to Hla Oad. Okur's house is right on the northeast edge of town. She'll tell you the ghost is that of Julie Aumine, and that she'll rest only when the four smugglers who killed her are dead and her amulet is returned to her husband.

I really hope it's not going to turn out that Okur had some big personal beef with the smugglers.

The smugglers—Dudley, Larisus Dergius, Ralos Othrenim, and Thervam Drelas—are hiding out in a cave called Yasamsi along the road south of Hla Oad. The door is off the southern edge of a swampy pool on the east side of the path. If you reach the Odai River bridge, you've gone too far.

The combat is challenging. These are advanced characters, and you'll probably have to deal with more than one of them at the same time. Dudley and Drelas (and anything the latter may have summoned) will be on top of you the moment you step inside. Dergius and Othrenim (who has the amulet) are deeper in the cave.

The booty's interesting—not so much the hodgepodge of stuff on the smugglers (though Drelas has some unusual Nordic trollbone items) as the huge collection of disparate items stored at the rear of the cave.

All yours now, chum. You probably won't want to cart this stuff off now, but make a mental note of it for the next time you need some quick cash.

You don't have to seek out the murdered woman's husband. Just get the amulet back to Okur and she'll take care of everything. All that's left to do is return to Kaye one final time for your reward: scrolls of Hellfire, Summon Flame Atronach, and Fifth Barrier.

LALATIA VARIAN'S QUESTS

In which pretty much all the procedural rules established in the previous three quest series are trampled underfoot.

Admission to the five "Oracle Quests" is limited to characters that have reached Rank 3 (Acolyte) in the Cult and who not only agree to the terms of a disclaimer, but swear a special oath to serve Varian.

Also, Varian sometimes doesn't tell you exactly what she wants. She doesn't always know herself. Rather, she relates a vision or prophecy and you're expected to draw out its buried meaning and then go do the quest.

You'll have to complete each quest in sequence to get the next one. You can't back out.

LALATIA VARIAN

And these quests are hard. No ingredient deliveries whatsoever.

Ring in Darkness

Varian has had a vision. She has seen the legendary Ring of the Wind.

Does she say where it is? She does not. That is not the way of visions. Rather, she says she has seen the wind upon a dark elf's hand, the fire gleam on a Dwarf's face, and darkness upon a ring of water and heard "no name whispered in the mouth of stone."

When the Oracle talked in riddles in the Silver Staff quest, Kaye translated it into English for you. Now you have to go find a translator yourself. Varian asks you to consult with a Dark Elf savant and a Dark Elf scout.

The quest's interpretive portion can actually be quite short and sweet. A few people can help you with this, but Llaalam Dredil, who can be found on Castle Ebonheart's second floor, is a Dark Elf savant. He translates "no name" as "Nammu" – a cavern west-northwest of the Daedric ruin Yansirramus that has a great, water-ringed stone spire at its heart.

So we know where we're going, but not how to get there. Who's heard of Yansirramus? Hands? Anyone?

Your best bet is to boat it to Tel Aruhn and make your way straight west across the north tip of Zafirbel Bay. Swim or Levitate and use the town's tallest tower as your on-shore reference point. Two islands west, you'll pass Yansirramus to the south. When you hit the mainland, jog north a short distance and you'll see a little lagoon with stone pads leading to a door. This is Nammu.

It starts out as a standard smuggler's cave, with two long prongs. The right-hand one is ordinary. Galmis Dren, who has the ring, is down the left one—high on a catwalk on the great stone pillar. Kill this battlemage and take the ring. Note his Dwemer helm (which explains why the Oracle said she saw a dwarf's face.).

But don't manhandle the other person up here. Speak to Jon Hawker to learn this Redguard trader was Dren's prisoner, and give him the Divine Intervention scroll you received from Varian so he can make his escape.

Read carefully what he tells you (something seems unspoken, yes?) and look at the presents he leaves with you. They are spectacular. The magical glove Zenithar's Warning casts Demoralize Creature, Demoralize Human, Silence, and Blind, and its companion, Zenithar's Wiles, casts Charm.

"It is strange — such valuable gifts," reads your journal entry. "How did he hide them from Galmis Dren?"

You've just had first-hand experience with Zenithar's wiles. Hawker isn't Hawker, but an earthly manifestation of the god.

Take anything you can carry away from here—many potions and scrolls can be found at the right end of the catwalk—and return the ring to Varian to discover you can keep it for yourself. (It boosts your Agility by 30 points)

And be sure to mention to her the story about Hawker for an extra Reputation point, for a total of two on this mission alone.

The Boots of the Apostle

**BOOTS OF
THE APOSTLE**

This time, Varian offers up a prophecy on the location of another legendary treasure: The Boots of the Apostle.

Though you're asked again to consult with a Dark Elf savant or scout on its meaning, and Llaalam Dredil can help you again, you shouldn't need much help. After all, the Berandas the Oracle mentions can only be the stronghold on the coast near Gnisis. "Wings of twilight" can only refer to powerful Daedra that must guard the item. And "dust sleeps in the shoes that Talos wore" can refer only to the item not being in use (i.e. buried in a chest or found on a body).

(Before he became Tamriel's emperor, Tiber Septim was known as Talos Stormcrown.)

Nevertheless, Berandas is not exactly easy to find from Gnisis. It's located southeast of the town across the Ouada Samsi, and no bridges are nearby. The best route is to jump in the water at the silt strider port and make your way south along the east bank. You'll eventually pass under a stone arch, and right after it is a shallow slope where you can climb out. Head east to a path, then south, and Berandas will rise up to meet you.

Like most strongholds, Berandas is a dark and forbidding place, but it seems to have fallen into disrepair—there is much evidence of collapse—and the two upper levels are largely empty. You won't run into serious opposition from the Daedra guardians until you reach the underground section. Here, you'll have to fight a Dremora and then a pair of Winged Twilights to reach the body of the dead hero who has the boots.

Don't be in a huge hurry to run back to Varian. Berandas's underground level appears simple, but a little levitating reveals a couple of hiding places. (Think you don't have a Levitate spell? Ah, but you do: that's the Boots' special enchantment, unless you're a Khajiit or Argonian, since you can't wear boots.)

One is high up in the final chamber, where you'll stumble upon a captive healer. Speak to Ama Nin and give her the Divine Intervention scroll she requests. She'll leave you with two enchanted items of clothing (Mara's Skirt and Blouse). We're unsure how many male characters will wear this cute satiny outfit, but everyone can use the extra reputation point you'll get for helping the lady.

Nin, of course, is another earthly manifestation of a member of the Cult's pantheon—this time Mara—and she's not the last you can meet.

But the last is even better hidden.

Get back to Varian to learn the Boots are yours to keep.

Ice Blade

It's nice to finally get an Oracle quest you don't have to translate first.

This one's pretty cut-and-dried: raid the Dunmer strongold of Rotheran in southern Sheogorad, rescue Adusamsi Assurnarairan, and, if possible, get the Ice Blade of the Monarch she'd gone there to recover.

Take a ship to Dagon Fel and head west and then south out of town. Follow this road for a good ways, with the mountains on your left, and then turn east at first opportunity. When you see the giant Dwemer ruin of Mzuleft ahead of you to the left, follow the path to the south. Rotheran's dead ahead.

It's another unconventional stronghold. (There are at least a couple of these in the game.) This one has a communal hut on the roof and a full-scale arena inside—to say nothing of a throng of Dunmer, who all act as though they want to eat your heart like an apple.

Don't give them the satisfaction. Kill 'em all—including sorcerer Llaren Terano, who's down in the far right corner of the corridor, and the baddies in the arena proper. (Don't hurt the two slaves here.)

From Terano's body, take the Ice Blade, Assurnarairan's ring and robe, and the key to the slave cells.

Free all the slaves in the cells off the Arena. You'll find Assurnarairan in with the Khajiits. She seems kind of messed up—she says something about Terano poisoning her mind with spells—and takes her ring from you and uses it to warp out with barely a "thanks."

ICE
BLADE

Report back to Varian for your reward. You'll get one Reputation point for the rescue and another for bringing the sword back. And you'll keep the Ice Blade. (This enchanted claymore has an evil reputation for choosing its own master—rather like a certain ring—but that's just the stuff of legend. It'll work fine.) You'll even get back Assurnarairan's ring.

Urjorad's Revenge

Long story short: Healer Urjorad went off to the Daedric shrine at Ashalmimilkala to avenge his master's death at the hands of Carecalmo, the shrine's High Elf priest, Among other things, he took with him a powerful artifact called the Scroll of Fiercely Roasting.

It's not explicitly stated when the quest starts, but you can read between the lines that the only thing believed to have been fiercely roasted at the shrine was Urjorad himself.

You're bound for Ashalmimilkala—on a coastal island west of the stronghold Hlomaren—to recover the scroll. That is all you have to do.

But if you're up to it, for extra credit, you can try to kill Carcecalmo and his bodyguard, a powerful knight named Meryaran. It's even cool if you use the Scroll to roast them.

That may prove to be difficult. This is an altogether tricky mission.

Getting into the shrine is tough enough. The structures that comprise the ruin are densely packed; the water around them can make movement awkward.

It doesn't get any easier when you're inside. First you've got to deal with the bodyguard, a ferocious spell-casting fighter who is sited close to the entrance.

Then you realize that the shrine—tiny at first glance—isn't small at all. Additional tunnels, some of them flooded, lead in an irregular ring to the late Urjorad and to Carecalmo himself. And while Carecalmo may be ancient, as Varian says, he is hardly feeble.

Finally, you'll need to Levitate to reach the Scroll of Fiercely Roasting— on a stone near Urjorad's body.

In short, you can bob and weave your way to the Scroll and get out, but even that is going to be a challenge.

Now, if you're dividing your time between the cult and the Morag Tong, it's conceivable you've already exterminated Carecalmo in one of the Tong's "Special Duties" quests.

If so, you've made your life that much easier, and you're halfway to the bonus reward for this quest: +1 Reputation, +5 Faction Reputation and +5 Disposition, plus the enchanted Gauntlets of Glory.

For getting this far, you deserve them.

Skull-Crusher

Once again, Varian has had a vision.

It concerns a lost artifact called Skull-Crusher—a potent but infinitely light warhammer. The weapon was stolen in the First Era. But legend has it that Skull-Crusher can betray thieves and return to its makers. If true, the great hammer still waits somewhere to be reclaimed and its curse lifted so that you may carry it. Varian says you are destined to do so.

But where is it? She does not know. It was created at an unknown site on Vvardenfell by a master weaponsmith and an enchanter. In her vision, Varian saw this site: a Daedric ruin with a forge of molten stone. The ruin has been sealed by fallen rocks. But the forge can still be reached through the Halls of the Dead.

Or maybe you'd rather go pick some corkbulb.

Varian says a Dark Elf scout and savant might offer some insight. The "sealed Daedric ruin" topic leads scout Nalasa Sarothren (at the Elven Nations cornerclub in Vivec) to suggest Anudnabia, a ruin near Sadrith Mora. And our Dunmer savant, Llaalam Dredil, back at Castle Ebonheart, equates the "Halls of the Dead" with any

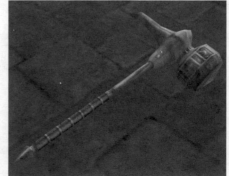

SKULL CRUSHER

Dunmer ancestral tomb.

Put two and two together: To find the Halls of the Dead, you need to find a Dunmer tomb near Anudnabia.

But where's Anudnabia?

Travel by ship to Sadrith Mora. You won't get any clues in town about the direction of the sealed shrine, but even a little exploration will turn up a Daedric ruin with a blocked door just over the ridge to the east of town. This is nowhere marked as Anudnabia, but it can't very well be anything else.

The ancestral tomb must be nearby. If you look carefully, you may even be able to see the cowl around the tomb door from the ruin. The entrance to the Omaren Ancestral Tomb can be found just northeast on an island.

From here on, everything's pretty deliberate. Enter the tomb, find your way through a hole in the crypt wall, and levitate across the chamber beyond the waterfall to reach the entrance below to the Forgotten Vaults of Anudnabia. Defeat the Storm Atronach and get the key from the chest. It opens the door as well as the chest on the other side. Both the door and the chest inside are trapped, so be prepared. Once you're through the door, use Levitate to reach Skull-Crusher in a chest suspended over the forge.

STORM ATRONACH

When you return to Varian, you'll learn the weapon is yours to keep. She finds no curse. Perhaps there never was a curse. Or perhaps it has been sacrificed to the greater good. In any case, your Reputation goes up by two points. And you get a nice ring. If your Blunt Weapon skill is greater than or equal to 40, you get Foe-Quern, with a +5 Fortify Blunt Weapon skill enchantment. If your Blunt Weapon skill is less than 40, you get Foe-Grinder, with a +20 Fortify Blunt Weapon skill enchantment.

(Consequently, to get the maximum skill bump, you'll want to monitor closely your Blunt Weapon skill in earlier quests. When it gets to 39, switch to a non-Blunt weapon. That way, you'll get the nicer ring.)

And that is that. You're done with the Oracle quests, and can tie up any loose ends you have outstanding with other cult quest-givers. Varian tells you that, if you're needed again, she'll send for you.

But don't hold your breath. She won't do this within the game. Not within this game, anyway.

Wulf at the Door

We're not quite done.

Once you obtain Wraithguard from Lord Vivec as part of the Main Quest, an aged Imperial warrior named Wulf will appear in Ghostgate's Tower of Dusk. (Note: Wulf will not appear if you obtain Wraithguard by one of the back-channel methods.)

Wulf was not in the game previously, and no one will mention him to you.

Speak to him. He'll ask you to carry an old coin to Red Mountain as a favor. Accept the coin. When you leave the tower, the old man disappears from the game as suddenly as he appeared.

You may just pass over this as a meaningless encounter. It has none of the usual hallmarks of a magical event.

WULF

The coin itself isn't a magical artifact, but when you accept it, you immediately acquire a new permanent power: Luck of the Emperor, which fortifies your Luck by 20 for 120 seconds.

Wulf isn't really Wulf, but a manifestation of the god Tiber Septim—and the god-emperor has just blessed your journey to Red Mountain.

All this doesn't require membership in the Imperial Cult. But cult members experienced in meeting members of the Imperial pantheon on the earthly plain may be best equipped to recognize it for what it is.

And even if you don't, Varian will. If you do belong to the cult, you can talk to the Oracle about the incident afterward using the topic "Wulf." She'll give you an explanation, your Reputation will jump by two points and the story will enter the realm of Morrowind rumor and legend. You can have it repeated back to you by simply asking anyone for "the latest rumors."

TRIBUNAL TEMPLE

The Tribunal Temple is the native religion. They worship three God-Kings, Almalexia, Sotha Sil, and Vivec, who are known together as the Tribunal. Most people usually just call it 'The Temple.' They accept outlanders as members, but few outlanders join except for the services.

Favored Skills

Unarmored	Mysticism
Alchemy	Conjuration
Restoration	Blunt Weapon

Advancement

Rank	Personality	Intelligence	One Favored Skill at	Two Other Favored Skills at
Layman	30	30	0	0
Novice	30	30	10	0
Initiate	30	30	20	0
Acolyte	30	30	30	5
Adept	30	30	40	10
Curate	31	31	50	15
Disciple	32	32	60	20
Diviner	33	33	70	25
Master	34	34	80	30
Patriarch	35	35	90	35

Faction Reaction

HATED ENEMY	ENEMY	HOSTILE	FRIENDLY	ALLY	BELOVED ALLY
Clan Berne	Mages Guild	Blades	House Hlaalu	House Redoran	
Clan Aundae	Imperial Cult	House Telvanni			
Clan Quarra		Ashlanders			
		Thieves Guild			
		Imperial Legion			
		Fighters Guild			

The Tribunal Temple likes folks with unyielding personalities who can serve as forceful advocates for its holy cause. You need a Willpower and Personality of 30 to sign up.

If you meet that spec, getting into this Dunmer church—a competitor to the Imperial Cult—is as simple as talking to Feldrelo Sadri at the Balmora Temple or any of the five quest-givers: Endryn Llethan and Tholer Saryoni (in adjacent offices in the High Fane in Vivec), Tuls Valen at the Ald'ruhn Temple, Tharer Rotheloth at the Molag Mar Temple, and Uvoo Llaren at the Ghostgate Temple.

In conversation, just select "join the Temple" and choose between joining or a short overview of what the Temple's about ("Faith, Family, Masters, and all that is good").

Advancing in rank from Layman up to Patriarch is similar to advancement within other factions. Your Willpower, Personality, and reputation within the Temple will each need to progress steadily and this progression will start to accelerate when you reach Rank 4 (Adept).

It doesn't matter which of the quest-givers you contact first. All of them, plus Sadri, will require you to first submit to "The Pilgrimages of the Seven Graces."

The Pilgrimages of the Seven Graces

Think of it as a rite of initiation. You must visit and activate seven shrines—all but one in the western half of Vvardenfell. None of these quests are hard—though some can be a bit nerve-wracking—and you'll be led through this process by the hand.

In conversation with your contact, select "Seven Graces" and you'll receive a book called "The Pilgrim's Path." Equip it to read it. It's a 19-page guidebook (a portable quest-giver, as it were) that lays out each shrine's significance, location and what must be done to complete each pilgrimage. Reading the book will add the shrine locations to your map.

Each shrine can be activated only by a special "token." This token can take the form of an item (which must be in the player's inventory) or an action.

If you succeed, the shrine will respond and you'll often receive either a half-day or full day blessing.

The Fields of Kummu Shrine

In fields northwest of Suran, Lord Vivec is said to have worked as a beast of burden to help harvest the crop of a muck farmer whose guar had died. Pilgrims still travel there to pray for the humility that Vivec showed that day.

THE FIELDS OF KUMMU SHRINE

Hope you have nice weather, for this trip takes you through some of the prettiest country-side in Morrowind. The shrine lies on the south side of the road that runs between the north shore of Lake Amaya and the mountains. (If you reach the path that leads north to the Sarano Ancestral Tomb and south to Alof's dock, you've gone too far east.)

You'll need a unit of muck in your inventory to activate the shrine. Any muck will do. You can buy it at Ibarnadad Assirnarari: Apothecary in Suran. And, if you don't mind dealing with a few slaughterfish and mudcrabs, you can find it in quantity on an island just southwest of the shrine.

In return, you'll receive a day-long Feather spell as your blessing.

To Stop the Moon: The Shrine of Daring

The first of the three Vivec shrines is just to the north, on the southwest corner of the upper level of the Temple canton.

This shrine marks the spot where Lord Vivec stopped a rogue moon—which now serves as the Temple's Ministry of Truth—from crashing into his new city. The token: a potion of Rising Force (Levitate) in your inventory. If you don't have one, you can buy it from any number of alchemists and enchanters in the city. (Home-brewed potions aren't accepted. Shrines in Morrowind, and some people, are kind of snobby that way.)

And the blessing? A half-day Levitation spell. Try not to be too high in the air when the spell vanishes.

The Palace: Shrine of Generosity

Two shrines dedicated to the memory of those who died in the last great war against Dagoth Ur are found atop the stairs to the Palace of Vivec—the southernmost of Vivec's cantons.

You simply have to donate 100 gold at one of them. You have that, don't you?

You'll get a day-long blessing that adds 10 points to your Mercantile skill. So if there's something you've been meaning to buy for that special someone (meaning yourself), now's the time.

THE SHRINE OF COURTESY

The Puzzle Canal: The Shrine of Courtesy

The Puzzle Canal is a fairly simple puzzle room in which you'll have to satisfy two shrines.

You may think you've made it into the Puzzle Canal when you haven't. It's reached through the palace's extensive sewer system. But the outflow grates on levels 1, 2, 4, and 5 of Vivec's pyramid-like palace simply take you into sewers very like the ones under other Vivec cantons.

However, in the Level 3 sewer, another grate can be found in the connecting corridor—the crossbar in the "H" layout of the sewer—and this takes you into the actual puzzle.

Climb the stairs in front of you when you resurface here and try to activate the shrine in front of you. You'll get a message: "Breath the Water of his Glory."

Or, in plain English, go drown yourself.

Seriously. Descend a nearby set of stairs into the water and let your breath run out and your health start to drop. Just before you die, surface to save yourself, climb the stairs and look back toward where you entered.

A bridge now exists where none existed before.

The Temple doesn't ask much of you, does it?

Naturally, if you can Levitate or if you've recently done the Pilgrimage to Stop the Moon, you don't need to try to kill yourself over this puzzle. You can just float across the gap.

However you get across the gap, climb the stairs beyond and try to activate the shrine before you. You'll learn that, on this spot, Vivec gave a silver longsword to Daedra Lord Mehrunes Dagon, rather than fight an unarmed opponent. You're expected to reenact that scene with Krazzt, the peaceful Dremora who stands beside the shrine.

Now, we'll just bet that you're fresh out of silver longswords.

It's OK. See the chest on the left? It contains a silver longsword, and it's recyclable. Take it, speak to Krazzt and allow him to take the sword from you. Activate the shrine again to complete the pilgrimage and receive a double blessing of day-long Water Breathing and Swift Swim spells.

Now just find your way out the way you came in. Once again, the next shrine is close by.

The Mask of Vivec: Shrine of Justice

Next, we're headed north to the Gnisis area to visit shrines in that town's Dunmer Temple and at the Koal Cave just to the south.

Take the silt strider to Gnisis. The temple is the low, domed building on your right as you head west through town. The Mask is on an altar on the upper level, and the shrine itself is up a short ramp in the center of the room.

Don't touch the Mask. It is regarded a holy relic—said to have formed over Vivec's face when he and his followers took refuge in Gnisis from renewed storms of ash and blight from Red Mountain. If you take it, the nearby Ordinator guard will see you, you'll be expelled from the Temple, and charged with a crime.

The Temple's got a lot of little rules. If you break them, you'll get the boot but can atone and be readmitted…once.

Do it again, and you're kicked out of heaven for good.

You'll need a Cure Disease potion in your inventory to activate the shrine, and any kind of potion (save for those crummy homemade ones) will do. If you don't have one handy, you can buy a Cure Common Disease potion from Zanmulk Sammalamus in the second room on the left as you enter the Temple.

While you're there, buy some Dreugh wax, too. You'll need it at the next shrine.

When you activate the Gnisis shrine, it casts Cure Blight, Cure Common Disease, and Cure Poison on you.

Don't leave just yet. This particular shrine is more than it appears. Once you have activated the shrine, try to activate the middle of its five segments. It will slide down to reveal the true Mask of Vivec. (Apparently, the Temple keeps only the replica on display.)

You can activate this mask with the same results as the shrine—and an additional benefit. You'll learn the spell Vivec's Touch—a low-cost spell that cures blight and disease in others (and not in you)… and always succeeds. This is useful for later Temple quests where you have to cure someone.

Koal Cave: The Shrine of Valor

When you're done in the Gnisis Temple, return to the silt strider port, jump in the river, and head south along the river's left bank. You'll soon pass under a stone arch and, beyond, find a spot where you can climb out easily. Head east over a rise and continue under an arch until you reach a path leading southeast.

This path will eventually straighten out and head straight east. Continue to follow it across an intersection marked with small stones and blue flowers, and as soon as you pass the next hill, turn right. You should see ahead of you one of those rope guardrails that are set up along roads to prevent travelers from blundering off cliffs at night. Follow it down to the water's edge and on the right, under another stone arch, you'll see the door to the Koal Cave.

THE SHRINE OF VALOR

The shrine is just inside the door. Activate it and you'll get a full-day blessing that fortifies all of your armor skills.

You forgot the wax? Well, you can get the wax in this cave, but you'll need to kill a Dreugh here to get it, and they're tough.

Moreover, Koal is a big place and you will have to swim through a lot of dark and sometimes confusing tunnels to rooms that don't always have nice air bubbles at the top (hence, it's not a bad idea to take care of this shrine right after the previous one and it's water breathing and swift swim blessings).

Naturally, there is also a pay-off: You can loot the bodies of a pilgrim and an adventurer who ventured into the cave's interior and died in the attempt—and the latter has great armor.

If you explore the cave and kill the Dreugh Warlord before you activate the shrine, you'll also get an enchanted dreugh cuirass. This will only work once, however, and only if you haven't activated the shrine yet.

The Ghostfence: The Shrine of Pride

The last shrine lies in enemy territory—inside the Ghostfence. To be sure, it's not far inside, and even without the spoon-fed directions from "The Pilgrim's Path," it's easy to find.

But a player just starting out may find whole the experience pretty intimidating. It's like getting a little preview of the endgame.

Start your trip in Balmora, where you should pick up any supplies you need—healing, anti-fatigue, and invisibility potions, Divine Intervention scrolls, and Mark and Recall spells may all be useful—and, most particularly, a soulgem to activate the shrine Any size soulgem is OK, and it doesn't matter if it already has a soul in it or not. Galbedir at the Mages Guild in Balmora has a bunch for sale.

THE SHRINE OF PRIDE

Leave town by the south gate and head east to the Foyada Mamaea. This volcanic trench is a freeway pointed straight at Ghostgate—the monastery that guards the only ready access to Red Mountain's crater. Just follow it north and northeast. The path should be obvious—though the trench widens around the Daedric ruin Assanatamat, where you may have to dodge some combats. Just keep up your speed and your health, and you should be fine.
.

Once you reach Ghostgate, use the switches to open the gates and head on in to Red Mountain. Go straight up the mountain north toward the crater. You'll soon see a path off to the right. At the end of this spur, you'll find the shrine between two dead trees. Activate it with the soulgem for a day-long blessing of Fortify Magicka and Shield. You'll find that an especially useful blessing later in the game, when you're inside the Ghostfence on a regular basis. It's a good idea to lay in a supply of cheap soulgems and stop at the shrine on each of these journeys.

Get back to any quest-giver or Sadri—it doesn't matter who made the initial contact—and you're done.

Once you've completed the "Seven Graces," many of the remaining Temple quests are open to you. You can get assignments from Endryn Llethan at the High Fane in Vivec, Tuls Valen at the Ald'ruhn Temple, Tharer Rotheloth at the Molag Mar Temple, or Uvoo Llaren in the Ghostgate Temple. (Sadri can bring you into the Temple, but offers no quests of her own.)

ENDRYN LLETHAN'S QUESTS

Disease Carrier

You'll find Llethan in his office at the northern end of Vivec's High Fane. Facing the tunnel, it's the door on the left.

Llethan seems preoccupied. Always pacing about and tending toward just-the-facts briefings, it's like he's got something else on his mind. (Maybe it's just having the boss, Archcanon Tholer Saryoni, in the office right next door!)

ENDRYN LLETHAN

But he does have work for you. It's not a happy job. Your first assignment is to make a sick woman get out of town.

Tanusea Veloth, a Vivec holy woman, has the "Divine Disease." That's the Temple's nice name for Corpus. It has not killed or disfigured her, but she can pass the sickness on to others. You're to persuade her to move to Divayth Fyr's Corprusarium in Zafirbel Bay.

Llethan knows only that Veloth is in the Arena canton. Talk to people there, and you'll learn she's in the Arena pit. (She's the woman off by herself toward the east end of the stands.)

You can take up leaving Vivec as a personal favor or as a practical matter, but she's having none of it. Veloth seems to be in denial.

Now, don't go killing her. Sooner or later, you will have first-hand experience with Corpus if you follow the Main Quest, and the woman's situation should stir your compassion.

In fact, three approaches will work here. You can persuade and bribe Veloth to get her Disposition up to 80 and she'll agree to <ahem> go live in a dungeon. Proud of yourself?

If you don't have the conversational skills to bring that about, remember Llethan's suggestion that a demonstration of your devotion might sway her thinking. You can dig up a copy of "Saryoni's Sermons" – a book Veloth mentions in conversation. If you have it in your inventory when you talk to her, you'll quote from the book and impress this deeply religious woman with your piousness enough that she takes you seriously.

(It's a common book, and you'll find it all over the game. However, you can find a copy easily at Jobasha's Rare Books in Vivec's Foreign Quarter.)

Or, as a last resort, yes, you can kill her. You'll complete the quest, but you'll get no real reward when you return to Llethan. If you follow one of the talking paths, he'll give you a Potion of Cure Blight Disease—just to be on the safe side. (But not to worry. You can't get Corpus from Veloth.)

Note that if you talk Veloth into quitting Vivec, she doesn't disappear immediately—she's an old lady and moves a bit more slowly than you—but should move to Tel Fyr the next time you leave Vivec. You can visit her there and have a little chat. Apparently, she's trying to convert Fyr himself to the Temple!

Silence

Didn't you just get back from a pilgrimage? In fact, didn't you just get back from seven pilgrimages? Now Llethan is sending you on one to the Sanctus Shrine west of Dagon Fel.

Could it be any farther away? And wait until you hear what you have to do along the way: You have to keep your mouth shut. Llethan swears you to silence.

SANCTUS SHRINE

If you give your destination to a ship's pilot or ask to barter with a shopkeeper, you've broken your vow. If you ask a scout for directions, you've broken your vow. Even if someone else talks to you unbidden—as occurs when the person you're escorting reaches their destination—you've broken your vow.

The one exception to the no-talking rule: Dealing with the guards if you're charged with a crime.

You'll have to make the most of the trip over land and all of it under your own power. To cross the straits to Sheogorad, you'll have to Levitate, water-walk, or swim. And you'll have to stay away from people who might inadvertently pipe up with a disastrous comment (and, hence, civilized areas in general).

Make sure you've got everything you need before you give Llethan the go-ahead. Then take the vow and zip it. Zip it good. Activate the shrine to receive its twin day-long blessings of Fortify Endurance and Fortify Willpower.

Then, released from your vow, travel to Dagon Fel, where you can grab a ship home and talk people's ears off.

However, there's a much faster way to do this. Initially, don't take the vow of silence. Assuming you don't yet have the spells, buy one Mark, one Recall, and two Divine Intervention scrolls. Take a boat to Dagon Fel, make your way west to the shrine and cast the Mark spell at this location. Use a Divine Intervention spell to zap to the nearest Imperial Cult shrine (at Buckmoth Fort outside Ald'ruhn) and then zap to Vivec via the guild guide teleport service at the Mages Guild.

Now, talk to Llethan and take the vow of silence. Cast the Recall spell and you'll zap directly to the spot where you cast Mark at the shrine. Activate the shrine, use your second Divine Intervention spell to zap out to the Imperial Cult shrine again and return to Vivec.

If the first solution holds too much frustration, and the second seems too much like cheating, here's a third: Talk to someone (Llethan, even) on purpose and blow the quest. Llethan won't hold it against you. Of course, you won't get any of the bumps in Reputation or Disposition that you'd earn by completing the quest, or the four skillbooks Endryn gives you, but at least you'll be able to move to the next one. That's a small good thing.

The Shoes of St. Rilms

In a dream, a priest saw this missing Temple relic in the depths of the Daedric ruin Ald Sotha. If you've reached the rank of Curate, Llethan will ask you to bring it back.

Ald Sotha is a relative rarity among Daedric shrines—located in the southern reaches of Vvardenfell and close to Vivec. (It's on the mainland just to the northeast.)

The scrolls you'll get from Llethan are four Restore Health, two Invisibility, and one Heroism. The Invisibility potions will help if you're not quite ready to take on the opponents here.

The opponents are heavy duty—Llandrale Varam, in the shrine proper, is a Level 25 mage—but they're not thick on the ground and you should be able to penetrate to the shrine quickly. Just keep moving and don't allow yourself to be drawn into unnecessary combats in the flanking chambers.

The shoes are in a locked (level 50) wooden chest at the rear of the altar in the shrine. It's the one on the altar proper—not one of the two on floor level.

If you do take on Varam, note that the various "Sanguine" items in her inventory will be needed to complete an overarching quest for the Morag Tong, so don't lose track of them if you have any plans to join the assassins guild.

And note, too, that fighting isn't your best move: Since you'll need to more or less clear out Ald Sotha in a late Morag Tong quest, there is little purpose in trying to do so now if you have a lower-level character. Do what needs to be done, and make a run for it.

Kill Bjadmund

Finally, Llethan asks you to kill the leader of a cult that meets under Vivec's St. Delyn Canton. He'll give you some respectable combat scrolls—Hellfire, Elemental Burst: Fire, and The Fifth Barrier—and send you off to a shrine called Ihinipalit.

The shrine has to be in the canton's Underworks (sewers). As usual, the sewer entrance is through the trapdoor in the Canalworks level, and the sewage outflow vents. Ihinitpalit is just down the hall.

You'll be attacked by everyone here and all the things they summon as soon as you open the door. But you don't have to kill everyone, just Bjadmund. He's the bald fellow with the battleaxe.

The loot is fair—decent armor on the men and fancy clothes on the woman.

Return to Llethan. He's been pretty stingy with the rewards so far, but this time he'll give you an Ancestral Wisdom Staff.

But ask him for more duties, and he has none. He'll send you on to colleagues Valen and Rotheloth for more work. They have difficult tasks for you... but at least they let you talk.

TULS VALEN'S QUESTS

Compassion

Valen can be found right inside the door of the Ald'ruhn temple. He is every bit as quick to the point as his colleagues as he dispatches you to the shrine Maelkashishi on an errand of compassion.

Vivec often showed mercy to his enemies, and you are now to show mercy to an enemy of the Temple—a Sheogorath worshipper named Bulfim gra-Shugarz—by curing her blight disease.

TULS VALEN

Valen doubles up on the lessons, apparently wanting you to show frugality as well. He gives you a potion of Cure Blight Disease for the Orc, but comments that it is expensive and that he'd prefer you learned a spell like Rilm's Gift (which cures both common and blight disease) and returned the potion unused. The real lesson seems to be: Show compassion if it doesn't cost you too much!

You can learn Rilm's Gift from Folvys Andalor upstairs.

The Daedric shrines are stacked up like fast-food restaurants in this part of Vvardenfell; Maelkashishi is the second one east of Ald Velothi. (Ashlamawia is the first.)

But that town's not served by fast transport, and as you're probably supposed to cure the Orc this month, you're better off taking ship or silt strider to Khuul and heading south.

You'll need to be careful on a few counts. First off, this road is lousy with bandits and renegade Ashlanders and they can be hardy and creative opponents. However, the rewards are too small to make casual combat worth your while, so don't engage. Just outrun them.

Second, the path isn't obvious. Daedric shrines don't show up on signposts—too many letters! – and at one turning, you may not be able to see the road.

Once out of town, make your first left. A signpost marks this crossing, but offers no sign for this particular road. Follow the road to a grove of twisted trees. In this grove, watch for chokeweed bushes. They turn up between the trees first on the right and then on the left. Right after the bushes on the left, leave the road and head southeast. You may not see the path immediately, but it will appear on your map. Follow it through the low green hills for a short stretch and Maelkashishi will appear in a depression on your left.

Finally, be careful inside the shrine. The Orc is at the base of the stairs. If you're just starting out, get in, do the cure and get out. Either the potion or a spell will do the trick, and though Valen will be properly outraged, killing the Orc will also complete the mission.

However, if your character is more advanced, and you can Levitate, definitely explore. This shrine has some good loot, and it's full of surprises. (It's basically a Daedric skyscraper.) Just don't break your neck if you leave via the Forgotten Galleries. It's looong way down.

Get back to Valen for a Restoration skillbook ("The Four Suitors of Benitah").

The False Incarnate

ELVIL VIDRON

There's a guy named Elvil Vidron who's trying to cut in on your action. He's telling people that he's the Nerevarine and is predicting Many Bad Things. Your job: Do that Persuasion voodoo that you do so well, and show him the error of his ways.

Your quickest route is silt strider to Balmora and then Suran. You'll find Vidron outside near Desele's House of Earthly Delights. It turns out he's not a lunatic; he's just confused about the dreams he's been having.

You and me both, brother. You can bring him around by getting his Disposition up to 65, or by showing off your fancy Moon-and-Star ring if you've received it already in the Main Quest. (If you've already been acknowledged by the Temple as the Nerevarine, Valen's instructions will be slightly different.)

Or you can, um, cut Vidron to ribbons.

However, this fellow doesn't really need to be murdered, just corrected, and you'll get less reward if you go that way. (Talk sense into him, and you'll get high-level Restore Health potions.)

The Magic Rock

Valen sort of phones it in this time. He doesn't even give you real instructions for this pilgrimage—just to read the inscription on the shrine in Maar Gan, imitate Lord Vivec, and to talk to the priest if you need help.

Consequently, you go into this strange little quest more or less in the dark. You won't figure out what to do until you step off the silt strider in Maar Gan—a fortified village north of Ald'ruhn—and visit the large hut in the east part of town.

The shrine here isn't the usual three-sided pillar. It's a boulder. When Mehrunes Dagon held it threateningly over his head, Vivec is said to have taunted the Daedra Lord to make him throw the rock at Vivec, rather than at Vivec's people.

OK, let's play Taunt the Daedra. You be Vivec and... OK, that Dremora over can be Dagon. Is that OK with you, Dremora? (The shrine actually has a Dremora standing around, looking like it could really use a cup of coffee.)

All you've got to do is use the "Taunt" command to bug the Dremora (who is named Anhaedra) until it attacks you.

Don't worry; it doesn't use the boulder.

You don't have to kill it. You don't even have to fight it. Once the Daedra attacks, evade or block its blows and activate the shrine for its blessing (day-long Fortify Speechcraft and Personality spells). And you can talk to priest Tralas Rendas if the Dremora somehow managed to get in a good whack or two and you need to heal up.

However, don't launch a preemptive strike against the Dremora, as you'll have to wait for its body to reform and then repeat the ritual.

Valen seems to have gotten his act together by the time you get back with the good news. He turns over a Block skill book ("The Death Blow of Abernanit"). Hope you're reading these. This one's an epic poem with no fewer than five footnotes!

Into Hassour

It's conceivable you've already stumbled onto this high-end Sixth House base and completed this mission as part of the Main Quest.

And if so, terrific. You'll discover you've wrapped up your work for Valen, who will turn over blight-curing potions and scrolls and kick you along to his colleagues.

If not, and you've reached the rank of Disciple, Valen sends you off on a commando raid against Hassour. Shut down this base, and you'll stanch the flow of Sleepers and Dreamers in the Balmora and Pelagiad areas.

You'll find the entrance in the west wall near the southwestern tip of the Foyada Mamaea—the opposite end of the volcanic trench you used to reach Ghostgate in the last of the "Seven Graces" pilgrimages.

Spooky place! Take the left-hand passage and turn left again at the first intersection to reach the shrine. (And be sure to strike the bells you find down this second hall for a little laugh.) The Ash Slaves and Dreamers shouldn't prove much of an obstacle, but the shrine's priest is a lesser Dagoth (Fovon) and a formidable opponent.

The loot here is excellent, and the 6th House Bell Hammer is formidable for an unenchanted weapon.

THARER ROTHELOTH'S QUESTS

Swamp Fever

If one of Vivec's cantons somehow floated away, it might have wound up like Molag Mar—bumping hesitantly against the harsh coast of the Molag Amur.

The appearance and layout of this settlement—more stronghold than town, as its residents tell you—is almost identical to that of a Vivec canton: Waistworks, Canalworks, Underworks. But the sewers are oddly extensive. And the top level, where most of the services are located, is oddly open to the air—air far less hospitable than Vivec's.

You'll find Rotheloth in the temple on this level. For your first quest, he'll send you to Tel Mora to cure a Redguard named Lette of swamp fever.

THARER ROTHELOTH

Don't even think about walking. Have you seen what it's doing outside? Do you know how far that is? Take ships to Sadrith Mora and then Tel Mora. Chances are Lette will be one of first people you see after you get off the boat; she's wandering in a daze across a narrow channel from the village. Get over there and give her a potion of Cure Common Disease or cast a spell. Anything that cures her is OK.

Grab the next boat back to Sadrith Mora and Molag Mar. Rather amusingly, Rotheloth gives you the "clearly heretical" Restoration skill book, "2920, Rain's Hand."

Riddles in the Dark

Another pilgrimage. This time, if you've reached the rank of Curate, you're to travel to Mount Kand to prove your bravery and wisdom.

The trip itself shouldn't be a challenge—especially if you've already played the Imperial Cult quest Silver Staff, which follows the same route. The road is marked and clear, even in bad weather, and the mountain lies directly north of Molag Mar.

But on that occasion, you were searching the slopes. This time you're going inside the caverns.

Like other Temple pilgrimages, this one follows the exploits of Lord Vivec. Under Mount Kand, he answered riddles from three Daedra. The Flame, Frost, and Storm atronachs are still down there, repeating their riddles into eternity, and you'll have to answer them correctly, in that order, and then activate the shrine beyond the Storm Atronach to receive Vivec's blessing (Fortify Endurance and Intelligence).

If you get one wrong, it'll start a fight. The atronachs apparently take their little riddles very seriously. You'll either have to kill the atronach and then wait for it to respawn so you can get the riddle again, or run, leave the caverns entirely, and return for the atronach to reset (after 72 hours).

But you shouldn't have any problems. While the second and third riddles are quite tricky, the answers are multiple choice and all can all be found in the "The Yellow Book of Riddles." This book turns up randomly, but should be available from a few booksellers—including Dorisa Darvel in Balmora. That's a quick trip from Molag Mar by silt strider.

The riddles start easy. The Flame Atronach wants:

A metal neither black nor red
As hheavy as man's golden greed
What you do to ssstay ahead
With fffriend or arrow or ssssteed

The double-meaning of the answer is the giveaway. It's "lead."

The Frost Atronach's riddle is a variation on an old classic:

"If you lie to me, I will slay you with my sword. If you tell me the truth, I will slay you with a spell."

If this seems bewildering, it's probably because it lacks context. But just think it through from the perspective of someone who wants to survive, and you'll see that one answer ("spell") kills you, the other ("sword") sets up a paradox that saves you. ("Don't kill me!" is just an emotional response, and it doesn't work.)

If you were to say "spell," the Daedra could either say you were telling the truth and kill you, or lying, and kill you.

But if you say "sword," the Daedra can't kill you with his sword, because that would mean you were telling the truth—in which case he'd have to kill you with a spell. But he can't kill you with a spell, either, because that means you were lying.

Finally, the Storm Atronach offers this scenario:

An atronach is dead. The Altmer says the Dunmer did it. The Dunmer says the Khajiit did it. The Khajiit says the Dunmer lies. The Orc swears he didn't do it. If only one of them is telling the truth, who killed the atronach?

The Orc.

He swears he didn't do it. But if you accept that either the Altmer, the Dunmer, or the Khajiit is telling the truth, everyone else is lying. If the Orc is lying, he's guilty in each case.

Don't make the trip harder than it is. The winding passage into the mountain's heart is extremely dark, and there is one pit before you reach the Frost Atronach's cavern that can injure or trap a careless player who can't Levitate to safety. Hug the right-hand wall, use the potions of Night-Eye that Rotheloth supplies and make sure you can float out of trouble.

Note that you don't have to fight the atronachs after you answer correctly. It's OK if you do, but it's not necessary. You can simply walk around the atronachs and fighting just raises your risk. That's already high enough.

Delvam Andarys

However many necromancers you may kill in Morrowind, another always seems to pop up somewhere else. So it is now with necromancer Delvam Andarys at Mawia. Rotheloth asks you to eliminate him.

DELVAM ANDARYS

Mawia's quite close to Molag Mar, and you can walk it. Just east of town, you'll find a north-south channel between two islands. Follow this channel south. You'll pass the Hlaalu Ancestral Tomb on the island to the west. Follow the beach on the eastern island around to its southern tip. To the south, you'll see a dome on the next island to the south and a series of flat stones leading like lilypads to a door. This is Mawia.

Easy, right?

Actually, it is—right up until you face the necromancer himself under the dome. You'll face the odd ghost and bonewalker on the way in, but the place is virtually empty. It's like Andarys just moved in, and hasn't had time visit the discount stores in Vivec to buy furniture.

Take Andarys' little enchanted short blade, Shimsil, and his Ring of Regeneration. And check out his library; it contains a lot of sly and not-so-sly references to vampires, and thus neatly foreshadows your next quest.

Galom Daeus

Unless you have played some of the Mages Guild quests, or stumbled onto one of their lairs, you probably haven't had much to do with the vampires of Vvardenfell.

Yes, vampires. See the "Vampires" section of miscellaneous quests for details. You can become one. In fact, there is a chance that you're going to become one.

Part of the Temple's anti-undead policy is a campaign to remove vampires from Vvardenfell. In this difficult quest, Rotheloth sends you to the vampire lair Galom Daeus to kill Raxle Berne, the leader of one of the island's three vampire bloodlines.

GALOM DAEUS

To help bring this about, he'll give you some enchanted vampire-killing equipment: the warhammer Veloth's Judgment (which compares closely to the deadly Dwemer hammer Sunder from the Main Quest endgame), a Belt of Balyna's Soothing Balm, and a Warden's Ring.

But he's not much help in getting you there. Rotheloth does put a nearby location called Uvirith's Grave on your map, and gives you accurate directions from that point. However, the usefulness of this reference point depends on where you are in the game. If arrive here after you have started building a stronghold, you should see the Telvanni tower rising at this site.

If you haven't, this is just a featureless patch of ash.

Don't try to find your way on foot from Molag Mar. It can be done, but not easily. Many of the trails in the Molag Amur range weren't made by man, but by nature, and following them is a thankless task.

Your best bet is to take ships from Molag Mar to Ebonheart to Sadrith Mora to Tel Aruhn, and then walk south down the coast. When you reach Tel Fyr, look west. On the beach, you'll find the yurt of some renegade Ashlanders. Just south of the tent is a grove of dead trees interspersed with steam spouts. And just west of this grove is a path into the interior pointed almost directly at Galom Daeus.

Beyond another group of dead trees and steam spouts, you'll come to a long lava river. Follow its banks as it runs west and northwest, under a swinging bridge, to end in a deep enclosure. To the west, across another lava pool, you'll see a Dwemer ruin. Detour around the north end of the pool and enter Galom Daeus—home of the Berne vampire bloodline.

Galom Daeus consists of two sections—the entry area, which is filled with lesser vampires (who will attack you on sight) and peaceful but uncommunicative "cattle" who are kept for vampire-feeding purposes.

Berne is in the Observatory. When you're done with him, take the rare book "Secrets of Dwemer Animunuculi" from his desk. If you're in House Telvanni, or planning to join, you'll need this book to complete your stronghold. If you're in the Mages Guild, you can show it to Edwinna for a reputation reward.

And while you're at it, Levitate up to the upper level of the Observatory and grab "Private Papers of Galur Rithari" and perhaps that Daedric shield as well. The shield, though immensely heavy, is also immensely strong... and it's worth a fortune. The papers will come in handy in a vampire-related miscellaneous quest.

Now, that said, note that there are compelling reasons to hold off on this quest until late in the game.

First off, it's extremely tough and best played with an advanced character.

Moreover, if you play any of it, you may restrict your future choice of quests.

The reason: It's very good bet that, in the course of this quest, you will become infected with

RAXLE BERNE

the Berne strain of vampirism—one of three in Morrowind. If you notice this, you can take care of it with Cure Disease potions.

However, if you miss it and become a vampire, you're limited to the Vampire quests offered by the Berne clan.

And, naturally, if you kill Berne, who is the quest-giver for the Berne clan, you'll cut yourself off from even the Berne quests, and limit yourself to the three Vampire faction quests that can be performed by any vampire.

We recommend that you wait, select the Vampire clan you want to join (if you want to join one at all) and then come back to this quest later.

UVOO LLAREN'S QUESTS

A Case of the Droops

Back to the grim solitude of Ghostgate. You'll find Llaren in the monastery temple, which is positioned on an upper level between the towers of Dawn and Dusk.

Llaren breaks you in gently with a couple of simple missions. The first involves curing an Ashlander outcast named Assantus Hansar. Hansar and a couple of pals have a little camp partway up the slope south of the monastery. You'll find your patient there. A spell or potion will work fine.

UVOO LLAREN

However, you may have to perform major surgery on his two friends, who are the usual sort of angry outcast Ashlanders and immediately attack you.

Report back to Llaren for three Cure Common Disease potions.

Kwama Eggs Again?

Another basic errand—though a very long one. Here, you're transporting sustenance—Kwama Eggs and Mazte—to hermit Sendus Sathis on Shuran Island, located just west of the stronghold Rotheran.

No fast travel is available out of Ghostgate, and you face a long jog back to Balmora, a guild guide zap to Sadrith Mora, a ship ride to Dagon Fel, and another long walk south.

Accomplished Levitators and mountain climbers may want to risk a direct route around Red Mountain. We sympathize, but withhold our recommendation, since this amounts to taking a census of the region's cliff racer population.

What you should do, learning the lesson of the Silence quest, is plant a Mark spell at Ghostgate before you leave, and then bounce back there with a Recall spell when you're done. In fact, once your character is sufficiently advanced that the inevitable small combats of travel begin to lose their purpose, you should do this for every mission that requires a long haul. Why walk when you can mingle with the ether?

Rotheran's easy to reach. Head west out of Dagon Fel, then south. Make your first left, continue east until you see the Dwemer ruin Mzuleft rising ahead of you and then head south to Rotheran. Just before you reach Rotheran, you'll see some gentle slopes that take you west over the hills to the water. (Be careful on the water side; the dropoff is steep.)

Swim west to the next island. You'll find Sathis on high ground, looking rather more like a castaway than a hermit.

And wouldn't you know? After all your effort, he complains about the food.

Cast that Recall spell and get back to Ghostgate.

The Hair Shirt of St. Aralor

The honeymoon is over. Now Llaren's quests start getting hard. You shouldn't try any of the next three missions until you reach at least Level 10, or even Level 15.

A Temple guard named Feril Salmyn, searching for Lost Kogoruhn, has become lost himself. He's thought to be dead, but the Temple wants to recover a relic known as the Hair Shirt of St. Aralor from his body.

This may confuse you a bit if you've already performed the Seven Tests of the Seven Visions as part of the Main Quest and have already visited Kogoruhn. After all, it's not "lost" to you. (Just remember that the way the Nerevarine sees the world isn't the way the rest of the world sees it.)

But it's the same place. It's just getting there that's changed.

Plant a Mark spell at Ghostgate, and we'll look at your options.

The old Dunmer fortress of Kogoruhn—original home to House Dagoth—lies fairly close to the north edge of the Ghostfence. The south edge of the Ghostfence is directly over your head. And you well may be thinking, "Hey, why don't I just follow the Ghostfence?"

Well, you can, after a fashion. There is a stretch of eastern slope in the foyada to the south that you can climb, and eventually make your way around to the north side of Red Mountain.

You'll be sorry. East of the Ghostfence is savage and unpredictable country—full of wrong turns, long diversions, territorial cliff racers, crazy Ashlanders, unclimbable slopes, and ankle-breaking falls. You are much better off retreating to Balmora, riding the silt strider north to Maar Gan, and following foyadas across the northern Ashlands. From Maar Gan, you'll take them southeast, northeast, northwest, east (which curves around to head north), east again, and you're there.

Alas, Salmyn is dead. You'll find his body, along with the itchy Hair Shirt, out of doors in a walled enclosure in the southwest corner of the fortress.

Light up that Recall spell and zap back to the Ghostgate Temple. Note that no reward accompanies the Shirt's return. But think of it rather as a reward deferred. Once you are named Temple Archcanon, that, and other Temple artifacts you have recovered, become yours for the asking.

The Cleaver of St. Felms

Now you're right in the thick of it. A Buoyant Armiger carrying the Cleaver of St. Felms fell in the Red Mountain citadel Tureynulal. You have to go in and recover this potent weapon before the enemy realizes what it has.

Getting from Ghostgate to Tureynulal is a real hassle. The foyada that leads straight up the mountain becomes impassably steep. The left-hand foyada goes to the citadel Endusal. And the one to the right one goes back down the mountain. Where does this leave you?

The path back down the mountain is the correct path. Near the bottom of this foyada, you'll see that the eastern slope is shallow enough for you to climb. Do so, and head northeast until you find yourself in a third foyada filled with small boulders. Climb this one to the top. You may have to struggle a bit around over a steep, smooth area, but it can be done.

At the top, you'll see a citadel on the left. This is Odrosal. Cross the swinging bridge across the foyada you just climbed and follow this new path along the Ghostfence. It's a long one. When you see the Salvel Ancestral Tomb on the right, start looking for a foyada on your left. (Yeah, there are tombs in here, and this is kind of a strange one. There is also a Daedric shrine and at least one mine!)

This foyada leads almost straight south to Tureynulal.

The Armiger's body is on the citadel's lowest level. From the entrance go straight ahead, down the stairs, right, down the stairs again, and through the trapdoor to the Bladder of Clovis. (Don't ask.) The body is in the far corner. Take the Cleaver, invoke your Recall spell, and get the hell out of Dodge.

The Crosier of St. Llothi

The Buoyant Armigers need to stop leaving their weapons behind. They've lost another one. This time, you're going into Dagoth Ur's own tower—down in the crater itself—to retrieve the Crosier of St. Llothis.

You can Levitate down there most easily, but if you're on foot, you'll be happy to learn this quest uses much of the route from the last one.

Follow those instructions, but this time don't make the left turn after the ancestral tomb that took you to Tureynulal. Stay on the path and continue west along the Ghostfence.

This path will soon end in a "T" intersection at another foyada. Turn left and follow this path up the hill. You'll see a swinging bridge ahead of you. Climb out beside it, and head east. Follow the "S" curve up the hill. When it straightens out, you'll be heading south, downhill, with a Dwarven statue ahead you. After the statue, turn right. The crater is ahead of you. Just before you reach the edge, turn right again, and you'll see a path leading down into its depths.

That big ball of stone conceals the door. This is exactly like the first Dwemer ruin you visited early in the Main Quest. To open the ball, turn the crank on the pipe over to the left. But be quick; you have only a small window in which to get back and activate the door before the ball rejoins to conceal it again.

The Crosier is in the Inner Tower. But, curiously, the route to it is almost all downward. At the bottom of the fifth flight of stairs, you'll reach the Inner Facility. Within, descend one more flight, enter the door straight ahead of you and use the trapdoor in the ceiling to enter the Inner Tower. The Crosier is on the floor at the right—right between a Dagoth and the body of the Armiger.

THOLER SARYONI'S QUESTS

Once you hit Rank 7 (Diviner) and have completed all of Endryn Llethan's quests, he will invite you to meet with Temple Archcanon Tholer Saryoni and supply a key to Saryoni's private quarters in Vivec's High Fane. You can reach this room either from Llethan's office or the Hall of Wisdom.

Note that this is different from a similar invitation you will receive from Danso Indules—that rather nervous fellow you've doubtless seen pacing at the mouth of the High Fane tunnel—as part of the Main Quest. That meeting, which sets up the Main Quest endgame, has different requirements and results. (However, if you meet the requirements for each, you can combine the two meetings.)

Speak to Saryoni about "duties," and the Archcanon tells you he is old and plans to retire soon. (What is it about you that makes people quit their jobs and move to an island in the distant reaches of Sheogorad the moment you poke your head in the door?) He's identified you as a potential successor, but first requires that you complete...

The Pilgrimages of the Four Corners

The who of the what?

When the Tribunal Temple began to supplant the Daedra in the hearts and minds of the Dunmer, it relegated these exotic magical creatures to two categories. The three "good" Daedra became known as the Anticipations, and the four "bad" Daedra as the Four Corners of the House of Troubles.

In the spirit of keeping your friends close and your enemies closer, you are dispatched to the four corners of the Bad Daedra world. You must perform these quests in the order below, as each sets up the one that follows. Otherwise, they will have no effect.

CLANFEAR

Outside Dagon Fel

The first corner is Malacath, the Daedric patron of Orcs, who tests the Dunmer for weakness. A shrine to this god can be found in Sheogorad southwest of Dagon Fel. To complete the pilgrimage, you must take four Daedra hearts there and recite Vivec's poem, "Four Corners of the House of Troubles."

Now, you've probably seen a few Daedra hearts in your time in Morrowind. Maybe you even heard that they have magical properties and kept one for a rainy day.

Well, now it's pouring.

But take heart (four of them, actually). Some alchemists have Daedra hearts for sale. Check with shops like Nalcarya of White Haven in Balmora and Anis Seloth in Sadrith Mora, with Gils Drelas in Therana's Chamber in Tel Branora's Upper Tower, and with Craetia Jullalian in Vivec's Mages Guild.

Or you can go Daedra hunting. This involves a lot of long-distance travel—most of the shrines are up north—and it can be disappointing. Hearts can be recovered only from the tougher Daedra: Clannfear, Daedroth, Dremora, Golden Saints, Hunger, and Ogrim. Even these will yield them only about 60 percent of the time.

However, at one location in Morrowind, you can find Daedra roaming in the wild in quantity. You may already have stumbled across it in an earlier quest when you were traveling to the Sanctus Shrine from Dagon Fel. Located northwest of that town just off the coast, this medium-sized island is home to two Hunger, a Golden Saint, a Daedroth, and even the rare Ogrim.

If you're lucky, you might find all four hearts here, and you're already reasonably close to your destination.

If you've spent much time on Sheogorad, there's a good chance you already know exactly where to find the shrine. From Dagon Fel, and make your usual exit west and south. Follow this road for a good ways and make your first right.

You'll see an Orc standing some distance down the road. This fine fellow, who goes by Blak gra-Murg, probably won't be hostile. Nor will he be especially communicative. You know how it is with Orcs.

But by his very presence, he's revealed you're in the neighborhood. (Remember: Malacath is the patron of Orcs.) Go to the end of this road, bear right, and follow this road past four additional, heavily-armored Orcs to a dead-end and a huge statue: Malacath.

The statue is the shrine. Activate it in the usual way to donate your Daedra hearts and get the poem (which you don't have to recite in front of the Orcs; it appears on its own) and your Fortify Strength blessing. Boat it or cast Recall to zap back to Saryoni for a briefing on how to turn the next corner.

Ald Sotha

In this shrine just northeast of Vivec, you're reenacting Vivec's rescue of Sotha Sil from the armies of Daedra Lord Mehrunes Dagon.

It should be pretty simple. In all likelihood, you're already familiar with Ald Sotha's layout from previous visits, and recall that the path to the shrine is all downhill. You don't even have to hunt up a token for this pilgrimage.

And the opposition? What opposition? If you have to square off with one Dremora, that'll be a lot. Get in, activate the statue of Dagon for the poem and a big old blessing (Fortify Destruction, Axe, and Attack), and get out.

BAL UR

Bal Ur

Bal Ur, rarely visited in Morrowind, is an extensive riverside shrine north of Suran. Here, Vivec is said to have tricked and defeated Molag Bal—the third corner of the House of Troubles

If you're willing to get your feet wet, Suran's a short jog northeast from Vivec. Pass through town and climb over the slope to the north, and you'll find yourself looking down into the shrine.

Note that Bal Ur has two entrances—one into a small upper level (from which you'll need to Levitate down into the main body of the shrine) and one in the shrine proper. The worshippers down here don't like you, and will fight with little or no provocation.

You could probably use a little help. As you approach the statue, you'll face a Bone Lord and a Golden Saint, and the shrine's priest, a 27th level witch named Derar Hlervu, isn't exactly a slouch either. Given the twisting path of the stone walkway over the lava, you won't be able to rush her—the tactic of choice with summoners—so Levitate over and put the hurt on her quickly.

Again, no token is required for this shrine. The statue's blessing is nice—a cheap Command Humanoid spell that always succeeds—and Hlervu's ebony mace, and the glass halberd and helm on the altar guarantee the quest will pay for itself. (The shrine also has a hidden upper level, which can be reached only with Levitation, but apart from a few nice scrolls, it's oddly short on loot.)

Ald Daedroth

The previous two quests were fairly straightforward exercises in combat that didn't require much travel.

But the last of the Four Corners quests recalls the first. Again, you have to journey to the northern reaches, and,

ALD DAEDROTH

again, you'll have to find a token to activate the shrine.

The place: the remote Daedric shrine of Ald Daedroth

The token: The Gambolpuddy.

Very funny. Can we have the real name, please?

That's it. Saryoni acknowledges that the name is bizarre, but says creations of the Daedric god Sheogorath all have in them a touch of madness. All you know is that the <cough> Gambolpuddy is in Ald Daedroth, and that it somehow will renew a pact that Vivec struck with the Sheogorath a long time ago.

Travel by guild guide or ship to Sadrith Mora and then by ship to Tel Mora. Make your way northwest to the camp of the Ahemmusa Ashlanders, and then west along the coast. When you can just make out the outline of the shrine Kushtashpi ahead of you, head north. It's a long way to swim—flying is better, if you can manage it—but you'll eventually see Ald Daedroth on your right.

If you are following the Main Quest, you'll have to visit this shrine sooner or later to make it a safe home for the Ahemmusa Ashlanders. When you drop in for the first time, you'll discover that Sheogorath cultists are having a wild party—a scamp is the bartender—and that Ordinators and spellcasters from the Temple are crashing it. Pitched battles are raging outside and in the corridors within. Ultimately, you'll either have to negotiate with one or both sides, let them fight it out and beat up on the weakened winner, or just clear the place out entirely.

As a result, depending on what you may or may not have done previously, you can have several different times on this visit to Ald Daedroth. If you've finished the save-the-Ahemmusa mission, it will be a walk in the park.

If you haven't, it's an invitation to a riot.

Your best bet to cut across all these potential complications is simply to make a run for the Gambolpuddy.

Ald Daedroth is huge, but cleanly laid out, with left and right wings and an Inner Shrine (where you'll find the statue of Sheogorath) that leads to the Antechamber. You'll be able to avoid battles along the way. In the uppermost of the Antechamber's rooms, you'll find a pair of bedrolls in the far left corner. Under the pillow of the bedroll closest to the outer wall is the Gambolpuddy—an enchanted glove that fortifies or drains four attributes. Take it back to the statue in the Inner Shrine, save your game, and then activate the statue.

Why save here? It's always a good idea to save regularly, but it's an especially good idea here because the statue's half-day blessing can be a curse. It will randomly add or subtract from four of your character's attributes: Intelligence, Willpower, Luck and Personality. If you save first, you can always reload and then roll the dice again.

(Then again, either way, the blessing should wear off shortly after you get back to Tel Mora—and you can always sleep off a bad roll.)

Then get back to Saryoni to have your completion of the "Four Corners" quests acknowledged.

An alternate approach: You can receive Gambolpuddy as a gift.

You just have to befriend Ra'Gruzgob—an Orc in Ald Daedroth so bombed on Moon Sugar that he thinks he's a Khajiit.

He'll ask you how you like his tail. He doesn't have one, but tell him it looks fine anyway. That'll help you bump up his Disposition. If you can get it up to 70, he'll offer to tell you a "little secret." Ask him about "little secret," and he'll ask for Moon Sugar. Get him Moon Sugar—there should be some over by the bar—and he'll tell you the little secret is under his pillow.

Assarnibibi

A few more "ifs": If you have now reached Rank 8 in the Temple, and if you have completed all four "Four Corners" pilgrimages in the correct order, Saryoni will invite you to perform one more quest.

He'll send you to Mount Assarnibibi, "where Molag Bal oversaw the 99 lovers of Boethiah that gave birth to Almalexia." Almalexia, Vivec, and Sotha Sil are the earthly gods who constitute the Tribunal.

What on earth does Almalexia do on Mother's Day?

In any case, you have to pray at the shrine, get the Ebony Mail, and return it to Saryoni.

Like Mount Kand, Assarnibibi is in the Molag Amur range, but farther north and east. Travel to Molag Mar via ship or silt strider, and just follow the signs from the silt strider port as you head east along the shore and then northeast up a long foyada. You may have to tangle with a cliff racer or two en route, but you're up to that, aren't you?

ASSARNIBIBI

You may be expecting a steep climb—something more like what you did at Mount Kand—but the actual assent is rather gradual. At the top, you'll see the shrine within a ring of five great standing stones.

Simply activate it. Nothing terrible happens. You'll get the Ebony Mail and all that remains is to get back to Saryoni for promotion to Archcanon. He tells you to keep the mail, and quits to write some more of those earnest sermons.

You inherit his title, but don't expect to inherit his office. It looks as though he's staying put.

ORAG TONG

The Morag Tong is an assassins guild sanctioned by the Empire to provide three varieties of execution: public executions, private executions, and House Wars executions. Constrained by ancient traditions and rigid codes of conduct, the Morag Tong only recruits candidates of proven skill and honor. Morag Tong only accepts legally approved contracts called 'writs,' but rumor hints at the execution of secret extralegal 'grey writs.' The Morag Tong is the sworn enemy of the Dark Brotherhood.

Favored Skills

Marksman	*Acrobatics*
Short Blade	*Sneak*
Light Armor	*Illusion*

Advancement

Rank	Speed	Agility	One Favored Skill at	Two Other Favored Skills at
Associate	30	30	0	0
Blind Thrall	30	30	10	0
Thrall	30	30	20	0
White Thrall	30	30	30	5
Thinker	30	30	40	10
Brother	31	31	50	15
Knower	32	32	60	20
Master	33	33	70	25
Exalted Master	34	34	80	30
Grandmaster	35	35	90	35

You can perform three different types of quests for the assassins guild: authorized executions (known as "Writs"), conventional Morrowind quests (here called "Special Duties") and item-retrieval missions ("The Threads of the Webspinner") that comprise an over-arching quest.

Finding the Morag Tong

But your first Morag Tong quest isn't one of these. It's sort of an informal quest. You have to find the guild's headquarters.

It isn't easy. To join, you'll have to speak to Grandmaster Eno Hlaalu... and he doesn't like the limelight. The HQ is hidden. And really hidden, not hidden-in-plain-sight like the Thieves Guilds.

Finding it isn't that different from finding anything else on Vvardenfell. Talk to people in the Morag Tong branches in Ald'ruhn, Balmora, and Sadrith Mora. You will learn the HQ is in Vivec. In Vivec, you'll hear it's in the Arena Canton. In the Arena Canton, you'll learn it's nearby.

And a very few people will tell that you either that's it is hidden under the Arena, or to investigate the Arena's storage area.

Sure enough, if you exit the Arena's main storage room by its southeast door, you'll find yourself in a small room with a trapdoor in the floor. This leads down into a three-level suite of otherwise inaccessible rooms with its own magic shop and trainer.

In a bedroom at the back of the top level, you'll meet Eno Hlaalu.

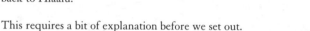

Joining the Morag Tong

You may not even have to talk to the Grandmaster about "join the Morag Tong." You've impressed Hlaalu by simply finding him, and he will allow most players who are just starting out in Morrowind to join the guild straight away.

But he does require you to pass another test.

It's your first official quest. Hlaalu gives you a "writ" – a written assassination order. You're to kill Feruren Oran, a spellsword at the Elven Nations cornerclub in Vivec, and report back to Hlaalu.

This requires a bit of explanation before we set out.

ENO HLAALU

Morrowind draws distinctions between outright murder and killing in self-defense, but executions don't receive such advance dispensation. Typically, your crime will be reported, and you'll be wanted. Imperial guards will stop you and impose fines or jail time. As a Morag Tong operative, regularly committing what the game regards as murders, you'd quickly build up a significant criminal record while just doing your job.

However, while its leader may hide like a criminal, and the organizations shares its last name with the criminal syndicate Camonna Tong, the Morag Tong isn't itself a criminal organization. A guild like the Fighters, Mages, and Thieves guilds, has the authority to perform executions in lieu of open warfare between the Great Houses.

How then to distinguish the executions you perform from any crimes that you may or may not commit (we admit nothing) on your own time?

"Writs" like the one you've been issued for Feruren Oran double as a "Get Out of Jail Free" card. A writ presented to any guard will subtract one assault and one murder from your criminal record.

Hence, membership in the Morag Tong does not amount to a free license to kill—you're still responsible for your actions as an individual—but the writs prevent you from footing the bill for business you conduct for your employer. That's a savings of 1,040 gold per pop—the typical penalty for a murder—and it changes radically the way you'll be viewed by the game world.

Then again, if you somehow lose a writ—say, while sorting through your possessions at dungeon-bottom while over-encumbered—you'll have to go back and find it or it's gone, gone, gone. The guild doesn't issue duplicate writs.

The Elven Nations is located in the northwest corner of the upper level of the Hlaalu Canton. You'll find Oran downstairs. He's quite capable of defending himself, so watch your step. His possessions are meager, but do take his steel dai-katana once he's dead.

Return to Hlaalu to report your success, and you're in. You can begin other writs immediately.

Writs

Writ quests like the one you just completed comprise a healthy chunk of your initial work for the Morag Tong. Usually offered in pairs, they're straight assassinations – "go here and kill this person" – and don't have special requirements beyond the completion of previous writs.

They're also not connected to any particular quest giver. You can get them from, and report your success to, any Morag Tong member of Rank 7 (Master) or better. (This doesn't need to be the same person.) In Vivec, you'll deal with Hlaalu. In Balmora, the quest-giver is Ethasi Rilvayn. In Ald'ruhn, it's Goren Andarys. In Sadrith Mora, it's Dunsalipal Dun-Ahhe.

These quests are offered without alternate approaches and usually with little background—just the victim's names and where to find them.

Odaishah Yasalmibaal and Toris Saren

Saren is local, so you may want to start with him. From an influential family, he lives in Saren Manor, located off Redoran Plaza in Vivec's Redoran Canton. He packs a nice weapon—an enchanted Wild Shardblade—which you should collect before you move north.

It's a fairly long haul to reach Yasalmibaal. An Ashlander who has been ordered killed by a Telvanni noble, he lives alone on a rocky island northwest of Tel Fyr. He's in his yurt, and he's not carrying anything special.

Return to a quest-giver (the Sadrith Mora guild is the most convenient) for complete the quest and receive payment: 500 gold for each execution.

Sarayn Sadus, Idroso Vendu, and Ethal Seloth

Again, you have a quest in the neighborhood. Sadus is hiding out in a cave called Zaintirari, located west of Tel Fyr.

It's a toughie. Sadus isn't alone, and you'll have to fight off his bandit buddies. But the loot is quite good. Dils Heladren, your first bandit victim, is decked out in bonemold armor.

The second assignment is a double-header, and in this case, you do get some background. Vendu and Seloth are apparently killers. However, the evidence isn't enough to convict them, Duke Vedam Dren is unwilling to help... and someone's paying the Morag Tong a lot of money to see that justice is served.

SARAYN SADUS

They're together—in Temporary Housing, just off Telvanni Plaza in that House's Vivec canton. There's no real loot here. Get to a quest-giver (Hlaalu in Vivec is easiest) for your pay-off: 1,500 gold for the three executions.

Guril Retheran and Galasa Uvayn

Retheran is on the downstairs level of the Flowers of Gold cornerclub in Vivec's Redoran Canton. Like Saren, he comes from money. His equipment comes from money, too: Check out his enchanted Fiend Tanto and, more particularly, his Glove of Sanguine Horny Fist (which raises the wearer's Hand-to-Hand skill by five points).

Hlaalu will want to see this item.

Uvayn, poor woman, made the mistake of offending a Redoran lord. A capable spellcaster and worthy opponent, she's in the Hlaalu Treasury in Vivec and has a Dire Flameblade.

Visit Hlaalu again and he'll pay you 1,000 gold for each of the hits.

If you assent, he'll also take possession of the Glove of Sanguine Horny Fist you found on Retheran. But if you don't mean to give it up yet, don't mention it to him, or his Disposition toward you will take a hit.

This is first of the 27 "Threads of the Webspinner" that you can recover as part of an over-arching quest—and the only such item you'll find in a "Writs" quest. We'll cover these in detail in the next section.

Mavon Drenim and Tirer Belvayn

Y'know, somebody could have mentioned this to you before you left.

Drenim and Belvayn are not your ordinary assassination targets. They are powerful spellcasters and the moment you walk into their respective lairs—Drenim's in the Upperworks of Vivec's Telvanni Compound, Belvayn's in the dungeon Shara—they will be all over you.

Ignore the shambling horrors they summon. Ignore Drenim's assistants. Stay focused on the mages, and take them out fast. Wizards are weak at close combat, and once they're gone, whatever they've conjured vanishes with them.

Take Drenim's Hellfire Staff and Belvayn's Silver Staff of War.

On top of the fights, Belvayn set up shop in an out of the way spot. You're basically told that Shara's on an island southwest of Sheogorad.

That's a little like giving directions to a city in Mexico by saying it's southwest of Texas.

The nearest reference point is Ashmelech, which is fairly obscure in its own right. From here, head up the path to the northeast and swim across the channel to the next island. Beyond the great standing stones, paths head east and northwest. Follow the eastern path and, when it splits east and northwest, follow the northwest branch. Shara will quickly turn up along the west side of this path.

Visit a quest-giver to get 1,000 gold for each killing.

Mathyn Bemis and Brilnosu Llarys

Bemis leads a gang of outlaws quartered in the Hlaalu Ancestral Vault in the Hlaalu Compound in Vivec. Most of the tomb will seem abandoned. Three of the bad guys are all in the big room at the north end. The fourth, Arven Nalyn, is elsewhere in the Ancestral Vaults and you may have finished him off already. If not, you might meet him on the way out, or during the fight with Bemis. In any case, he's not your target.

Arven Nalyn can be tackled by himself. But the other three baddies attack en masse, and that can make this a messy fight.

The loot is good. Nalyn will fill out, and upgrade, your suit of bonemold armor. A search of Broris Fals' corpse turns up a Fiend Battle Axe. Bemis himself had a Cruel Sparkblade.

MATHYN BEMIS

Llarys is just a general no-goodnik who hangs out with outlaws and Daedra worshippers at the stronghold Hlormaren west of Balmora. After the long and chaotic battle in the tomb, this may seem more like dealing with a rebellious teenager. Your mark is not in the stronghold's dark depths, but up on the roof, so you have lots of room to maneuver, and while she has some help and conjures new fighters, you should be able to get to her quickly.

Again, great equipment: Llarys has two pieces of ebony armor and the Dwemer halberd Stormforge.

Get back to a quest-giver to collect another 1,000 for each execution.

Navil and Ranes Ienith

The names should be familiar. You may already have killed them.

This quest is identical to Thieves Guild quest Kill Ienith. You must seek out the brothers Ienith (enforcers for the Camonna Tong) behind two seriously locked doors in the cellar of the villa of Dren Plantation, northeast of Pelagiad, and do what assassins do.

Note that the brothers' tactics are tricky. You may think you've found only Navil. But Ranes appears behind you during the fight.

Return to a quest-giver to collect the 2,000 gold payment.

You're done with Morag Tong writs—for now. You won't be able to perform additional quests of this type until you've finished the Main Quest mission Destroy Dagoth and made Grandmaster (See Special Duties).

THE GRANDMASTER WRITS

Larrius Varro

LARRIUS VARRO

Return to a Morag Tong quest-giver once Dagoth Ur is dead, you've completed all the previous writs and made Grandmaster, and you'll learn many new writs have been issued owing to the "recent troubles."

The guild has saved the four most difficult of these for you.

These people will be extremely hard to kill.

Moreover, these are also some of the most honorable men (and one of the craziest women) on Vvardenfell. And if you happen to belong to your victim's faction, there may be hell to pay once you kill them. So don't look on these quests as integral to gameplay, but as high-level challenges.

Then again, by now, maybe you don't care what people in the game think of you. You're the fulfillment of prophecy. You're practically a Morrowind God in your own right. My right hand is lightning and my left is thunder. My eyes are flame. My heart is ashes. Look upon me and tremble.

Where were we? Oh, yeah. The first of the new writs finds you handing the local Imperial Legion commandant his head. Varro can found in the Fort Moonmoth barracks.
He puts up a heroic struggle. Even with your Dagoth-Ur-killing artifacts in play—the hammer Sunder or sword Keening—he'll take quite a while to go down.

His armor is surprisingly ordinary—plain Imperial steel—but his weapon is Temreki, Shackler of Souls.

Ya gotta love a sword that has a name.

Return to a quest-giver for the 4,000-gold payoff.

Baladas Demnevanni

Does anyone really want to kill Demnevanni? A Morrowind without this sorcerer would be a less interesting place.

Your quest-giver strikes a rare cautionary note and reports that your target is "formidable," and this is true. When you confront him on the top floor of his home (Arvs-Drelen in Gnisis), Demnevanni will stand up against you longer than most of his wizardly brethren. And if you give him breathing space, he'll surely summon something nasty.

It's appropriate that you don't get many real benefits from killing this Dwemer expert beyond the 5,000 gold from your quest-giver. He carries the plainest of items – only the Dwemer summoning ring you obtained for him in the Telvanni quest Dahrk Mezalf should stand out—and his study and home are unadorned with the trappings of influence and wealth. Demnevanni seems to have lived a life of the mind.

Dram Bero

Your quest-giver will tell you only that Bero, a reclusive member of the Hlaalu Council, lives somewhere in Vivec.

You'll learn in the Main Quest and Hlaalu faction quest that Bero's in St. Olms Haunted Manor. If you haven't reached that point in the Main Quest, or don't belong to House Haalu, you can find him independently with the same sort of aggressive questioning you used to find the Morag Tong to begin with.

The manor is on the south side of St. Olms Plaza. The empty shelves and the lone goblet on the counter within are meant to suggest to the casual eye that it is vacant. But the aggressively locked door down a ramp at the rear reveals this as a false front.

Pick the lock, and you may find yourself in a pleasant dining room. Bero and Omesu Hlarys (presumably his bodyguard) are in a room off the hall ahead of you.

When Bero dies, you'll get a message about having broken a thread of prophecy and indicating you can restore a saved game or continue to live in a doomed world—Dagoth Ur's recent demise notwithstanding.

Don't worry about this. Before the defeat of Dagoth Ur, Bero's death would be a quest-breaker. That is, he was one of the people you had to deal with to complete the Main Quest.

But that quest is done, and now you're just seeing what you can see and doing what you can still do.

Return to a quest-giver to claim your 3,000 gold.

Therana

Conceivably, Telvanni councilor Therana is already dead. Killing her is a valid option in your quests to be named Telvanni Hortator and Archmagister.

Heck, the Nerevarine stuff aside, you might have killed this loon during the Telvanni faction quests because she kept attacking you whenever you did things for her.

Someone else seems to share your low opinion. The quest-giver tells you Therana is dangerous and unstable, and you must end her insanity.

Therana's in her Upper Tower chamber in Tel Branora at the southern tip of the Azura's Coast region. The rules for fighting other enchanters apply equally here. See a quest-giver for the 10,000 gold pay-off.

Finally, Therana has proved her worth.

THERANA

THE THREADS OF THE WEBSPINNER

The Glove of Sanguine Horny Fist you found on Guril Retheran's body at the Flowers of Gold cornerclub wasn't just another enchanted item with an elaborate name. It is one of 27 created by Daedra Lord Sanguine for Morag Tong patron Mephala.

Twenty-five of these are scattered across Vvardenfell. (In addition to the glove you found, Hlaalu already has recovered the Amulet of Sanguine Enterprise, which adds five points to the wearer's Mercantile skill.)

If you return to Hlaalu the remaining items, you'll receive an elaborate reward from Mephala.

Fifteen of the 25 Threads can be recovered in the course of the "Special Duties" quests covered later in this section. While you are required to recover only two of them that way, the other 13 can be easily incorporated into those missions.

The remaining 10 Threads, covered below, require their own missions.

Note that you don't have to rush this stuff back to Hlaalu. You don't need to turn it in until you're ready to collect the reward. The Threads are designed to be used by the player. Each item supplements one of your 27 skills with a constant five-point bonus and you can wear seven of them at the same time (two rings, one amulet, two gloves, one pair of shoes and one belt).

Different strategies can work here. You can accentuate the positives and make your character more of what it already is. You can identify your weak skills and use these items to shore them up. Or you can store them items someplace convenient and use them to best support your activity of the moment.

However, that said, don't wait too long to return to return the Threads or you'll miss the opportunity to do so. If you complete the Grandmaster quest under "Special Duties," Hlaalu will retire. When you leave the area, he will vanish from the game, and with him will vanish the possibility for your reward.

Sanguine Glib Speech

Have you been to Khuul? Probably not. It is a remote fishing village on the West Gash coast northeast of Ald Velothi. A collection of weather-beaten dockside shanties and a single shop, Thongar's Tradehouse, Khuul's most distinguishing characteristic is its unobstructed view of the great natural stone arches to the southwest.

AMULET OF GLIB SPEECH

Nevertheless, one of the Threads of the Webspinner has found its way to this out-of-the way place. The Amulet of Sanguine Glib Speech (which adds five points to the wearer's Speechcraft skill) belongs to Shotherra, who you will find just inside the door at Thongar's.

Recovering a lot of the Threads won't raise any issues with the authorities. A Thread's current owner—always a Dark Brotherhood agent or Mehrunes Dagon worshipper in these quests—usually will attack you with enthusiasm and, as usual, you're within your rights to defend yourself.

However, this item and two others are held by peaceful characters. So you'll wind up killing them. Sad, but necessary.

Sanguine Golden Wisdom

In this case, the Thread is the Ring of Sanguine Golden Wisdom, which adds five points to your Alteration skill, and its owner is a mage named Talis Veran.

Ebernanit, in the trackless gray wastes of the northern Ashlands, is one of the tougher Thread locations to find. Your best bet is to follow the northern coastline east, past the Urshilaku Ashlander camp, to the stronghold Valenvaryon, and then chart a course straight southeast. You'll soon see the ruins in a low crater.

Sanguine Green Wisdom and Sanguine Smiting

At Ald Daedroth, two more cultists are wearing additional Threads. You can find Gnaw Tooth and his pal Domba deep inside the great Daedric shrine, located northwest of the Ahemmusa Ashlander camp.

GNAW TOOTH

Descend into the outer shrine, bear right in the main room and enter the right wing. At the bottom of the next set of stairs, turn left and go to the room at the end.

Mr. Tooth and Mr. Domba act as though, for all the world, they would like to split your head open and feast upon your brains. After you speed their passage into the next world, take from Gnaw Tooth the Ring of Sanguine Green Wisdom, which adds five points to your Restoration skill, and from Domba the Belt of Sanguine Smiting, which adds five to your Blunt Weapon skill.

Sanguine Impaling Thrust

Gluronk gra-Shula on the second floor of Sadrith Mora's Gateway Inn has a Thread as well: the Belt of Sanguine Impaling Thrust, which adds five points the wearer's Spear skill.

A Brotherhood agent, this Orc assassin should appear to your right immediately after you open the north-wing door. Like the Brotherhood agent in Khuul, she's a peaceful type, so this is more or less a holdup—OK, it's entirely a holdup—and goes in the books as a crime.

Sanguine Leaping

The Shoes of Sanguine Leaping, which adds five points to the wearer's Acrobatics skill, are in the possession of Dro'Zaymar, a Khajiit who lives at Canal South-Three in Vivec's St. Delyn Canton—a working-class district just west of St. Olms.

As with Shotherra and gra-Shula, you'll have to kill or knock out this Dark Brotherhood agent to get the Thread. However, unlike the other assaults, you may be able to get away with this one, as it occurs behind closed doors in a private apartment and so escapes notice.

But that doesn't mean you have to feel good about it.

Sanguine Safekeeping

A forbidding journey for those unfamiliar with the Vvardenfell interior.

To reach the shrine Ularradallaku in the southern Ashlands, make your way to the Dwemer ruin Endusal. Then bear south, with the pale-blue shimmer of the Ghostfence on your left, cross a swinging bridge, and you'll soon see the shrine rising up above you to the west.

ꙮ The Morrowind Prophecies ꙮ

Your destination is the Daedric shrine Ularradallaku. It lies inside the Ghostfence, north of the citadel Endusal. (It's amazing how much normal activity continues inside this hostile environment.)

From Vivec, your quickest route is silt strider transport to Ald'ruhn, and then a quick jog south and east across the mountains to Ghostgate. Inside the Ghostfence, follow the main foyada up the mountain, make your first left, and follow the foyada over the rise to Endusal. Head north, over a swinging bridge, to reach the shrine.

Before you reach Mehrunes Dagon worshipper Inganar, who has the Thread, you'll have to beat down two fire atronachs and afterward, possibly, two of Inganar's pals.

Take the Glove of Sanguine Safekeeping (which adds five points to your Security skill) and get back to friendlier terrain.

Sanguine Silver Wisdom

You'll find the Ring of Sanguine Silver Wisdom (which adds five points to your Illusion skill) in the sprawling Daedric ruin of Assurnabitashpi—found along the desolate north coast west of the Urshilaku Ashlander camp. Look for Dark Brotherhood agent Earmil in the underground shrine. Don't fret if you can't find him immediately. The shrine is deceptively large—it has two levels, each with its own entrance—and he will eventually turn up.

Sanguine Stalking

You'll find the Shoes of Sanguine Stalking, which add five points to your Sneak skill, on Dark Brotherhood agent Thovasi Alen in the small shrine of Assarnatamat.

Be warned: The surface ruin, in the Ashlands northeast of Balmora, is quite extensive and what with ash storms and persistent attacks from scamps and cliff racers, it's difficult to find the door by day and almost impossible at night. Make good use of your map, and search at the eastern tip of the site.

Sanguine Unseen Wisdom

ERUNDIL

Ostensibly, Indoranyon is a stronghold. That's certainly what it looks like from the outside.

But when the interior loads, you may wonder if the game has done something wrong. Inside, it's barely a stronghold at all. This dungeon, located on Vvardenfell's east coast north of Tel Aruhn, is a huge, sometimes treacherous and sometimes just confusing mish-mosh of cave, shrine and bandit hideaway... and with just a little bit of stronghold mixed in.

That's just the most obvious way in which you've been fooled.

A less obvious way is that you didn't actually enter through the door. Rather, you were teleported from the circle of candles outside the door to... uh, somewhere else. And so rather than finding your way into the stronghold's recesses to find your quarry—Mehrunes Dagon worshipper Erundil—you must find your way back a corresponding circle of candles on the inside of the door, so you can teleport out again.

You may walk in circles a bit, and a Levitate spell is useful here and there, but your path isn't that complicated, and you'll soon find yourself in a large chamber with the exit on the far side and Erundil on a platform off to your right.

Get over there quickly and take him out—he's a sorcerer—and get his Ring of Sanguine Unseen Wisdom (which boosts your Mysticism skill by five points).

When It's Over

When you're ready, turn all 26 Threads items into Hlaalu. He's already got the Amulet of Sanguine Enterprise, so you only need to get 26 more. (If you've killed him, you've blown the quest.)

Your reward from Mephala is a unique three-pronged spell, perfect for an assassin, that simultaneously casts Chameleon, Fortify Attack and Fortify Skill Shortblade. It's very inexpensive in terms of Magicka—less than a fifth of what the spells would cost separately—and it never fails.

SPECIAL DUTIES

Once you reach Rank 2 (Thrall) in the Morag Tong, you are eligible to receive these quests from Grandmaster Eno Hlaalu.

Contact

MIUN-GEI

When talking to Hlaalu, select "special duties" and then "Dark Brotherhood."

You've probably already heard about this group. It broke away from the Morag Tong many years ago, and the two organizations are deadly enemies. Hlaalu wants you to contact them through a Vivec enchanter named Miun-Gei.

You'll figure out why two quests down the road.

This can work out three ways.

Miun-Gei has shop in the Lower Waistworks section of the Foreign Quarter. Get his Disposition up to 70, and he'll reveal his Brotherhood contact is a Khajiit named Tsrazami who can found in Vivec's Market Canton.

If you don't talk the talk, you can still get the information. Check the chest of drawers in Miun-Gei's bedroom downstairs and you'll find a letter from Tsrazami, which you can return to Hlaalu.

However, if you've somehow managed to kill Tsrazami, the enchanter can't help you. Tsrazami was his lone Brotherhood contact. Even so, you'll complete the quest. Make your way back to the Grandmaster talk about "Dark Brotherhood" again to put it to bed.

Sanguine Fleetness

Hlaalu has learned that a Dark Brotherhood member named Hrordis has the Belt of Sanguine Fleetness—another of Threads of the Webspinner. You are to pay Hrordis a little visit at the Halfway Inn in Pelagiad and relieve her of the belt.

The inn's the last building on the left as you climb the hill toward Fort Pelagiad. Hrordis is in the middle room upstairs. She looks like little more than a kid. But you can't persuade her to give up the belt and you can't steal it, so bite your lip, kill her and take it. (The Belt adds five points your Athletics skill.)

By now, you're probably used to walking away scot-free from killings in the name of the Morag Tong. But this isn't an execution and the crime probably will be detected. That means a 1,040-gold fine or jail time. If you're short on funds and you go to jail—you shouldn't be, with good money coming in from writs—you'll need to retrieve the Belt from your prison's evidence chest.

Darys

With or without Tsarazmi's help, Hlaalu has not been idle. Talk to him about "special duties" and "Movis Darys" to learn he wants you to turn this Brotherhood agent and bring him into the Morag Tong.

MOVIS DARYS

You must persuade Darys to join the Morag Tong, or kill him. Turning Darys requires either his good Disposition (70) or your good intimidation. However, killing him completes the quest as well—and may better satisfy your instincts about him. (Once a spy, always a spy.) And Hlaalu will pay for the kill as if it was a Writ.

While you're here, make sure you get the Belt of Sanguine Denial. Movis Darys will give it to you if you're persuasive enough, and he'll have it on his corpse if you kill him. This item, which adds five points to your Block skill, isn't required to complete the quest, but you'll have to do it eventually, and why make an unnecessary second trip?

Carecalmo

Hlaalu says worshippers of Mehrunes Dagon are harboring Dark Brotherhood members. You're to deliver an ultimatum to a cultist named Carecalmo: Knock it off, or prepare for a war.

You may never get to the ultimatum. When you find Carecalmo at Ashalmimilkala, a beautiful, waterlogged shrine on an island west of Balmora, he may just attack you out of hand.

If so, kill him without bothering with the ultimatum. Even if you do persuade him to listen, he's only going to attack you again when you unveil the Hlaalu's proposal. (People tend to have strong reactions to ultimatums.)

And what a shock! Carecalmo just happens to be wearing another gaudy item from the Threads of the Webspinner Collection! Get the Belt of Sanguine Martial Craft (which adds five points to your Armorer skill) and return to Hlaalu.

Sublime

This quest could easily have been included in the "Threads of the Webspinner" section—except that Hlaalu asks you directly to get this item.

So go get it. This time, you're off to retrieve the Ring of Sanguine Sublime Wisdom from Anel Rethelas, who can be found in the Daedric ruins of Yasammidan west of Ald Velothi.

Just follow the rocky coastline. You'll cross two bridges to reach the Dwemer ruins at Arkngthunch-Sturdumz. Yasammidan is just down the hill and across the water to the west.

Access is slightly tricky. Underwater debris prevents a direct approach from the east, so you'll need to swim around the shrine and come in from the west.

Rethelas will meet you on the ramp that leads down into the shrine proper. Get the ring, which boosts your Alchemy skill by five points.

But don't stop there. He wasn't alone. Below, at the altar, you'll find Mindeli Saren. She has another Thread—the Belt of Sanguine Stolid Armor, which boosts your Heavy Armor skill by five points.

Report back to Hlaalu.

Depending on your rank in the Tong, the Grandmaster may not have another quest for you for a good bit. This is a good opportunity to catch up on any outstanding Writs and recover Threads not available through Special Duties quests.

When you reach Rank 7, return to Hlaalu for another mission.

Assernerairan

The Tong isn't the only secretive organization that thinks Vivec's underpinnings are ace for a base. The Dark Brotherhood has one under St. Olms Canton in the shrine Assernerairan. Durus Marius, a Brotherhood leader, is said to be there now. Hlaalu asks you to go kill him.

DURUS MARIUS

You can find this base on your own. It's in the city's Underworks (sewers), which are reached through a trapdoor in the Canalworks. You can't miss the guarded door. Hope you're ready for a fight.

All you are required to do here is kill Marius—he's the one who looks as though he should be a hero—but that may prove easier said than done. You'll find yourself attacked with a high degree of simultaneity by three Brotherhood members and whatever they've summoned.

If you're up to it, you may find the best approach is to kill them all and let the Daedra gods sort them out.

The result will be you're going to bring home a whole wagonload of new Threads. Marius himself carried the belts of Sanguine Sureflight (+5 on your Marksman skill) and Sanguine Hewing (+5 on Long Blade), while Relas Arothan had the belts of Sanguine Balanced Armor (+5 on Medium Armor) and the Belt of Sanguine Deep Biting (+5 on Axe).

Sanguine sure seems to have liked making belts.

Seems like a lot? You ain't seen nothing yet. Get back to Hlaalu for a 2,000-gold payoff, and prepare to deal a killing blow to the Dark Brotherhood.

Ald Sotha

The Brotherhood's headquarters is also close by—in the ruins at Ald Sotha near Vivec. You are going there now to kill leader Severa Magia.

To find this shrine, follow a steady course northeast from Vivec through some pretty countryside and you'll run right into it. Inside, it's a relatively straight shot down the central ramp to the lower level and the shrine beyond.

Magia, the Brotherhood's "Night Mother," may be hard to find. She's in the southwestern room of the lower level, but watch out for the Dremora or Daedroths on either side of the entrance.

Once Magia and Llandrale Varam are dead, you're in Threads City. From the body of Magia, you can recover the Amulet of Sanguine Nimble Armor (+5 to your Light Armor skill), the Gloves of Sanguine Swiftblade (+5 to Short Blade) and the Ring of Sanguine Fluid Evasion (+5 to Unarmored). From Varam, who is at the Shrine, you'll get rings of Sanguine Red Wisdom (+5 to Destruction), Sanguine Transcendence (+5 for Conjuration) and Sanguine Transfiguring (+5 to Enchant).

That's six Threads. Get back to Hlaalu for the coda.

Grandmaster

In which you reach Rank 8 and become Exalted Master of the Morag Tong. It doesn't involve the Threads of the Webspinner at all.

Hlaalu wants to quit.

Traditionally, the new Morag Tong Grandmaster executes the old one, and Hlaalu is prepared to fight with you. But he offers you the opportunity to depart from tradition and allow him to retire gracefully. He'll then name you the new Grandmaster, and that'll be that.

ENO HLAALU

You just need to talk your way through the dialogue to this point. Nothing else is required.

Of course, maybe you like tradition and think Eno Hlaalu is a big baby. And killing him will work as well—as long as you've already reached Rank 7 (Master).

But note that, if you haven't finished the "Threads of the Webspinner" quest, Hlaalu's death or retirement will spoil your chances to do so. (You can't turn in your finds when there's no one to turn them in to.)

This isn't the end, however. Now that you've reached the top, you can perform the last four writs. See "The Grandmaster Writs" section for details.

And sharpen your sword. For while these assassinations are quite legal, they are nevertheless murder.

Chapter Six:
Miscellaneous Quests

Our third category of quests in Morrowind is "everything else." "Miscellaneous Quests" covers assignments that don't fit into the Main Quest or Faction Quests—though they sometimes cut across their paths.

These quests are everywhere. They come from people you meet along the road and out in the middle of nowhere. They spring from rumors.

There are many more of them than you might think, and they are sometimes more substantial than you might imagine. While some are as trivial as helping a pretty woman who has lost her ring (or so she says) or a man who has lost his pants, you may also find yourself supporting the reconstruction of a lost shrine. You can have a little romance.

You can even walk Morrowind's dark edge as a vampire.

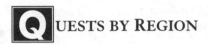 UESTS BY REGION

ALD'RUHN

The Empty Pockets of Ienas Sarandas

The financial affairs of Ienas Sarandas are in some disarray. You can learn this through the rumor mill, and confirm it by talking to merchants. No fewer than five of them, when questioned about "work," will tell you that Sarandas owes them money. Each offers you a reward if you can either collect payment or recover the goods.

Three of the shops are clustered just outside the town's Manor District. Bevene Releth: Clothier is owed 50 gold for a firejade amulet, and will pay 25 gold for its recovery. Daynes Redothril: Pawnbroker is owed 150 gold for two rings—made of ebony and glass, respectively—and will pay 50 gold to get them back. And Tiras Sadus: General Merchandise is owed 50 gold for a racer suede belt, and will pay 25 gold.

The other two shops are off on the lowest floor of the Manor District. Sarandas owes 120 gold to Llether Vari: Enchanter for a pair of designer shoes enchanted with Light, which will pay 50 gold. And he owes a staggering 360 gold to Bivale Teneran: Clothier for a brocade shirt and silk pants. Teneran's offering 50 gold as a collection fee.

When you visit the shops, ask after Sarandas himself. He's apparently a nice young fellow. But you'll learn that his parents recently died, and that his inheritance and the fast crowd that came with it have made him foolish. (He's a gambler, and you'll learn elsewhere that he has a taste for the sauce.)

The money's gone, but the goods can be recovered in a range of different ways to satisfy these five small quests.

Now speak to Sarandas himself. His house is on the right at the base of the stairs south of the Manor District. If you raise his Disposition to 60, or have a Speechcraft skill of 50 or better, ask him about "overdue payments" and then choose the "Offer a sympathetic ear and friendly advice" option.

You'll shame him into returning the items. In fact, he'll give them to you right off his back, and you can bring them back to the respective merchants. In each case, you'll get your cash reward and a 20-point Disposition bump (which amounts to a discount on future purchases).

And now you're a local legend (if you weren't already). Ask anyone in Ald'ruhn about "latest rumors" repeatedly and you'll eventually learn that Sarandas has donated his house to the Tribunal Temple and is studying to be a priest. (In fact, you can go visit him at the Ald'ruhn Temple. No, you do not get a share of his estate.)

In fact, you can do this all over town, talking repeatedly about "latest rumors" and raising everyone's Disposition to a maximum of 70. This has real advantages when you're shopping, looking for information or raising money for the Imperial Cult (as in the quest BuckmothAlms).

A few curves in this route can bring you to variations on the solution without the high Disposition requirement

If you have flin, greef or Cyrodilic brandy in your inventory when you talk to Sarandas, select "Offer a drink of brandy and a sympathetic ear."

If you have a copy of "Saryoni's Sermons" in your inventory, select "Offer a quote from 'Saryoni's Sermons' and a sympathetic ear." (You should be able to use a copy found nearby without stealing it.)

Finally, you either knock Sarandas out or kill him and just take everything and return it. However, you won't get the "latest rumor" Disposition bonus (because you're a thug) and, if you kill Sarandas, attempts to elicit "latest rumors" will actually lower the speaker's Disposition.

Where O Where Has My Husband Gone?

On the west slope of the hill just west of the silt strider port, you'll find Falanu Indaren. She and her husband, Drerel, were attacked by wild nix-hounds while traveling through the area. She played dead; he ran. Now they're separated, and you have to go find her hubbie.

Indaren thinks he went west, and she's right. Kill the Nix-Hounds in the immediately area—usually one north of Indaren and two more over the hill to the west—and start your search. Follow the foyada where you found the two Nix-Hounds to the north and northwest.

After you turn northwest and pass a dead tree, you'll see some stones high up on the southwest slope. Drerel Indaren is up there. Speak to him and he'll follow you back to his wife and give you a Block skillbook ("A Dance in the Fire, Chapter 2").

FALANU INDAREN

(This will work equally well if you stumble upon Drerel Indaren before you find Falanu.)

Rhymes with Rich

If you leave Ald'ruhn by the south exit and head west, you'll run into one Viatrix Petilia. She is a pain in the neck. This will be apparent immediately from the way this well-to-do pilgrim talks to you—as though you're her servant.

"You there! Yes, you. I'm in need of an escort. You'll do in a pinch."

Specifically, Petilia has to get to Ghostgate within two days. Agree to escort her and she'll start to follow you.

It's a pretty long haul as escort missions go, but the road is open, the enemies relatively few, and if you don't get too far ahead of your employer, the trip should take not even half a day. Of course, if it does take longer, she'll let you know, and might eventually decide to find her way on her own.

"Do you have any idea where you're going at all? I'm in a hurry, and you're as slow as a three-legged guar."

Head east, past Buckmoth Fort, and you'll connect up with a foyada just north of the Daedric shrine Ramimilk. Follow this northeast and east to the Ghostfence. Then follow the Ghostfence south to the Foyada Mamaea and north to Ghostgate.

Resist the temptation to strand Petilia someplace really nasty. You'll need to take her to the shrine inside the Ghostfence. It's at the end of the right-hand spur off the main path up the mountain. (If you've performed the Pilgrimages of the Seven Graces for the Tribunal Temple, you've been here.)

She'll pay you off—not well, given what's she put you through—and make another nasty remark if you talk to her again.

The rich really are different.

Semi-Naked Barbarian in the Middle of the Road

HISIN DEEP-RAED

This one's a bit of a walk. Head straight west out of town and follow the road into the West Gash region. (Right after you pass the Maar Gan road, the ground will change from gray to brown.) Continue west through a rocky gorge to a "T" intersection with the Gnisis road. To the east, you'll see Hisin Deep-Raed.

This barbarian is a state. Deep-Raed apparently was on…well, intimate terms with the witch he was escorting. He doesn't say exactly what happened, but it wasn't good. She cursed him with a disease that paralyzed him and left him virtually naked in the middle of the road.

Now, you could kill him. He can't fight back, can he? But killing him won't get you anything that Deep-Raed won't give you freely when you release him from the enchantment.

So either give him a Cure Disease potion or cast a Cure Disease spell on him, and he'll give you a family heirloom—an enchanted fur helm called The Icecap.

You'll leave him even more naked than before, and still muttering about the witch.

Taking a Load of Shirt

From the spot where you found Deep-Raed, make a giant U-turn by heading west, southwest, and south. You'll see an Argonian standing beside the road. His name is Rasha, and he has "pressing business" that demands your attention.

He wants you to deliver five exquisite shirts to Bivale Teneran: Clothier in Ald'ruhn. Teneran will pay you. Rasha asks you to swear to Zenithar to seal the deal. Agree, and head back to Ald'ruhn the way you came. (Do it quickly if you're in need; until you hand over the shirts, you won't receive service from anyone in town.)

You already know Teneran's shop is on the lower level of the Manor District. (She was one of Sarandas' creditors.) Talk to her about "Rasha's shirts" and receive an enchanted Belt of Iron Will.

A Favor for a Thief

By quest-giver location, this is almost more of a Gnisis mission, but since you're out this way on Ald'ruhn business anyway, and since it takes you back there, we've affiliated it with the latter community.

LUCAN OSTORIUS

Maybe we should have affiliated it with the moon instead.

Lucan Ostorius can be found between the compact Daedric shrine of Dushariran (inhabited by some very tough Orcs) to the east, the Ashimanu Egg Mine and the very nasty Sixth House base of Mamaea (a destination in another Miscellaneous quest) to the west, and a small camp of mabrigash (Ashlander witchwomen) to the south.

Unfortunately, none of these reference points is exactly obvious. Even the stretch of road on which Ostorius is standing doesn't connect to anything. So we need to rewind a bit.

Remember the spot where you came through the rocky pass out of the Ashlands and saw Deep-Raed?

Well, if you turned west at that point, instead of east, you'd be on the road that passes closest to Ostorius. Follow it west, northwest, and finally north. Once the road turns north, you'll come to two signposts. The second has no pointer for the road to the east, which leads to the eggmine. From the eggmine, you just need to climb over the rise to the east and look north and you should see Ostorius.

He was supposed to meet someone at this out-of-the-way spot, and has missed his contact. Ostorius asks if you're heading to Ald'ruhn and wonders if you can do him a favor. (He'll put it a little differently if you're in the Thieves Guild.)

Agree, and deliver the four weapons he gives you to Yak gro-Skandar at The Rat in the Pot cornerclub—located to the right of the stairs—by speaking to him about "Lucan's shipment." You'll get 100 gold out of it and, if you're in the Thieves Guild, your reputation within that faction will increase five points.

You can rip off Ostorius—selling the weapons or keeping them for yourself.

But be prepared for payback if you do—or even if you just procrastinate. Should you enter Ald'ruhn and leave without completing delivery, Ostorius will appear behind you and attack.

Mamaea

A spin-off from the Main Quest.

Early in that story, Caius Cosades will send you to Ald'ruhn to elicit information from a wealthy Ashlander-turned-trader named Hassour Zainsubani. Zainsubani will mention in passing that his son, Hannat, is exploring an ancient complex at Mamaea, and that he'd be grateful for news of the boy.

HANAT ZAINSUBANI

Hannat has found an unusual way to experience Mamaea. He's a prisoner there. Once the sequence with his father is complete, you can rescue him.

You may have stumbled onto this strange place—a giant Sixth House base—while looking for Lucan Ostorius. (See the previous quest.) It's divided in three large sections—Sanctum of Awakening, Sanctum of Black Hope and Shrine of Pitted Dreams—and all will be well-supplied in Dreamers, Ash Slaves and Corprus Stalkers.

Hannat's locked in a cell deep in the second section. You won't want him following you as you explore the most dangerous regions, so let him sit tight until you're done and pick him on the way back out.

Great prizes await those who penetrate to the shrine: the spooky heavy Daedric helm Face of Inspiration, ebony boots and a great enchanted dagger called Fang of Haynekhtnamet.

Once you've cleaned up the place to your satisfaction, release Hannat. He'll follow you back outside. The next time you're in Ald'ruhn, pop in to the Ald Skar Inn to see his father. The grateful Hassour, down the stairs at the right rear of the inn, will supply a rich man's reward: ebony, an enchanted shortsword, and an enchanted unarmored-combat ring.

ALD VELOTHI

Into Palansour

The wild northern reaches of Vvardenfell are thick with thieves and smugglers caves. Dealing with most of them is pretty simple. You get in, club anyone who looks as you funny, fill your pockets with their belongings, and get out again.

Palansour, along the coast south of Ald Velothi, is a little different. Someone, or something, has already gotten in here, and set up one of Morrowind's more obscure quests.

To reach this cave, head straight south from Ald Velothi's tower and along the eastern edge of a ravine. Follow the rope guard rail to a swinging bridge, and cross it. Do not cross the second bridge. Looking south from the end of the first bridge, you'll see a low rise. This conceals the entrance to Palansour.

Scamps! Three scamps! And an Ogrim! They've killed almost everyone—even the guy in the boat outside the water-level back door! And they've taken their victims' clothes off! And they've been <gulp> cooking!

You won't get a clear explanation of how this smuggling operation went awry until you reach the lone survivor. Inwold, the incompetent sorcerer responsible for this disaster, can be found in a locked cell high in the south wall of the main chamber. He asks you to bring him a Levitation potion so he can escape. (You should find three such potions in the cave.)

In return he'll offer you the fancy hat and skirt the scamps made him wear.

Doesn't sound like much of a reward, does it?

Nope, and you should act on that thought. You can take both, either one, or neither. If you take neither, and let the sorcerer walk out of here with dignity (well, a little dignity; he is in drag), your Reputation will go up a point.

DIN

A Symphony in Slaughterfish

South and west of Ald Velothi, and man wearing the armor of the Imperial Legion stands on top of a mountain and says wild things.

You can help him, but first you have to find him. And in this tangled countryside, this can be a bit difficult.

From Ald Velothi, make your way west along the coast toward the Dwemer ruin Arkngthunch-Sturdumz. Shortly before you reach the bridges leading to the ruin, you will see a path down the hill to the south. Follow it to a signpost. At the bottom of the hill, head west to another signpost.

Our objective is the top of the tall mountain to the southeast. From your current location, you can either head south and circle around behind the mountain to find a path up or, with greater ease (though greater distance), circle up behind the next hill to the west and cross the swinging bridge east to the mountain.

You'll find a man named Din standing close to the rope guide rail. Din is plainly mad. Every sentence out of his mouth seems to be from a different conversation.

But while some of the things he utters are threatening, he doesn't actually seem dangerous. Speak to him about "catch some slaughterfish" and then about "muddled," and you'll get options to cure him.

If you can't cast Cure Disease, have Din follow you to the healer Mehra Drora at the Gnisis Temple. As you approach, he'll suddenly become sane enough to give you some gold and boost your rep within the Legion.

If you can cast it, do so, and spare a potentially harrowing trip through confusing country. It'll be like nothing ever happened.

And, suddenly, Din is just a normal guy again. He was much more fun when he was totally nuts.

SYNETTE JELINE

A Ring and a Prayer

On your way to Din, at the second signpost, you probably noticed a woman and a man standing by a pool off to the ring.

The woman, Synette Jeline, can send you on a little quest to recover her lost ring, which apparently has rolled into the water. (If your character is male, this will be accompanied by some flirting and a few choice words to heighten your ardor. If female, the offer is much more straightforward.)

Accept, and, if your character is male, Jeline also proposes to discuss your reward that night after she's done dancing in Gnisis .

How could you say no? This girl is a tomato. (She's got kind of a young Judy Garland thing going on.) You might notice her friend, Tavynu Tedran, hanging around nearby. Of course, she's invisible, so is tough to notice. Still, this is something most guys are jumping into with both feet.

Well, it's all baloney. You're not about to get lucky in Gnisis. This is a robbery. Didn't you think it was strange that Camonna Tong and Thieves Guild were included among Jeline's few conversation topics? She and her compatriot just want you in the water so you'll be more vulnerable to their attacks.

Once you get hold of the ring, sweet little Jeline will start chucking throwing stars at you and Tedran taking shots with a bow and arrow.

Just kill them, and take their stuff for your reward. Tedran has a fair amount of gold, and Jeline a couple of enchanted weapons.

Oh, the ring itself? Probably not worth the effort. It's worth only 30 gold.

AHEMMUSA ASHLANDER CAMP

Dream of a White Guar

Urshamusa Rapli, an Ashlander at the Ahemmusa Camp, has seen you in her dreams. Not those kind of dreams, goofball! Symbolic, Ashlander-type dreams. She also dreams of a White Guar, which she believes to have been sent by the gods to help her troubled tribe, and asks you to find it.

Agree, and she'll give you a clue: She saw the guar at a fork in a path, a spot "where the rocks grow from the earth like the fingers of a hand."

Now, where have you seen a path around here? If you made your way northwest from Tel Mora, maybe not at all. But if you head west, past Rapli, you'll eventually see a trail opening between two low rises, bordered by stones and blue flowers. Follow it west, south and west again to "T" intersection marked by five stone "fingers." (Along the way, you'll pass the fellow who'll give you the next quest.)

The White Guar should be right nearby. Approach, and it should start to move west. Follow it. When it finally stops, check out the rocks nearby and you'll find a corpse and, on the corpse, the Amulet of Ashamanu.

With the amulet, get back to Rapli and talk to her about the White Guar and then about the amulet. It turns out that, many years ago, Ashamanu was a healer who gave her life to save others; it's said she'll give it again and again so that the Ashlanders may live on.

You'll give Rapli the amulet, and she'll give you the enchanted Shield of the Undaunted.

They tried to kill Athanden! You bastards!

Now get back to that fellow you passed along that westerly path to the five stone fingers. Athanden Girith tells you that he's been robbed by a pair of "bastard Ashlanders" and promises you a generous reward from his friend Berwen in Tel Mora if you recover his guar hides.

Back at the Ahemmusa camp, talk to anyone about the attack and they'll immediately identify the bandits as a pair of outcasts—Emul-Ran and Kashtes Ilabael—who have a camp to the south along the water.

They're easy to find. And they admit to the theft, since they think you're not going to escape with your life. Show them the error in their ways, and take the 10 hides off Emul-Ran's body. Cart them back to Girith for his thanks, and see Berwen at Berwen: Trader in Tel Mora for three Fortify Health potions and the enchanted Ring of Hornhand.

BALMORA

Bloodbath

If you've reached Level 6, you can learn about this tough quest by asking people in Balmora about "little secret." You'll hear that Larrius Varro at Moonmoth Fort wants to talk to you. About what, no one seems to know.

When you first talk to him in the fort barracks east of town, you may wonder if Varro himself knows. He chooses his words so carefully that he winds up saying nothing—which is precisely his design.

LARRIUS VARRO

Question him a bit to indicate your interest, and he'll open up. Varro wants you to do something he can't—identify and eliminate five members of the Camonna Tong criminal syndicate. He doesn't know their names or where to find them. He knows only their callings—scout, pawnbroker, savant, thief, and smith—and that they're all in Balmora.

You can ask around Balmora about "bad people," but, c'mon, you can't assassinate people by poll. Folks with a Disposition of 50 or better will point you to the Thieves Guild at the South Wall Cornerclub. (If you haven't figured it out already, the Guild and the Camonna Tong are at war.) Pump a Guild member's Disposition up to 50 (30, if you're in the Thieves Guild), and you'll get a list of your targets.

We'd give you the names, but you don't need names. They're all at the Council Club, and three are in the same room. (Another is upstairs at the entrance, and the other is in the cellar.) And except for proprietor Banor Seran, who you don't have to kill, this constitutes the entire population of the tavern.

So it's going to be clean and convenient, but it's not going to be easy. All five targets are well-equipped Level 9 characters and you may well have to face more than one at a time. Get in, hit hard, and get out.

You're an instant fugitive, so don't talk to guards before you see Varro. Don't even get close to them. Varro has a lot of pull as Legion champion and will take care of things—removing the crimes from your record and supplying the promised "nice present" from the Emperor (a Ring of Surroundings with the Chameleon enchantment). Your reputation also goes up a point—your deed quickly enters the rumor mill, where it is blamed on the Thieves Guild—and Varro's Disposition goes up 20 points.

You've done the job. And you've given him his bloodbath.

Barbarian at the Bridge

Varro can offer you one other bit of work. If he has a Disposition of 40, you can ask him about "careless travellers" and he'll mention a Nord highwayman who has been waylaying the unwary near Hla Oad.

FJOL

You'll find Fjol at the south end of the bridge north of that fishing village. Talk to him about "murderous outlaws." If his Disposition is less than 40, he'll volunteer that he is a murderous outlaw and demand 100 gold. If it is 40 or better, he'll still ask for your money, but now he'll make it sound as though he's doing you a favor.

Give him the money, and you're done. You can report Fjol's location to Varro, without reward.

Don't give him the cash, and you're in for a fight, and a 100-gold reward when you report back to Varro.

The Lost Dunmer Mine

How do you lose a mine? Don't know, but it happened in the Odai River valley south of Balmora. The once-productive Vassir-Didanat Ebony Mine has become the Vassir-Didanat Cave.

No road runs past the mine's door. Its rich stores of raw ebony remain untapped. The equipment sits idle in deep darkness. Fire atronachs, nix-hounds, and alits walk its silent halls.

To reach the mine, leave Balmora by its south exit and follow the north bank of the Odai southwest, past the Shulk

Egg Mine, to a swinging bridge. Cross the bridge and head straight east cross-country. Tall cliffs will rise up before you and you'll soon see the mine entrance flanked by three giant boulders.

You can explore it. If you have an experienced character and a good light source, you could get rich quick on the ebony in here.

But you don't have to explore. If you simply enter the lost mine, you've re-discovered it and set up the conditions for the quest. "Vassir-Didanat Mine" will now appear in your topics menu, and three Hlaalu councilors will promise great rewards if you reveal to them the mine's location.

Of course, certain people will simply promise rewards and not deliver, and you'd best hear all offers before you spill the beans. For instance, Nevena Ules, who can be found at Ules Manor, right across the water from Suran, talks a good game, but never gets specific.

On the other hand, Dram Bero, found at St. Olms Haunted manor in Vivec, will offer you your choice of a half-dozen Deadric weapons. And Velanda Omani, at Omani Manor northeast of Vivec, will pay you 2,000 gold.

Your choice.

The Last Words of Ernil Omoran

North of Balmora, under a stone arch a short distance off the Caldera road, you'll find the body of Ernil Omoran.

What killed him? The Alits you may find hovering nearby? Maybe. The drug Skooma? Maybe. He has a Skooma pipe in his inventory—along with an ambiguous (but not suicidal) note addressed to a "Tsiya."

But you really can't know.

Take the pipe and the note.

There is a Tsiya in Balmora; she has a house fronting on the river on the west side of town. You'll have to let yourself in via lockpick or spell. You'll find Tsiya upstairs. Speak to her about "Note from Ernil." She will ask if you found anything on the body. Tell her yes, and you'll exchange the pipe and the note for gold and moon sugar.

Tsiya is clearly embarassed about the pipe, claiming it is for a friend, but not so embarassed that she doesn't take it.

Strange, and somehow sad.

Pillow Talk

A super-obscure quest, though a very minor one.

Remember Drarayne Thelas from the early Fighters Guild quest Rat Hunt? Right, the pillow freak. She had a whole bunch of pillows in her little house on Balmora's east side, and apparently she ordered even more.

Morrowind doesn't send you out very often to explore its many shipwrecks. (Just one other quest involves exploring one.) But if you visit the Abandoned Shipwreck north of the Sanctus Shrine, you'll find in the cabin an invoice for 40 more pillows bound for Thelas.

They're on board. On the lower level, you'll find four crates, each containing eight pillows. The last eight are lying uncrated around the stairs to the upper level.

You don't suppose…

No, you don't. Though you can collect all 40 pillows, you can't actually give them to Thelas. (Think about it: Would you want someone dumping 40 salt-water-soaked pillows in your parlor?)

However, Thelas will acknowledge the pillow invoice—it's useful for tax purposes, we figure—and give you an "extra-comfy pillow" as a reward.

This does nothing at all—except change the message when get you you awake from sleep.

CALDERA

Heirlooms

Approaching Caldera from the south, you'll see a woman standing at the base of the hills just east of the southern part of town.

Aeta Wave-Breaker has been robbed. A gang of bandits, led by the Khajiit Dro'zhirr, took her jewelry, including two family heirlooms. She'll ask you to get them back and indicates that the thieves have a hideout somewhere east of the town (which guards in town will confirm).

The bad guys are in the cave Shushishi. This may be a struggle to find. These hills don't want to be climbed. And the door, facing west, is located at the end of an almost sheer-walled canyon to the northeast. (You'll have better luck climbing the hills farther south, and then following the ridge north to the canyon. You can drop down using rocks protruding from the canyon's eastern wall.)

You can fight your way into this good-sized cave or simply run your way through. You'll have to go almost to its end to find Dro'Zhirr. For a bandit, he's very much a businessman, and he'll take you up on a proposal to split your 300-gold reward. Of course, you can just kill him and take the jewelry. Either way will work. When you've got them, return to Aeta and talk to her about her "family heirlooms." She'll give you the 300-gold reward. Whether you take Dro'zhirr his share is your decision.

A Pattern Emerges

North and west of Caldera, you will run across another semi-naked barbarian with another story of seduction and betrayal. (Check out Deep-Raed's similar tale in "Semi-Naked Barbarian in the Middle of the Road" in the Ald'ruhn section.)

Hlormar Wine-Sot is on the right at the intersection for the road to Ald'ruhn. He'll claim that he was on his way to Caldera when he was seduced by a witch, that she cast a paralyzing spell on him and took all his possessions—including his enchanted axe Cloudcleaver—and then abandoned him to the scorn of passers-by. He's still a bit bee-stung from the spell, but thinks he met her at a camp to the northwest.

HLOMER WINE-SOT

With Hlormar following you, make your way northwest along the Ald'ruhn road, and then north at the first intersection. You'll find the "witch" along this road.

Talk to her about Hlomar. It turns out she's a healer named Sosia Caristiana. She says she enlisted Hlomar an her escort on the road to Caldera. He got "entirely too friendly for his own good." She cast a Sleep spell on him, took his stuff as a lessson and took Cloudcleaver so it didn't wind up buried in her skull.

Ask about Cloudcleaver and learn Caristiana is not willing to return the axe quite yet, as Hlomar still looks fit to be tied. However, she'll meet him three days hence at the Caldera Mages Guild, when he's had a chance to cool down, and turn over everything. Convey this to Hlomar as "Sosia's offer."

This does not lighten the barbarian's mood. He forces you to take sides.

Side with Caristiana and he'll attack you. You'll have to kill him. (You'll also have to kill Caristiana if you want the axe.) She will give you 2 healing potions and a fatigue potion, though.

Side with Hlomar, and he'll beat the snot out of Caristiana, with or without your help. Take Cloudcleaver from her body (Caristiana also has an enchanted Steel Staff of Chastening), and speak to Hlomar about Cloudcleaver for another choice: Give him the axe or keep it. Keep it, and he attacks you. Give it to him, and he'll supply fighting tips that boost your Strength by two points.

The Note That He Never Wrote

See that boulder right across the road from where you met Hlormar Wine-Sot? The Orc Bugrol gro-Bagul is hiding behind it. Apparently, he's being sought by the authorities in Caldera in connection with an unspecified "something bad." If you select "help me" in conversation, he'll ask you to take a note to his co-conspirator—I mean, friend—Bashuk gra-Bat.

BUGROL GRO-BAGUL

Her house is back in Caldera, on the left side of the street right after the road to the Governor's Hall. She'll give you a note to take back to him. (You can read the notes without annoying the orcs; both are elegantly stupid, and gra-Bat's is insulting.)

Cart this note back to gro-Bagul, and he'll give you a diamond (he thinks it's just a rock, and is rather proud of himself for deceiving you).

Now, if you want to know what these two Orcs did, no one's going to come out and tell you. But you can sort it out from correspondence found in the various people's houses. Check the note from Irgola you'll find in Bashuk's place, and another at Valvius Mevureius' house (on the right as you re-enter Caldera).

The state of disarray here—there is even a bottle under the bed! – should tell you something.

J'ZHIRR

EBONHEART

Special Delivery

You're a postman. If you ask Llaalam Dredil on the second floor of Castle Ebonheart about "running an errand," he will ask you to deliver a letter to J'Zhirr at the East Empire Company and return with his response.

This is dead simple. You'll find the Khajiit in the East Empire Company Hall down by the Ebonheart docks. Talk to him about a "delivery from Llaalam Dredil," and he'll take the note and give you one for Dredil. Return to Dredil and talk to him about "running an errand" again. He'll take the note and pay you off with 75 gold.

You can read the notes. They seem innocent enough on the surface. But note that the biggest price increase is for Dwemer artifacts. And what could Dredil be doing for the East Empire Company that's worth 10,000 gold? It won't be the last time you see this letter.

An Enchanting List

Few of the Miscellaneous quests are chained together in sequences, but this one is.

If you've proved yourself adept at small, menial tasks by completing the Special Delivery quest above and the Rats! quest in Vivec, you can get a third, more advanced quest from Bolrin—the little owl-like wood elf in the East Empire Company Hall in Ebonheart.

Speak to him about "further assistance" and then "information gathering" to learn that the East Empire Company, jealous of Vivec enchanter Audenian Valius' high profits and exclusive clientele, wants to know what he's selling and to whom he's selling it. You're to obtain a list.

You may already have seen the list; it's on the shelf in Valius' back room. It's easy enough to grab it, but there's one small problem. See, Valius is an enchanter, and he's enchanted this list to summon a Hunger if someone other than he picks it up. Oops. You're immediately attacked by the Hunger guardian and quite possibly by Valius himself on your way out. Get the document back to Bolrin, and he'll reward you with a very substantial payoff: 700 gold!

ERABENIMSUN ASHLANDER CAMP

A Runaway Slave

This isn't an Ashlander-related mission, but the Erabenimsun Camp is the closest reference point, and you may even stumble upon it while performing another mission.

Just south of Tel Fyr, there is a path west into the Vvardenfell interior. It's a little slice of Hell, with lava, dead trees, steam vents and dead gray hills.

In this god-forsaken place, just south of the beginning of a lava river, you'll find a lone Argonian named Reeh-Ja.

Initially, all he's likely to say is that he wants to go home.

REEH-JA

Reeh-Ja is a runaway slave and, as such, reluctant to talk about his plight to just anyone. But if you can coax his Disposition up to 50, he'll confess that he's trying to get to the Argonian Mission in Ebonheart. (If you've had dealings with the Mission on quests for the Imperial Cult, you already know it's involved in spiriting escaped Argonian slaves out of Morrowind.)

You can be a hero, a villain or just another indifferent passer-by.

If you're feeling up to it, you can escort the slave either to Molag Mar,where you can pick up a silt strider or ship, or all the way to Ebonheart. It's a long road—you're traveling almost from coast to coast—but it is clear, wide and, soon, well-marked. Head west and southwest along the lava river and you'll see a signpost ahead of you. From here, just keep following the signs for Vivec, Pelagiad and Balmora, then Vivec and Pelagiad and finally just Pelagiad, where you'll pick up signs for Ebonheart.

Note that you'll face a pretty fair amount of low-to-moderate level fights until you get out of the mountains. Balance your desire to clear the path ahead with the need to stay close to your charge—both to keep him moving in the right direction and to gaurd against surprise attacks by cliff racers.

The mission is in the Hawkmoth part of the Ebonheart fort complex. Take Reeh-Ja to consul Im-Kalaya. He'll give you a Blood Belt (which has a nice magical health boost), and your reputation within the Twin Lamps abolitionist movement will jump 10 points.

You can also sell out Reeh-Ja. If you're feeling sleazy, or simply don't relish the long trip, return Reeh-Ja to Savile Amayn at Tel Aruhn's Slave Market, where he's worth 150 gold alive and 50 gold dead. (However, if you go this route, you're better off not speaking about Reeh-Ja to Im-Kilaya in any future encounters, as this reduces your rep with the Twin Lamps as much as saving the slave would have advanced it.)

Or you can leave Reeh-Ja to his own devices. After all, it is a long road to Ebonheart and if you're out east to begin with, you probably have other tasks at hand.

In any case, he's not going anywhere without your help.

Hides in Plain Sight

Apparently these guar-hide holdups are a pretty common thing. Marsus Tullius has the same complaint as Athanden Girith up north.

But this time, the situation's a bit more complicated.

MARSUS TULLIUS

You can find Tullius northwest of the camp. It's a little easier to find him if you go a little out of your way. Remember the area where you found Reeh-Ja? Well, if you find your way back to the coast, and then head north, you'll come upon a long inlet with a lot of mudcrabs on its beaches. West of the end of the inlet, you'll find Tullius standing out in the open.

He says two Ashlanders jumped him, took the hides and vanished. Can you get them back? Does Tullius deserve to get them back?

The nearest Ashlander camp—the only one nearby, in fact—is the Erabenimsun camp to the southeast. It's easily reached by returning to the coast, heading south, then inland at first opportunity and south again through a defile between two hills.

The Ashlanders here report that those responsible, Tinti and Hairan, are "honorable warriors," and speculate that the trader offended them or poached from the tribe's guar herds.

Put this together with what Tullius has already told you about finding a large guar herd to the south, and this sounds a plausible explanation.

You can confirm this by talking to the warriors themselves, who are both in camp. They are adamant: they simply took back what already belonged to the tribe.

This can play out a few ways.

If you've already completed the part of the Main Quest that makes you an Ashlander, the warriors will recognize you as a brother and simply offer you the hides.

You don't have to take them. (After all, their actions seem just.) If you decide not to take them, you'll receive a Herder's Belt as a sign of your friendship.

However, if you're still an outlander to the Erabenimsun, and you just have to have the hides now, you'll have to tan the warriors' own hides and take the guar ones. But given that the Ashlanders were within their rights to reclaim the goods, that may not sit right with you.

Then again, one of the warriors may attack you and settle the issue. You can either fight it out then and there or run away and return after he's cooled off.

But a nice compromise is to let Tullius cool his heels for a while. Don't take the hides right away. Wait until you're a clanfriend and the Ashlanders are willing to give them to you. Tullius refers you to his father in Tel Aruhn for payment. Stentus Tullius is the guy walking around town who looks just like Marsus. Speak to him about "Marsus Tullius' hides" to get your 200 gold.

GNAAR MOK

A Most Peculiar Woman

Follow the signs for the main Ald'ruhn road out of Caldera, and you'll run into a merchant named Pemenie. Her escort on her trip to Gnaar Mok has taken a break and she asks you to fill in. In return, she offers you the Boots of Blinding Speed.

Then again, every time it comes up, she sounds like she's on the verge of reneging.

But a quest is a quest, so agree and start toward Gnaar Mok. Once you cross the plank bridge to the village, she'll turn over the boots. What a surprise!

Or is it? Ask about "Pemenie the trader" in Caldera or Gnaar Mok, and you'll learn she has a bounty on her head.

PEMENIE

"…although no one would bother trying to collect it. She's a slippery one. Often deals in shoddy items. Great promise, but low reward. You know?"

Maybe you should try on your new boots. You may be in for a surprise.

GNISIS

Man Without Pants

Just slightly east of the silt strider port, you'll find Hentus Yansurnummu standing thigh-deep in the river. He tells you Hainab Lasamsi stole his pants while he was bathing, and asks you to get them back.

Hainab does indeed have Hentus' pants. You can pickpocket them (he's not wearing them). You can kill Hainab or knock him out and take the pants. Or you can talk Hainab into giving you the pants if you get his Disposition up to 80.

Deliver them back to Yansurnummu for his thanks and some hackle-lo.

HLA OAD

Freedom

Hla Oad may be only slightly less player-friendly than Red Mountain, but that doesn't mean you can't get quests here. It just means you may need to think about how you want to perform them.

For instance, you may know by now that the cellar of the seedy shop Fatleg's Dropoff is home to a barely-concealed base for the Camonna Tong criminal syndicate. The trapdoor is in the near left corner. Descend, head right at the base of the stairs, and at the base of the next stairs you'll find Relam Arinith. Talk to him about "doing some business" and then "deliver this slave." He'll invite you to escort Rabinna, the Khajiit beside him, to Vorar Helas on the east side of Balmora, and admonishes you to be careful with the slave.

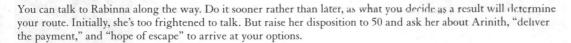

"Rabinna here might not look like much, but it's what's on the inside that counts," says Arinith. "Know what I mean?"

Unfortunately, yes. Rabinna is a drug mule.

Once you strike the deal, she'll follow you automatically. It can be a mite tricky getting her onto the wooden walkway that leads to the trapdoor, but once there, it's clear sailing.

But do you really want to do this?

You can talk to Rabinna along the way. Do it sooner rather than later, as what you decide as a result will determine your route. Initially, she's too frightened to talk. But raise her disposition to 50 and ask her about Arinith, "deliver the payment," and "hope of escape" to arrive at your options.

Deliver her to Helas, and you're killing her; he'll attack her once she is in close proximity. But take Rabinna to Im-Kilaya at the Argonian Mission in Ebonheart, and you can help her escape.

The former path (north up the coast to the stronghold Hlormaren, then east to Balmora) will earn you 400 gold and a ring of Medusa's Gaze—even if Rabinna dies along the way, as long as you rescued the moon sugar. The latter path (south across the river to Seyda Neen and then Ebonheart) also earns you 400 gold, and a 10-point boost in your reputation with the Twin Lamps.

KHUUL

SASON

What's A Missing Wife or Two?

As you can probably attest from personal experience, the road south from Khuul is a dangerous one, and you are not its only victim.

Once you're past the silt trider port, make your second left. (The first takes you to the bandit cave Ashir-Dan.) This unmarked road leads to a grove of trees where you'll find a man named Sason who says his wife, Malexa, was abducted by cultists. He suspects they haven't gone far.

So, naturally, you're going to look in the nearest Daedric shrine. That's Maelkashishi, which is in a depression just to the southeast.

Only, it's the wrong place.

This is Daedric Shrine Country. Cultists have many potential altars for their unholy rituals. And, in fact, Malexa is at another shrine, Ashalmawia—located east of Ald Velothi and southwest of your current location. You can't miss it— it's sited on a high rock—and if somehow you do miss it, it's visible from Ald Velothi's tower.z

Like Maelkashishi, you may have been in Ashalmawia before—a House Redoran mission takes you there—and you may not have had skill to explore it thoroughly.

You don't have to do so this time, either. Just kill the cultists in the altar area to clear the path out. Malexa is reached through the locked and trapped door to the right of the altar. Simply talk to her and have her follow you back to Sason for a reward 200 gold and a five-point boost in your reputation with House Redoran. (Sason is a member.)

If you happen to find Malexa without first getting the quest from Sason, that's OK. Just bring her back to him as outlined to get the same credit.

Then again, an advanced player will want to descend the stairs to the left of the shrine and the hard-to-spot flight behind the stone table to reach the Sunken Vaults—in essence a whole other shrine-within-a-shrine. (However, note that, if you're in House Redoran, you have to kill Gordol, the bad guy down here, in the quest Cult Elimination.)

MAAR GAN

Rich Man, Poor Man

Leave Maar Gan to the west, along the road to Ald'ruhn, and you'll soon come upon "poor" pilgrim Fonus Rathryon.

FONUS RATHRYON

Rathryon is on his way to Koal Cave south of Gnisis, but has gotten lost and needs a guide. If you help him, he'll pay you 150 gold. (Apparently, by "poor pilgrim," he means a lost pilgrim.)

You can do this on foot, but it's an indirect and rather hazardous trip. A better move is to retreat with Rathryon to Maar Gan, take the silt strider to Gnisis and find your way south.

You may know the route from previous visits. The land route is long, but you can take a shortcut across the river, swim south down the east bank until you reach a stone arch and then make your way east to the shrine. Don't dawdle, though—Rathryon has a schedule, and he won't hesitate to let you know about it. Wait too long, and he'll leave your company.

PELAGIAD

Beluelle's Silver Bowl

A quest in reverse.

Most quests begin with a person—the quest-giver. This one begins with an item—what would ordinarily be a quest objective—and you have to find the person to whom it belongs.

Few people are likely to stumble onto this quest, as the game doesn't direct you to the cave where it is found. And fewer are likely to make the connection and realize that there is a quest in there at all. Success here relies largely on the player's sense of enterprise.

It starts in the smuggler's cave Ulummusa. You can find this by taking the main road out of Pelagiad, turning north at the "T" intersection and then making your first left.

It's a very small cave, with just two smugglers—one with the interesting name of Godrod Hairy-Breeks. The sense of humor extends to the name of his magical, fatigue-damaging belt (Northern Knuck Knuck).

But that's the only real booty here. Even the locked chest at the rear contains only mundane items.

But did you look on top of the chest? There you'll find Beluelle's Silver Bowl. Take it. You'll get a journal entry, which you should read (always a good policy) to see the inscription.

Separate and distinct from the other junk here, this is clearly someone's property, and should be returned.

But where is Armond Beluelle?

Ask about "Beluelle's silver bowl" back in Pelagiad to learn that a Piernette Beluelle has a farm off to the east, and that Ygfa, the healer at Fort Pelagiad, might be able to offer better directions.

Skip Ygfa; she means well, but her directions aren't the best and following them takes you well out of your way. Instead, head west out of Pelagiad and this time turn south at the crossing. When the road splits, follow the left fork toward Vivec. After you cross two wooden bridges, the road turns north and northeast, At the next intersection, head southeast on this unmarked road. Beluelle's farmhouse is the first house on the left.

She'll describe at some length how her husband—now serving with the Legion in Argonia—received the bowl and how it came to be stolen. You can return it, try to get a reward, or keep it.

But Beluelle has no reward to offer except her gratitude, which takes the form of a 20-point Disposition bump if you return the bowl.

In fact, you can translate this good deed into higher Dispositions all over Pelagiad by talking to people about it afterward. Conversely, if you acted badly toward the lady, you can send Dispositions all over Pelagiad into the toilet by talking about that...which would be dumb.

Kiss the Girls (and Kill the Boys)

New arrivals on Vvardenfell may have their first less-than-positive experience in Morrowind with Nels Llendo.

But only if you're a guy.

If you are daring or foolhardy enough to try to walk to Balmora from Seyda Neen, you will run into this bandit on the road south of Pelagiad. And if you talk to him for any time, there is a chance you're going to get your head handed to you.

See, he's so polite that you won't even know you're being robbed until he actually introduces the subject of money changing hands. By then, it's too late to get out, you may not have the 50 gold he requires, and you won't be able to beat him in combat. Usually, this combination equals dead, wounded, and worn out.

The best advice for the beginning player is simply to stay away. Come back once you have some experience under your belt.

Then, it may actually be worthwhile. At least you'll be able to defend yourself. And if you do pay him off, as soon as you leave the area, Llendo will remove himself to the common room of the Halfway Tavern in Pelagiad, where he will offer training in Short Blade, Security,y, and Sneak.

NELS LENDO

Now, if your character is a woman, it's a whole different deal. In that case, all Llendo wants is a kiss. Refuse and his ardor drops by 10 Disposition points. Kiss him and it'll go up by 30, he'll talk like Pepe Le Pew for a bit, and he'll suggest you stop by his lodgings at Pelagiad's Halfway Tavern.

Don't get your hopes up, girls. There is no hanky-panky that we're aware of going on at the Halfway Tavern. The invitation is for training—the same for gals as for the guys.

Victim of Love

MAURRIE AURMINE

Is the Love Bug going around in the Pelagiad area? Seems that way. First there was Nels Llendo getting all kissy. And now, down the road a piece, Maurrie Aurmine is getting hot and bothered over some bandit.

You'll find the smitten Aurmine by leaving Pelagiad to the west and turning north at the "T." When the road forks, take the right fork (the Balmora road) and you'll soon find the lady on the right-hand slope.

She's been robbed, but she's not mourning her lost jewels so much as the disappearance of the handsome Dunmer bandit. "Nelos Onmar...a name that will stay on my lips for eternity," she says. Aurmine asks you to find him—she suspects he is in Pelagiad—and gives you a glove for him as a token of her love.

Sigh. When's one of these girls going to like you? (Soon, soon. See the "Romance" section.)

Make your way back to the town and check out the Halfway Tavern. Sure enough, Onmar's here. He's the fellow to the right of the bar. He seems touched by this news, takes the glove and gives you a note for Aurmine. (You can read it; it is restrained and yet passionate.)

Return to Aurmine and speak to her about "note from Nelos." She's in seventh heaven and, overflowing with love, tries to fix you up with one of her friends. If your character is male, this will be Emusette Bracques at Plot and Plaster in Tel Aruhn. If female, Barnand Erelie at Sethan's Tradehouse in Tel Branora.

That's a long way to go for a blind date. But it's also an opportunity to pick up a reward of high-level Restore Health potions. (You'll recall that Aurmine had nothing to give you.)

In Tel Aruhn, Plot and Plaster is up a long staircase from Aryne Telnim: Smith at the north end of town. In Tel Branora, Sethan's is up the stairs on the right side of the tower. In each case, your "date" reports that the couple has apparently run off together, and that their love is now the stuff of song.

Erelie looks old enough to be your Dad, but that Bracques is a honey.

"Always happy to chat with people I like," she may say, looking at you steadily. "And I like you."

That Love Bug thing seems to be catching.

At Play In or Near the Fields of Kummu

This one's a good walk compared to other Pelagiad-area missions. Once again, leave town to the west and head north on the main road. At the fork, take the unmarked road on the left.

This will take you west through a long green valley with few notable features. Shortly after you pass the Lleran Ancestral Tomb, the road begins to turn northwest, and up ahead, you'll see a woman. Pilgrim Nevrasa Dralor has gotten lost on her way to the Fields of Kummu shrine. She'll pay you 150 gold to escort her there. Plus, if you ask her about the Fields of Kummu, you'll get some cool lore about Lord Vivec.

Step one is get back to the fork. From there, follow the sign for Balmora and head north. You'll be on this road for long time, along the way passing the cave Adanumuran. At a four-way intersection, head east toward Suran along the north shore of Lake Amaya. The shrine's just a short distance away, on the south side of the road.

SADRITH MORA

It's a Ghoooost!

Talk to folks at the Gateway Inn or ask in town about "latest rumors" and you'll invariably learn the inn is haunted. Speak with prefect Angaredhel in the lobby of the Gateway—it's the large structure just in from the docks—about "work" for a briefing.

A ghost keeps appearing in the South Turret room. As often as it is driven out, it returns. The room is unrentable, the guests are in a panic and Telvanni officialdom has inspected the site and more or less shrugged its shoulders.

If you like, you can visit the room and beat up on the ghost. But it won't achieve anything permanent. You're going to have to track down the cause.

From the rumors you'll get the sense that this is sorcerous mischief, rather than an honest-to-goodness haunt, and from the prefect in the inn's lobby you'll get the name Arara Uvulas, the Mouth, or spokesperson, for Telvanni Councilor Neloth.

You'll find Uvulas at the Telvanni Council House north of the docks. (She's the second "Mouth" on the right as you enter the council chamber.) She'll echo the rumor that this isn't an authentic haunt, and suspect involvement of a Conjuration expert—someone adept at calling up ghosts.

You may feel you've hit a dead-end here. If so, you're just not talking to the right people. No one knows more about spellcasters than other spellcasters, and where better to find spellcasters than at the Mages Guild at Wolverine Hall—the fort-type structure south of town?

ANGAREDHEL

Any Mage-type character here should respond to "Conjuration expert" by mentioning that Uleni Heleran teaches Conjuration at the guild. Ask about her specifically, and you'll learn that you don't simply have an expert witness, but a potential suspect: Heleran has a mischievous character, "some sort of bad feeling" for the inn and its prefect, and lately has adopted the habit of transporting magically into Wolverine Hall.

Heleran herself can be found in the far right-hand corner of the guild. If you had any doubt of her involvement, you won't after you've spoken to her. You can break down her defenses by raising her Disposition to 50. (She requires a Disposition of 40 if you belong to the Mages or Fighters guild, the Imperial Legion or the Imperial Cult. If you don't belong, and you're having trouble getting Heleran to open up, you can join the Mages Guild by speaking to Skink-in-Tree's-Shade in the same room.)

She then takes responsibility, agrees to knock it off (though one comment may make you wonder) and gives you a silly note for Angaredhel. (The whole business seems to been a dust-up over the "Hospitality papers" needed for non-Telvanni to operate in Sadrith Mora.)

Get back to Angaredhel and talk to him about "work" again.

You have three choices here. You can refuse to explain how you stopped the haunting. This completes the quest and wins the reward: one of three enchanted rings (Fighters, Mages and Thieves) that enhances two attributes important to members of that character class.

But this annoys the bejesus out of Angardedhel and instead of the 30-point Disposition boost you'd otherwise receive, his plummets 20 points. You won't get the one-point Reputation bump, either.

However, Heleran is well-liked here and not ratting her out has benefits. Afterward, you can raise Telvanni dispositions all over Sadrith Mora—and Dispositions of everyone at Wolverine Hall—by talking to them about the case, with the usual benefits when you go shopping or need to drag out some information.

On the other hand, you can blame Heleran and either pass along or withhold the note. (The note seems to enrage the prefect, but has no actual effect.) You'll satisfy Angardedhel, but won't be able to the town-wide Disposition bump.

And if you've killed Heleran, no explanation is required—except perhaps to the Mages Guild members who witnessed the deed.

SEDYA NEEN

Can You Help Out a Fellow Imperial Who's Down on His Luck?

VODUNIUS NUCCIUS

The first person you're likely to run into once you clear customs in Seyda Neen at the beginning of Morrowind will quietly offer you a quest. You may not even realize it at the time.

Ask Vodunius Nuccius for a "little advice," and he'll suggest you take the silt strider to Balmora. "Fast and cheap," he says. "No trouble with wild animals. And smugglers. And bandits. And outlaws."

Oh, and you're to tell silt strider operator Darvame Hleran than Nuccius sent you.

Cross the bridge to the north and climb the hill to the strider port to the west. Hleran's up on the boarding platform. Don't travel just yet. Mention Nuccius and learn they have a little business arrangement, and that Nuccius is unhappy on Vvardenfell.

Armed with this insight, return to Nuccius and ask about "Vodunius Nuccius." He confesses that he's not happy and that, if he had the money, he'd be gone. On that score, he wonders if you'd buy his cursed ring.

Don't expect wonders. It's a pretty ordinary ring. But this quest isn't about getting some cool item. It's about helping someone in need, and you've done that.

A Nicer Ring

Even before you ran into Nuccius, you may have acquired the raw material of another small quest.

In the customs house, you took everything you could lay your hands on. Don't lie. We were watching. And it's OK. The game expects you to take the stuff. It even encourages you to do so. Maybe you even plundered the little storage room down the stairs. Also OK. And between the two buildings, you probably grabbed an Engraved Ring of Healing from the barrel and thought you'd come across a real find.

The ring belongs to someone. If you talk to Fargoth, the little wood elf north of the bridge, you'll learn his ring has been stolen. If you return the ring to him, he'll have a word with the proprietor of Arrille's Tradehouse. This will improve his Disposition by 40 points when you shop there, and that translates into lower prices.

FARGOTH

In Fact, So Nice I Stole It Twice

Now, what's the point of making friends in the game if you can't turn around and immediately stab them in the back?

You're about to do just that.

Ask Arrille at Arrille's Tradehouse about "latest rumors" and he'll mention that Hrisskar is having money problems.

Hrisskar's in the bar upstairs. Talk to him about "recover some gold," which leads to "Fargoth's hiding place," and a plot is born.

See, Hrisskar has had a run of bad luck gambling, and has been shaking down little Fargoth to make ends meet. He hasn't been as profitable recently, though, and your new buddy wants to find out where Fargoth is hiding his good loot. Agree to find his stash. And then go kill mudcrabs or something for the rest of the day.

At nightfall, return to Seyda Neen and make your way to the lighthouse south of town. Climb to the very top, and stand in the corner closest to town.

Watch and wait.

Before long, you'll see a little man creeping along—first to a tree, then a wall, then toward the lighthouse, then back to the tree, and, finally, to a muck pond.

He lingers there for a moment, and then he leaves.

You've found Fargoth's hiding place.

Get down to the muck pond. It contains a hollow log. Inside, you'll find 300 gold, a journeyman lockpick and, if you'd previously found it and returned it to Fargoth, his Engraved Ring of Healing. (If you've been watching and waiting anyplace other than the lighthouse top, Fargoth won't appear.)

Take it all. Get back to Hrisskar, who takes the gold, gives you 100 gold back for your trouble and lets you keep the other stuff you've found.

And, no, you can't trade the ring in a second time. But nice try.

Declare the Pennies on His Eyes

If you ask about "latest rumors" in the village, you'll learn that tax collector Processus Vitellius is missing. If you cross the bridge to the north, swim across the inlet to the west and search among the rocks to the northwest, you'll learn he is dead.

Take the 200 gold and tax records you'll find on his body, return to the village, and speak to Socucius Ergalla in the Census and Excise Office about "murder of Processus Vitellius." (He's the older, bearded fellow who generated your character. Never thought you'd see him again, did you?)

Ergalla asks whether Vitellius had the tax money he'd collected. You can say "no" and keep the gold, and, because you're a big old liar, the quest will end here. Or you can turn the money in. (If you had the gold, but spent it, Ergalla will admonish you get it back.) And if you've recovered it one way or the other, Ergalla will see that you're trustworthy and commission you to find Vitellius' killer.

Start by chatting up the people in town. You'll learn Vitellius was not well-loved here, but that he did have a girl-friend—Tavere Vedrano at the Lighthouse. She's distraught at the news and discloses that she's seen Vitellius angry only once or twice. Ask about "seen him get angry," and you'll learn he argued over taxes with Foryn Gilnith.

Gilnith has one of the shacks down by the water. Question him about the murder and he'll cop to it, arguing that Vitellius was overcharging on taxes and skimming the cream for himself.

Here, again, you have a choice. You can accept Gilnith's story and spare his life, or you can kill him.

Morally, it's hard to know what to do here, as no real evidence has been offered of Vitellius' supposed corruption.

But if it's early in the game (and since you're in Seyda Neen, it may be), the lure of the prom-ised bounty of 500 gold may weigh heavily upon you. Either way, you'll get Vitellius' ring, which you can return to Vedrano for two health potions.

**PROCESSUS
VITELLIUS**

SURAN

Smart Slave

Suran, barely more than a name on a map in the Main Quest and a waystation in other faction quests, really comes into its own into the Miscellaneous quests.

A nice way to start here is by putting in at Desele's House of Earthly Delights. It's the first door on the right after you get off the silt strider.

After you've seen the, uh, view, have a chat with the drunken bounty hunter at the bar.

Daric Bielle holds forth on "stupid slaves" – stupid, apparently, because they don't stay in one place long enough to be caught by this idiot and because they insolently insist on hiding. He's been tracking one escape slave named Haj-Ei for months without luck, and has even hired an Argonian guide, Hides His Eyes, whose main achievement seems to have been to introduce Bielle to the House of Earthly Delights.

Are you thinking what I'm thinking?

No, you're probably still thinking of dancers at the bar! Snap out of it.

If your character is Argonian, or has Intelligence of 90 or better, this is a really short quest. You'll get the critical topic as soon as you agree to find the slave. Just fast-forward to the end of this walkthrough.

If you're a non-Argonian of lesser intelligence, tell Bielle you can find his slave. Then go talk to people around town about Haj-Ei and Hides His Eyes. You may need to bump up their Dispositions a bit to hear what they have to say. On the Hides his Eyes front, you'll hear that there's something not quite right about him. On the Haj-Ei front, you'll be referred to slave trader Dranas Sarathram.

Sarathram is at the Suran Slave Market—just up the stairs immediately opposite the western entrance to the town. Flatter or bribe him until his Disposition reaches 60 and then ask about "Hides His Eyes" to learn this is simply a translation from the Argonian.

In Argonian, Hides His Eyes might be known as "Haj-Ei."

Well, la-de-da.

Run off with your new "Hides His Eyes is Haj-Ei" topic to applaud the Argonian's cleverness. He's on the top floor of the Suran Tradehouse, which is tucked away on the southeast side of town.

You can tell him that you'll keep his secret, which solution will kick your reputation with the Twin Lamps abolition-ist movement up by five points.

Or you can say that you must report him to that incompetent back at the House of Earthly Delights.

This will start a fight. Privately, we hope that you lose. But if you survive, check in Bielle for a reward of 150 gold. Of course, you can just skip talking to Hides His...er, Haj-Ei...and go straight to Bielle. He won't believe that the Argonian is the slave he's been hunting, but he's drunk enough to give you the cash anyway. Then everyone is happy.

A Plot Foiled

North of Suran, and west across a swinging bridge, a pair of additional missions await. Northwest of the bridge, you'll run into an Argonian named Tul. Talk to him about "aid a poor Argonian" to learn he's recently escaped from cruel masters at the nearby Dren Plantation. He has heard of a Redguard who helps escaped slaves has a place nearby, and begs you to take him there.

Depending on what other slave-related quests you've completed, you'll get slightly different wording in your dialogue and options. But Tul must be referring to Sterdecan's Farm, which you may have already visited on a similar errand. It's close by—a short jaunt to the northwest. You'll find this out if you ask the locals about a "Kindly Redguard."

TUL

You may think twice about this mission. There's something slightly off about Tul. His courtesy is a little over-the-top—even for a grateful escaped slave. And, if you check your journal, you'll note the comment there that he seems rather too fit and healthy for a mistreated slave.

Perform the mission. But I wouldn't turn my back on him.

The farm is just across the road from the Sandas Ancestral Tomb. You'll find Sterdecan out in his fields.

As you approach, Tul will speak to you again. Suddenly, he is no longer the fawning slave, but a Camonna Tong opera-tive sent to assassinate the abolitionist Sterdecan. He'll give you a chance to leave. If you don't (and you shouldn't), he'll attack. Kill him, and speak to Sterdecan, who says such attempts are not uncommon and gives you a First Barrier ring.

I'll Be A Quarter-Mile Away for You

Continue west along the road from Sterdecan's Farm. The river to the south will gradually broaden and turn into Lake Amaya. You'll come to an intersection, with Alof's Farmhouse off to the left and the Sarano Ancestral Tomb down a dogleg to the right.

At the intersection, you'll find a man named Thoronor. He was on his way to Vivec with his friend, Edras Oril, when Oril wandered off to investigate an animal sound. Some hours have passed without a sign of his friend, and Thoronor is worried.

And rightly so. Conceivably, you've already encountered the source of the sounds. Two mating kagouti are in the area, and Oril has been trapped by them in a rocky enclosure north of the path a short ways east of Thoronor's location. (The quest will also work if you find Oril first.)

If you've already encountered the creatures and taken care of them, great; Oril should agree to accompany you back to his friend. If you find him with the kagouti still on the prowl, you'll have options: kill the critters, cast a concealing spell (like Invisibility or Chameleon) on Oril so they can't see him as you travel, or just throw up your hands.

Once you reunite the friends, Thoronor will give you an Amulet of Slowfalling.

Wimp Alert

Just across the river from Suran, right next to Dirara Drom's Farm, you'll find a man named Paur Maston. He was supposed to meet his business partner here, but he was late, and Vanjirra seems to have gone on to Molag Mar without him. It's a dangerous trip, he says, and asks you to be his escort.

Let me get this straight: your lady business partner went to Molag Mar without you, but you want an escort?

True enough, south and east of Suran, the color of the earth changes from brown to gray as you enter the Molag Amur mountain range. The trees are dead. Steam gushes from the ground. Lakes and rivers are filled with lava.

PAUR MASTON

But this trip is as safe as it could be. The worst creature you're likely to face is a skeletal warrior from the Raviro Ancestral Tomb, which you'll pass when the beach vanishes and your path turns inland. And the worst thing you'll put Maston through is swimming over to the north side of the river below Suran so you can follow the coast, and finding his way around the odd piece of driftwood on the beach.

You'll find Vanjirra near the bridge into Molag Mar. Speak to her about "reward" and she'll give you a Light Amulet.

The Death of a Warrior (Or Maybe Just of You)

While you're at the Suran Tradehouse, speak to bartender Ashumanu Eraishah about "latest rumors," and you'll hear about a heavily-armored, sword-waving madman on a hill to the east.

That sounds like just our kind of trouble.

If you're on foot, it's a fairly lengthy trip. This huge Orc warrior, who calls himself "Umbra," after his great sword, is actually very close to Suran as the cliff racer flies. But the Molag Amur range east of the town is unclimbably steep on much of its western side, and you'll need to head south into open terrain, then east past the Inanius Egg Mine, then briefly north and finally northwest, up a long foyada, to reach him.

If you can Levitate over the mountains, do so. Use as reference point the top of the stairs (the street stairs, not the slave market stairs) located just south of Suran's northern entrance. Simply turn east and fly straight over the mountains from this point and you'll find Umbra waiting below you at the top of the foyada.

UMBRA

Don't worry. He cuts a threatening figure. But he won't attack you on his own, and you don't have to fight him until you feel you're ready.

By the way, Umbra's not crazy; he's just depressed. He has killed so many times, and has seen so much death, that the world no holds any surprises for him. All he wants is a warrior's death in close combat, and has not found it. If you follow his dialogue through to "nothing is left," you can volunteer to introduce him to his maker.

Ah, but there's a problem. Umbra is not just going to lie down and take it. He wants to go out fighting, and unless you have an advanced character—Level 12 or so would be nice for a melee fighter (less for a good wizard) – it is entirely possible he'll take you out before you take him. He's Level 20 and has weapon, armor, and Block skills of 90.

And he's got one of those endgame-type swords, with which he may not have to hit you with twice.

The great thing is that, when you do finally kill him, you get to keep that sword

Getting back to Suran is surprisingly easy. You can climb over the mountain from this side without a struggle and let yourself slide gently down the other side.

Don't be surprised if you're smiling. In dying, Umbra may make you feel grateful to still be alive.

TEL BRANORA

Something's going on outside Tel Branora. A spellcaster and five bonemold-clad retainers stand in a bunch to the southwest of the great tower, as if waiting for their cue.

None of them say why.

It you ask her about "little advice," leader Trerayna Dalen says only that the matter is between her and Therana—an eccentric member of the Telvanni Council—and that she wants no help and will brook no interference. And most of her subordinates say only that it's a "high Telvanni" affair.

In other words, mind your business, bub.

This little gathering has not gone unnoticed by Therana's guards. But Therana won't allow them to leave the tower to deal with this "petty annoyance," and one of them, Mollimo of Cloudrest, who patrols the curving ramp that leads to the Upper Tower entrance, is willing to pay you 1,000 gold to remove it.

"Don't be fooled by her thugs," he cautions. "The armor is impressive, but there's not much inside it."

And this is true. Though you're only being paid to take care of Dalen, the others will attack you when you attack her. They are as mosquitoes to the swatter. If you have a decent character and wade in with a significant weapon or spells, you should be able to wipe the floor with the whole bunch in no time.

Get back to Mollimo for your reward, but no additional information.

What was Dalen thinking?

TEL VOS

"Bottled Magics"

Tel Vos is a strange place even for a Telvanni tower. The base for Telvanni Councilor Aryon, with whom you can have significant dealing in the Main and Telvanni faction quests, it is founded on the ruins of an Ebonheart-like castle, entered through the south tower.

But Aryon's actual quarters are high in the great vine-like growth that has overwhelmed the fortress and, as they say, you can't get there from here. Ask about "someone in particular" in the Services Tower to learn that door faces south in the central spire, and that you'll have to fly.

TRERAYNA DALEN

Once through that door, you'll find Turedus Talanian, who is in charge of Aryon's mercenary guards. Speak to him about "work," and, for all you've been through to get here, you'll discover the mission comparatively mundane. Talanian wants to improve relations between Tel Vos and the Zainab Ashlander tribe, and figures trade is a good way to go.

But he doesn't know what the Zainab want, and will give you 100 gold to find out.

The Zainab camp is a short ways south and west across the Grazelands. Don't be too surprised to learn that the tribe wants for nothing.

Now, there is a little trick to dealing with these Ashlanders. If you asked after "little secret" in conversation back in Tel Vos, you learned that the Ashlanders are fiercely proud—especially the men—and reluctant to admit to shortcomings.

However, speak to any female of the Zainab about "trade goods wanted" to learn they could use "bottled magics " (potions) to cure the common and blight diseases the men get while hunting or tending the guar.

Make your way back to Tel Vos and Talanian to receive not only the promised 100 gold, but an Amulet of Levitating, which will make it easier for the magic-challenged to visit Telvanni towers in the future. Your Reputation also goes up a point and everyone here loves you. Aryon and Talanian's Dispositions rocket 30 points and you'll also get a 20-point bump for other retainers and service providers.

A mundane task, yes, but apparently an important one.

URSHILAKU ASHLANDER CAMP

Vengeance

You'll be able to get this quest only if you have become an Ashlander Clanfriend in the Main Quest by retrieving Sul-Senipul's Bonebiter Bow from the Urshilaku Burial Grounds.

Visit the camp on Vvardenfell's north central coast and speak to the trader, Kurapli, about "discuss" and then about "personal vengeance."

Kurapli tells you that an Ashlander outcast named Zallay Subaddamael killed her husband. If you kill Subaddamael, she will give you her husband's enchanted Spirit Spear.

Subaddamael has done something a bit unusual even for a renegade Ashlander. There are many outcasts from the three Ashlander tribes, but they tend to stay on Vvardenfell. This one must be scared. He has taken refuge on Sheogorad.

Kurapli suggests you might get information about the fugitive or his hiding place in Dagon Fel.

Some hiding place. Everyone in Dagon Fel seems to know about Subaddamael or his encampment at Aharasaplit or both. The camp (which, like most outcast "camps," consists of a single yurt) is at the west end of a long beach on Sheogorad's south coast—just north of the island where you may have taken food to hermit Sendus Sathis for the Tribunal Temple.

Subaddamael's in the tent. Do and the deed and get back to the trader for your reward.

VIVEC

JACQUELINE

Jacqueline the Ripper

Jack the Ripper is alive and living in Vivec. You can get this up from the rumor mill, and then get the grisly details from Elam Andas in the Office of the Watch in the Temple's Hall of Justice.

Seven people have been murdered in Vivec recently. In each case, the victim's throat was cut with a dagger. Five victims were outlanders; two were Temple guards. (Before the Ordinators were killed, the official thinking was that it might be the handiwork of an anti-Imperial fanatic, and that's still possible.) All were armed, and yet only one seems to have put up a fight. And nothing was removed from any of the bodies.

Of the Outlanders, three were found in the Foreign Quarter, one in the water near the Arena and one in the Hlaalu Compound. The two Ordinators were found near the Hlaalu victim; it's believed they interrupted the killer. But neither had drawn a weapon and Temple security is deeply troubled by the implications. It means the killer either is exceptionally stealthy or a powerful spellcaster.

Finally, none of the murders was witnessed. But a incident occurred in the Hlaalu compound at about the same time as the killings that may shed light on them: An outlander reported being threatened by a Dunmer woman yielding a dagger, and wearing skirt and netch leather armor.

You should now be able to ask people in the Hlaalu, Arena and Foreign quarters cantons about "woman with a dagger."

No dice on the first two. But in the Foreign Quarter, you'll hear about a Dunmer woman having been seen in the Underworks.

That's not much of a clue. No mention is made of a dagger or netch armor, and while Dunmer turn up rarely in the Foreign Quarter, there's a lot more to Underworks than sewers and rats.

And yet it's all you've got, so check out the sewers.

If this is your first visit to the Foreign Quarter Underworks, note that the Canalworks here has two separate sections and is much more extensive than in other cantons, with shops, a large tomb, a healer, and an Imperial Cult altar.

The Dunmer woman is in the Underworks. This red-haired "dreamer prophet" will attack you on sight. When she's dead, report back to Andas for your choice of either an Indoril helm and cuirass (standard Ordinator eequipment) or the enchanted Belt of the Armor of God.

I'm Sorry I Called You A Flat-Head (You Ignorant Fool)

The other fellow in the Office of the Watch has a much simpler quest for you. Tarer Braryn explains that he got drunk last night, ran into Mages Guild Guildmaster Trebonius Artorius and called him a "Flat-Head."

Now Braryn has the rash to end all rashes. Potions and spells do nothing. He's hoping that a little gift and his apologies, relayed to Artorius ("the ignorant fool") by someone with a way with words, will make the problem go away.

And he'll pay you 50 gold to be that someone.

The Mages Guild can be found in the Foreign Quarter Plaza. Artorius is on the left at the bottom of the stairs.

Now, fact is, he is kind of a flat-head, as you'll learn if you do much work for the Mages Guild.

But when you speak to Artorius about "apologies" with Tarer's copy of "Aedra and Daedra" in your inventory, he takes the gesture in stride—giving you a Rising Force (Levitation) potion and a special Cure Common Disease potion for Braryn.

Braryn's rash is better for it, and he's so happy with the way everything went that he doubles your fee to 100 gold.

The Long Road to an Iron Shardskewer

Another Vivec rumor concerns Miun-Gei, an enchanter with a shop on the Lower Waistworks level of the Foreign Quarter, who apparently is having trouble with a fellow peddling wares outside his store.

Pay a visit to the enchanter and speak to him about the "annoying fool" who chases his customers away. He'll ask you to see what you can do.

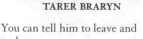

TARER BRARYN

The fool, named Marcel Maurard, should be right nearby. Speak to him about "line of work" to learn he's a would-be actor who is selling magical baubles to make ends meet. You can tell him to leave and you can threaten to kill him. (You don't want to actually kill him.) But he's not going anywhere.

Maurard does give you a clue on how he might be enticed to leave: find him a theater troupe.

You now have the topic "theater troupe." If you ask around town using it, you'll learn that Hlaalu Councilor Crassius Curio has written a new play and would like to have it performed.

Seek out Curio. Sooner or later, this colorful character ("You can call me Uncle Crassius") is likely to become an integral part of your game. But if you haven't already met him, you'll find him on the lower level of Curio Manor off Hlaalu Plaza in the Hlaalu Compound.

Curio confirms that his play, "The Lusty Argonian Maid," is almost done, and that he needs an actor with "wit, grace, charm and a firm...oh, never mind." And don't forget to ask him about his "new play." He'll give you a bit of it to read...and it's quite a read.

(He seems to have his eye on you for a part—Curio will flirt with you mercilessly throughout Morrowind—but senses that you have other concerns.)

Now you can return to Maurard and talk to him again about "theater troupe." He's gone. And now nothing's left but to return to Miun-Gei to chat about "annoying fool" to trumpet your success.

He'll reward you with an Iron Shardskewer. You'll probably have to look it up: it's an enchanted spear.

Voodoo Economics

Poor Balen Andrano. The proprietor of Redoran Trader on the Waistworks level of the Redioran canton has hit a run of bad luck. Shipments are few, prices high, and competition stiff—especially from Jeanne: Trader, which has been taking away a lot of his customers.

Andrano proposes to change his competitor's luck by practicing real voodoo economics and planting a magical artifact—an ancient Dwarven bone—in a chest near her bed.

If you agree, that will be your job.

CRASSIUS CURIO

It's pretty simple. Jeanne: Trader is found in the western section of the Foreign Quarter's Canalworks level. The proprietor is at the front of the shop; the bed and chest are in the back room and hidden from view. You'll just need to unlock the door, unlock the chest, put the doggy bone inside and leave. If Jeanne sees you, though, you're busted, and the quest's over. You might want to pick up a Chameleon potion for this part of the quest. Return to Redoran Trader and speak to Andrano about "change her luck" again to receive a Sleep Amulet.

And, do you know, you've even set up a mini-quest for yourself. Now you can go back to Jeanne's shop, talk to her about "terrible haunting" to learn of the Dwarven spirit that scaring off her customers and play the hero all over again. (The Ordinator may be fighting it as you speak. It's actually pretty funny.) She'll ask you to get rid of the ghost. You can either kill it, or remove the bone from the chest in back. Then talk to Jeanne again for her thanks and a Steel Shardmauler.

(You may now feel inclined to give Andrano a litle of his own medicine. But there is no bed in his store. And, even if there was, the bone has lost its power.)

Dead Men Smoke No Skooma

BALEN ANDRANO

Now here's a "Tales from the Crypt" episode if there ever was one.

Ask for "latest rumors" in the St. Olms Canton and you'll hear about Moroni and Danar Uvelas. Moroni works long hours in the Brewers and Fishmongers Hall; Danar spends all their money feeding his skooma addiction and hanging out with similarly-inclined pals in the canton's sewers.

And now he's gone missing.

Many of the trade halls are on St. Olms' Waistworks level; the Brewers and Fishmongers Hall is the westernmost. Moroni is behind the counter. Talk to her about "gone missing" and agree to find Danar.

From the rumor, you already know to look in the sewers. Actually, there is quite a lot down here: the folks at the Assernerairan shrine, the usual rats and, potentially, the Khajiit informant Addhiranirr from the Main Quest.

And that corprus stalker.

Actually, that's new.

Kill the stalker and search its remains to confirm your worst fears: it's Danar Uvelas. Take his ring and return it to Moroni (using the "gone missing" topic) to receive a Potion of Cure Common Disease.

Moroni has lost her husband for good this time. But she seems to recognize that, in fact, she lost him a long time ago.

A Contract Killing

Maybe it's just the green-eyed monster talking. But Alusaron, who has a Smith's shop off Foreign Quarter Plaza, says rival Ralen Tilvur is up to "something shady." Talk about "competition" and "big orders" to learn Tilvur has a new contract to deliver more swords and armor than Alusaron sells in a month.

It's a contract Alusaron would like for himself, and if you talk further about "get that contract," he'll enlist you to steal it. (That way, he can have the correct order ready when Tilvur defaults.)

Sounds like Alusaron is the one up to something shady.

If you agree, Ralen Tilvur: Smith is at the other end of the plaza. It's kind of weird. The shop is really small, you and Tilvur are the only people in it, and you more or less have to pick the lock to his private quarters while he watches. Don't be too surprised when you learn the crime has been reported. What did you expect?

The contract is on top of the chest of drawers downstairs. It's huge. Return it to Alusaron and he'll reward you with an enchanted Firebite War Axe.

Slander!

In the Foreign Quarter Plaza, you'll find a man named Domalen handing out leaflets. Read the one he gives you. It looks like something you might find posted on the Internet. With lots of exclaimation points and capital letters, it tears into an apothecary named Aurane Frernis as more or less a demon alchemist.

Frernis has a shop on the Lower Waistworks level. Talk to her about the leaflet. She'll say it's all slander, and ask you to get to the bottom of it.

Get back up to the plaza and talk to Domalen again about the leaflets.

Don't demand to know where they're from; he won't say. But tell him its contents are lies, and he'll distance himself from them. He just distributes them. Galuro Belan, a struggling apothecary in the Telvanni canton, makes them up.

Get over to Belan's shop on the Waistworks level of the Telvanni canton, and confront her. She should admit to being behind the flyers and offer you 100 gold to keep your mouth shut.

You're in the catbird's seat here. You can expose her, keep her secret, or say you're going to keep her secret, take her 100 gold, and then expose her to Frernis for another 100 gold. (Sounds like Frernis is going to sue, too.)

If you say you'll expose her lies, Belan moans that you'll ruin her. But she did that herself.

DOMALEN

AURANE FRERNIS

Flower Picking!

If you've completed the Slander! quest above, Frernis will send you to Daedric shrine Ald Sotha to collect five Roland's Tears—a rare magical curative distinct from the ordinary Gold Kanet flowers among which it appears.

In return, she promises to make you something "rare and wonderful" from the leftovers.

In other words, you're being invited to lick the spoon.

You've probably been to Ald Sotha by now. It's northeast of Vivec, and most easily reached by taking the bridge from the Telvanni canton east to the mainland and then heading north. (If you haven't visited the shrine, watch out for dead-eyed spellcaster Nathala Herendas and scamps in the surface ruin.)

Gold Kanet flowers grow in various spots around Ald Sotha, but in profusion on the small peninsula just east of the ruin. About seven Roland's Tears can be found among them.

You don't get to lick the spoon after all. It turns out that Frernis ran through all her ingredients. But she does supply a Luck potion.

The Invisible Teenager

Outside Lucretinaus Olcinius: Trader in St. Delyns Plaza, you'll be approached by Cassius Olcinius, who says a wizard has made him invisible.

In fact, Olcinius is semi-visible. (He's like a spectre; you can see through him, but still see him.)

But this is small consolation to the young man. People walk into him and knock him down. No one will speak to him; they take him for a ghost. He's scared to see wizard Fevyn Ralen, who put him into this state, and too embarassed to talk to his father (the trader Olcinius).

Of course, you have no cause to be scared or embarassed. Go into the store and talk to his father about the boy. He's too busy to tackle the matter himself, but will supply 75 gold. (This has all the earmarks of a father placing career over family.)

Then visit Ralen's store, Telvanni Mage, on the Waistworks level of the Telvanni canton, and talk to him about the case.

Man, this kid's a loser.

It turns out that Cassius, trying to escape the world, asked Ralen to make him invisible. But he never paid the 400-gold bill (or told you about any of this on his own) and Ralen won't undo the spell until he gets his money.

He's probably learned his lesson already, and you can pay off the debt yourself, if only to save yourself from a second trip, and Cassius will become fully visible again. Return to Lucretinaus and he'll reimburse you and give you 100 gold for your help.

Or, if you can't afford this, you can go back to his Dad, mention "debt to pay," and he'll give you the money and you can come back to the wizard again, mention "debt to pay" yet again, and get this kid out of your life.

But if you go this route, don't forget to visit Lucretinaus one last time to collect your 100-gold reward.

Rats!

If you ask about "latest rumors" in Vivec's Telvanni Compound, you'll hear about a rat problem. It's especially acute for Audenian Valius, who owns the Telvanni Enchanter shop on the Waistworks level.

But simply killing the two beaver-sized rats in his back room doesn't satisfy Valius. He asks you to go after the source of the problem in the canton's sewers.

Get down to the Canalworks level and use the trapdoor to reach the sewers. You'll find 10 more rats down here. Wipe them out, and return the Valius for a grand soul gem.

Made in Mzuleft

Drop into the Glassworker's Hall off St. Delyn Plaza and speak to Alarvnye Indalas about "exotic items" and "dwarven limeware."

She'll complain that getting these items has become difficult. She believes Bolrin at the East Empire Company in Ebonheart is manipulating the prices, and says he won't issue many licenses for its sale. (Actually, Llaalam Dredil is the culprit, as you know if you read his letter in the Special Delivery quest.)

In fact, Indalas is aware of a limeware shipment that is even now sitting on the Chun-Ook at the dock in Ebonheart. She wonders if you might be persuaded to liberate it.

Just jog over to Ebonheart, board the boat and climb down the hatch to the upper level.

You'll need to be a little stealthy here. The two guards are cool with your presence, but will take violent exception to your picking the lock on the trapdoor to the lower level, so slip into the alcove in the stern and do this from a concealed position.

You'll find the limeware—five cups and five bowls—in the crate closest to the prow. Take it when the solitary guard here isn't looking.

This stuff is worth 1,500 gold back at the Glassworker's Hall in Vivec.

Alternatively, it's worth 500 gold here in Ebonheart. With the stolen goods in your inventory, go see Bolrin at the East Empire Company Hall and speak to him about "dwarven limeware," and he'll reward you for detecting holes in company security.

Steal This Letter...

Once you've delivered that letter for Llaalam Dredril in Ebonheart setting new high prices for the East Empire Company (Special Delivery), you can get this quest from Mevure Hlen at the Tailors and Dyers Hall on the St. Olms Canton's Waistworks level.

She'll say that "prices are a bit high" as a result of East Empire's control over imports to Vivec, and that while other goods do come in at Ebonheart, they get so tied up in "bureaucracy" that shipping them here is unprofitable. They're searched by Duke Vedam Dren's men and often are held up in customs for weeks. Nice little business the Duke and the Company have set up for themselves.

Hlen wants to know who sets Company prices. Once again, if you looked at Dredil's letter before you handed it to

J'Zhirr, you could tell her that right now. But she wants the actual price list.

It's still in East Empire Company Hall, but now in a locked chest behind the locked door next to J'Zhirr.

The room's guarded, so there's no room for subtleties. Just pick the door lock, get caught, pay the small fine, enter the room, close the door, and pick the lock on the chest. Then bring the list back to Hlen (who is outraged) and claim your reward: a two-point boost in your Mercantile skill.

MEVURE HLEN

...But Burn This One

In the southernmost of the two planters in Hlaalu Plaza, you will find a love letter from Gadayn Andarys to Eraldil. It is awful. ("Your eyes are really, really brown, in that good wood elf kind of way.") It is so uniquely awful that you should just leave it where it is, so it can fertilize the plants.

If you feel the impulse to see who produced this embarrassment, Andarys is nearby. He runs Hlaalu General Goods just to the west. Speak to him about "love letter" and you'll find that he speaks far more eloquently about his feelings than the letter would suggest. But he lacks the courage to speak to Eraldil, and, like Cyrano, asks you to serve as his representative.

You'll find Eraldil walking around on the Waistworks level. Ask her about "love letter." She's not interested. In fact, she's rather nasty about the whole thing, and suggests Andarys would be better suited for her lowborn cousin Glathel, a waitress at the Elven Nations cornerclub.

Get back to Andarys. He's troubled by Eraldil's refusal, but doesn't give up. His "backup plan" is to slip her a mickey—a love potion.

You can deliver the potion or point him to the cousin. If the latter, Andarys sees the light, and you'll be doing him a favor. He does look up Glathel and when you see him next (well, after 10 days or so), they'll be married (which has to set some sort of record) and and he'll be quite ecstatically happy. He'll reward you with a Flamemirror Robe and some low, low prices.

On the other hand, if you bring the love potion to Eraldil (under the guise of "apology from Gadayn"), she'll be as unpleasant as before—she's definitely high maintenance, this one—and you just know it's going to end badly.

Return to Andarys. He has high hopes. (He volunteers to name their first child after you.) He gives you a Light Ring. But if you come back later, he's in Hell. Suddenly the love potion is your idea. And Eraldil is a harridan. And Andarys' prices tend to skyrocket.

We told you so. You should have found a way to tell Andarys.

What to Do with Rollie the Guar and Other Deep Mysteries of Life

Northeast of Vivec, on the road north of the gro-Bagrat Plantation, you will find Teris Raledran and his pack guar, Rollie. They need an escort to Agrippina Herrenia's clothing store in the Canalworks level of Vivec's Foreign Quarter.

The good news is that you only have to take the good-tempered Rollie a short distance. Guar aren't permitted inside Vivec. And he does seem like a heck of a guar: Raledran's talks to him all the time. You can try talking to him, too...but he always quiets down just when he seems ready to chat.

The bad news is that you may not realize this right away and thus will spend a considerable amount of time trying to coax this sizeable creature through narrow gaps (like the bridges west of the gro-Bagrat Plantation) and up river banks that the poor beast finds hopelessly intimidating, and may wind up killing it (for a reduced reward) in simple frustration.

TERIS AND HIS GUAR

So give that up that plan right now. Before you get to Vivec, you need to find a spot where you can leave the guar.

Head south, with Raledran and Rollie in close pursuit. At the gro-Bagrat Plantation, make your way west to an intersection. Do not try to cross the bridge further west. Rather, start down the side road to the south, and Raledran will pipe up with a comment about the need to leave Rollie behind. The guar will settle down and you and the trader can proceed across the bridges and then south into the city on your own. At Herrenia's store, Raledran will pay you off—200 gold if Rollie survived, or 100 if, in a fit of pique, you reeled off and belted Rollie with your Iron Shardskewer.

Jobasha the Abolitionist

Not a quest so much as an unadvertised opportunity.

Behind the scenes, Morrowind counts the slaves you free. Once you've freed more than 30, Jobasha at Jobasha's Rare Books on the Foreign Quarter'sLower Waistworks level will give you skillbooks devoted to the skills Armorer ("The Armorer's Challenge"), Acrobatics ("Realizations of Acrobacy") and Marksman ("The Marksmanship Lesson").

You can get these books by talking to Jobasha about "Twin Lamps" when he has Disposition of 70. You'll get the "Twin Lamps" topic after you have freed five slaves, then talk to a freed slave about "go free."

The Silent Despair of Tinos Drothan

To find Tinos Drothan, cross the bridge that leads east from Vivec's Telvanni canton to the mainland.

Climb over two rises east of the bridge, and you'll find yourself on a north-south road. Head north to an intersection. Take the left-hand path, which does a little jigger to the west, and then continues north. Almost immediately, you'll see a large tree on the left side of the path. Just before you reach this tree, head west. You'll go over two rises and then walk almost directly into Drothan.

He is grumpy, and will tell you to be on your way. If you didn't get one of those little journal-update messages after he speaks, you might think he was simply another Dunmer with a Mount Kand-sized chip on his shoulder.

But get his Disposition up to 50, and Drothan will reveal why he's mad at the world: his escorts just ran off with his shipment of raw glass. He asks you to recover is cargo and kill the thieves in exchange for some "trader's secrets."

Drothan says the villains, Alvur Hleran and Dondir, went southeast to hole up in a cave and count their loot. Only one cave is located nearby: Beshara. You'll find it by backtracking and turning left at the first intersection you came to (not the one leading to Drothan).

Beshara turns out to be rather large and home to a whole den of thieves, with some spellcasters among them. But they're spread out, and none should present much challenge individually. You should be looking at Drothan's 10 units of raw glass in no time. It's in a locked chest in the innermost extremity of the cave. Alvur Hleran has the key, or you can just pick the lock.

The loot's fairly low level, but you can come out of the mission with an Invisibility scroll, an Acrobatics skillbok ("Realizations of Acrobacy") and some gems. Drothan will add a boost to your Mercantile skill—with the size of the boost determined by whether you've killed both bandits.

ENNBJOF

What Comes from a Little Matze

Sometimes getting a quest requires carrying the right item at the right time.

Consider the long trek that springs from simply having the beverage Matze in your inventory when you speak to Ennbjof at The Lizard's Head, a tavern on the Telvanni canton's Waistworks level.

Ask him about "little secret," and he'll ask if you can spare a jug of the stuff. Hand over the Matze, and what you get back may startle you: a rusty old key and a story about the burial of Olmgerd the Outlaw and the enchanted battle-axe Stormkiss. The site: a small island off the west coast of the peninsula between the Daedric shrine Zaintiraris and Tel Branora.

There can only be, what, a couple dozen of those, right? And a few of them contain tombs.

Well, the one you're looking for is the Marvani Ancestral Tomb.

Conceivably, an advanced character could plunder this site on their own, without advance knowledge, but the key Ennbjof supplies lets you past the main obstacle—a door with a Lock Level of 80.

From the bridge into Molag Mar, scale the hills south of the town. You will see the Zaintiraris shrine to the south and the Redas Ancestral Tomb and renegade Ashlander settlement Kaushtababi to the east.

Make your way carefully around the shrine—potentially, there will be a good deal of fighting here—to the high, rocky ground at the south end of the island. Continue south across the channel to a rocky island. The entrance to the tomb is off the beach on this island's southeastern side.

The Marvani Ancestral Tomb appears to be a standard tomb, with usual urns and eternal flames, the usual small treasures, the usual skeletons and ancestral ghosts.

You'll eventually reach a small room with two locked and trapped doors. The one straight ahead is opened with the key that's almost invisible in back of the ashbed in the unlocked room on your left.

And that very locked door on your right can be unlocked only with the key you got from Ennbjof back at The Lizard's Head.

Enter, and descend.

This is where the tomb turns unusual.

After you've gone down three flights, you may be wondering what you've got yourself into over a drink of Matze. The descent continues for nine flights. When it ends, you're at the door to Tukushapal, the burial chamber of Olmgerd.

Within, a maze. Morrowind doesn't do this often, and when it does, the mazes are simple. This one is also simple. It has two paths. The right-hand one, unguarded, dead-ends after a short distance. The left-hand one, guarded by skeletons, leads only slightly circuitously to the door to the Sepulcher.

Olmgerd was a king's son, and he has a king's son's tomb. They built a whole Viking ship down here to carry him into the next life, one equipped with money, jewels, potions and food. You came for Stormkiss, but you may want to stay for the Imperial Dragonscale Helm, Cuirass, and Tower Shield and the ebony bracers.

And if you can Levitate, this would be a good place to do it. Be guided by the hum of crystals as you climb. High above, on a hidden platform on the north side of the chamber, you can find the terrifying Daedric helm Face of God and a Daedric Warhammer.

VOS

If You've Seen One Half-Naked Barbarian...

Why do these disasters always seem to come in threes? The saga of witches and the barbarians who love them continues southeast of Vos.

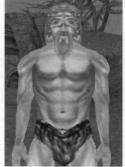

BOTRIR

The easiest way to reach the Barbarian Botrir is to follow the coast south to the stronghold Indoranyon and then follow the road west to a "T" intesection. Head north toward Hanud, and you'll soon come upon another muscular guy standing beside the road wearing not much.

He uses colorful language to describe his plans for the witch he was escorting to Tel Aruhn. ("I"ll tear her throat out and wear it as a belt!") To hear him tell it, Iveri Llethri seemed "real friendly," and then, all of a sudden, she put him under a spell, stole his possessions—including his prize axe, Widowmaker—and left him in the road in his fur undies.

Now, given our previous experience with barbarians and witches—the barbarians can't keep their hands to themselves—you may want to see a "Russian hands and Roman fingers" topic before you commit to the atrocities Botrir has planned.

But you've said only that you're going to help him get his axe back. That's pretty natural, right?

Botrir thinks Llothri went northwest. The road you're on does not go northwest. This means you are traveling cross-country, which can be a dicey proposition when a nebulous direction like "northwest" and any real distance is involved.

Mercifully, the witch hasn't gone far. Climb the hills to the northwest and look west down the valley on the other side, and you should see a campfire.

That's the witch.

Maybe the barbarian's in the right this time. After all, Llothri will start summoning creatures the moment she detects your presence. Botrir will attack when he sees her. You can either race ahead and kill the witch yourself, or help Botrir do it or sit back and watch. In any case, when it's over, grab the axe and speak to the barbarian about it. You'll have a choice of returning it (which adds a point to your Axe skill) or keeping it (which starts a fight). It's a nice weapon, but you're going to wind up with enough nice weapons to decorate every room in your stronghold. The skill point's probably worth more.

WILDERNESS

SATYANA

In the Vault

This quest, found in the Arenim Ancestral Tomb, required its own category. Located on a large northwest-southwest penninula located southeast of Tel Fyr, it isn't near anything. The closest landmarks are the Daedric shrines Kaushtarari to the north and Shashpilamat to the south, but neither of those names is likely to pop up on the radar of any but the most dedicated explorers. If you don't want to make a special trip, you're best off combining it with a visit to Tel Fyr, the Erabenimsun Ashlander camp or the hidden monastery Holamayan.

You'll know the moment you enter the tomb's north-facing door that you've found something rather different: You're not alone. A woman named Satyana stands at the base of the stairs.

Talk to her. She's looking for her father's amulet — this is her family's tomb—and she'll ask for your help. Refuse, and she'll attack. Accept, and she'll follow you through the tomb at fight at your side. That pretty much defines your relationship.

A-lootin' you will go. Beyond the gallery southwest of Satayana, you'll reach a "T" corridor. In the room at the end of the left-hand corridor, you'll find a key on the floor near a skeleton. This opens the large locked room at the end of the right-hand corridor.

Within, you'll find the amulet and the Sword of Agustus—an enchanted claymore—on a skeleton. Satyana will demand the amulet, and, once more, you have a choice between refusing and fighting or assenting and keeping the peace. If you choose the latter, she'll continue to fight at your side as you loot her family's tomb, but won't leave the tomb itself.

QUESTS BY THEME

THE DAEDRIC QUESTS

It's an Elder Scrolls tradition that you can summon a Daedra lord on a certain day with a certain ritual to receive a quest.

That tradition has been simplified for Morrowind. You can get any of the game's seven Daedric quests on any day by simply visiting the appropriate shrine. Most of the time, you'll have to activate the great statue within to receive the mission.

These quests carry no requirements at all, and you can visit the shrines in any order.

All you have to do is find them.

You won't have a lot to go on. No one tells you that you can get quests by activating the statues. No one tells you in which of the many, many Daedric shrines the quest-giving statues are located. Some are in unconventional places and difficult to find.

And one is just about impossible.

The completion of all seven quests carries no special reward. But the more you complete, the more high-level weapons and tools you'll acquire.

The Shrine of Azura

Visiting the Shrine of Azura for the first time will help you understand why worshippers make pilgrimages. It's magificent. Even if you don't want the quest, you should see this shrine just to see it. It's like a Statue of Liberty for Morrowind.

The shrine is found beneath the huge statue of Azura that adorns the southeast corner of Vvardenfell. Don't worry. While the interior resembles the interiors of the dangerous Daedric shrines, it's empty and you're safe here.

Activate the statue to learn that the gods Azura and Sheogorath have made a bet. Sheogorath argues that solitude makes people go crazy, Azura that it lends itself to reflection.

To test this, Azura dispatched one of her priestesses to live on a distant island for 100 years. If she succeeds, Azura's theory will have been proved correct, and she'll win her bet.

The time is almost up. But Sheogorath, sensing he's about to lose, isn't playing fair. He's sent his minions to the island to pierce the priestess' solitude. You are to remove those minions without disturbing the priestess and return to Azura with proof of Sheogorath's inteference.

Azura is not at her most helpful. She tells you the island is north of Dagon Fel, but her bump of direction seems to be off, and you won't find much more than Andre Maul's tower if you head that way.

In fact, the island is to the west. From Dagon Fel, take the road west, over a rise, to a beach. Cross the channel to the north, take the first left and continue west past the bandit cave Habinbaes. The path will eventually turn south, but don't follow it that way. Instead, follow it up the slope to the west to the base of one of those great mushroom trees.

Turn north. Below you, you'll see a beach and, across a narrow channel, an island.

Here, you'll find fire and storm atronachs and an Ogrim to the northwest, two Hungers on a rise to the northeast and, farther north, a Daedroth and a Golden Saint.

Kill all of them.

Odd. This Golden Saint had a name: Staada. You'd be right to wonder if there's anything else distinctive about her. Search her body to find Sheogorath's Signet Ring, which is just the evidence of that god's meddling that Azura requires.

(This is also a great place to collect Daedra hearts, which you'll need for the "The Four Corners of the House of Troubles" quests if you plan to join the Tribunal Temple.)

Don't enter the shack to the north. If you do, priestess Rayna Drolan, will speak to you and Azura will lose her bet. Just get back to the shrine and activate the statue again with the ring in your inventory, and Azura will reward you with Azura's Star—a re-useable soul gem.

The Shrine of Boethiah

The lost shrine of Boethiah is one of the most obscure locations in Morrowind. You're unlikely to find it on your own. While you can learn about it from one character in the game, he's in the middle of nowhere. And you'll probably discount what you hear, as he's totally unreliable on most other topics.

M'AIQ

But about Shrine of Boethiah, M'Aiq the Liar happens to be right on the mark.

You don't have to talk to M'Aiq first, and can proceed directly to the statue. But it's worth a stop if you're in the Sheogorad area, as he's a lot of fun.

To reach him, leave Dagon Fel by its eastern entrance and follow the path past Sorkvild's Tower as it curves south. You'll pass the Senim Ancestral Tomb to the west and emerge on a beach as the Dwemer ruin Nchardahrk looms up ahead of you.

This beach is actually fitted with a natural sight pointing directly at M'Aiq's island. Stand at the water's edge and look northeast. Close by, you will see two stone pillars and beyond them, farther out in the water, two more. Adjust your position to line up these two sets of pillars and swim between them, and they'll lead you directly to featureless rock where the Khajiit paces back and forth.

M'Aiq is part Easter Egg, part tipster. The Easter Egg part is a wonderful source of wholly unbaked information on all kind of things that do not exist in Morrowind, including becoming a lich, dragons, horses, multiplayer, nudity, naked liches, rope-climbing, and weresharks.

You may find what M'Aiq says on "multiplayer" just tantalizing enough to send you looking for the characters he mentions (Im-Leet and Rolf Uber) in hope of unlocking a hidden multiplayer mode.

Trust us. The characters do not exist. There is no multiplayer. This is just game-designer wickedness.

It's not the only such enticement. M'Aiq even refers to one of the game's real secrets—the Mystery of the Dwarves—and to another weird Easter Egg (a talking mudcab merchant). But what he has to say on the former subject is nonsense, and by the time you work your way down to "the Shrine of Boethiath" entry in his topic menu, you probably won't take a thing he says seriously.

Nevertheless, this topic produces a journal entry. As is often the case, it's more precise than the info you get from the actual dialogue. M'Aiq reports that a sunken shrine to Boethiah can be found off the west coast of Vvardenfell near Hla Oad.

Now, many players may spend the day diving off Hla Oad, come with nothing but pearls and slaughterfish scars, reasonably decide M'Aiq is lying about everything and give up. But the shrine is there, fairly close to the Daedric shrine of Ashurnibibi.

Hop down the west coast on a series of boats, and then follow the coast north from Hla Oad. Ashurnibibi is across a wooden bridge at the southern tip of a penninsula. As you turn south to approach the ruin, look for three small rocks in close formation just off the shore to the west. Dive west of them to find the lost shrine.

A broken statue of Boethiah is at its center. Talk to the fallen head—the body won't listen—and the god will speak to you.

He sounds depressed, and why not? His shrine is underwater. His priests won't take his calls.

Boethiah asks you to rebuild his shrine in exchange for a mighty sword called Goldbrand and, in a pretty straightforward riddle, sends you to Caldera to find a sculptor.

Ask around in town. You'll be referred to trader Verick Gemain, who has a shop just north of the Shenk's Shovel tavern, and he mentions that there's an Orc sculptor across the road at Ghorak Manor

Ghorak Manor is a strange place. You get the feeling you've stumbled onto something vaguely criminal, but maybe it's just a haphazard way Orcs live. You'll find the sculptor, such as he is, near a big hunk of rock on the top floor. Speak to Duma gro-Lag about "sculptor," and ask him to recreate the shrine. He'll agree, and ask for plans and 2,000 gold.

It's pretty much just like starting a stronghold.

Don't be flummoxed over the plans. It's just a book and, like the lion's share of Morrowind books, can be found at Jobasha's Rare Books in Vivec's Foreign Quarter. Take it and the money to gro-Lag, and he'll tell you the statue will go up on Khartag Point—located on the Vvardenfell's west coast near the stronghold Andasreth. When it appears, simply activate it to receive Boethiah's praise and the katana.

It's been a long, long road, but you really have something to show for it!

The Shrine of Malacath

The Shrine of Malacath is in Assurdirapal—a Daedric shrine on the northeast coast of the long, narrow island just west of the Sanctus Shrine. The easiest way to reach it is simply to head west and south from Dagon Fel to the beach on the northwest tip of the main Sheogorad island, and then swim west.

In the inner shrine, activate the statue and Malacath will tell you about a dark elf named Oreyn Bearclaw who is falsely credited with feats of heroism actually performed by his Orc friend, Kharag gro-Khar. The god wants you to destroy Bearclaw's legend by killing the last of his line. Succeed, and you'll get the Helm of Oreyn Bearclaw. (Note to Malacath: Rename the Helm of Oreyn Bearclaw!)

Now, this seems hardly fair to Bearclaw's descendant. But gods don't have to be fair—they're gods—and it's not negotiable.

OREYN BEARCLAW

Drop a Mark spell at the shrine so you can Recall back there quickly, and then head for Vivec as directed by Malacath. Talk to people there about Bearclaw to find his legend lives on, and that his descendant, a battlemage named Farvyn Oreyn, apparently is cut from the same heroic cloth. Ask about Farvyn in turn to learn he and his servants are on a mission to Gnaar Mok.

They're singing Farvyn's praises in Gnaar Mok as well. Ask around town to learn he arrived the previous day to clear out marauding netches and is now south of town.

And sure enough, you'll find Oreyn and two retainers south of town near a pair of dead netches. The retainers (one of them in Orc-ish armor—a nice touch) don't have anything distinctive to say, but Farvyn fesses up quickly when you use Kharag gro-Khar's name.

Perhaps he's not such a bad sort after all.

This impression, and any fragile thoughts of mercy, will evaporate immediately the moment you declare yourself and Oreyn orders your death. (It doesn't matter whether you say you're there at Malacath's behest to end the lie, or try to back out.)

You only have to kill Oreyn, but all three guys attack you, so take them all out if you like. They all have enchanted stuff. Then zap back to the shrine for quick activation of the statue and receipt of the Helm.

The Shrine of Mehrunes Dagon

This small, deep shrine lies just west of the Dwemer ruin Arkngthunch-Sturdumz, which is just west of Ald Velothi. Just detour south around the Dwemer ruin to reach the Daedric one. It's called Yasammidan.

Dagon is one of the four bad Daedra. Baaad. When you activate the statue, he debates squashing you like a bug, but admires your boldness in approaching him. Out of that admiration comes an offer: You may prove your worth by retrieving Dagon's Razor from the Alas Ancestral Tomb.

The tomb is at the center of the Molag Amur mountain range. But, like Yasammidan, it's comparatively easy to reach if you know the terrain. The closest landmark is the Erabenimsun Ashlander camp. From the camp, simply make your way west and then south up the foyadas to the tomb door.

The tomb is small. You should be in and out quickly. In the room at the bottom of the entry stairs, make a left and then a right, search the body of Varner Hleras on the altar and take the Rusty Dagger.

Now, hold on a second. Didn't Dagon say to bring back his Razor?

Well, OK, have it your way. Put back the Rusty Dagger. Now search the rest of the tomb. Do you see anything remotely like a Razor here?

We didn't think so.

In this case, the disparity between what you were told and what you find requires a small leap of faith. One man's Razor might be another's Rusty Dagger.

Take the dagger back to Yasammidan, activate the statue again and, behold, the dagger is replaced in your inventory by Mehrunes' Razor—a savage little blade which is now yours to keep.

The Shrine of Mephala

TAROS DRAL

Have you found the Morag Tong's hedquarters? It's well hidden. It can be reached only through a locked trapdoor in the storage area on Canalworks level of Vivec's Arena canton.

Once inside, climb the stairs, make a right at the top to enter the small, statue-less shrine and speak to Taros Dral about "sensitive matters."

He doesn't say much up-front—simply that the god Mephala, the assassins guild's patron, has given him information which must be acted upon.

There is good reason for his discretion. If you agree to help, you'll learn you're to poison Balyn Omarel—an important member of the guild who has been performing executions on his own. Dral will supply Treated Bittergreen Petals to put in Omarel's food.

Omarel lives in Balmora—on the second floor of the northernmost house in the middle rank of structures east of the river. You'll have a heck of a time getting through the front door unnoticed. The occupant is wandering around out front and, if he sees you, he will challenge you, which blows the quest. Would that there were a back door of some kind.

Actually, there is one. Approach the house from the south and east, walking up the easternmost of Balmora's north-south streets toward Caius Cosades' place. At the north end of the street, climb the stairs to the roof of Cosades' building and jump over the parapet onto the neighboring roof (Omarel's) to the west.

Remaining on the eastern side of this roof, unlock the trapdoor you'll find in the southeast corner and drop down into Omarel's apartment. With the poison in your inventory, activate the cauldron you'll find against the west wall and make your escape via the trapdoor. Drop down onto a bannister of the staircase at the building's southeast corner and return the same way you approached.

Back at Morag Tong headquarters, speak to Dral again. He'll tell you to speak to the shrine. Do so, and you'll receive the Ring of Khajiit, which supplies the wearer with speed and stealth. Oh, and if you decide to go back to Omarel's place, you'll see the results of your actions. He lies dead in the middle of his room, obviously having keeled over during his dinner. Might have been something he ate.

The Shrine of Molag Bal

Contact Molag Bal by activating his statue in the shrine Yansirramus, two islands west of Tel Aruhn. (You can reach him through the Bal Ur shrine in one the vampire quests, but not this one.)

You should be able to get down to the statue easily, but nosing around in the side chambers will get you into fights.

Bal complains about a lazy Daedra named Menta Na who, though created to terrorize the mortal world, has retreated from it into the caves at Kora-Dur. The god supplies a key and asks you to kill Na (though he puts it far more elegantly) to obtain Bal's favor.

Drop a Mark spell at the shrine before you leave. You have some ways to go.

Kora-Dur is found east of the stronghold Kogoruhn. The stronghold is a fairly straight shot northeast along the foyadas near Maar Gan, but finding the cave is a bit of a challenge. It's not hidden, but branching paths and the shallow, climbable slopes in this section of the northern Ashlands leave the impression that it is one of many possible destinations.

From the stronghold, head northeast. The path will turn north at a little Ashlander camp, and eventually curve around to head east. After you pass Bensamsi (a Sixth House shrine) on your right, bear southwest. (If you can see the Dwemer ruin of Bthuand rising up on your right, you've gone too far east.)

The path soon splits west and south. Take the south path (the one with all the dead trees). This curves up a hill to the door of Kora-Dur.

The door's ultra-locked, but, thanks to Bal, you've got the key. The ruined shrine within is laid out simply (though it's just complex enough to get you to walk in circles) and, as usual, you'll find your target, a Daedroth, at its innermost chamber.

Consistent with what Bal told you, the loot represents the rather modest acquisitions of a bad guy who doesn't get out enough, but you will find a Daedric staff here.

Who's idea was the potted plant?

Cast Recall to zap back to Yansirramus and collect the Mace of Molag Bal. He adjures you to use it to "bring strife and discord with you wherever you may travel."

Just what we had in mind!

BIG HEAD

The Shrine of Sheogorath

Sheogorath's shrine is close to home. Just descend into the sewers in Vivec's St. Delyn canton, enter the Ihinipalit shrine and, after killing off any surviving cultists (which sure beats waiting in line), activate the statue there to offer your services.

Again, plant a Mark spell here before you leave. Close as the shrine may be, the quest sends you to the ends of the earth. Sheogorath asks you to recover the Fork of Horripilation from a mad hermit near Ald Redaynia and use it to kill a giant bull netch that lives nearby.

When you arrive in Dagon Fel, ask around town about "mad hermit" to learn that Big Head lives north of Ald Redaynia.

Ald Redaynia, an abandoned Velothi dome on high ground at the western tip of the Sheogorad region, is indeed the closest ready reference point to the hermit's shack. But it's not actually close, and using it as the starting point for your search will take you out of your way.

A better route is head northwest from Dagon Fel, hopping between islands. Use the route you used to reach the Isle of the Daedra in Azura's quest. Then, from the west coast of that island, chart a course to the west-northwest.

You'll see the next island almost immediately; it has a long sandbar and tidal pools along its southern coast. The next one is much larger and slightly farther away. Watch the stone pillars in the water; they get taller closer to the island. Big Head's shack is up a rocky path from the southeast coast.

It's a strange place. Big Head has stacked five stools almost to the ceiling. And he has a spectacular collection of polearm weapons—ranging from mundane halberds to enchanted spears.

The poor fellow really is out of his mind, but not dangerous (despite all the hardware), and fragments of what he says do make sense. (He'll tell you that the netch is hiding, and this is true in the sense that it's not nearby.)

Talk to him about "Fork of Horripilation," and he'll invite you to take it.

But if you check the cool pole-arm weapons in the corner, you won't find it among them.

Check the dinner table instead. It's the little one that looks like a, uh, barbecue fork.

Remember, Sheogorath incorporates a touch of madness in all his creations.

Now, how are you going to kill a Giant Bull Netch with an enchanted barbecue fork?

Very carefully. Remember, Sheogorath didn't say you had to actually fight the netch with the fork. He just said you had to kill the netch with it. You can fight it with your best weapons or spells as long as you have the fork equipped when it dies.

But how do you figure out when to switch over to the fork for the killing blow?

Head east to the island with the sandbar. You'll find the netch there. It really is a monster. Save your game, equip your favorite weapon and count the number of blows it takes to kill the creature.

Now, restore your game and hit the netch the same number of times, minus one.

Given the range of possible damage from a hit, it's conceivable you'll kill it again. But if you don't, switch over to the fork and finish what you started. It shouldn't take too long.

Magic users can use another approach. Cast a damage-over-time spell (like Toxic Cloud) on the netch. It will start to lose health. Before it dies, equip the fork. When it does die, you'll get credit simply because you were holding the right weapon at the right time. Who's to know you never actually used it?

Zap back to the shrine and activate the statue. Sheogorath will take the Fork and give you the Spear of Bitter Mercy.

It is most decidedly not a barbecue spit.

THE ROMANCE QUESTS

In the course of Morrowind, you can help a few people get their romantic lives in order. But your own is rather empty. Hlaalu Councilor Crassius Curio flirts with you religiously—almost to the point of sexual harassment. And Synette Jeline, who gets all blushy and turned on, is actually trying to rob you.

Well, here, your character can finally have a little relationship.

AHNASSI

Smooth Moves

Visit Pelagiad's Halfway Tavern and speak to Ahnassi. She's the Khajiit at the base of the stairs to the second floor.

You don't have to be a Khajiit. You just have to be male and put Ahnassi in a good mood. If she digs you—her Disposition must be at least 50—she purrs and praises your "smooth moves."

(Alas, female characters will have to make do with the likes of kissing bandit Nels Llendo.)

Talk to her about "smooth moves" and "her profession," and she'll make a bold declaration. Select "Give Ahnassi the gift of friendship." Ahnassi is tickled by your response, and begs you to visit her often and tell her things and ask her things.

It's very sweet. How could you not like a girl who likes you so much?

You can turn her down—actually, you can turn her down repeatedly, with no downside—but her passion remains undiminished. Ahnassi's ready whenever you are.

In fact, the only way you can screw up this sequence (aside from dying in the course of one of the quests) is by hitting Ahnassi. Do it just once, and it's over. Ahnassi will no longer respond to any of the romance options.

The Girl Upstairs

Ahnassi is just dying to tell you one particular secret. When you and Ahnassi become friends, you learn that a tavern guest named Hrordis has a magic belt and is a worshipper of the cruel Daedric prince Mehrunes Dagon—the implication being, seemingly, that it's OK to pound her into a fine mush and take her Belt.

If you've been working your way through the Morag Tong quests, you already know Hrordis (in the middle room upstairs) has the enchanted Belt of Sanguine Fleetness, which fortifies the Athletics skill.

This is one of two quests, also available by other routes, to which the Romance sequence can offer early access.

(Note: If you do get the Belt, don't lose track of it. It is one of 27 "Sanguine" items required for an over-arching Morag Tong quest called "The Threads of the Webspinner.")

But this is just a nice tip from your new girlfriend. Go beat Hrordis to death and take the Belt, or don't; it doesn't have an impact on your romance.

HRORDIS

The "new friend" topic opens two more: "share a gift" and "share a care." You'll be using these choices a lot over the course of your relationship.

The gift is just a little something for you: a Feather potion. The "care" allows Ahnassi to tell you about something weighing heavily on her mind.

Bring Me the Head of Daren Adryn

Someone has badly frightened Ahnassi. A Camonna Tong thug named Daren Adryn is pressuring your favorite thief to join that criminal syndicate. Ahnassi has foresworn violence, but action from some quarter is needed to save her, and she looks to her new friend to take it.

DAREN ADRYN

You'll find Adryn in Nadene Rotheran's shack in the west coast fishing village of Gnaar Mok.

You can talk to him about Ahnassi, but you needn't bother; it only starts the inevitable fight. Just pop him and make your escape. Three other Camonna Tong operatives are in the shack, but you don't need to take them down.

But if you do clear out the shack, don't lose sleep over it. When you get back to Pelagiad, Ahnassi pulls some strings and manages to have your criminal record expunged—not simply for the recent crime or crimes committed in her behalf, but anything you currently have on the books.

In other words, if there's anyone in your game who badly needs killing, but whom you've given a reprieve because you can't afford the consequences, you're getting a "get out of jail free" card here. Use it wisely.

Naturally, this makes it all the more important that you avoid Pelagiad's ubiquitous Imperial guards until your well-connected girlfriend can do her thing.

Ahnassi also has more tangible presents for you: a spiffy outfit, and, hidden in the clothes, a Short Blade skill book, "36 Lessons of Vivec, Sermon 30."

The Small But Expensive Mistake of Belrose Dralor

And on top of that, she has a new secret to tell. Redoran agent Belrose Dralor has not exactly been Mr. Security lately. The key to two chests in the Redoran Treasury in Vivec is in his wife's clothes chest.

Both Dralor Manor and the Redoran Treaury are located off Redoran Plaza. The key is in an unlocked chest of drawers in the manor's top-floor bedroom. The chests are on the table on the lowest level of the treasury.

But the contents are the least of the rewards available here. If you manage to avoid getting hacked into small, slippery pieces by the guards, who will respond vigorously when you actually take stuff, you can come away from the treasury with a huge haul of high-end armor and weapons.

The simplest way to avoid said hacking is teleportation spells—either Divine Intervention or a Mark-and-Recall combo.

Like your robbery of Hrordis, this daring burglary is not required to further your romance. But ya gotta like having a girlfriend who functions more or less as a hidden Thieves Guild quest-giver.

The Husband

J'DHANNAR

You knew it was too good to be true.

"Ahnassi feels strange telling her good friend this thing," she says (via the "share a care" topic). "But Ahnassi has a mate."

Actually, she says J'Dhannar is a former mate. But she still has feelings for him, and these are the source of your next quest.

J'Dhannar is a skooma addict living in Vivec. Ahnassi tried to get him to give up the junk, and thinks you may succeed where she failed.

Ahnassi directs you to the St. Olms canton, but that's as far as she (or anyone else) can take you.

You'll find J'Dhannar where you almost always find drug addicts in Vivec: the lower levels of the city. Specifically, you will find him pacing in the large, southern section of St. Olms' extensive Canalworks.

You now have the topic "cure skooma addict." Use it. J'Dhanner rages at you and Ahnassi as fools. (He also manages to let drop the fact that he's not simply Ahnassi's mate, but her husband—a little detail your girlfriend seems to have omitted). And he insists skooma addiction has no cure.

Of course, addicts are not their own best doctors. A healer like Vaval Selas at the St. Olms Temple or savant like Velms Sadryon at Library of Vivec would have a better grasp of skooma lore.

Either a healer or savant will mention a book—non-Khajiit races will supply the title: "Confessions of a Dunmer Skooma-Eater" – and direct you to Jobasha's Rare Books in the Foreign Quarter Waistworks. Buy or steal a copy. (If stealing, "Confessions" is not on display, but in a chest of books in the southwest corner of the shop's lower level.)

Return to J'Dhannar with the book in your inventory, get his Disposition up to 50 and try the "cure skooma addict" topic again. This time you'll get through to him—at least enough that he agrees to read it and releases Ahnassi from their bond.

Housekeeping

The news is even better by the time you return to Pelagiad: J'Dhannar is returning to the Khajiit home province of Elswyr and has stopped using skooma. And Ahnassi now invites her "VERY special friend" to visit her at her home in Pelagiad. She supplies directions—it's across the street and a soft left from the tavern—and the key. She'll vanish from the Halfway Tavern when you leave, and appear at the house when you arrive.

Nice place. Roomy, yet cozy. Lots of food and drink. Nothing too cheap or too extravagant.

It even has a fireplace.

You'll also notice that the only bed is made for two.

From this point on, you'll find Ahnassi at home. You now have a base of operations in Pelagiad for as long as you need it. You can rest here safely. You can use or take Ahnassi's possessions. (There is nothing really special among them, but Ahnassi won't mind if you do.) And you can store loot here without Ahnassi asking you to please get it out of the living room before company arrives.

Meeting Ahnassi's Friend

You live with Ahnassi. She whispers secrets in your ear. And now, via the "share a gift" topic, she invites you to meet one of her friends.

However, it's not a social occasion. Senyndie, found at the Arena Fighters Quarters in Vivec, is a "secret master" of Acrobatics – "master" because she has the highest Acrobatics skill of any character in the game (100) and "secret" because her mastery isn't otherwise advertised within Morrowind. (Can you find the other secret masters? See the Freeform section) You know about it only because you're tight with Ahnassi.

As a result, Senyndie can train you to a higher level of the Acrobatics skill than anyone in the game. And because you're a friend of a friend, she likes you. Senyndie's Disposition goes up 40 when you mention Ahnassi, which means you get lower rates. And she gives you a free Acrobatics skill book ("The Black Arrow, Volume 1").

Flowers for Ahnassi

Now, while we don't want to sow discontent, we have to point out a certain inequity in this relationship: It seems to be mostly about you. You get the quests. You get the cool presents. You get trained in Acrobatics by a secret master.

What about Ahnassi? You did save her life from the Camonna Tong guy. But what have you done for her lately?

You're about to get a chance to make it up to her. Fire up that "share a gift" topic to learn she just wants two flowers: a Coda Flower for her and a Gold Kanet for you. She doesn't tell you where to find them. You've got to figure that out for yourself.

You won't have to look far for the Gold Kanet. They grow at the crossroads west of Pelagiad.

The Coda Flower requires a walk. A knowledgeable apothecary can tell you it is found in Draggle-Tail plants that grow along the Bitter Coast—that hump of swampy shore roughly between the village of Seyda Neen and the stronghold Hlormaren.

What pharmacists won't tell you is that the plants have to be flowering to yield a Coda.

You'll find at least five mature Draggle-Tail plants in the Seyda Neen area—one in a muck pool southwest of the lighthouse, another southeast of the entrance to bandit cave Addamasartus and three more in pools along the road north of town. Some of these won't produce a Coda, but you're sure to find at least one flower.

Then again, if you're useless at this stuff, you can simply buy one or both flowers from Peragon at Moonmoth Fort east of Balmora. He's in the far left corner of the main room. Ahnassi won't know the difference. But it's much faster just to visit Seyda Neen.

Return to Ahnassi with the flowers. She is delighted, and says "thank you" three times.

The Many Dark Moods of Mavon Drenim

You're not getting off so easy. Right after the thanks, Ahnassi observes that it's her turn to "share a gift" again. This time, she wants you to steal wizard Mavon Drenim's Flamemirror Robe from his lair in the Telvanni compound in Vivec.

The lair is on the top floor of the Velothi dome in Telvanni Plaza. Drenim is an intimidating foe—extremely quick to anger and attack. (He seems to know you've arrived almost before you do.)

MAVON DRENIM

Don't try to go toe-to-toe with him. Race for the closet on the right side of the room, grab the robe, and teleport out. Or sneak in under the cover of a potent Chameleon spell. Or just show your face so Drenim and his two colleagues start chasing you and, once they're some distance away from the closet (ideally, one whole floor), circle back and grab the goods.

Ahnassi accepts the robe gratefully. And wait until you see what she has for you in return: 20 throwing stars. Made of ebony.

FURIUS ACILIUS

Elvul's Black Blindfold

Ahnassi has one final secret. The "share a gift" topic now reveals that Elvul's Black Blindfold, a magic glove that leaves enemy archers in a befuddled darkness, can be found beneath the Imperial Commission in Castle Ebonheart.

It's heavily guarded, but Ahnassi seems to think a secret entrance, located underwater in the sea off the castle complex, offers a way around the guards. That doorway is set into a boulder north and just west of the channel that leads under beneath the long, high bridge into Castle Ebonheart. (It's the same entrance you may discover in the second-to-last quest for the Imperial Legion.)

You'll surface in a cave beneath the castle. From here, make a left at the intersection, and use the door to enter the shrine under the Imperial Commission. The Blindfold is in a chest of drawers in the room right next door.

But guess what? Ahnassi was wrong. The secret entrance isn't an end run on the guards. You could have gotten to this point just as easily by entering Castle Ebonheart through the front door. You're still going to have to open the room's locked door in full view of two extremely resilient Imperial troopers. (You can try to pickpocket Rufinius Alleius for the key—he's upstairs—but this is ultra-difficult.) And woe to you should you fail to open the door to his room stealthily.

However, that said, the secret entrance does have a purpose. Depending on when you begin your relationship with Ahnassi, it can provide access to a marvelous enchanted cuirass called the Lord's Mail way before Varus Vantinius actually sends to look for it in an Imperial Legion faction quest.

If you head straight up the tunnel from the pool, rather than turning left toward the shrine, you'll run into a fellow named Furius Acilius. You're after that shimmering armor he's wearing. You'll have to kill him for it. But even if you don't—Acilius may prove too tough—you can still find a couple of well-concealed glass weapons in the cave that make this route worthwhile.

That ends of the "live" portion of the romance sequence, though not the romance itself. You can still rest and store stuff at the house in Pelagiad. Ahnassi continues to appear there, but from this point on she'll simply repeat the same affectionate things.

But one thing does happen now and then: Two containers of food and drink refill themselves.

We can only assume that, on those occasions when you're off doing Nerevarine-type things, Ahnassi goes shopping.

THE VAMPIRE QUESTS

So You've Decided to Become a Vampire

Becoming a vampire in Morrowind is pretty simple: Fight vampires, get bitten by one and avoid getting killed in the process. This means you should either have a character powerful enough to take down a vampire—say, Level 10—or accomplished at running away…or both.

You have a choice of vampire clans, but you may not realize this initially.

Heck, you may not even realize for a while that Morrowind has vampires. They exist on the game's fringe, and you're required to face only one in the Main Quest. His name is Calvario, he's in the Nerano Ancestral Tomb, and he's a Berne vampire. Berne is one of three competing vampire clans or bloodlines.

It will take a little exploration to find the others.

Most of Morrowind's vampires can be found in 12 lairs, each affiliated with one of the clans. In addition, five vampires are independent contractors—linked to a specific clan by blood but operating on their own.

The Berne clan, led by Raxle Berne, is based at the Galom Daeus observatory in the northern central part of the Molag Amur mountain range. In addition, Berne vampires can be found in the Raviro Ancestral Tomb west of Molag Mar, the Othrelas Ancestral Tomb near Balur Salvu's farm outside Vivec, and the Andrethi Ancestral Tomb southeast of Hlormaren.

In addition, four of the five rogue vampires are Berne. That goes for Marara in the Drethan Ancestral Tomb, Merta in the Reloth Ancestral Tomb, Irarak in the Ginith Ancestral Tomb, and Calvario in the Nerano Ancestral Tomb. Marara's base is on an island south of the Dwemer ruin Ncardahrk. Merta's is southeast of Khuul. Irarak's is just off the Gnisis-Ald Velothi road and southeast of the Dwemer ruin Arkngthunch-Sturdumz. Calvario's tomb is southwest of the Ahemmusa Ashlander camp.

The Aundae clan, led by Dhaunayne Aundae, is the opposite of the Berne. It's about as far away as it can be from the populous west. Based at the tomb Ashmelech on an island southwest of Sheogorad, the Aundae vampires have additional lairs in the Sarethi Ancestral Tomb northwest of Dagon Fel, the Dulo Ancestral Tomb west of Galom

Daeus, and the Aralen Ancestral Tomb south of the Zainab Ashlander camp.

Finally, the Quarra clan, led by Volrina Quarra, is based at the Dwemer ruin Druscashti southwest of the Urshilaku Ashlander camp. You'll also find Quarra vampires in the Serano Ancestral Tomb near Galom Daeus, the Hleran Ancestral Tomb west of Ald'ruhn, and the Alen Ancestral Tomb southeast of Khuul.

The rogue Mastrius at the Salvel Ancestral Tomb is also a Quarra vampire. He's inside the Ghostfence—on the foyada northeast of the Red Mountain citadel Odrosal.

Once bitten by a vampire, wait for three full days, and then go to sleep. (A little tip: Do this after you used a mode of fast travel to get as close as possible to the clan's headquarters; you won't be able to use fast travel afterward.)

When you wake up, you'll be a vampire in the bloodline of the vampire that bit you.

If you've been infected, but are having second thoughts about becoming a vampire or somehow wound up in bloodline other than the one you wanted, don't worry. It can be cured with a simple Cure Common Disease potion any time before the three days are up.

Curing vampirism itself? Regardless of what you hear in Morrowind, it can be done. But not with a potion. It will be your last act as a vampire—once cured, you can't become one again—so we'll handle it last.

Now, why would you want to be a vampire?

Reason # 1: To do the vampire quests.

A vampire can perform up to 11 of the 17 vampire quests in a given game. Three of these are specific to the vampire clan you've joined. Joining a bloodline, which occurs automatically when you become a vampire, locks out the six quests for the two other bloodlines.

The other eight quests are open to any vampire.

Reason # 2: To play as an incredibly powerful character.

Being a vampire is not like belonging to a faction. It is a state of being. In fact, it is a state of super-being. All vampires receive 20-point boosts in the stats Strength, Willpower, and Speed and 30-point boosts in the skills Sneak, Athletics, Acrobatics, Hand-to-Hand, Unarmored, Mysticism, Illusion, and Destruction.

On top of those increases, each clan has one additional stat and three additional skill bonuses—one of these in a skill or stat you don't already have and the other three reinforcing those that all vampires receive.

Berne vampires receive a 20-point boost in the Agility stat and additional 20-point boosts in the Sneak, Unarmored, and Hand-to-Hand skills.

Aundae vampires receive a 20-point boost in the Short Blade skill and additional 20-point boosts in the Willpower stat and the Mysticism and Destruction skills.

Quarra vampires receive a 20-point boost in the Blunt Weapons skill and additional 20 point boosts in the Strength stat and Hand-to-Hand and Heavy Armor skills.

Vampires are also immune to Paralysis and Common Disease, and they have a high resistance to normal weapons (50%).

And in addition to your regular spells (which you keep), vampires acquire two additional incantations: Vampire Touch (an extremely valuable spell that drains your opponent's health while restoring your own) and a more potent, longer-lasting version of the Levitate spell.

You'll grow to love your Vampire Touch spell, because it's one of the only ways you'll be gaining back health in your undead state. See, as a vampire, you don't heal while you sleep. Instead, you're awakened by a rather disturbing dream, and you'll find that your health hasn't risen at all. There are actually a number of these dreams that can appear to you when you sleep, involving everything from murdered parents to dead babies to your lips being sewn shut. It's worth sleeping just to read these twisted tales. Plus, your fatigue and magicka will still replenish normally, so sleep does have its advantages.

The upside of all this: You are capable of killing pretty much anybody who even looks at you funny. If all you want to do is kill people and take their stuff, this is a phenomenal character.

The downside. While you're incredibly powerful, you're also incredibly lonely. While you're a vampire, very few people will talk to you. The undead-hating Dunmer will shun you. Some people will attack you. In fact, aside from Mages Guild members (who have a practical interest in vampirism), the Telvanni (who just don't care, but seem to have a pseudo-scientific interest) and other vampires, you will be in a world of one. You won't be able to do much of anything except kill people, and while you'll be able to perform some Telvanni and Mages Guild quests, quests that take you outside those respective spheres may prove impossible to complete.

In a nutshell, being a vampire kills much of Morrowind's gameplay, and, as a vampire, you kill pretty much everything else. As a result, the game's story is effectively on hold.

Whether this is a temporary or permanent state of affairs is up to you. If you're a vampire just so you can perform the vampire quests, it shouldn't be a problem. Most of the vampire quests occur within a self-contained world, with little interaction with or impact on the "normal" world around it. Consequently, you can do the vampire quests, take the cure, and if you haven't gone on any homicidal rampages, the world you left will not have changed when you return.

But if you don't stop there, and proceed to play Morrowind as a vampire, we can't be held responsible for what happens. If you go through the game killing folks indiscriminately, eventually, you're going to kill someone important and "break" the Main Quest—that is, make it impossible to play through the story as it was designed to be played.

This does not make it impossible to finish the game. By brute force and great skill, a very powerful character can still complete the Main Quest. But, as outlined in the Main Quest chapter, this forces on you a so-called "back-path" approach that includes a good deal of extra work and special requirements.

THE BERNE QUESTS

RAXLE BERNE

Blood of the Vampire

The Berne clan is based at Galom Daeus in the northern central section of the Molag Amur mountain range. You can make this trip on foot from the western regions, but this Dwemer ruin is reached most easily by traveling by boat to Tel Aruhn and then finding your way down the coast to a point just south of Tel Fyr, where you'll find a path leading inland to a lava river. Follow the lava river west to its end. To west, you'll see another lava pool and, beyond it, Galom Daeus.

The vampires here won't attack you, since you're one of them, but the Dwemer steam centurions may not be so forgiving

You will find clan leader, or "Ancient," Raxle Berne in the Observatory. You have probably never been greeted with so little respect by a quest-giver. He seems to regard you as only slightly more advanced than the slave "cattle" the clan keeps for feeding purposes.

However, he'll lay out the three clans and their respective strengths. And if you select "serve me," he'll offer you a mission—though he seems to have already made up his mind that you won't return.

Berne says Quarra clan Ancient Volrina Quarra draws much of her power from drinking the blood of Quarra clan elders. If you can get him that potion, he'll allow you to draw on the services available at Galom Daeus.

When you set out for Druscashti, you'll quickly discover several practical limitations to being a vampire.

One is that you're not free to move around outside during the day. From dawn to dusk, you can take damage from sunlight.

It's not exactly the "night good, day bad" deal of conventional vampires; there are degrees in between, depending on how much sunlight is hitting you at a given moment. Full sunlight will burn you down at amazing speed. But if it's raining or an ash storm is raging, the amount of damage you take is reduced. And if you dive into water, the effect of the sunlight is diluted and you won't take quite as much damage.

You'll find you've turned into the Addams Family, hoping for bad weather. But it's a dicey proposition, as you never know when the weather is suddenly going to turn nice. As a side note, as if sleeping wasn't bad enough with the twisted visions you receive, sleeping outside is a really bad plan. The sun burns sleeping vampires quite nicely, thank you.

Another factor is limitations on fast travel. Ordinarily, to get to Druscashti, you'd take silt strider to Maar Gan. But the inability to talk to most people effectively means silt strider and boats are out. Even your erstwhile pals at the Mages Guild will deny access to the guild guide teleportation service. (A side note: If you need to use a fast-travel mode to make your initial trip to your clan's headquarters, postpone actually becoming a vampire until close to your destination. You won't be able to afterward.)

This has the effect of making everything seem really far away.

Together, these two considerations produce a third. It's now more important to know where things are along your planned route. You can't camp in the wilderness, and you can't afford to be caught out in the open while searching the wilderness for an egg mine or bandit cave in which to weather a beautiful day.

Until you get the hang of this new way of doing things, play it safe. Wait until nightfall to head for the Quarra base at Druscashti. As you make your way northwest up the Foyada Bani-Dad from Maar Gan, it's the second of two Dwemer ruins overhanging the eastern side of this trough.

Once inside, two quick rights take you down to the lower level. Once through the door, make your first left, and you'll encounter the first of two formidable vampires, the ebony-equipped Siri, and, down the stairs in the large room beyond, the glass-equipped Quarra. You won't be able to kill them—they're levels 24 and 30, respectively—but you may be able to sneak past them.

The blood potion is in the right-hand of three kegs against the outside wall. It's locked but, if you're an accomplished pickpocket, Quarra has a key.

Take the Blood of the Quarra Masters and return to Galom Daeus. Talk to Berne about "Quarra Blood Potion." He'll take it, and grant access to the two vendors in Galom Daeus' entry area: Arenara (who has a great selection of advanced weapons and armor and can also perform repairs) and Germia (who sells thieves' tools).

Revenge of the Vampire

Berne is surprised by your success, and offers another task. Talk to him about "an errand for you" to learn about the vampire Merta—a Berne lieutenant until she went solo and set herself up in a tomb west of Mar Gaan.

For Merta's audacity in leaving the clan, and for taking "cattle" Berne sees as his, he orders you to kill her.

MERTA

She's in the Reloth Ancestral Tomb—a small crypt that actually proves to be not so much west of Maar Gan as it is southeast of Khuul. (It's just southwest of the Maelkashishi shrine.) You'll find Merta in its innermost chamber. Her Poisonmirror Robe is a nice bit of loot, and you'll get better from Berne when you report in the news of Merta's death. The Berne Amulet he gives you casts a Recall spell that zaps you back to Galom Daeus on demand.

War of the Vampires

Berne now charges you to kill "worthless vampires" from the Quarra and Aundae clans.

Variations on this freeform campaign serve as the third quest for each of the clans. Don't worry about the "worthless" part. (Berne basically thinks all other vampires are worthless.) It doesn't matter which vampires you kill—just how many. And Berne doesn't say exactly how many.

The magic number is "12."

You don't have to go back to Druscashti to find them. Lower-level vampires are close by. The Dulo Ancestral Tomb, set into the western side of the same mountain as Galom Daeus, is home to five anonymous Aundae vampires. The Serano Ancestral Tomb, just a quick jaunt northeast and northwest from Galom Daeus, has five anonymous Quarra vampires.

Ten down, two to go.

You can pick up both remaining kills at the Aralen Ancestral Tomb. It's a long and winding trip through the northern Molag Amur, but still shorter than any of the other trips you could make.

From Galom Daeus, head northeast to the crossroads and follow the signs for Vos and Tel Vos north. You'll eventually emerge into the Grazelands just southeast of Massama Cave (a large abandoned glass mine) and southwest of the stronghold Falensarano. Follow the road around the stronghold and continue north. After the road bends east, you'll find the Aralen tomb to the south.

Return to Berne and ask about "future rewards." He'll now allow you feed off the clan's "cattle" using your Vampire Touch spell. Just don't kill any of them. That really, really makes him angry.

That's the extent of the Berne vampire's missions. See the "All Clans on Deck" section for more quests.

THE AUNDAE QUESTS

A Vampire with a Heart

Ashmelech is one of those places that isn't really close to anything. Sorry. We could name a few ancestral tombs and one Velothi dome, but they probably wouldn't mean anything to you.

The best way to reach the Aundae vampires' headquarters is to travel by boat to Khuul and then head east along Vvardenfell's northern coast. You'll pass the Urshilaku Ashlander camp and the mountaintop stronghold Valenvaryon. Then the coast will begin to dip south.

After the dip, start looking for a large silt strider carcass a short distance in from the shore. Stand at the southeast end of the carcass, and head straight north across the water. You'll soon see a beach. At the northeast end of the beach, you'll see a road. And when you start up the road, on your left, you'll see the entrance to Ashmelech.

**DHAUNAYNE
AUNDAE**

There is a long way and a short way down through this huge underground complex to clan leader Dhaunayne Aundae. If you follow the right wall from the entry ramp, you'll come to a gaping hole in the corridor floor. This is the express elevator to Aundae. Invoke your Levitate spell and descend.

She's about as unpleasant as all clan quest-givers—to her, you are a "little monster" – but select "plan to serve me" and then "about my family" and she'll reveal a softer side.

Aundae says that, in her former life, she was a high-born Altmer with a husband and a young son. The same vampire who made her a vampire killed her husband, but the child was permitted to live.

"I am curious what became of the boy, although he has likely gone the way of all mortals now," she tells you. "Still, it would be amusing to know his fate."

It's rather touching. Aundae puts a disinterested face on her inquiry, but she can't hide her feelings. Agree to help, and she'll give you a signet ring with her family crest—which she says any high elf should recognize—and direct you to her family's last known address: Sadrith Mora.

You'll find more drawn swords than leads until you get the Mages Guild in Wolverine Hall. Speak to Tusamircil over by the left-hand wall about "family crest." He recognizes the ring as similar to one worn by Sinyaramen. He's unlikely to talk to a vampire, but Tusamircil suggests that delivering the potion he ordered might get him to open up.

It's a good idea, so agree.

The hitch: Tusamircil doesn't know where to find Sinyaramen.

But Iniel, just to his left, will help you put two and two together. She, too, has seen the crest—at the Gateway Inn.

Get uptown to the Gateway. Sinyaramen's on the second floor. As Tusamircil guessed, he won't deal with you without inducement, but you have inducement in the form of the potion. Ask about "family crest," "killed by your kind" and "Vilandon."

Vilandon was Sinyaramen's grandfather—a hunter of vampires after one killed his parents, and finally himself a victim of a vampire named Kjeld.

Got all that?

Return to Aundae and talk to her "about my family" again. She will eloquently order Kjeld's death.

Family is an odd thing, is it not? Defined by blood, separated by blood, joined by blood. In the end, it is all just blood.

Kjeld is a Quarra vampire quartered behind a trapped door on the upper level of Druscashti. When you've killed him, report back to Aundae and speak to her about "Kjeld," and she'll award you access to clan services. Now Mororurg will sell you potions and ingredients, and Gladroon will sell and repair weapons and armor.

It's not quite like home, but, for now, it will have to do.

Chapter Six: Miscellaneous Quests

The Vampire Hunter

A vampire hunter has been poking around in Ashmelech. Aundae's spies have followed him back to Ald'ruhn. You're to go there and kill him—in broad daylight and with people around, so that his death may serve as a cautionary example for others who might follow in his footsteps.

ANO VANDO

What, the spies couldn't even get the guy's name?

No matter. Just as the Mages Guild helped you out in Sadrith Mora, it will do so again in Ald'ruhn Ask about "vampire hunter" there, and you'll learn the hunter's name is Ano Vando.

As if you'd have any trouble figuring it out. Vando's walking back and forth near the Mages Guild, carrying this glittering ebony shield.

Whack him. Check the time first (noon's good, just so there's no confusion) and make sure someone's standing nearby as a witness. If you bring it off correctly, you'll get a journal entry and can zap back to Ashmelech to talk to Aundae about "vampire hunter" for your reward. As in your second Berne and Quarra quests, you'll get an amulet you can use to Recall back to clan HQ. You might be tempted to grab Vando's mace (Light of Day) and/or shield (Darksun) from his corpse. After all, you've learned they pack a good punch. Don't try to use them, though. These things are most definitely anti-vampire, and will send your health plummeting if you try to equip them. You might stash them somewhere for later use, though, if you decide to give up the undead lifestyle.

"A Great Number" of Dead Vampires

That's what you're expected to produce in your third quest. Aundae basically asks you to wage war on the other two clans, with a promise of future rewards if you really pile up the bodies.

All three clans have this quest, and it's pretty much the same in each case. Here, you need to kill 12 Berne or Quarra vampires (or any combination thereof), and you can take them wherever you find them.

The only difference is a level of convenience. The Berne vampire can find easy 10 victims without even leaving the neighborhood. The Aundae vampire has to shlep a good distance just to reach the nearest lair, and the challenges within that lair are considerable.

It's the Quarra base Druscashti—a Dwemer ruin southwest of the Urshilaku Ashlander camp. To find it, you'll probably just have to retrace some of the steps you took to find Ashmelech to begin with.

Minus the unfortunate Kjeld, who you've already killed, you should find two remaining vampires on the upper level and four on the lower.

Unhappily, two of the latter four vampires—Siri and Volrina Quarra—are murderously tough opponents who should only be tackled by a very advanced player. If that's you, wonderful. Great armor and weapons will be your reward. But chances are, it isn't, so the effective yield of Druscashti is four vampires. Eight to go.

You can knock off five more by continuing west along the coast to Khuul and then making your way southeast to the Alen Ancestral Tomb. Just take the road southeast toward Khuul's silt strider port, then east toward a renegade Ashlander camp, and south and then west to the first of two close-set intersections. Make a left here and follow the road over the rise into a grove of trees. Hang another left in the grove and follow the short path to the tomb door.

Be careful. The Quarra vampires here aren't at all tough, but there are five of them in a small area, and you'll probably be getting hit by one as you kill another.

Three to go.

Two rogue Berne vampires can be found in the general neighborhood—theReloth and Ginith tombs, respectively— but unless you cleared out Drucashti, it's not enough to complete the quest and so not worth the effort of tracking them down individually.

However, you can wrap up the mission at a third Quarra location farther south. The Hleran Ancestral Tomb is located in the western Ashlands off the road west of Ald'ruhn. A short distance from town, the road starts uphill and you'll see a steam geyser and a signpost on your left. The path to the south isn't marked. Follow it as it turns west into a ravine. You'll find the Hleran tomb at its end.

Use your amulet to zap back to Ashmelech for a reward identical to that in the other clans' version of this quest: You can now use your Vampire Touch spell to feed on the clan's "cattle."

But that's the end of the formal Aundae quests. See the "All Clans on Deck" section for additional quests that can be performed by any vampire.

THE QUARRA QUESTS

Cult of the Vampire

VOLRINA QUARRA

If you've been following the vampires' mini-dramas, we're betting you know where Druscashti is by now. After all, the dwarven ruin used by the Quarra clan as its main base really takes it on the chin in the other clans' quests.

Here's your chance to give the Quarra their turn in the sun. (Well, so to speak!)

Coming from the south, you'll find the vampire lair just up the Foyada Bani-Dad from Maar Gan; it's the second Dwemer ruin overhanging the east slope. (The first is Bthungthumz.) Coming from the east or west, it's southwest of the Urshilaku Ashlander camp.

Seek out Volrina Quarra on the lower level and speak to her about "use to me." She'll explain that a vampire named Irarak (a rogue from the Berne clan) has set up shop near Gnisis and is being worshipped as a god. Quarra considers this a mockery, and wants Irarak dead.

The Ginith Ancestral Tomb, where Irarak holds court, is actually a bit closer to Ald Velothi than to Gnisis. So, we'll start from there.

It's down in a little thicket of "Miscellaneous" quests just south of town. From Ald Velothi's tower, follow the coast west toward the Dwemer ruin Arkngthunch-Sturdumz. But before you cross the bridge to the ruin, turn south, down the hill, and west again at the signpost. Whip around the hill ahead of you on its northern side and the Ginith tomb will soon appear on your left.

It's a small tomb and following either wall from the entrance will take you quickly to Irarak's audience chamber.

And this is interesting: You're actually welcome here. Irarak's four young followers all identify you as a vampire, but seem unthreatened. While not yet vampires, they seem to be looking forward to the day when Irarak bestows on them his "dark gift."

This sounds as though it has been ripped from today's headlines.

Speak to Irarak about "Brood of Lord Irarak," "provide comfort," and "material gains"—and you'll sort out that this is a racket. I guess it's easier than running around at night and biting people.

This also forces a decision: Kill Irarak, or extort money from him. If the former, everyone gangs up on you. If the latter, you'll get 1,000 gold—and then you should kill him anyway to satisfy Quarra. (If you let him live, you'll get kicked out of the clan on your return.)

Back at Druscashti, Quarra makes good on her promise of access to services. Areas, found up the stairs at the end of the lower level's first long hall, sells a range of items. But Kjeld, in a trapped room on the upper level, has a nice selection of weapons and armor and repairs them as well.

Amulet(s) of the Vampire

Speak to Quarra again about "use to me" and "raw materials," and, after she says the usual disparaging vampire-quest-giver things, she'll give you another job.

It's actually a whole bunch of jobs. She's making magical amulets for clan members, and needs supplies:

- *five extravagant sapphire amulets*
- *two portions of void salts*
- *a daedra heart*
- *ectoplasm*
- *vampire dust*
- *a skull*

In other words, she needs everything.

This isn't a simple mission, but it isn't as elaborate as it may first appear. You could wait for all this stuff (minus the skull) to turn up in loot, but shortcuts are available if you know where to find them.

Three sapphire amulets can be found in crates in the smuggler's cave Yasamsi near Hla Oad and two more in crates aboard the Obscure Shipwreck in the far western reaches of Sheogorad. (It's near the island where you'll find the mad hermit Big Head in the quest from Daedric god Sheogorath.) There's no guarantee you'll find them there (they're part of the leveled loot lists), but you've got a shot of getting them in these crates. If they're not there, there are some NPCs who are also carrying them. You can get one if you off Nelos Onmar (who we meet on a miscellaneous quest). Other folks include Cienne Sintieve (an alchemist in Ald'ruhn), Miner Arobar (in Arobar Manor in Ald'ruhn), and Domesea Sarethi (in Sarethi Manor in Ald'ruhn). Sounds like they had a run on these things in Ald'ruhn.

The easiest way to get the four ingredients is simply to buy them from Telvanni and Mages Guild vendors. You'll have to visit two or three to put everything together.

And once you start looking for a skull, you'll suddenly see them all over the place. You'll find them under an Imperial Steel Helmet in Ald Daedroth, on a shelf in the Caldera Mages Guild and in quantity just outside the Arano Ancestral Tomb near Tel Branora—and lots of places in-between.

You'd think that, with all this hard work, Quarra might break form with the other clans and give you a distinctive reward. But nooo....You don't even get one of the amulets she's making. You get one of her old rejects. It allows you to Recall to instantly to Druscashti without first setting a Mark should you get into trouble.

The Only Good Vampire

For the final Quarra quest, you're expected to kill a dozen vampires from the two rival clans. It's the same deal you'll get as an Aundae or Berne vampire—though rather less demanding than the Aundae version and not quite as unde-manding as the Berne.

Your best bet is simply to head east to the Aundae headquarters at Ashmelech. (See "The Aundae Quests" for directions.) In that underground vampire town, you will find no fewer than nine vampires. Eight if you're less ambitious and don't include the Level 30 Dhaunayne Aundae on the list.

Pick up the rest up north at another Aundae lair—the Sarethi Ancestral Tomb northwest of Dagon Fel. Then return to Quarra and she'll allow you to feed on the clan's "cattle." Tastes like chicken!

And with that, you're done with the formal Quarra quests. See the "All Clans On Deck" section below for quests for all vampires.

ALL CLANS ON DECK

Any vampire can perform these quests. Aundae, Berne, Quarra—it's all good. And you don't have to perform any of the clan-specific quests first. In fact, you might want to try some of these first as a way of weaning yourself from the normal world to the vampire one.

SANVYN

Something for the Kid with Everything

If you ask after the latest rumors in Ald'ruhn—try the Mages Guild—you'll learn about a rich kid who wants to be a vampire. Visit Llethri Manor and speak to Fathasa Llelthri for the big picture. (Oddly enough, she's willing to speak to you.) Her son. Sanvyn, thinks vampirism is the ticket to power and respect. She'll ask you to convince him that vampires aren't as strong as he believes them to be.

Quietly, she has just given you the solution.

Sanvyn is just down the hall. Speak to him about "submit myself," and chose your responses for maximum irritating effect: "You are a foolish boy," "You are ridiculous young man, "Stupid child," "You are too weak to be a vampire" and "You know nothing!"

Each dig will lower his Disposition by seven points (compared to five for the other, more measured choice) and raise his Fight by five (compared to two). By the end of your little chat, he'll want to tear your lungs out and use them for a bagpipe. If he doesn't start a fight afterward, just keep up a string of taunts until he does.

And here's the key: Remember his mother's words, and let him win. Don't fight back. (He's just a kid, and you'd probably kill him.) Once your health has been halved, he'll decide you're a big weenie, declare that all he's heard about vampires has been lies, and stop fighting.

Little monster, indeed. Return to Fathasa and talk to her about "convinced my son." She'll give you a magic ring pro-tects the wearer against fire damage, which is handy for a vampire.

Just Shoot Me

In Tel Mora, ask for the latest rumors, and you'll pick up some buzz about a powerful vampire who has been killing folks right and left. Go see Marara, found in the Drethan Ancestral Tomb southwest of Ald Daedroth, and ask her what's up with that.

Like Umbra, the Orc warrior you may have met in the mountains near Suran, she's weary of her long life and wants it to end. However, again like Umbra (and somewhat bewilderingly), she's unwilling to just put her head on the chopping block, but insists she be bested in combat by one of her kind.

So you can't just do her a favor. It's a fight for your life as well as hers.

If you're up to it, you'll get the enchanted Ring of Marara, which casts Reflect, Fortify Acrobatics (10 points), and Resist Normal Weapons (40%).

But despite Marara's talk about her treasures, you won't find huge amounts of loot here. The most notable feature of this small tomb is that it has two entrances—one of them via an extensive smuggler's den called Shallit.

MASTRIUS

Betrayal of the Vampire

Probably the most obscure of the vampire quests. You won't find Mastrius until you're well inside the game, and well inside the Ghostfence. And by then, of course, you may have your sights set on bigger fish.

This Quarra vampire is the lone resident of the Salvel Ancestral Tomb—found along the foyada that extends northeast of the Red Mountain citadel Ordosal. Speak to him about "my imprisonment" and "way to escape" to learn he is a prisoner—confined here by the Daedra god Azura for reasons unstated—and that he may have found an escape hatch. He begs you to release him, and offers you the world.

Mastrius asks for two things: a powerful shield called Spellbreaker, and a daedra's heart.

The shield is in the Dwemer ruin Bthuand. It's located in the northern Ashlands, just inland from the central section of the coast and just west of the Daedric shrine Zergonipal. If you performed the Daedric quest for Molag Bal, then you've already been in close proximity. As in the quest, the best approach is via the stronghold Kogoruhn.

Bthuand's an odd place. As wonderfully well-preserved as most other Dwemer ruins have been, this one seems to be falling down. The scribs here are all dead. The only living thing (if you can call it living) is a handful of centurions.

The decay is used to conceal the shield; you'll find it behind some fallen stones in the ruin's inner extremity. And you should be able to find a daedra heart after killing one at the neighboring shrine.

Now, Azura must have had her reasons for penning Mastrius in here, so you'd be wise to approach this mission with caution. In fact, it's probably a good idea to approach any Level 29 vampire with caution. Note the telling foul-up he makes if you speak to him again without having returned with his items.

When you do return to Mastrius with shield and heart, he'll ask for one more thing: your strength to break the spell. If you agree, he'll drain half your health and stamina.

And then he'll attack you.

Hey, we told you to keep an eye on him.

Kill him, and you can pick over his possessions at your leisure. Spellbreaker is yours, as is the late Mastrius' full suit of ebony armor.

Killing Shashev

A vampire in Vivec? It's not exactly traditional territory for a Creature of the Night. But if you're not averse to travel, you can pick up a couple of simple quests in Vvardenfell's largest city.
Find Sirilonwe in the labyrinthine Mages Guild (off Foreign Quarter Plaza) and speak to her about "someone killed." She'll ask you to rub out a rival named Shashev and bring back his key.
We weren't kidding about the travel. Shashev is at Ald'ruhn's Ald-Skar Inn.
Once the job is done, just get back to Sirilonwe with Shashev's key and talk to her once again about "someone killed." She'll tell you to keep anything else you found on Shashev's body. (That includes a nice magical ring that casts Paralyze and Poison.)

SIRILONWE

Dust of the Vampire

With Shashev pushing up Gold Kanets, speak with Sirilonwe again—this time about "vampire dust." She'll ask for three portions of this magical ingredient for a spell she's researching.

You can find the dust in the remains of dead vampires (which your quest-giver prefers) or from alchemist and apothecary shops.

The former solution requires a trip out to the nearest vampire lair—the Othrelas Ancestral Tomb to the northeast. (This Berne lair is along the water near Balur Salvu's farm.)

The latter will involve a bit of shopping . Anarenen at the Ald'ruhn Mages Guild. Anis Seloth: Alchemist in Sadrith Mora, and Brarayni Sarys in Tel Aruhn should all sell you the stuff. Except they won't sell you anything. Because you're a vampire. Ah, well. No one will miss a couple of alchemists.

If you're more of a thieving frame of mind, vampire dust can be found just lying around here and there. Aurane Frernis:Apothecary in the Foreign Quarter Lower Waistworks has a portion on the table. Another can be found in Arvs-Drelen in Gnisis. And if you've built a stronghold, you can visit the Telvanni version, Tel Uvirith, and find all three portions in Menas' house!

With dust in hand, return to Sirilonwe for an Amulet of Gem Feeding.

Who Ya Gonna Call? Vampire!

When ordinary people want someone dead, they call the Morag Tong. When mages want someone dead, they call a vampire.
Or so it would seem. If you speak to Raven Omayn, the "Mouth" for Councilor Dratha, at the Telvanni Council House in Sadrith Mora, she'll give you another hit. Talk to her about "Rimintil," and she'll ask you to kill him.
No details. Apparently he's just not one of Dratha's favorite people.
You'll find your target in Tel Vos' Central Tower. Return to Omayn with Rimintil's blood on your hands, and you'll win a lovely Flamemirror Robe. Rimintil got a ton of Dwemer armor on him as well, which is a nice added bonus.

Blood of the Vampire II

Word seems to have gotten around about that Quarra Blood Potion. Raxle Berne asks you to get it for him in the first Berne clan mission. And now, provided you've been successful with Rimintil, Omayn wants it as well.
No problem. If you've performed the regional Miscellaneous quests in Seyda Neen, you're already a pro at stealing the same item twice. Poor Fargoth....

Anyway, back to the Blood Potion. If you haven't already taken it for Raxle Berne, the potion is still in a locked steel keg on the lower level of Quarra lair Druscashti.

If you have, it's in Galom Daeus—in Berne's inventory. You'll have to pick his pocket (very difficult) or kill him. (If you're planning to do the Tribunal Temple quests, you'll have to kill Berne eventually anyway.)

Return to Omayn for a Flawed Dwemer Jinksword. Flawed? Not to worry. It just means the intended enchantment didn't come off as planned—but your natural resistances should make it uniquely useful to you.

Taking the Cure

You probably heard the debate about whether a cure exists for vampirism long before you became a vampire. Under the topics "vampirism cure" and "vampirism," a good number of people will offer their thoughts about whether vampirism is a disease and, if so, whether it can be cured.

Well, it can.

This quest may actually start back in the "normal" world. No one actually gives it to you. But either through persistent inquiry, you will eventually learn about a book called "Vampires of Vvardenfell, Volume II."

The most likely source is Skink-in-Tree's-Shade at the Mages Guild in Sadrith Mora, who actually sends you off to look for the book in one of the Mages Guild faction quests, but Estirdalin (at the Balmora Mages Guild) and Smokey Morth (at the Varo Tradehouse in Vos) will tell you about it as well.

It's quite rare. Copies can be found in Vivec in the Tribunal Temple's secret library and at Jobasha's Rare Books, in the wizard lairs Mawia, Odiniran and Vas, in Tel Vos' Central Tower, and in the observatory at Galom Daeus.

And, if you've got big ones, you can go look in Kagrenac's Library in the Red Mountain citadel Tureynulal.

This can lead in turn to an even rarer document – "The Private Papers of Galur Rithari, Buoyant Armiger" – which can be found only in the secret library in Galom Daeus and Tureynulal.

The papers actually spell out the solution, but that solution is also implicit in "Vampires of Vvardenfell, Volume II" and you can guess at it without much trouble: You have to go to Bal Ur.

This Daedric shrine is located north of the mountains west of Suran. Pass through the shrine and enter the

Underground and speak to Derar Hlervu. He'll tell you to talk to the statue.

When you do so, as with Rithari, Bal sets you a task: You must go to the cave Dubdilla, located south of Vos, and kill Bal's daughter, Molag Grunda, and her atronach consort, Nomeg Gwai. She's disobeyed her father by hanging with this guy, and her Dad is in bad need of anger management.

When they are dead, simply return to the shrine, activate the statue again, and your vampirism will be removed.

You are more or less what you were. You have lost your vampire super-stats and skills as well as your resistances and spells, but any level and skill increases you achieved as a vampire remain intact.

You may be nervous about walking in direct sunlight for a while. But that will pass.

And you may be thinking about the clan quests you missed, and wondering if you can become a vampire again and join another bloodline.

What do you think this is, a record club? Don't bother. You are cured now and forever. You can't become a vampire again—until your next game.

FREEFORM

You're done. Or rather, you think you're done. You've finished the Main Quest, Faction Quests, and the Miscellaneous Quests. You've communed with gods old and new. Maybe you've even been a vampire for a while. And now you're wondering what else is out there.

Actually, quite a bit.

You don't need to do only what you're told. Seize the initiative. While Morrowind uses many of its locations in organized quests, it doesn't use anywhere near all of them. As a result, the game supplies raw material for many quests of the player's own devising.

Most of these little adventures won't have a formal story—it's just you seeing, going, and conquering—but some will acquire scraps of one in documents you'll find along the way.

In fact, you really don't know what you're going to find out there until you find it. But here are some of the things in Morrowind that will make you go "hmmm!"

Radical Abolitionist

Quests allow you to save a fair number of Morrowind slaves from their harsh lives, and the game rewards you for showing a sense of enterprise and saving 30.

But there are more than 160 slaves in the game—not counting the feeding "cattle" in the main vampire lairs—and you can free the majority of them.

Where there's a key, there's a way. (Except for skeleton keys. Slaves don't recognize these as keys and so don't invite you to free them.)

You can find keys that release slaves at the following locations: Abebaal Egg Mine, Addamasartus, Aharunartus, Assarnud, Caldera ebony mine, Dren Plantation, Habinbaes, Hinnabi, the stronghold Hlormaren, Kudanat, Minabi, Panat, the stronghold Rotheran, Saturan, Sha-Adnius, Shushan, Shushishi, Sinsibadon, Yakanalit, Zainsipilu and Zebabi.

In addition, while you can't free slaves that are for sale, you can buy slaves from Savile Imayn in Tel Aruhn and then set them free. You can't buy slaves from Brallion in Sadrith Mora or Dranas Sarathram in Suran.

And you can't personally end slavery on Vvardenfell. Some slaves can't be released. This includes those in Sadrith Mora and Molag Mar, at the Suran Slave Market and Desele's House of Earthly Delights in Suran, and some at farms in the Ascadian Isles.

But you can make a difference.

The Bookworm Quests

A pleasant pastime in later stages of Morrowind is tracking down the game's many books.

The be-all-and-end-all for obscure books in Morrowind is Jobasha's Rare Books on the Lower Waistworks level of Vivec's Foreign Quarter. The three other dedicated booksellers and the handful of pawnbrokers and general-merchandise stores that deal in books can't touch him.

But even Jobasha doesn't have everything. The super-rare stuff is in private libraries.

You already know about the Tribunal Temple's secret library in Vivec, the Dwarven inventor Kagrenac's library in the Red Mountain citadel Tureynulal, and the one in the Holamayan monastery. Those are the big collections.

But smaller ones can be found in the homes of spellcasters like Divayth Fyr. In his Hall of Fyr, you'll find Starlover's Log, The Posting of the Hunt, and Tal Merog Ker's Researches (open on Fyr's desk). These last two will be of special interest to players aspiring to possess the Spear of Bitter Mercy. (See the Daedric Quests in the Miscellaneous Quest section.)

Other unique books without quest tie-ins include the manuscript version of Saryoni's Sermons (in a chest in Lliralal's Shack near the Sanctus Shrine) and War of the First Council (under the bed in Caius Cosades' place in Balmora).

Then there are two obscure multi-volume series: The Mystery of Princess Talara and Poison Song. Unhappily, unlike many of the multi-volume series, these collections are nowhere available as boxed sets. You'll have to hunt most of the volumes down individually—a somewhat tricky business because, depending which volume you find first, you probably won't know how many there are.

There's no reward. Or, rather, the books themselves are their own reward. Both series are real page-turners—with great endings.

The Mystery of Princess Talara

This lively story is spread over five volumes. You can get four of them in Caldera.

The first four volumes are skill books. "The Mystery of Princess Talara, Part I" is an Acrobatics book found in Dro'Shavir's house in Caldera, Madren Ulvel's house in Sadrith Mora, Desele's House of Earthly Delights in Suran, and in random loot.

Part II is a Restoration skill book that can be found in Caldera at the home of Valvius Mevureius. It's also carried by the healer Chark, who's out east in the shrine Esutanamus, and it appears in random loot.

(If you get Mevureius' copy, save yourself a trip and pick up the non-skill book Part V while you're there. It's also available at Codus Callonus: Bookseller in Ald'ruhn.)

Part III, a Destruction skill book, is the most common of the five. It's in Caldera's South Guard Towers, the dome atop the stronghold Hlormaren, Tyravel Manor in the northwest part of Balmora, the shrine Ramimilk, the cave-cum-shrine Ibar-Dad, and in random loot.

Part IV, an Illusion skill book, is the hardest to find. One copy is in Omni Hard-Mouth's house in Dagon Fel and another in the Urshilaku Burial Caverns. Specifically, it's in the southeastern leg of the X-shaped Fragile Burial, reached through the Astral, Karma, and Laterus burials.

And, like all except Volume V, it's in random loot. If you can wait that long.

Poison Song

More obscure is the Poison Song series.

Only the first of the seven volumes of this Sixth House-related horror story is at a quest location—near Irarak in the Ginith Ancestral Tomb northwest of Gnisis. The game directs you to this crypt only on Volrina Quarra's quest to kill Irarak, and you'll get that quest only if you're a Quarra vampire.

And only one copy exists of volumes II, III, IV, and VII.

At least you don't have to travel to the ends of the earth to find them. They're concentrated within civilized areas. Five volumes can be picked up at three locations in Sadrith Mora, two at a single location in Pelagiad, and two at Ules Manor just west of Suran.

Volumes I and III are at Nevrila Areloth's house in the eastern central part of Sadrith Mora.

Volumes II and V are at Trendus Dral's house in the south part of town.

Volume VII is at Madren Ulvel's house in the western central section. (She also has Part I of the Princess Talara collection above.)

Then you just have to run by Ules Manor to pick up volumes IV and VI. (Additional copies of volumes V and VI can be found at Adanja's house in Pelagiad.)

Do yourself a favor and wait until you have all seven volumes to read them. You'll enjoy them individually, but much more as a whole.

CAVES

They're everywhere. We count around 40 caves that have not been specifically used as quest locations. Most are occupied by smugglers and bandits. (Sorcerers have taken over a handful, like Odaishah, but they tend to prefer the Velothi "towers.") And while rarely a source of surprises, the caves are almost always an excellent one for loot.

They range from the huge Punsabanit, just northeast of Rotheran, down to the compact Sinsibadon, which is located between Suran and Telasero … and consists largely of stairs!

Lack of formal quests notwithstanding, you've almost certainly been to one or two of these. Located east and west of Sedya Neen, respectively, the bandit caves Addamasartus and Aharunartus will be the source of many players' first real weapons, the place they will kill their first bad guys and free their first slaves. The loot is only modest, but it will seem like a fortune to the player just starting out.

The loot gets better. In Nissintu, west of the stronghold Marandus, you'll find a great cache of scrolls on catwalks suspended over its underground lake. In Dun-Ahhe, a watery sorcerers lair just north of the Cavern of the Incarnate, a swim leads into a little diamond mine. Ahinipalit, west-southwest of Tel Fyr, and Odirnamat, northest of the stronghold Rotheran, yield uncommon loot in bolts of cloth. Located along the coast northwest of Gnisis, Ashinabi is a big, two-section smugglers den with some swimming required, an underwater exit, and a Sixth House tie-in. (They're smuggling ash statues!)

And in some cases, a cave is worth visiting simply to see it. Kumarahaz, north of Tel Branora, has at its core a multilevel series of platforms. And at the elbow of Kudanat, west of Caldera, you'll find a splendid dark grotto. It even has a waterfall.

DWELLINGS

An Abandoned Shack

At first glance, this hovel on an island just southwest of Gnaar Mok barely rates a second look.

But humor us. Give it a second look and a third.

The upside-down bowl on the table conceals two pearls.

Most of the sacks contain saltrice, but the cloth sack against the southern wall contains 100 gold.

There are two musical instruments here—a lute in plain sight and a drum behind the barrels to the right of the door. They're not valuable—just a bit unusual.

That flower on the table is a Coda—one you'll have to travel fairly far to find for one of the Romance quests.

Semi-concealed by the south end of the hammock is the "gag" book "No-h's Picture Book of Wood."

And if you take the book, you'll find a sad and ethereal note that you can otherwise find only in a bottle far out at sea. (See "Under the Sea.")

How did it find its way here? We can only assume that the ghost who wrote it delivered it himself.

All It Lacks is Ginger

Just northwest of Khuul is one of the prettiest places in the game: a deserted island with a waterfall, a bedroll, and great views of the shimmering sea to the east and the great natural stone arches to the west.

A campfire is burning, and a plate and utensils are laid out for dinner. It's as though someone just stepped away for a swim. But they never come back, and their place is yours.

It is perhaps the most uniquely restful location in all of Morrowind. No distracting dungeon doors. No slaughterfish (though a critter will start appearing on the beach once the player hits Level 3). Just you and the world.

Now, it's not just here entirely for the view. The trunk contains a nice selection of loot keyed to the player's current level. But it is well-locked (lock level: 45) and the key is nowhere in evidence.

It's here, but hidden under the Pilgrim's Lantern. Even when you know that, getting it is a bit tricky. You'll have to pick up the lantern from the east. From the west, the overhanging Roobrush bush keeps getting in the way. Nature is beautiful, but it can be a pain in the butt.

Argonian Name Explained!

You've doubtless wondered at the origin of some of the elaborate Argonian names. Nine-Toes. Hides-His-Eyes. Hides-His-Foot. He-Only-Stands-There. Skink-In-Tree's-Shade. Rarely do the Argonians explain their origin.

But one of them does.

From Vivec's Foreign Quarter, follow the road northwest to a "T" intersection. Turn right and pass a bunch of netches. Make your next right. (Teris Radledran and his guar will be waiting here, unless you've already escorted Raledran to Vivec in a Miscellaneous Quest.) Just before you reach Nilera's Farmhouse, the road will turn east and come to another "T" crossing. Turn right. Immediately, you'll see a fork. Follow the left fork east until you see a small shack over a rise on your right.

This is Traveling-New-Woman's place. Talk to her about "background" or "Traveling-New-Woman" and she'll give you the skinny on her name. It's a good yarn.

Ashlanders

Ya gotta love 'em. While the established Ashlander tribes you'll deal with in Morrowind are suspicious of you at first whiff, and courtly once you've proved your worth, the rogues whose solitary tents dot the northern and eastern countryside are unfailingly aggressive. They like kidnapping people. They like attacking you.

And given that they don't have any real loot, they won't exactly rank high among potential destinations for a freelancing adventurer. We mention them merely to let you know they're out there for killing (hey, did we actually say that?) and that there is something to be said for having a safe place to sleep out in the Grazelands.

Eight named renegade settlements aren't referenced by quests: the Ashamanu Camp west of Tel Aruhn, the Elanius Camp northeast of the stronghold Falensarano, the Mamshar-Disamus Camp east of the stronghold Kogoruhn, the Massahanud Camp southwest of the stronghold Indoranyon, the Salit Camp west of Vos, the Shashmanu Camp south of Khuul, the Sobitbael Camp just west of Tel Fyr, and the Yakaridan Camp just southwest of Vos.

The only one that really merits the description "camp" is Salit, just across the water west of the shrine Esutanamus. (It has two tents!) And the only thing that distinguishes the Ashlanders there from their brother renegades is that there are more of them.

You may have given up on seeing anything unusual at these settlements, but one camp does have a couple of interesting quirks.

For one, the Ashamanu Camp is a Mabrigash (Ashlander witch-woman) settlement, like the Shashurari Camp involved in the Imperial Legion quest to free hermit Jocien Ancois.

For another, it has a prisoner of its own. Make that "had." You'll find Imperial pauper Arlowe lying lifeless in the camp. The women here are mute as to his fate, but you can guess. Check his inventory for a unique warhammer called the Banhammer.

Bal Isra, Odai Plateau and Uvirith's Grave

You may stumble onto one or more of these locations in the early stages of the game…and wonder why there's nothing there.

Don't worry. There isn't a problem with your game. It's just that there's nothing there yet.

These are the spots where the player's stronghold—and two complimentary, rival strongholds—will rise once you complete certain Faction Quests for your chosen Great House.

Bal Isra, along the main Ald'ruhn-Maar Gan road, will eventually be the site for Redoran stronghold Indarys Manor. The Odai Plateau, a section of high ground on the north bank of the Odai south of the Shulk Egg Mine, will be the location for the Hlaalu stronghold Rethan Manor. And Uvirith's Grave, a gray and green bump in the ash wasteland northeast of Galom Daeus, will become the Telvanni stronghold Tel Uvirith.

DWEMER RUINS

You've hit most of the main Dwarven ruins, but a few may have eluded you. Aleft is due west of the Band Egg Mine south of the stronghold Hlormaren. Mzahnch is north of Ball Fel. The large ruin Nchardumz is southeast of Mount Assarnibibi (and should not be confused with Nchurdamz farther southeast). Nchardahrk is northeast of the stronghold Rotheran.

The only unusual one is Bthanchend—and not so much for what it contains (fairly standard Dwemer-ruin loot) as for its location. It's inside the Ghostfence, just west of the citadel Vemynal, where it effectively serves as a red herring. (It isn't a Dagoth citadel, but it is sited among them.)

Did you know that Dagon Fel has its own little dungeon? The Vacant Tower, near the water on the east side of the village, is a Dwemer ruin in miniature.

The loot's good, too. At the bottom, you can find a Blind Ring and Amulet of Spell Absorption, and, up top, Dwemer Scarab Plans used in a Mages Guild quest.

Of course, the tower's not quite vacant. Khargol gro-Boguk, a drunken "secret master," has taken up residence there, so you can get trained as well. See the "secret masters" section for details.

And there's one other ruin. See "Grottos" for details.

FARMS

Gro-Bagrat Plantation

The farms out in the Ascadian Isles in southern Vvardenfell are peaceful, pretty, and dull. Once you've done the quests in this region, there's not much to find here.

With one exception. An early Imperial Cult quest sends you to pick flowers at this skooma smuggler's home in the lush farmland north of Vivec.

At that time, you are encouraged to stay away from the Orc himself, and it is good advice. If you do somehow manage to get past two heavily-locked doors into his basement, he kills you so fast it'll make your head swim.

Ever wonder why? Pay him another visit. That basement isn't just a storage room. It's a skooma lab!
Flora and Fauna

Don't you like those flower-picking and ingredient-finding missions? We do, too. Communing with nature in Morrowind is cool.

(But if anyone asks, we never said this. We just said we like pounding on bad guys and taking their stuff, understood?)

A potential diversion for the player who thinks he's seen everything is to track down in the wild those ingredients that haven't turned up in quests.

Among Morrowind's indigenous plants, the rarest are certain varieties of bittergreen—none of which actually yield bittergreen petals. We don't know why anyone would need to know this, since you can't pick them, but all can be found growing at Venim Manor in Ald'ruhn.

Somehow, this seems appropriate.

The rarest plants that yield ingredients are the black, red and green lichens. Black lichen can be found all across Vvardenfell and is most common in the sorcerers lair Ashirbadon.

Red lichen is equally rare, but harder to track down, because it doesn't grow in named locations, but in the wild—most notably in the Ashlands near the Redoran stronghold, Indarys Manor.

Less rare, but still uncommon, is green lichen, which grows almost exclusively in the West Gash and Sheogorad regions, but does appear in small quantities in Vas and the Halit Mine.

Of course, you could buy all these lichens in shops. But where's the fun in that?

Then there's Meteor Slime. You won't find it for sale in any shop. It comes only from a potted plant on a bookshelf at Jobasha'a Rare Books in Vivec. The plant has a name – "Charles" – and the slime cures poison and blight disease and fortifies Willpower. Go figure.

Fauna is a iffier business. Chances are that, if you've played through Morrowind as it was designed to be played, you've seen all the species.

GROTTOS

Ten of these flooded caves are spread across Morrowind: Akimaes Grotto (southeast of Seyda Neen), Eluba-Addon Grotto (southeast of Ald Daedroth), Ilanipu Grotto (just south of stronghold Rotheran), Madas Grotto (northeast of Ald Redaynia), Malmus (northwest of Dagon Fel), Mudan Grotto (southwest of Vivec), Mul Grotto (northeast of Bal Fell), Nimawia Grotto (south of Balmora), Vassamsi Grotto (southeast of Tel Mora) and Zalkin Grotto (west of the Holamayan monastery).

The locations are always obscure—grottos are entered underwater—and you could go through a whole game without seeing even one. Moreover, Morrowind doesn't direct you to them, and most contain little to attract treasure hunters beyond pearls, the occasional drowning victim and the odd bit of loot (though Vassamsi actually has a fair amount of armor.)

Naturally, there is one exception. The relative blandness of the first nine grottos is merely to set you up for the wondrousness of the tenth, which is essentially a quest without portfolio.

The peninsula west of Vivec is typical of the farmland around that city: safe, green, empty. Its only distinguishing feature is a small island that lies off its southwest coast, almost within sight of the towers of Ebonheart.

If you swim over, you'll see a second island just to the south. And from the westernmost tip of this island, with your viewing distance set to maximum, you'll see two more islands far to the west. Swim to the northern of these two islands.

Nondescript, right? A couple of mudcrabs. Some plants. A tidal pool.

But if you check underwater on the south side of the island, you'll also find a little door.

Welcome to Mudan Grotto.

Inside, swim between the two large rocks to your left, and through the archway just to the left. A second archway is to your right. Descend steeply to a third portal and, up ahead, you'll see a familiar form—the circular door of a Dwemer ruin!

Hey, if Morrowind can have a lost Daedric ruin (Boethiah), why not a lost Dwemer ruin as well?

Inside this "Lost Dwemer Checkpoint," you're still underwater, so the first order of business is getting some air. You can do that by heading straight ahead and then either left or right from the entrance and climbing the stairs. Pick around in the loot up here—and note the location of the locked and trapped table in the room closest to the ruin's entrance—and then descend again. From the entrance, swim down the stairs opposite the door, make your first left and use the hatch to enter the Right Tower.

Here, you'll find the body of a hapless adventurer named *ahem* Peke Utchoo who drank poison instead of a healing potion and died without knowing where the key in his inventory would take him.

It should take you back to that locked underwater table. It contains a second key which opens the hatch to the vault—located at the end of the hall and up the stairs from the ruin entrance. And here, if you can beat down (or just avoid) the steam centurion, you'll find the real prize: a Dragonbone cuirass that's one of Morrowind's great lost artifacts. (A lot of lesser loot can be found on surrounding shelves.)

MINES

Along with hard cases and terrible weather, one of Vvardenfell's defining industries is kwama eggs. Thirty-plus egg mines dot mountainsides and country roads all over the island. If you know where they are, you'll never want for food—or for kwama foragers to hop up and bite you in the butt while you're eating it

And yet there is more to mining in Morrowind than the incredible, edible kwama egg. And looting these non-egg mines can be an extremely profitable pastime.

The Caldera Mine is simply the best known of the raw ebony mines. Elith-Pal Mine (west of the Zainab Ashlander camp), Mausur Caverns (south of the Red Mountain citadel Vemynal), Sudanit Mine (west of Ghostgate), Vassir-Didanat Cave (south of Balmora) and Yanemus (northeast of Ghostgate) also produce this black gold.

And where do you suppose the glass weapons and armor come from? They're refined from raw glass extracted at the Dissapla Mine (north of the stronghold Falensarano), Dunirai Caverns (southeast of Ghostgate) Halit Mine (west-northwest of Falensarano), Massama Cave (southwest of Falensarano) and the Yassu Mine (north of Ghostgate).

And Abaelun Mine, south-southeast of Ald'ruhn, is a diamond mine.

These minerals turn up in smaller quantities in other places as well. Diamonds appear in the bandit caves Punammu (west of Dren Plantation) and Assarnud (near Gnisis) and the wizard lairs Abanabi (southwest of Sadrith Mora), Maba-Ilu (southeast of Molag Mar) and Dun-Ahhe (in the Ashlands well east of Kogoruhn).

Glass also apears in small amounts in Maba-Ilu and, of all places, in the Dwemer ruin Nchurdamz (southwest of Holamayan).

And ebony also appears in Abanabi, Maba-Ilu, the Sepulcher in the tomb Tukushapal (reached through the Marvani Ancestral Tomb south of Molag Mar), and the bandit cave Zenarbael (east-northeast of Galom Daeus)

SECRET MASTERS

Your romance with the Khajiit thief Ahnassi can eventually bring you into contact with a woman named Senyndie. She has the highest Acrobatics skill of any character in the game (100) and, consequently, can train you to very high levels.

Senyndie is one of 27 "secret masters" in Morrowind—each a trainer gifted in a discipline that corresponds to one of your 27 skills. But she's the only master with whom the game actually directs you to train.

There are 26 others. You might be able to guess at the identity of some from references to them in skill books, and one, Security expert Hecerinde, figures in a Thieves Guild quest. But, in most cases, you would have to find them entirely on your own.

Organized by skill, the masters are:

Acrobatics: Senyndie, at the Fighters Quarters on the Waistworks level of the Vivec's Arena canton.

Alchemy: Abelle Chriditte, in the Propylon Chamber at the stronghold Valenvaryon.

Alteration: Seryne Relas, at her home in Tel Branora.

Armorer: Sirollus Saccus, on the lowest level of the Hawkmoth Legion Garrison in Ebonheart.

Athletics: Adibael Hainnabibi in Adibael's Yurt at the Kaushtababi camp, south of Molag Mar.

Axe: Alfhedil Elf-Hewer, on the upper level of the stronghold Falensarano.

Block: Shardie, in the courtyard of Buckmoth Legion Fort outside Ald'ruhn.

Blunt Weapon: Faralenu Henim in The Abbey of St. Delyn the Wise, off St. Delyn Plaza in Vivec.

Conjuration: Methal Seran, on the lowest level of the Ald'ruhn Temple.

Destruction: Leles Birian, east of Piernette's Farmhouse (which is located east of Pelagiad).

Enchant: Qorwynn, near the exit from the stronghold Indoranyon.

Hand-to-Hand: Taren Omothan, in the southwestern bedroom on the lowest level of the Holamayan monastery.

Heavy Armored Defense: Seanwen, at Arena Fighters Training in Vivec.

Illusion: Erer Darothril, at Dirty Muriel's Cornerclub in Sadrith Mora.

Lightly Armored Defense: Aerin, in the Andus Tradehouse in Maar Gan.

Long Blade: Ulms Drathan, at the Armigers Stronghold in Molag Maar.

Marksman: Missun Akin, in Missun Akin's Hut atop the stronghold Falasmaryon.

Medium Armored Defense: Cinia Urtius, on the deck of the boat at the Tel Fyr dock.

Mercantile: Ababael Timsar-Dadisun, in his yurt at the Zainab Ashlander camp.

Mysticism: Ardarume, in the west wing of the Gateway Inn in Sadrith Mora.

Restoration: Yakin Bael, at the Vos Chapel.

Security: Hecerinde, at his home in Balmora.

Short Blade: Todwendy, at the Lucky Lockup Cornerclub in Balmora.

Sneak: Wadarkhu, at Druegh-jigger's Rest in Gnaar Mok.

Spear: Mertis Falandas, on the lower level of the Tower of Dusk at Ghostgate.

Speechcraft: Skink-in-Tree's-Shade, at the Mages Guild in Wolverine Hall in Sadrith Mora.

Unarmored Defense: Khargol gro-Bogúk, in the Vacant Tower in Dagon Fel.

SHRINES

As many shrines as there are in Morrowind, 14 without quest "hooks" are still out there, daring you to mispronounce their names.

They are: Addadshashanammu, south of Gnaar Mok; Almurbalarammi, east-southeast of Molag Mar; Assalkushalit, north of Dagoth Ur's citadel (and how unlucky is that?); Dushariran, east of the stronghold Berandas; Esutanamus, northeast of Tel Vos; Ibishammus, in the Underworks of Vivec's Foreign Quarter; Kaushtarari, south of Sadrith Mora; Kushtashpi, west of the Ahemmusa Ashlander camp; Onnissiralis, just northwest of the Sanctus Shrine; Ramimilk, southeast of Ald'ruhn; Shashpilamat, just north and west of Sadrith Mora; Tusenend, southeast of the Erabenimsun Ashlander camp; Zaintiraris, south of Molag Mar; and Zergonipal, south-southeast of the stronghold Rotheran.

Most of these follow what are by now familiar shrine models, but nevertheless incorporate the odd neat wrinkle.

Some have better loot than others. Dushariran has a huge haul of potions behind the altar. In the trapped private chamber at the rear of Ramimilk, you'll find an ebony staff.

While nothing is concealed behind the caved-in tunnel at Shashpilamat, the shrine does have another small section. Return to the surface and head east to find the entrance.

Perhaps the most interesting of the bunch is Kushtashpi. Just follow the barren brown hills west from the Ahemmusa camp to reach the site. The entrance is up a flight of stairs on the shrine's western side. Within, stairs lead down into darkness, a smooth-walled tunnel and a broken bridge. You should be able to jump across the gap from the left balustrade or the large stone block on the right. Then it's clear sailing into the shrine proper.

In addition, there is one major shrine that isn't a quest location.

Bal Fell

You can hear a good amount about this giant Sheogorath shrine in Morrowind, but no one actually sends you there. You'll get the scoop, usually in bits and pieces, from scouts and savants in Vivec and Suran, and in its entirety from Jobasha at his Foreign Quarter book shop and Artisa Arelas at The Abbey of St. Delyn the Wise.

The upshot is that Bal Fell has a history (it goes back to the First Era), a reputation (an evil one), and an air of mystery. (Legend suggests it was built atop an ancient Daedric site.) And it's the subject of current interest among Telvanni wizards who are sponsoring competing teams of adventurers there.

Located at the western edge of the sea of islands between Vivec and Tel Branora, Bal Fell is most easily reached by swimming or flying east from a point just south of Omani Manor on the Ascadian Isles peninsula east of Vivec.

The shrine is huge—comparable in size and layout to Ald Daedroth. The competition has reduced the number of enemies—hence the dead scamps in the foyer—but also the loot, and nothing can be found in the wings or Outer Shrine save fallen rocks.

Fortunately, none of the other adventurers has penetrated to the Inner Shine, and Bal Fell's great prize is yours for the taking. In a trapped chest on the altar, you'll find Ten Pace Boots, which temporarily boost your Speed and Athletics skill by 20 points and also cast SlowFall.

As for the legend of an ancient Daedric site here, there's no evidence of a ruin below the ruin.

But this is what editors are for, isn't it?

SIXTH HOUSE BASES

Another source of late-in-the-game fun is mopping up the remnants of the Sixth House cult.

Dagoth Ur's death kills off any ash vampires in the Red Mountain citadels, but Sixth House bases remain in full swing. And there are a lot of them.

You've probably already cleared out most of the big bases. The Main Quest takes you into Ilunibi (at Khartag Point on the west coast), and Faction Quests take you into Assemanu (just west of Vivec), Hassour (at the foot of the Foyada Mamaea), Mamaea (east of the stronghold Berandas), Yakin (southwest of the stronghold Indoranyon), and Hanarai Assutlanipal's cellar in Ald'ruhn!

However, you may not be aware of the extent to which this Dagoth Ur cult had established itself. If you've played Morrowind more or less by quest, no fewer than a dozen Sixth House installations survive. They are: Ainab (on the northern coast of Vvardenfell southwest of the stronghold Rotheran); Abinabi (south of the Urshilaku Ashlander camp); Bensamsi (northeast of Kogoruhn); Maran-Adon, just south of the Cavern of the Incarnate; Missamsi (northeast of Moonmoth Legion Fort); Piran (northwest of Mount Kand); Rissun (east of Bal Fell); Salmantu (southeast of Sadrith Mora); Sanit (west-southwest of the Ahemmusa Ashlander camp); Sennananit (just north of the stronghold Hlormaren); and Sharapli (east of Ghostgate).

But these are all more or less second-tier installations. The only big Sixth House base that is at all likely to survive—simply because no one explicitly sends you there—is Subdun.

It's conceivable that you've already visited this island base if you made a concerted effort to shut off the flow of Dreamers and Sleepers—the Subdun station "broadcasts" in the Gnisis, Ald Velothiu, and Khuul areas—but we're playing a hunch that assigned tasks will keep players so busy that you won't come up for air until late in the game.

To reach Subdun, take silt strider to Gnisis and make your way east and south to the north side of the stronghold Berandas. From here, head west to the coast and then south along the coast, under a stone arch, to a peninsula. Follow the peninsula out to the muckspunge plants at its tip. From here, swim a short distance west to a horseshoe-shaped island. The entrance to Subdun in right off the beach.

Subdun is huge cave with the emphasis less on fighting than on outwitting its tricks and traps. The main tunnel is concealed by stalactites at one point, and you can't escape certain rooms or reach others without Levitate, so make sure you have the spell or scrolls before you set out.

In the shrine, the fighting comes in like gangbusters, and you'll go up against a range of nasties—ending in priest Dagoth Draven. He is perhaps the last of his kind. Extinction has certain merits after all.

STRONGHOLDS

You've explored some of them. The Main Quest sends you into the vastness of Kogoruhn on an easter-egg hunt and Faction Quests into Andasreth, Berandas, Falasmaryon, Indoranyon, Rotheran, and Telasero.

But that leaves four strongholds that no one ever tells you to enter: Falensarano, Hlormaren, Marandus, and Valenvaryon.

Strongholds are the closest thing in Morrowind to conventional hack 'n' slash dungeons. These ancient Dunmer fortressses, built to fend off Nord incursions in an era before the Great Houses coalesced, were finally abandoned when the Tribunal Temple designated Vvardenfell a religious preserve, and have been taken over by a variety of different groups.

Falensarano, set amid the rocky greens of the southern Grazelands, seems at first to be of a piece with the pleasant land around it. The upper level is virtually empty, apart from a "secretmaster," and that may make you feel safe.

You're not safe. The tomb-like lower level is home to two witches and a warlock and a cast of supporting Daedra. The spellcasters are aggressive in their summoning and indomitable in their pursuit. If things don't go well, you'll find a vertical escape hatch in the depths of their lair. (A Levitate spell is required to use it.)

A Morag Tong "writ" quest does take you to the roof of Hlormaren, located mid-way up the west coast, but not inside. It's big. Hlormaren has the usual dome, Propylon Chamber, upper and lower keeps, but also an underground level, where you can free a ton of slaves, and a sewer system that puts the Vivec cantonal sewers to shame (and incorporates a secret riverside exit).

Marandus, like Andasreth, is a sort of generic bad-guy hideout. Exploration is a very straightforward affair—a suite of handsomely-appointed bedrooms, a wide variety of respectable (though not exceptional) loot ... and scattered among them no fewer than 16 disagreeable people eager to nail your hide to their wall. If you'd rather defer that little pleasure, go straight to the dome on the roof. It's unoccupied, the loot's decent, with one of the chests guaranteed to contain an ebony weapon.

Valenvaryon is more of a curiosity than a destination. Built on a mountaintop between the sea and the northern Ashlands, it's actually more of a scenic overlook than stronghold. It has the requisite Propylon Chamber, the stone parapet and small roof structures. But these turn out to be huts for the Orc caretakers, and you won't find an actual dungeon here.

Speaking of Propylon Chambers, you've probably already guessed that these rooftop structures, humming with unharnessed power, are teleport stations. But when you try to activate the pillars within, you are told you don't have the necessary "index."

You've stumbled onto a kind of quest—barely documented and extremely open-ended.

The chambers once were used to supply the strongholds. But the keys to their mechanisms—a unique index for each chamber—have been scattered all over creation. You can find them and use the Propylon Chambers, but with very little help from the game

In all of Morrowind, only one person has a lead on one of the indices. Talk to Crazy-Legs Arantamo at Simine Fralinie: Bookseller in Vivec's Foreign Quarter Canalworks about "little secret." He'll tell you that the owner of one index went to the Maelkashishi shrine southeast of Khuul and never returned.

Sure enough, you'll find the index for the stronghold Falensarano on top of a scroll, near a corpse, on the highest level of the shrine's Forgotten Galleries.

Now, that said, some of these little stone doorstops are relatively easy to find. Rotheran's and Telasero's are in their respective strongholds. Rotheran's is even close to the Propylon Chamber. Rols Ienith has it. He's in the Communal Hut on the roof. Just pick his pocket, knock him out or kill him, and take it.

Telasero's index is in a trough on that stronghold's lower level. Be careful how you go. As you know from a Faction quest, this place is a major-league Sixth House base.

But after those three, it starts to get harder.

The index for Andasreth is in the dome of neighboring stronghold Hlormaren. The dome has its own entrance off the upper roof, so you can Levitate up to it. (If you can't Levitate, you'll have to fight your way up from the entrance.) The index is on the middle shelf of a bookshelf against the left-hand wall.

The Berandas index is in nearby Arvs-Drelen—Baladas Demnevanni's home in Gnisis. Check out the top shelf of the bookshelves on the top level of this Velothi dome.

Valenvaryon's index is off to the west of the stronghold at the Urshilaku Ashlander camp. Check out wise woman Nibani Maesa's yurt; it's on the table.

And Falasmaryon's index is, well, semi-nearby, in Maar Gan. Just inspect the offerings before the magic stone at the local Shrine.

From here on, it's really tough.

Hlormaren's index is on a windowsill at Irgola: Pawnbroker in Caldera.

The Indoranyon index is in the Hall of Fyr in Tel Fyr, on a table right near Divayth Fyr.

And the Marandus index, the most annoying of the bunch, is in a lower-level storage room in Vivec's St. Olms Temple, surrounded by crates and rats. It's one of those things you'd stumble across long after you'd given up looking for it—if you ever found it at all.

But now you've got it, and you can start zapping where you once walked.

However, the Propylon Chamber has certain limitations.

First off, it sends you only to the two closest strongholds in the rough ring around Red Mountain. For example, the two propylons at Andasreth will send you to the strongholds Hlormaren and Berandas. From those destinations, you'd have to then hop over to neighboring propylons to make additional trips to Falasmaryon and Marandus, respectively. (In other words, you can't cut across the ring and move directly from Andareth to Indoranyon.)

So, yes, it's fast travel, but it's also a bit like running the bases. And since it nowhere connects to other fast-travel modes, like boats or silt strider, it's handy only when moving across Vvardenfell's difficult interior or exploring obscure sections of Sheogorad.

TOMBS

The remainder of the game's 80-plus tombs hold a few surprises.

You're not the only visitor in some. The Indaren tomb north-northwest of Kogoruhn has three smugglers and the Dralas tomb northwest of the stronghold Rotheran holds two more.

You'll run into unexpectedly high-level monsters in others. Tomb creatures typically grow in difficulty as the player grows in level, but, irrespective of your experience, you'll still find the Sandas tomb west of Bal Ur guarded by a pair of Skeleton Champions, and the Dralas tomb above by a Bonelord.

A few hold unusual items. The Andules tomb southeast of the stronghold Falensarano holds a Telvanni Mole Crab Helm, and the Beran tomb south of Tel Branora an enchanted glass poisonsword. The Hlervi tomb holds a Nordic Trollbone cuirass. It's tough to spot—it's high on a ledge above the corpse—and the tomb itself is plenty obscure. (It's on a small island well northeast of Sadrith Mora.)

And a couple hold serious treasures mentioned in the book "Tamrielic Lore." See the "Yagram's Book" section for these.

In addition, two unplundered tombs contain less tangible pleasures.

Hlervu Ancestral Tomb

Climb over the coastal hills right around the Shrine of Azura, and you'll drop into a pretty dale around the Ahallaraddon Egg Mine. Follow the path northwest and west. Head north at the first intersection and east at the second, and when you clear the rise, you'll see the tomb straight ahead of you. You'll find the last words of Malaki the Lightfooted on a scroll next to the skeleton in the far left corner of the second room.

Omalen Ancestral Tomb

Climb over the ridge north of the stronghold Kogoruhn—done most easily from the northeast corner of the roof—and look down into the northern Ashlands. Below, you'll see a large dead worm.

Climb down to the worm, stand at its northern end, and follow the valley north. When you reach a "T" intersection, don't turn, but climb over the rise directly ahead of you. On the far side, you should see the Omalen Ancestral Tomb.

Inside, you'll wind your way through a sinewy crypt and face a great deal of fighting—seemingly without commensurate reward.

The reward is uncovering a neat little Easter Egg. In the final room, you'll find the body of an adventurer killed, either by accident or by design, by some falling boulders. The poor fellow doesn't have much on him, but do read the long note he left behind. It's the whole reason for coming.

TOWNS

Molag Mar

This buttoned-up fortress town offers little in the way of diversions. There is a Buoyant Armigers Stronghold, where you train with a "secret master." (See that section for details.) And the Underworks here is large compared the cantonal sewers in Vivec, with spur corridors in its northeast and southwest corners, where it can be reached via manholes on the entry level.

Initially, you won't find anything down there beyond rats. But in the linking corridor between the two main channels, you'll find a dead body… and a corprus stalker! Now, how did that get down here?

Seyda Neen

Breaking Customs

Did you get into the Customs warehouse? It's right across from the door where you entered the game world.

An advanced character won't have much use for the stuff inside. But if you're just starting out and you can beat the lock on the door (Lock Level: 45), it's in your best interest to steal everything you can lay your hands on, use what you can and cart the rest over to Arrille's Tradehouse for selling. (Don't bother with the moon sugar and skooma; Arrille won't deal with you until you dump it.)

Granted, picking the lock may go down a crime. But the door remains unlocked. And your thefts go unwitnessed.

If you're really good with locks, you can nip into Arrille's own back room (Lock Level: 70) and rip him off. Just don't try to sell him his own stuff, as he'll recognize any of it right away.

Tel Mora

Did you pick up on a dirty little sub-plot at Jolda: Apothecary?

Blight Disease is an enduring concern in Morrowind until the Main Quest is complete. In It's the reason the Ahemussa Ashlander tribe wants to move to Ald Daedroth. It has contaminated many an egg mine. It is at the root of faction quests from the Hlaalu, Imperial Legion, Telvanni and Tribunal Temple.

And we bet you've come down with blight a few times, too.

In every crisis, someone seeks to turn others' misfortune to their profit. With the Blight, that person is Jolda.

The apothecary doesn't discuss her little plot, but it's well-documented. The notice tacked to the potion shelf in her shop (which is empty of Cure Blight potions) reports she is stocking them as quickly as she can.

But check out the five crates of Cure Blight potions in the upstairs storeroom and the note on the chest there. Jolda is hoarding the potions for some personal goal.

"When they are gone the tower shall be mine!" she writes.

Which tower? Tel Mora? Or nearby Tel Vos, which has a shortage of Cure Blight potions you'll address in a Telvanni quest. It's a mystery.

You can't do anything about this—at least, not anything the game world will acknowledge. (In other words, it's not a quest.)

But now that you know where to get 20 Cure Blight potions, we suspect Jolda's stockpiling days are over.

The Bosmer Who Fell to Earth

If you take the road northwest from Seyda Neen, you may see a man plummet to the ground.

Tarhiel's appearance is triggered when you approach his journal, which is lying on the path a short walk from town. You can't save him—he dies on impact—but you can follow in his wake.

The journal lays things out nicely: Tarhiel devised a spell that, in theory, would allow him to jump enormous distances without the disorientation of flying spells or the costs of fast travel. He had only to test it. You've just witnessed the result.

You might argue the project was doomed the moment he named the spell "Icarian Flight." (In the legend of Icarus, this son of Daedalus made a pair of waxen wings, but flew too close to the sun and fell into the sea.)

Can you do better? You can try out the spell yourself. Tarhiel has three of the scrolls in his inventory. Just save your game first.

The Icarian spell does indeed take you to staggering heights—at your apogee, you won't be able to see the ground—but it wears off before you land. That's why Tarhiel died, and that's why you'll die, too, if you don't take action.

A couple of things can save you. A slow-descent spell, like SlowFall, will reduce the damage you take when you hit the ground. And launching a second Icarian Flight spell will work as well.

Practical applications? Probably none in which Levitate wouldn't work at least as well. (Icarian Flight is less easy to control.) But it could conceivably be of use in quickly reaching the upper levels of very tall shrines and tombs like Tukushapal—assuming you don't mind ramming your head into ceilings. This doesn't do damage, but it may make you feel like a clod.

Vos

In the storage room of the Varo Tradehouse, you'll find a shipping note that refers to three crates of cheese that arrived earlier in the week. But there is no evidence of cheese in the storeroom—though there are three open crates.

Smart rats.

You can do proprietor Burcanius Varo a little favor and take care of the rodent problem here. Like the journals in the dungeon of neighboring Tel Vos, this isn't an actual quest, though it has some of the hallmarks of one. It's just a little thing you can do while passing through.

Vivec

Check out the Monster Lab off the Canalworks in the Telvanni Compound. God knows what the wizards are up to down here. In this proving grounds, you can fight off a whole Dwemer ruin's worth of centurions—three spider, two sphere and one steam. Your reward: six soulgems, some repair equipment and low-end Dwemer loot.

The loot's a little better in the Telvanni Vault in the Velothi dome in Telvanni Plaza. Skip the left-hand cell with the two Storm Atronachs. The chests beyond them contain next to nothing. But in the right-hand cell, you'll find the enchanted blades Saint's Black Sword and Foeburner, Maryon's Staff, a spear called Greed, and the axe Karpal's Friend.

And that's just the stuff that has names.

And the other Great Houses? You can loot the Redoran treasury in the Romance quest, but the Hlaalu vault may remain untouched. Located off the Treasury of the Hlaalu Waistworks, it contains nothing as exotic as your Telvanni finds, but does have a mess of gold and a full suit of glass armor.

UNDER THE SEA

Pearl Beds

One of the lesser-known ways to make money in Morrowind is pearl diving.

Kollop shells yield random pearls. These are spread all along the coasts of Vvardenfell and Sheogorad, and can also be found in sea caves like Koal and the various grottos. (See "Grottos.")

But they're available in greater concentrations at certain spots than others and because the pearls reappear over time, knowing these locations guarantees you a source of income.

One especially rich stretch of pearl beds can be found on the northern shore of Vvardenfell, beginning just east of where the Foyada Bani-Dad runs into the sea. Another is located farther east—southeast of the Daedric shrine Ald Daedroth.

Shipwrecks

Only twice do you have to explore a shipwreck for a Morrowind quest. Edryno Arethi sends you to recover

Daedric Wakizashi from the wreck of Prelude in a House Hlaalu faction quest. And while nowhere are you commissioned to perform this Miscellaneous quest, Drarayne Thelas will reward you the return of an invoice from the Abandoned Shipwreck.

But those are just drops in the ocean (ed.: *rimshot*). You'll find no fewer than 19 shipwrecks along the coasts. They are: Abandoned Shipwreck (north of the Sanctus Shrine), Ancient Shipwreck (south of Ald Daedroth),. Derelict Shipwreck (at the northern end of the Foyada Bani-Dad), Deserted Shipwreck (northeast of Bal Fell), Desolate Shipwreck (northwest of Dren Plantation), Forgotten Shipwreck (west of Ald Velothi), Lonely Shipwreck (southeast of Tel Fyr), Lonesome Shipwreck (north of Tel Mora), Lost Shipwreck (southeast of Tel Mora), Neglected Shipwreck (at Khartag Point on the Smuggler's Coast), Obscure Shipwreck (northwest of the Sanctus Shrine), Prelude Shipwreck (east of Bal Fell), Remote Shipwreck (southeast of Seyda Neen), Shunned Shipwreck (southwest of Gnaar Mok), Strange Shipwreck (northeast of Sadrith Mora), Uncharted Shipwreck (south of Vivec), Unexplored Shipwreck (southeast of Hla Oad), Unknown Shipwreck (west of Sadrith Mora), and Unmarked Shipwreck (west-southwest of Ald Velothi).

It's a wonder any goods make it to Vvardenfell at all.

Now, shipwrecks by their very nature offer rather limited adventuring possibilities. (It's getting there that's the fun.) Most consist only of a cabin and upper and lower levels. They're about loot, plain and simple, and some have more than others.

For instance, in the cabin of The Strange Shipwreck, you'll find an uncommon book—a diatribe against Orcs called "The Pig Children" – and in the hold a silver claymore and a chest full of soul gems.

The Ancient Shipwreck doesn't really have anything—save for the unique gag book "Capn's Guide to the Fishy Stick" on the upper level.

The Desolate Shipwreck has a crate of raw ebony.

And aboard the Abandoned Shipwreck, you'll find enough booze in the captain's cabin to fairly reckon it's the reason for the shipwreck!

But don't look for loot only on the ruined ships themselves. In some places, time and tide have moved stuff around. For instance, south of Vivec, near the Uncharted Shipwreck, you'll find a chest partly buried in the sea bottom.

And note, too, that certain small wrecks have escaped documentation. In the waters north of Dagon Fel and southwest of the stronghold Andasreth, you'll find capsized longboats on the bottom—each concealing a bit of loot.

Mainland?

Finally, you may wonder if the designers have snuck into the game a trace of the Morrowind mainland. They have not. The mainland comes up in conversation now and then, but that is all. No secret boat or teleport transports you there. You can try to swim across the ocean. But as endlessly as you may swim, the sea will stretch out just as endlessly before you. At least, as far as the game that we shipped is concerned. It is possible, and in fact quite likely, that you'll find plugins you can download and play that will introduce new lands elsewhere.

And the Imperial Prison Ship?

In the same enterprising spirit, you may want to catch up with Jiub—the Dark Elf prisoner who asks your name at the start of character creation—and wonder about the whereabouts of the ship that delivered you to Vvardenfell.

It is no longer in the game. We promise. Once you enter Seyda Neen's Census and Excise Office to figure out who you're going to be in Morrowind, it vanishes for good. It does not reappear at Holamayan or some other distant dock. Though it is a nice thought.

Sending Out an SOS

But this is not to say there's nothing to be found in distant waters. Floating in the sea well northeast of Dagon Fel, you'll find a bottle. Inside, a poetic letter from a drowned man to his former life. (If you can't find this in the water— and it ain't easy—the note also turns up on dry land. See "Dwellings.")

WIZARD LAIRS

Tel Fyr

Divayth Fyr's island tower and its Corprusarium dungeon are required stops in the Main Quest. Fyr also plays roles in two Faction Quests.

But long about the time you complete the second of these, it may occur to you that Tel Fyr is awfully big given the little you've had to do there, and start casting about (so to speak) to see what you might be missing.

Good move. There are several things you can do in Tel Fyr.

The most elaborate is to solve an undocumented locked-chest puzzle. You must unlock a series of seven or eight chests—each save the last containing a key that opens the next chest in line. It leads to a very nice prize, and the prize leads to an even nicer one.

You'll need a key to get going, natch, and you'll find Divayth's 637th Key right on Fyr's desk in the Hall of Fyr. Don't worry about stealing it from under his nose. He won't turn you into a newt. If you talk to his test tube babies, you'll get the sense that this kind of thing happens all the time.

But what does it open? Nothing topside. You won't find a lock for this key until you get down to the Corprusarium. You'll find the entrance on the tower's lowest level, behind the pillar in the room opposite the Golden Door.

From the first intersection, head left and you'll run right into a chest containing a Dwemer goblet and Divayth's 678th Key.

Head back the way you came and cross the intersection where you turned left. The path will turn north and you'll see a pool on your right. Looks empty? Looks can be deceiving. Jump in, look left and you'll see a chest hidden under the shelf of the path above. Inside, Divayth's 738th Key.

Leave the pool and backtrack a few steps and you'll see a gate on your left. Inside, on your left and another pool, another chest and, inside it, three Dwemer goblets and Divayth's 802nd Key.

Now, backtrack yet again. Head back toward the first chest you found. But before you reach it, turn left. In the far left corner of this room, you'll find another chest containing four goblets and Divayth's 897th key.

You've emptied all the chests in this section of the dungeon, and may be tempted to head into the Corprusarium Bowels. Not yet. Backtrack again—this time all the way back to Onyx Hall in Tel Fyr. At the Golden Door, make a right. In the room at the end of the hall, you'll find a chest behind the central pillar. Inside, you'll find five Dwemer coins and Divayth's 1,008th Key.

Now you can hit the Corprusarium Bowels. Use the entrance that's straight ahead from the main Corprusarium entrance, and once inside, continue straight ahead again to another chest. This one contains six goblets and Divayth's 1092nd Key.

Unfortunately, this doesn't open the other Bowels chest—the one near Yagrum Bagarn.

Yup, you have to go back to Tel Fyr again—this time back to Fyr's office in the Hall of Fyr. The key unlocks the lockbox on the left-hand bookshelf. Within, a Dwemer coin, Divayth's 1,155th Key and…well, this is interesting: a Daedric Sanctuary Amulet.

Now here, for a change, you have a choice.

You can return to the Corprusarium Bowels again, open Bagarn's chest and claim a very nasty warhammer called Volendrung and 50 Dwemer coins (which, valued at 50 gold apiece, are pretty pennies indeed).

Or you can save that for later and, instead, click the Daedric Sanctuary Amulet on your character and select "yes" when asked if you want to travel to Magas Volar.

Magas Volar?

This is a small, enclosed Daedric shrine where you'll face Lord Dregas Volar, a Dremora armed with a Daedric Crescent—an unholy two-handed blade from the Battlespire.

Take the initiative here, and charge him. In addition to dealing out a lot of damage, the Crescent blinds its opponents, and you'll be able to see Volar only between the blows he strikes. If you can keep him contained in the altar area, you probably won't have to see him to hit him.

Defeat him, and you get the Crescent—as well as a second amulet that zaps you back to Fyr's office. (Once used, the Daedric amulet vanishes and the Tel Fyr amulet loses its power. However, it retains its high value, so don't just toss it. Sell it.)

Now, after that run-around, we wouldn't blame you if you swore off opening a chest on the east coast of Vvardenfell for the rest of the game. (Of course, if you've picked up one of the handful of skeleton keys, you can cut to the chase and head straight for the lockbox in Fyr's office. Gentleman Jim Stacey gives you one of these open-anything keys after you complete your final Thieves Guild quest, but you can find four of them on dead bodies at any time. They're in the Redoran and Hlaalu Underworks, the undead dungeon Hanud, and on the upper-level keep in the stronghold Berandas.)

But two more treasures from the Yagrum's Book section below are close at hand, and Fyr will deal with their disappearance with the same equanimity with which he accepted your theft of his 637th Key. The Daedric Scourge is in the locked chest just to the left of the office door, and the Cuirass of the Savior's Hide is in the closet that's just down the hall to the left.

Finally, Fyr has a great little library and, if you're an incurable book collector, you'll find in the Hall of Fyr some books that exist nowhere else in Morrowind. See the "The Bookworm Quests" section for details.

Tel Branora

Did you check out the dungeon under the Lower Tower? It's pretty small, but it's got some respectable monsters: a clannfear, flame atronach, and bonewalker (with nastier variations on this last once you hit levels seven and nine).

The loot is respectable as well: an enchanted Heart Wall cuirass and a Helm of Wounding down the stairs and, hidden behind some rocks near the bridge, an enchanted Stormblade sword.

Tel Vos

The people in Vos, just down the hill east of the great tower, have only praise for Telvanni Councilor Aryon's new construction in the village.

But they must not know about what happened in the tower's new jail and dungeon.

Check it out for yourself. There are two entrances: the hut at base of the hill to the west of the tower (which lets you straight into the dungeon) or through the castle's southern tower (which gives access to the jail).

Collect the five scattered journal entries left behind by Beram, the foreman on the projects, and read them in order. (Two are in the jail and three in the dungeon.) It's a real horror story, and it ends badly.

There's no actual quest here; it's just a matter of exploring and confirming what actually happened. But you can collect some valuable limeware and odd bits of Dwemer loot—and even the score by killing the fire atronach the workmen released.

Velothi Towers

Two of the four remaining Velothi "towers" – they're actually just domes—are home to bad-tempered rogue Telvanni spellcasters. You'll find Sanni (with sorcerer Bravosi Henim) southwest of Ald Daedroth and Shishara (with sorcerer Medyn Gilnith) south-southeast of Ghostgate in the center of the southern Ashlands.

Mababi and Hanud are cut from different bolts of cloth. The former, northwest of Mount Kand, is a peaceful sort of place (though your mileage may vary). And the latter, just west of the stronghold Indoranyon, is essentially an undead dungeon, a la Ald Redaynia.

Yagrum's Book and Great Artifacts

The last dwarf (well, the top two-thirds of the last dwarf) has written a book. At the behest of his host Divayth Fyr, Yagrum Bagarn has assembled in "Tamrielic Lore" a list of great artifacts. You can find it beside him in the bowels of the Corprusarium. Read it, and use it as a guide to what you're missing.

Of course, it's just a rough guide. Yagrum didn't know the current location of these treasures. And you may have already stumbled across some of the items in the book. A lot are associated with quests.

But a lot aren't. Here's a run-down on those.

Bloodworm Helm: A real find for the enterprising necromancer, this helmet allows the wearer to summon skeletons and direct the actions of the undead. Current owner: Crazy Batou. He hangs out in the Maren Ancestral Tomb, a huge crypt just west of the Erabenimsun Ashlander camp.

Bow of Shadows: Invisibility and increased speed are said to accrue to the user of this fabled longbow. It now rests, with a lot of other loot, in the Venim Ancestral Tomb, just north of the Zainab Ashlander camp.

Cuirass of the Savior's Hide: Made with the peeled hide of the Daedra prince Hircine (awarded to the first mortal to escape his hunting grounds), this great breastplate has a special resistance to magicka. It's in a closet in the Hall of Fyr in Tel Fyr's tower.

Daedric Scourge: This potent ebony mace, with the ability to poison its victims and summon what it has killed, is in a chest in the Hall of Fyr—in the same room as Fyr himself.

Denstagmer's Ring: The name is a mystery, but the ring casts Resist Fire, Frost, and Shock spells. It can be found in a trapped cremation urn marked "D. Bryant" in lowest chamber of the Falas Ancestral Tomb just east of Gnisis.

Eleidon's Ward: A healing shield—said to have been created for a great Breton warrior using all the riches of a baron grateful for his daughter's rescue. It's now mounted on the wall above a bier in Ibar-Dad west of the Urshilaku Ashlander camp.

Note that this is just one chunk of the booty available here. Read Elante's Notes in her chamber for the big picture. (This will probably require killing Elante.) In this erstwhile cave, two rogue sorceresses have found the hidden Daedric tomb of Modrin Hanin (he of the book Hanin's Wake.) A barely-locked gate lead to the Daedric (and much more extensive) portion of the program. Beyond it, you'll need to swim through the tunnel to the left to get the key to the tomb through the tunnel to the right.

Fang of Haynekhtnamet: A dagger made from a magical beast's tooth—one that inherited some of the creature's magic. (It does shock damage to enemies.) It can be found in the Shrine of Pitted Dreams in the Sixth House base Mamaea, located north of the stronghold Berandas. (It's conceivable that you liberated this item in a Miscellaneous quest involving a rescue from Mamaea.)

Fists of Randagulf: The gauntlets of the great Skyrim warrior grant the wearer extra strength (the right one) and agility (the left). Both can be found in Soul's Rattle—the innermost recess of the massive Sixth House base Ilunibi. (Again, it's possible you picked this up when you went into Ilunibi on the Main Quest.) It's at Khartag Point, located on the Bitter Coast between Hla Oad and Hlormaren.

Masque of Clavicus Vile: This mask makes the wearer more charismatic. The higher your Personality, the better people will respond to you. It's currently in the possession of the necromancer Sorkvild the Raven, who has a tower east of Dagon Fel. But the Masque is not equipped, meaning a skilled pickpocket could steal it.

The Mentor's Ring: Created by a wizard to aid his apprentices in their studies, this band increases the wearer's Intelligence and Wisdom and so makes magic more efficient. It's in the Samarys Ancestral Tomb southeast of Hla Oad—in an urn marked "Lord Brinne."

The Ring of Phynaster: This marvelous ring carries enchantments that improve the wearer's resistance to Magicka, poison, and shock. It's in the Senim Ancestral Tomb southeast of Dagon Fel (and near the beach where you set out from to find M'Aiq in Boethiah's Daedric quest).

Staff of Hasedoki: A wizard is said to have placed his soul within this protective staff—now in the possession of Koffutto Gilgar, an Orc sorcerer who can be found in the Gimothran Ancestral Tomb. That large crypt is located in the mountains south of the stronghold Falensarano.

Vampiric Ring: This ring steals life from its victim and gives it to the wearer—essentially doing what you'll do with the Vampire Touch spell if you become a vampire. It's on the skeletal wizard who rules the Velothi dome at Ald Redaynia in western Sheogorad.

ODDITIES

The Talking Mudcrab Merchant

Make that the drunken talking mudcrab merchant.

It's northeast of Bal Fell—on an island directly across from the entrance to the Releth Ancestral Tomb. It's pretty funny, and it actually does sell stuff.

Namely, booze!

Stupid Player Tricks

The ability to take a great many small objects in Morrowind adds a level of creativity to the game.

You can write your name in tableware in a town plaza, or "SOS" on a beach.

You can use start a public-safety program and use spare copies of "The Anticipations," "Lives of Saints," and "The Consolation of Prayer" to create stepping stone across lava pools. (Hey, we like prayer and saints and stuff fine. But there are 90-plus copies of each of these books in the game, so you won't run out. And besides, we're trying to teach the lava to read.)

Or you can make a new book about your exploits, complete with maps, and upload it for use as a plug-in.

Actually, that's not stupid at all.

WEAPONS AND ARMOR

Great Stuff

Did you find:

- **Azura's Servant?** This unique Daedric shield can be found in Tel Vos' northeast tower. It belongs to Telvanni Councilor Aryon, so the usual issues may attach to its disappearance.

- **A Daedric dai-katana?** At 120,000 gold each, it's the seventh most valuable weapon in the game. The easiesr way to get one is from the remains of the dead warrior in the Maesa-Shammus Egg Mine.

- **Fury?** This unique enchanted claymore is on another dead warrior in the Hall of Maki in the stronghold Kogoruhn.

- **Sword of White Woe?** It appears in Suran's Guard Tower and the Eastern Guard Tower in Balmora (in each case owned by a Hlaalu guard), as well as in loot awarded only when the player reaches a specific level. (Level 18, in this case.)

- **The Spirit of Indoril?** Maybe not. This shield is found only in that same, level-oriented loot once the player hits Level 17. Other such items include the Staff of the Forefathers (16), Steel Staff of the Ancestors (13), Merisan Club (11), the shield Succor of Indoril, and the mace Icebreaker (8). To get them, you'll need to be in one of the right places at the right time.

Free Stuff

Usually, Morrowind makes you work for your weapons. First you have to perform an errand, or solve a problem, or kill something…or a bunch of somethings.

But in a few cases, you can stumble across excellent weapons more or less undefended in the wilderness. If you can reach them early in the game, they'll serve you especially well.

Two especially good ones are on the Odai Plateau and at the Dwarven ruin Arkngthunch-Sturdumz.

An ebony short sword can be found among the boulders near the southwest corner of would-be Hlaalu stronghold Rethan Manor. It's an excellent conventional weapon, and it's undefended. And since the stretch of the Odai River valley which you'll traverse to get there is a utterly peaceful place, this wouldn't be a bad excursion for a new arrival in Balmora.

The Dwarven mace is with some coins on a ledge on the southern side of Arkngthunch-Sturdumz. Just enter the surface ruin from the east, make your way around the building on the left and drop down onto the ledge.

This is a dicier proposition for a starting character. The nearest community, Ald Velothi, isn't served by boat, so you'll need to take silt strider to Gnisis or Khuul (Gnisis is better) and walk through rather rugged country.

And there is a 25 percent chance you'll arrive to find a cliff racer nursing the mace.